THE GOOD P...
LONDON
AND THE
SOUTH EAST

Edited by

Alisdair Aird and Fiona Stapley

Managing Editor: Karen Fick

Associate Editor: Patrick Stapley

Editorial Assistance: Fiona Wright

EBURY PRESS

Please send reports on pubs to:

The Good Pub Guide
FREEPOST TN1569
Wadhurst
East Sussex
TN5 7BR

or feedback@goodguides.com

or visit our website:
www.thegoodpubguide.co.uk

This updated edition published in 2012 by Ebury Press, an imprint of Ebury Publishing

Material first published by Ebury Press in 2011

A Random House Group Company

Text © 2011 & 2012 Random House Group Ltd
Maps © 2011 Perrott Cartographics

The Random House Group Limited Reg. No. 954009

Addresses for companies within the Random House Group can be found at
www.randomhouse.co.uk

A CIP catalogue record for this book is available from the British Library

The Random House Group Limited supports The Forest Stewardship
Council (FSC®), the leading international forest certification organisation.
Our books carrying the FSC label are printed on FSC® certified paper. FSC
is the only forest certification scheme endorsed by the leading
environmental organisations, including Greenpeace. Our paper
procurement policy can be found at www.randomhouse.co.uk/environment

FSC
www.fsc.org
MIX
Paper from
responsible sources
FSC® C016897

To buy books by your favourite authors and register for offers visit
www.randomhouse.co.uk

Printed and bound in the UK by CPI Group (UK) Ltd, Croydon, CR0 4YY

ISBN 9780091949624

Contents

Editors' Acknowledgements

We could not produce the *Guide* without the huge help we have from the many thousands of readers who report to us on the pubs they visit, often in great detail. Particular thanks to these greatly valued correspondents: Paul Humphreys, Phil and Jane Hodson, Chris and Angela Buckell, George Atkinson, Jeremy King, the Didler, Michael and Jenny Back, Tony and Wendy Hobden, Guy Vowles, N R White, LM, Phil Bryant, Alan and Eve Harding, Michael Doswell, Dennis Jenkin, Brian and Anna Marsden, Martin and Karen Wake, Michael Dandy, Gordon and Margaret Ormondroyd, John Wooll, Tracey and Stephen Groves, Ian Phillips, Ann and Colin Hunt, Joan and Michel Hooper-Immins, Roger and Donna Huggins, Phyl and Jack Street, Clive and Fran Dutson, Gerry and Rosemary Dobson, Simon and Mandy King, Martin and Pauline Jennings, Val and Alan Green, Michael Butler, Dennis Jones, Andy and Claire Barker, Pat and Tony Martin, Terry Buckland, Susan and John Douglas, David Jackman, Tony Hobden, Edward Mirzoeff, Reg Fowle, Helen Rickwood, Peter Meister, Ed and Anna Fraser, Steve Whalley, Barbarrick, Brian and Janet Ainscough, Ian Herdman, Sara Fulton and Roger Baker, Brian Glozier, John Beeken, Richard Tilbrook, David and Sue Smith, J F M and M West, Dave Braisted, Sue and Mike Todd, GSB, B and M Kendall, John Prescott, JJW, CMW, Chris Flynn, Wendy Jones, Mike Gorton, Mike and Eleanor Anderson, Mike and Mary Carter, Richard and Jean Green, John and Eleanor Holdsworth, Roy Hoing, Sheila Topham, Mrs Margo Finlay and Jörg Kasprowski, M G Hart, R K Phillips, Derek and Sylvia Stephenson, Dr and Mrs C W Thomas, Peter F Marshall, Comus and Sarah Elliott, Ian Malone, Andy and Jill Kassube, Rob and Catherine Dunster, John Pritchard, Mrs Susan Brooke, MLR, Barry and Anne, Dr and Mrs A K Clarke, Ryta Lyndley, Tony and Maggie Harwood, Dr Kevan Tucker, Tony and Jill Radnor, Christian Mole, Simon Collett-Jones, Les and Sandra Brown, Dr J Barrie Jones, Martin and Judith Tomlinson, Neil and Anita Christopher, Canon Michael Bourdeaux, Terry and Nickie Williams, Ross Balaam, Pete Flower, Hunter and Christine Wright, John and Helen Rushton, Bob and Margaret Holder, R T and J C Moggridge, Mr and Mrs P R Thomas, Giles and Annie Francis, David M Smith, Anthony Longden, Peter Crozier, Phil and Sally Gorton, Paul Rampton, Julie Harding, Chris Johnson, Tony and Gill Powell, Roger and Lesley Everett, Colin and Louise English, John and Gloria Isaacs, MP, R C Vincent, Mike Proctor, R L Borthwick, Martin Smith, Jim and Frances Gowers, Roger and Marion Brown, Margaret Dickinson, Theocsbrian, Conor McGaughey, Taff Thomas, Tim Maddison, Chris and Jeanne Downing, JCW, John Saville, Di and Mike Gillam, Nick Lawless, C and R Bromage, Charles and Pauline Stride, Ewan Shearer, Ian Barker, D and M T Ayres-Regan, Richard Fendick, Roger and Kathy Elkin, KC, MDN, Tim and Sue Halstead, Denys Gueroult, John and Joan Nash, Sue Rowland, David Lamb, Neil Kellett, Tim and Ann Newell, Bill Adie, Bruce and Sharon Eden, Stanley and Annie Matthews, Robert Lester, Andrew and Ruth Triggs, Mark, Amanda, Luke and Jake Sheard, Steven King and Barbara Cameron, Chris Evans, Ian and Helen Stafford, Robert Watt, Meg and Colin Hamilton, John and Sylvia Harrop, David Crook, Ann and Tony Bennett-Hughes, Lucien Perring and David and Gill Carrington.

Warm thanks, too, to John Holliday of Trade Wind Technology, who built and looks after our database.

Alisdair Aird and Fiona Stapley

Introduction

For decades, even centuries, London has been *the* city to visit; it is full of interest and provides an obvious draw for people from all over the world. The city has a phenomenal number of pubs – probably somewhere in the region of 6,000 – but to enjoy them at their best you should avoid peak times (mid-lunchtime or early evening) when they are often so full that customers spill out onto the streets. And whilst the service then is almost unfailingly efficient, you can't fully appreciate the charms or often extraordinary décor when they are packed to the gunnels.

There are some real architectural gems that will amaze first-time visitors, as well as pubs of real age and character with long, historical (and fascinating) backgrounds. There are restored coffee houses, converted former banks, pubs that were once stable blocks, a vinegar factory, a toll house, a historical coaching inn, a pub where the Great Train Robbery was planned, and even a former fire station. And despite this being a vast metropolis, some London pubs have an engaging country feel.

As you'd expect in a big city, prices are high, but pub food in central London is often surprisingly good value (if not a gastronomic experience) – though there are a growing number of places that now offer top-class modern cuisine. And whilst most pubs do support the local breweries, there are those that keep a fantastic range of ales from all over the country. There are also quite a few micro-breweries springing up and an extraordinary choice of bottled beers is available from all over the world. London pubs also tend to stay open all day, which is incredibly useful for parched and hungry visitors.

With a rich and long history, a stunning coastline and plenty of royal connections, the South East of England has long been a magnet for visitors – both from within and outside of Britain. There are seaside resorts, lovely villages and enchanting cities, some superb gardens (including England's oldest landscaped garden in Esher), exceptional historic houses as well as quite a crop of castles, antique and tea shops. In addition to these sights you can enjoy boat trips on rivers or on the sea, and take walks or strolls on the South and North Downs, amongst the horses and deer in the New Forest, across the Chilterns and beside the water – then relax in a high density of well-run, enjoyable pubs. It's not a cheap part of the country, but we've tried to make sure that we include pubs here that offer value for money – whatever the price range. Pubs by rivers, with stunning views, in flint cottages or in lovely old houses dating back hundreds of years, there's a place within these pages for every mood and every occasion.

What is a Good Pub?

The entries for top pubs featured in this *Guide* have been through a two-stage sifting process. First of all, some 2,000 regular correspondents keep in touch with us about the pubs they visit, and double that number report occasionally. We also get a flow of reports sent to us at **feedback@goodguides.com**. This keeps us up-to-date about pubs included in previous editions – it's their alarm signals that warn us when a pub's standards have dropped (after a change of management, say), and it's their continuing approval that reassures us about keeping a featured top pub for another year. Very important, though, are the reports they send us on pubs we don't know at all. It's from these new discoveries that we make up a shortlist, to be considered for possible inclusion as new top pubs. The more people who report favourably on a new pub, the more likely it is to win a place on this shortlist – especially if some of the reporters belong to our hard core of about 600 trusted correspondents on whose judgement we have learned to rely. These are people who have each given us detailed comments on dozens of pubs, and shown that (when we ourselves know some of those pubs, too) their judgement is closely in line with our own.

This brings us to the acid test. Each pub, before inclusion as a featured top pub, is inspected anonymously by one of the editorial team. They have to find some special quality that would make strangers enjoy visiting it. What often marks the pub out for special attention is good value food (and that might mean anything from a well made sandwich, with good fresh ingredients at a low price, to imaginative cooking outclassing most restaurants in the area). The drinks may be out of the ordinary – maybe several hundred whiskies, remarkable wine lists, interesting ciders, or a wide range of well kept real ales possibly with some home-brewed or bottled beers from all over the world. Perhaps there's a special appeal about it as a place to stay, with good bedrooms and obliging service. Maybe it's the building itself (from centuries-old parts of monasteries to extravagant Victorian gin-palaces), or its surroundings (lovely countryside, attractive waterside, extensive well kept garden), or what's in it (charming furnishings, extraordinary collections of bric-a-brac).

Above all, though, what makes the good pub is its atmosphere – you should be able to feel at home there, and feel not just that *you're* glad you've come but that *they're* glad you've come. A good landlord or landlady makes a huge difference here – they can make or break a pub.

It follows from this that a great many ordinary locals, perfectly good in their own right, don't earn a place in the *Guide*. What makes them attractive to their regular customers (an almost clubby chumminess) may even make strangers feel rather out-of-place.

Another important point is that there's not necessarily any link between charm and luxury. A basic unspoilt village tavern, with hard seats and a flagstoned floor, may be worth travelling miles to find, while a deluxe pub-restaurant may not be worth crossing the street for.

This year, for the first time, we have asked the top pubs featured with full entries to pay a fee. This is a necessary change without which we could not cover our research and production costs, because of the way people are now using the *Guide* – with fewer buying the printed version, and more using the Internet version or the iPhone app. However, selection of the pubs for inclusion remains exactly as before. No pub can gain an entry simply by paying a fee. Only pubs which have been inspected anonymously, approved and then invited to join are included.

Using the *Guide*

THE REGIONS

We have divided this *Guide* into two main regions: London, and the counties of the South East: Berkshire, Buckinghamshire, Hampshire, Isle of Wight, Kent, Oxfordshire, Surrey and Sussex. The featured top pubs are listed in alphabetical order of their town or village. Other pubs worth knowing in the region are then listed county by county.

The county boundaries we use are those for the administrative counties (not the old traditional counties, which were changed back in 1976).

We list pubs in their true county, not their postal county. Occasionally, when the village itself is in one county but the pub is just over the border in the next-door county, we have used the village county, not the pub one.

STARS ★

Really outstanding pubs are awarded a star, and in a few cases two stars: these are the aristocrats among pubs. The stars do NOT signify extra luxury or specially good food – in fact, some of the pubs which appeal most distinctively and strongly of all are decidedly basic in terms of food and surroundings. The detailed description of each pub reveals its particular appeal, and this is what the stars refer to.

FOOD AWARD ⑪

Pubs where food is quite outstanding.

STAY AWARD 🛏

Pubs that are good as places to stay at (obviously you can't expect the same level of luxury at £60 a head as you'd get for £100 a head). Pubs with bedrooms are marked on the maps at the back of the book as a dot within a square.

WINE AWARD ♀

Pubs with particularly enjoyable wines by the glass – often a good choice.

BEER AWARD ◖

Pubs where the quality of the beer is quite exceptional, or pubs which keep a particularly interesting range of beers in good condition.

VALUE AWARD £

This distinguishes pubs that offer really good value food. In all the award-winning pubs, you will find an interesting choice at under £10.

RECOMMENDERS

At the end of each featured pub, we include the names of readers who have recently recommended that pub (unless they've asked us not to).

Important note: the description of the pub and the comments on it are our own and not the recommenders'; they are based on our own personal inspections and on later verification of facts with each pub.

OTHER GOOD PUBS

The second part of this book is a county-by-county descriptive listing of the other pubs that we know are worth a visit – many of them, indeed, are as good as the featured top pubs (these are identified with a star). We have inspected and approved nearly half of these ourselves. All the others are recommended by our trusted reader-reporters. The descriptions of these other pubs, written by us, usually reflect the experience of several different people, and sometimes dozens.

It is these other good pubs which may become featured top pub entries in future editions. So do please help us know which are hot prospects for our inspection programme (and which are not!) by reporting on them. There are report forms at the back of the *Guide*, or you can email us at **feedback@goodguides.com**, or write to us at The Good Pub Guide, FREEPOST TN1569, Wadhurst, East Sussex TN5 7BR.

LOCATING PUBS

To help readers who use digital mapping systems we include a **postcode** for every pub (at the end of the directions for the top pubs and on the right for other pubs).

Pubs outside London are given a British Grid four-figure **map reference**. Where a pub is exceptionally difficult to find, we include a six-figure reference in the directions. The map number (featured top entries only) refers to the map at the back of the *Guide*.

PRICES AND OTHER FACTUAL DETAILS

The *Guide* went to press during the summer of 2011, after each pub was sent a checking sheet to confirm up-to-date food, drink and bedroom prices, and other factual information. By the summer of 2012, prices are bound to have increased, but if you find a significantly different price please let us know.

Breweries or independent chains to which pubs are 'tied' are named at the beginning of the rubric of useful information at the end of each featured top pub. That generally means the pub has to get most, if not all, of its drinks from that brewery or chain. If the brewery is not an independent one but just part of a combine, we name the combine in brackets. When the pub is tied, we have spelled out whether the landlord is a tenant, has the pub on a lease, or is a manager. Tenants and leaseholders of breweries generally have considerably greater freedom to do things their own way, and in particular are allowed to buy drinks including a beer from sources other than their tied brewery.

Free houses are pubs not tied to a brewery. In theory they can shop around but in practice many free houses have loans from the big brewers, on terms that bind them to sell those breweries' beers. So don't be too surprised to find that so-called free houses may be stocking a range of beers restricted to those from a single brewery.

Real ale is used by us to mean beer that has been maturing naturally in its cask. We do not count as real ale beer which has been pasteurised or filtered to remove its natural yeasts. If it is kept under a blanket of carbon dioxide to preserve it, we still generally mention it – as long as the pressure is too light for you to notice any extra fizz, it's hard to tell the difference. (For brevity, we use the expression 'under light blanket pressure' to cover such pubs; we do not include among them pubs where the blanket pressure is high enough to force the beer up from the cellar, as this does make it unnaturally fizzy.)

Other drinks We've also looked out particularly for pubs doing enterprising non-alcoholic drinks (including good tea or coffee), interesting spirits (especially malt whiskies), country wines, freshly squeezed juices, and good farm ciders.

Bar food usually refers to what is sold in the bar; we do not describe menus that are restricted to a separate restaurant. If we know that a pub serves sandwiches, we say so – if you don't see them mentioned, assume you can't get them. Food listed is an example of the sort of thing you'd find served in the bar on a normal day, and we try to indicate any difference we know of between lunchtime and evening.

Children If we don't mention children at all, assume that they are not welcome. All but one or two pubs allow children in their garden if they have one. 'Children welcome' means the pub has told us that it lets them in with no special restrictions. In other cases, we report exactly what arrangements pubs say they make for children. However, we have to note that in readers' experience some pubs make restrictions that they haven't told us about (children only if eating, for example). If you come across this, please let us know, so that we can clarify with the pub concerned for the next edition. The absence of any reference to children in the shorter entries for pubs also worth a visit means we don't know either way. Children's Certificates exist, but in practice children are allowed into some part of most pubs in this *Guide* (there is no legal restriction on the movement of children over 14 in any pub). Children under 16 cannot have alcoholic drinks. Children aged 16 and 17 can drink beer, wine or cider with a meal if it is bought by an adult and they are accompanied by an adult.

Dogs If the licensees of featured top pubs have told us they allow dogs in their pub or bedrooms we say so; absence of reference to dogs means dogs are not welcome. If you take a dog into a pub, you should have it on a lead. We also mention in the text any pub dogs or cats (or indeed other animals) that we've come across ourselves, or heard about from readers.

Parking If we know there is a problem with parking, we say so; otherwise assume there is a car park.

Credit cards We say if a pub does **not** accept them; some which do may put a surcharge on credit card bills, to cover charges made by the card company. We also say if we know that a pub tries to retain customers' credit cards while they are eating. This is a reprehensible practice, and if a pub tries it on you, please tell them that all banks and card companies frown on it – and please let us know the pub's name, so that we can warn readers in future editions.

Telephone numbers are given for all featured top pubs that are not ex-directory.

Opening hours are for summer; we say if we know of differences in winter, or on particular days of the week. In the country, many pubs may open rather later and close earlier than their details show (if you come across this, please let us know – with details). Pubs are allowed to stay open all day if licensed to do so. However, outside cities many pubs in England and Wales close during the afternoon. We'd be grateful to hear of any differences from the hours we quote.

Bedroom prices normally include full english breakfasts (if available), VAT and any automatic service charge. If we give just one price, it is the total price for two people sharing a double or twin-bedded room for one night. Otherwise, prices before the '/' are for single occupancy, prices after it for double. A capital B against the price means that it includes a private bathroom, a capital S a private shower. As all this coding packs in quite a lot of information, some examples may help to explain it:

£60	on its own means that's the total bill for two people sharing a twin or double room without a private bath or shower; the pub has no rooms with a private bath or shower, and a single person might have to pay that full price
£60B	means the same – but all the rooms have a private bath
£60S	means the rooms have a private shower
£60(£90B)	means rooms with private baths cost £30 extra
£35/£60(£90B)	means the same as the last example, but also shows that there are single rooms for £35, none of which has a private bathroom

If there's a choice of rooms at different prices, we normally give the cheapest. If there are seasonal price variations, we give the summer price (the highest), but during the winter you may find all sorts of cheaper rates and bargain breaks.

Meal times Bar food is commonly served from 12-2 and 7-9, at least from Monday to Saturday. If we don't give a time, assume you can get bar food at those times. However, we do spell out the times if they are significantly different. To be sure of a table, it's best to book before you go. Sunday hours vary considerably from pub to pub, so it makes sense to ring to check they are open.

Disabled access Deliberately, we do not ask pubs about this, as their answers would not give a reliable picture of how easy access is. Instead, we depend on readers' direct experience. If you are able to give us help about this, we would be particularly grateful for your reports.

SAT NAV AND ELECTRONIC ROUTE PLANNING

In conjunction with Garmin *The Good Pub Guide* is now available for your Sat Nav. Available as an SD card or download, it integrates quickly and easily into your Garmin Sat Nav and gives you access to all recommended pubs in the *Guide*. The Sat Nav guide will tell you the nearest pubs to your current location, or you can get it to track down a particular pub. Microsoft® AutoRoute™, a route-finding software package, shows the location of *Good Pub Guide* pubs on detailed maps and shows our text entries for those pubs on screen.

iPHONE AND iPAD

You can download an iPhone or iPad version of this edition from Apple's App Store. The iPhone is brilliant for us as it means users can report on a pub even while they are in it – perhaps adding a photo.

OUR WEBSITE: www.thegoodpubguide.co.uk

Our website includes every pub in this *Guide* plus many more. It has sophisticated search tools and shows the location of every pub on detailed maps.

CHANGES DURING THE YEAR – PLEASE TELL US

Changes are inevitable during the course of the year. Landlords change, and so do their policies. We hope that you will find everything just as we say but if not please let us know. You can find out how by referring to the Report Forms section at the end of the *Guide*.

Top Pubs

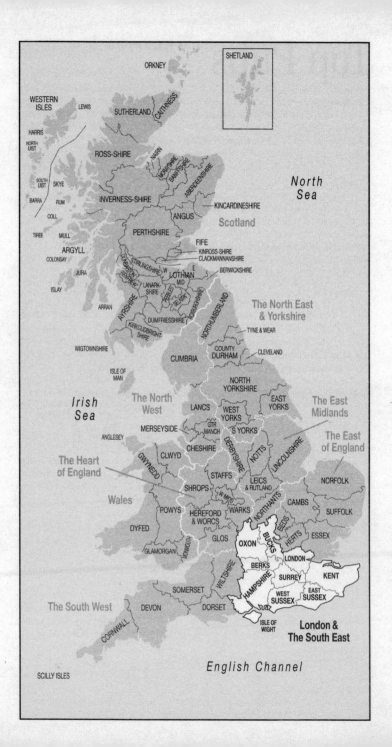

EDITORS' FAVOURITES

Unchanging old-world pubs in **London** are a timeless success with readers, especially the waterside Grapes in East London, cosy Harp, Old Mitre and nicely eccentric Seven Stars (all Central London). The Royal Oak in South London is a clever historical re-creation by Harveys and carries their full beer range. Great food pubs include the Thames-side Gun in East London (**London Dining Pub of the Year**), Old Orchard in Haresfield, Outer London (Brunning & Price's usual great all-round package) and for an outstanding burger the Bountiful Cow in Central London. Also worth a visit are the Black Friar, Chandos, Cittie of Yorke, Jerusalem Tavern and Olde Cheshire Cheese in Central London, the Doric Arch in North London and the Anglesea Arms (Wingate Road), Dove and the Windsor Castle in West London.

The South East's top pub for 2012 is the Cat at West Hoathly in **Sussex** (warmly friendly hands-on landlord). Other special pubs in this county are the smashing old Rose Cottage at Alciston, Jolly Sportsman at East Chiltington (**Sussex Dining Pub of the Year**, plus lovely little bar), charming Tiger by cottage-lined East Dean green, Partridge in Singleton (a fine newcomer) and timeless Royal Oak at Wineham. Also particularly worth a visit are the Cricketers Arms at Berwick, Hatch in Colemans Hatch, Three Horseshoes at Elsted, Bulls Head at Fishbourne, Queens Head at Icklesham, Lewes Arms in Lewes, Chalk Pit in Offham, Green Man at Partridge Green and Horse Guards at Tillington.

Top picks in **Berkshire** are the Hinds Head at Bray (**Berkshire Dining Pub of the Year**), Pot Kiln in Frilsham (super country dining pub), newly opened Horse & Groom at Hare Hatch (a model refurbishment), Hobgoblin in Reading (great beers), Royal Oak at Ruscombe (good all round), village-owned Shurlock Inn at Shurlock Row (another new entry) and Beehive at White Waltham (deservedly enormously popular). Also worth a visit are the Bell at Aldworth, Flower Pot in Aston, Bel & the Dragon in Cookham, Magpie & Parrot at Shinfield and the Royal Oak in Yattendon.

The best **Buckinghamshire** pubs include the Royal Oak at Bovingdon Green (**Buckinghamshire Dining Pub of the Year**), properly traditional Red Lion at Chenies, Royal Standard of England in Forty Green (great character), White Horse at Hedgerley (unchanging gem), Queens Head in Little Marlow (smashing all-rounder) and the Eight Bells at Long Crendon (another unspoilt charmer). Also well worth a visit are the Three Crowns in Askett, Three Horseshoes at Bennett End, Pheasant in Brill, Hampden Arms at Great Hampden, Full Moon in Hawridge Common, Red Lion at Marsworth, Chandos Arms in Oakley and the Bull & Butcher at Turville.

Pubs we've particularly enjoyed in **Hampshire** are the friendly and chatty Sun in Bentworth, Anchor at Lower Froyle (**Hampshire Dining Pub of the Year**), Yew Tree at Lower Wield (exceptional landlord), White Horse near Petersfield (remote, unspoilt), Plough at Sparsholt (hands-on licensees, nice food), Harrow at Steep (quite unchanging, in the same family for 82 years), and a great clutch of new finds, all with good food: smartly updated Hurdles at Droxford, bustling Hogget in Hook, warmly traditional Fox at North Waltham, waterside Mill House at North Warnborough and gently stylish Purefoy Arms in Preston Candover. Also worth a visit are the Flower Pots at Cheriton, Hampshire Bowman in Dundridge, Mill at Gordleton in Hordle, Running Horse at Littleton, Jolly Farmer at Locks Heath, Ship in Lymington and the Old Vine in Winchester.

Top pubs on the **Isle of Wight** are the Red Lion at Freshwater (happy balance between bar and dining) and rambling old New Inn in Shalfleet (**Isle of Wight Dining Pub of the Year**). Also worth a visit are the Folly in Cowes, Taverners at Godshill and the Seaview Hotel at Seaview.

Pubs that stand out in **Kent** include the lovely old Three Chimneys at Biddenden (**Kent Dining Pub of the Year**), Royal Oak at Brookland and Bottle House at Penshurst (both welcoming places for good meals), Dering Arms in Pluckley and Sankeys in Tunbridge Wells (very good fish and seafood at both), and the Tiger near Stowting (super country pub). Of five new top pubs this year, three that particularly stand out are the Pearsons Arms in Whitstable (great sea views from the restaurant) and two Brunning & Price pubs – the Nevill Crest & Gun at Eridge Green and the White Hart in Sevenoaks. Also worth a visit are the Timber Batts in Bodsham, Gate Inn at Boyden Gate, Shipwrights Arms in Oare, Crown at Stone in Oxney, Spotted Dog at Penshurst, Chaser in Shipbourne, Red Lions at Snargate and Stodmarsh, and the Fox & House at Toys Hill.

First-class **Oxfordshire** choices are the Lamb at Burford (civilised and friendly), Chequers tucked away in Chipping Norton, Blowing Stone at Kingston Lisle (**Oxfordshire Dining Pub of the Year**, a newcomer to the *Guide*), Blue Boar at Longworth (smashing old place), beautiful Old Swan & Minster Mill at Minster Lovell, Turf Tavern in Oxford (excellent city-centre pub), and the Swan at Swinbrook (civilised, good, inventive food). Half a dozen other memorable newcomers are the Black Boy at Headington (great Oxford oasis), civilised Oxford Arms in Kirtlington (good food), bustling well run George & Dragon at Long Hanborough, lovely Chilterns Maltsters Arms at Rotherfield Greys, Horse & Jockey at Stanford in the Vale (great all-rounder), and the charmingly updated White Horse at Stonesfield. Also worth a visit are the Saye & Sele Arms at Broughton, Black Horse in Checkendon, Chequers at Churchill, Duke of Cumberlands Head at Clifton, Radnor Arms at Coleshill, White Hart in Fyfield, King William IV at Hailey, and the Bell at Hampton Poyle.

A good batch of new top pubs in **Surrey** includes the thriving Richard Onslow at Cranleigh, Red Lion in Horsell (popular bistro-style food), handsome Refectory at Milford and the warmly welcoming Flower Pot in Sunbury. The Seven Stars at Leigh (enjoyable food) is on good form, as is the Inn at West End (fabulous wines and food) and the Three Horseshoes at Thursley (**Surrey Dining Pub of the Year**). Also worth a special visit are the Barley Mow at West Horsley and the Running Horses at Mickleham.

Bountiful Cow

Eagle Street; ⊖ Holborn; WC1R 4AP

Bustling and informal place popular with those wanting either a chat at the bar or a meat-related meal

Although there is a basement dining room by the open kitchen with red-painted walls and cow prints, most customers prefer the informal street-level bar in this part pub/part grill house. The chrome and white leather bar stools are grabbed quickly by those wanting a chat and a pint of Adnams or Dark Star on handpump and there are quite a few tables – though there may be a short wait for a free one at peak times. The raised area by the windows has booth seating and the smallish main room has red wicker dining chairs around wooden tables on the stripped floorboards, beef-related prints and posters on the painted brick walls and a mixture of happy chat and piped jazz. Service is quick and friendly, and the licensees also run the Seven Stars in Carey Street.

As well as their range of terrific steaks, popular food includes duck rillettes, smoked salmon, charcuterie, couscous with roast vegetables, club sandwich, dill cured herring with potato salad, and grilled chicken breast with pancetta and mashed potatoes. *Benchmark main dish: bountyburger £12.80. Two-course evening meal £23.00.*

Free house ~ Licensee Roxy Beaujolais ~ Real ale ~ Bar food (11-10.30) ~ (020) 7404 0200 ~ Children welcome ~ Open 11-11; closed Sun

Recommended by Richard Gibbs

Harp ◀

47 Chandos Place; ⊖ ⇄ Charing Cross, Leicester Square; WC2N 4HS

Narrow little pub with eight real ales, friendly service, a cheerful atmosphere, and nice sausage baguettes

You can really tell that the cheerful long-serving landlady and her friendly staff take delight in welcoming their customers and running this busy little pub. Even with just a few customers there is a chatty atmosphere and in the early evening it hums with customers spilling out into the back alley. It pretty much consists of one long narrow, very traditional bar, with lots of high bar stools along the wall counter and around elbow tables, big mirrors on the red walls, some lovely front stained glass and loads of interesting quirkily executed celebrity portraits. If it's not too busy, you may be able to get one of the prized seats looking out through the front windows. A little room upstairs is much quieter, with comfortable furniture and a window looking over the road below. The eight real ales on handpump are particularly well kept and quickly changing. There's usually three from Dark Star, one from Harveys, two from Sambrooks and one or two widely sourced guests – maybe from Ascot or Twickenham; five farm ciders and three perries and quite a few malt whiskies.

🍴 Bar food consists of good changing sausages such as boar and apple, pork, port and stilton, venison and redcurrant, lamb and mint and so forth, served in baps with lots of fried onions. These are served until they run out. *Benchmark main dish: sausage baguette £2.50.*

Free house ~ Licensee Bridget Walsh ~ Real ale ~ Bar food (12-4; not Sun) ~ (020) 7836 0291 ~ Open 10.30am-11pm(midnight Fri, Sat); 12-10.30 Sun

Recommended by Tim Maddison, Roger and Donna Huggins, Mike Gorton, Barbarrick, Joe Green, Tracey and Stephen Groves, Peter F Marshall, LM, Taff Thomas, Matt and Vikki Wharton, Phil Bryant, the Didler, Mike and Sue Loseby

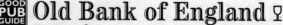

CENTRAL LONDON   Map B

Old Bank of England ♀

Fleet Street; ⊖ Chancery Lane (not Sundays), Temple (not Sundays) ⇒ Blackfriars; EC4A 2LT

Dramatically converted former bank building, with gleaming chandeliers in impressive, soaring bar, well kept Fullers beers and good pies

Well worth including in a tour of London, this former subsidiary branch of the Bank of England has a quite astounding interior. The italianate building itself is rather austere but its sternness stops here. The soaring, spacious bar has three gleaming chandeliers hanging from the exquisitely plastered ceiling, high above an unusually tall island bar counter, crowned with a clock. The end wall has huge paintings and murals that look like 18th-c depictions of Justice, but in fact feature members of the Fuller, Smith and Turner families, who run the brewery that owns the pub. There are well polished dark wooden furnishings, luxurious curtains swagging massive windows, plenty of framed prints, and, despite the grandeur, some surprisingly cosy corners, with screens between some of the tables creating an unexpectedly intimate feel. Tables in a quieter galleried section upstairs offer a bird's-eye view of the action, and some smaller rooms (used mainly for functions) open off. Seven Fullers beers are on handpump alongside a good choice of malt whiskies and a dozen wines by the glass. At lunchtimes the piped music is generally classical or easy listening; it's louder and livelier in the evenings. There's also a garden with seats (one of the few pubs in the area to have one).

🍴 Pies have a long if rather dubious pedigree in this area: it was in the vaults and tunnels below the Old Bank and the surrounding buildings that Sweeney Todd butchered the clients destined to provide the fillings in his mistress Mrs Lovett's nearby pie shop. Well, somehow or other, good home-made pies have become a speciality on the menu here, too: maybe steak in ale, fish, beef and venison and stilton, mushroom and red pepper. Other dishes include sandwiches, ploughman's, summer salads, sausages and mash, proper burgers, and fish and chips. *Benchmark main dish: pie of the day £9.75. Two-course evening meal £15.00.*

Fullers ~ Manager Jo Farquhar ~ Real ale ~ Bar food (12-9) ~ (020) 7430 2255 ~ Children welcome till 7pm ~ Open 11-11; closed weekends and bank holidays

Recommended by Michael Dandy, Peter Dandy, Barry Collett, the Didler, Chris and Jeanne Downing, Tom and Ruth Rees, Andy and Claire Barker

> Virtually all pubs in the *Good Pub Guide* sell wine by the glass. We mention wines if they are a cut above the average.

CENTRAL LONDON   Map B

Olde Mitre  £

*Ely Place; the easiest way to find it is from the narrow passageway beside
8 Hatton Garden; ⊖ Chancery Lane (not Sundays); EC1N 6SJ*

**Hard to find but well worth it – an unspoilt old pub with lovely
atmosphere, unusual guest beers and bargain toasted sandwiches**

You need to be in the know to find this hidden gem that's tucked away
down a tiny alley. These days, it's all too rare in London to find proper
hands-on licensees who genuinely care for their pub and their customers
– but Mr and Mrs Scott do just that and our readers love it. The cosy small
rooms have lots of dark panelling as well as antique settles and –
particularly in the popular back room, where there are more seats – old
local pictures and so forth. It gets good-naturedly packed with the city
suited and booted between 12.30 and 2.15, filling up again in the early
evening, but in the early afternoons and by around 9pm becomes a good
deal more tranquil. An upstairs room, mainly used for functions, may
double as an overflow at peak periods. Adnams Broadside, Caledonian
Deuchars IPA, Fullers London Pride and Gales Seafarer and guests like
BrewDog Trashy Blonde and Titanic White Star on handpump, and they
hold three beer festivals a year. No music, TV or machines – the only
games here are board games. There's some space for outside drinking by
the pot plants and jasmine in the narrow yard between the pub and
St Ethelreda's church (which is worth a look). Note the pub doesn't open
weekends. The iron gates that guard one entrance to Ely Place are a
reminder of the days when the law in this district was administered by the
Bishops of Ely. The best approach is from Hatton Garden, walking up the
right-hand side away from Chancery Lane; an easily missed sign on a lamp
post points the way down a narrow alley. No children.

Served all day, bar snacks are limited to scotch eggs, pork pies and sausage
rolls, and really good value toasted sandwiches with cheese, ham, pickle or
tomato. *Benchmark main dish: toasted sandwich £1.95.*

Fullers ~ Managers Eamon and Kathy Scott ~ Real ale ~ Bar food (11.30-9) ~
(020) 7405 4751 ~ Open 11-11; closed weekends and bank holidays

*Recommended by Jim Frame, Richard Endacott, Tracey and Stephen Groves, Ross Balaam,
John and Gloria Isaacs, Ian Phillips, N R White, Lawrence R Cotter, Anthony Longden, Barbarrick,
the Didler, Tom McLean, Chris and Jeanne Downing, Andy and Claire Barker, Matt and
Vikki Wharton, Taff Thomas*

CENTRAL LONDON   Map B

Seven Stars ◼

*Carey Street; ⊖ Temple (not Sundays), Chancery Lane (not Sundays),
Holborn; WC2A 2JB*

**Quirky pub with cheerful staff, an interesting mix of customers and good
choice of drinks and food**

There's a genuinely timeless atmosphere at this unchanging,
characterful little pub, which the licensees tell us was first established
in 1602. There's always a good mix of customers – though as it faces the
back of the Law Courts, it's a favourite with lawyers and court reporters;
there are plenty of caricatures of barristers and judges on the red-painted
walls of the two main rooms. There are also posters of legal-themed
british films, big ceiling fans and a relaxed, intimate atmosphere; checked

tablecloths add a quirky, almost continental touch. A third area is in what was formerly a legal wig shop next door – it still retains the original frontage, with a neat display of wigs in the window. It's worth getting here early as they don't take bookings and tables get snapped up quickly. Adnams Best and Broadside and a couple of guests such as Dark Star Hophead and Sambrooks Wandle are on handpump, and they do a particularly good dry Martini. On busy evenings there's an overflow of customers on to the quiet road in front; things generally quieten down after 8pm and there can be a nice, sleepy atmosphere some afternoons. The Elizabethan stairs up to the lavatories are rather steep, but there's a good strong handrail. Tom Paine, the large and somewhat po-faced pub cat, still remains very much a centre of attention. The licensees have a second pub, the Bountiful Cow, on Eagle Street, near Holborn tube station, which specialises in beef. No children.

Good, interesting food chosen and cooked according to the landlady's fancy and what's freshly available might include bruschetta with different toppings, a swedish dish of potato, anchovy, cream and dill, napoli sausage with mash, linguine with duxelle of mushrooms and truffle oil, vegetarian chinese stir fry, home-made meat pies, a large hamburger with trimmings, roast guinea fowl in lemony jus, chargrilled fish of the day, and posh ice-cream. *Benchmark main dish: goose pie £11.00. Two-course evening meal £15.00.*

Free house ~ Licensee Roxy Beaujolais ~ Real ale ~ Bar food (all day) ~ (020) 7242 8521 ~ Open 11(12 Sat, Sun)-11(10.30 Sun); closed some bank holidays
Recommended by LM, Tim Maddison, Eddie Edwards, Ian Martin, N R White, the Didler, Tracey and Stephen Groves, Andy and Claire Barker

EAST LONDON   Map A

Grapes

Narrow Street; ⊖ ⇄ *Limehouse (or Westferry on the DLR); the Limehouse link has made it hard to find by car – turn off Commercial Road at signs for Rotherhithe Tunnel, then from the Tunnel Approach slip road, fork left leading into Branch Road, turn left and then left again into Narrow Street; E14 8BP*

Relaxed waterside pub with timeless London feel, particularly appealing cosy back room, helpful friendly staff, well liked Sunday roasts, and good upstairs fish restaurant

You get a lovely sense of history if you catch the Canary Wharf ferry to this 16th-c riverside pub and enter via the steps that lead up from the foreshore. Though much brushed up, it remains almost exactly as it was when Charles Dickens used it as a model for his Six Jolly Fellowship Porters in *Our Mutual Friend* – all the more remarkable considering the ultra-modern buildings that now surround it. It has bags of atmosphere, a good mix of customers and friendly service. The chatty, partly panelled bar has lots of prints, mainly of actors, and old local maps, as well as some elaborately etched windows, plates along a shelf, and newspapers to read; the cosy back part has a winter open fire. Adnams Best, Marstons Pedigree, Timothy Taylors Landlord and a guest on handpump, and Addlestone's cider, are served from the long thin bar; board games. The upstairs fish restaurant, with fine views of the river, is highly thought of. The pub was a favourite with James Whistler, who used it as the viewpoint for his river paintings. In summer, the small balcony at the back is a fine spot for a sheltered waterside drink, with easterly views towards Canary Wharf. No children, but they do have a bowl of water for dogs.

🍴 Reasonably priced and generously served bar food includes sandwiches, soup, a tankard of whitebait, sausage and mash with onion gravy, very good fish and chips, home-made fishcake with caper sauce, and puddings like apple crumble and bread and butter pudding; Sunday roast is highly regarded (no other meals then). The fish restaurant is pricier. *Benchmark main dish: fish and chips £8.75. Two-course evening meal £23.45.*

Free house ~ Licensee Barbara Haigh ~ Real ale ~ Bar food (12-2.30, 6.30-9.30; 12-4 Sun; not Sun evening) ~ Restaurant ~ (020) 7987 4396 ~ Dogs welcome ~ Open 12-3, 5.30-11; 12-11 Thurs, Fri; 12-10.30 Sun

Recommended by Barry and Anne, N R White, Mike Gorton, John Saville, Andy and Claire Barker, Claes Mauroy

EAST LONDON   Map A

Gun 🍴 ♟

27 Coldharbour; ⊖ Blackwall on the DLR is probably closest, although the slightly longer walk from Canary Wharf has splendid Dockland views; E14 9NS

LONDON DINING PUB OF THE YEAR

Top-notch gastropub, pricey but worth it, great views from the riverside terrace, plenty of character and history, well chosen wines

There is a terrific long narrow terrace behind this busy riverside pub, with uninterrupted views of the Dome across a broad sweep of the Thames. Heaters and huge umbrellas make it welcoming even on cooler days. Inside, crisp white walls and smart white tablecloths and napkins on tables at one end of the front bar contrast strikingly with dark wood floors and the black wood counter and back bar with its row of red stools. Towards the terrace is a busy flagstoned bar for drinkers, with antique guns on the wall, and no tables, just a large barrel in the centre of the room. It shares a warm log fire in winter with a cosy red-painted room next door, which has comfy leather sofas and armchairs, a stuffed boar's head, some modern prints, well stocked bookshelves and views on to the terrace. Friendly aproned staff serve three real ales such as Adnams, Fullers London Pride and Greene King Abbot and a good choice of wines. There's a relaxed chatty atmosphere throughout. On summer days, they open up another terrace as a portuguese barbecue; piped music. They may occasionally close the pub on Saturdays for weddings, and will keep your credit card if you are sitting on the terrace and want to run a tab.

🍴 You can eat from both the bar and restaurant menu in the bar so there is a good choice of dishes, starting with oysters, devilled whitebait, steak or fish finger sandwich, macaroni cheese and shepherd's pie from the bar menu, moving up to braised beef and ox tongue soup with roast marrow bone, crispy pork belly with snails, garlic and peppered chicory, mushroom and spinach pasty, smoked haddock and salmon fishcake with poached egg and chive butter sauce, braised sweetbreads with morels and veal jus, and well hung black angus rib-eye steak with béarnaise sauce from the restaurant menu. *Benchmark main dish: shin of beefburger £13.50. Two-course evening meal £30.00.*

Free house ~ Licensees Ed and Tom Martin ~ Real ale ~ Bar food (12-3(4 Sat, Sun), 6-10.30(9.30 Sun)) ~ Restaurant ~ (020) 7515 5222 ~ Children welcome ~ Quiz Mon evening ~ Open 11am-midnight(11pm Sun)

Recommended by LM, W T Selwood, Andy and Claire Barker

Tipping is not normal for bar meals, and not usually expected.

NORTH LONDON   Map B

Drapers Arms 🍴 🍷

Far west end of Barnsbury Street; ⊖ ⇄ *Highbury & Islington; N1 1ER*

Streamlined place with good mix of drinkers and diners, thoughtful choice of beers, wines and imaginative modern food, and seats in the attractive back garden

The spreading bar at this simply refurbished but stylish Georgian townhouse has a mix of elegant dark wooden tables and dining chairs on bare boards, an arresting bright green-painted counter contrasting with soft duck-egg walls, gilt mirrors over smart fireplaces, a sofa and some comfortable chairs. Harveys Best and a couple of guests such as Dark Star Hophead on handpump, and carefully chosen wines by the glass (about 20), carafe or bottle. The stylish upstairs dining room has similar tables and chairs on a striking chequerboard-painted wood floor; piped music and board games. The back terrace is most attractive with white or green benches and chairs around zinc-topped tables, flagstones and large parasols; more reports please.

Good modern cooking might include sandwiches, ploughman's, smoked haddock and bacon chowder, grilled razor clams with red onions, garlic and thyme, pork, pigeon and foie gras terrine, rump of lamb with courgettes, saffron and garlic, steak and oyster pie (for two or three), and puddings such as buttermilk pudding with rhubarb, chocolate pot and chocolate chip cookie. *Benchmark main dish: onglet steak £14.50. Two-course evening meal £20.50.*

Free house ~ Licensee Nick Gibson ~ Real ale ~ Bar food (12-3(4 Sun), 6-10.30(9.30 Sun)) ~ Restaurant ~ (020) 7619 0348 ~ Children welcome, but after 6pm must be seated and eating ~ Dogs allowed in bar ~ Open 10-midnight(11 Sun)

Recommended by Richard Gibbs

SOUTH LONDON   Map B

Royal Oak

Tabard Street/Nebraska Street; ⊖ ⇄ *Borough, London Bridge; SE1 4JU*

Old-fashioned Harveys corner house with all their beers excellently kept; good, honest food too

This enjoyable corner house is slightly off the beaten track, in rather unprepossessing surroundings, and is the only London pub belonging to Sussex brewer Harveys – needless to say, they stock the full range as well as a guest such as Gales HSB. The brewery transformed the pub when they took over, painstakingly re-creating the look and feel of a traditional London alehouse – you'd never imagine it wasn't like this all along. Filled with the sounds of happy chat, two busy little L-shaped rooms meander around the central wooden servery, which has a fine old clock in the middle. They're done out in a cosy, traditional style with patterned rugs on the wooden floors, plates running along a delft shelf, black and white scenes or period sheet music on the red-painted walls, and an assortment of wooden tables and chairs; disabled ramp available on the Nebraska Street entrance.

Most pubs with any outside space now have some kind of smokers' shelter. There are regulations about these – for instance, they have to be substantially open to the outside air. The best have heating and lighting and are really quite comfortable.

🍴 A reasonable range of bar food includes impressive doorstep sandwiches, and generously served daily specials such as cod and chips, vegetable and stilton and steak and ale pies, rabbit in mustard sauce, poached salmon salad, and roast duck; Sunday roasts. *Benchmark main dish: ham, egg and chips £7.95. Two-course evening meal £15.00.*

Harveys ~ Tenants John Porteous, Frank Taylor ~ Real ale ~ Bar food (12-2.30, 5-9.30; 12-7.30 Sun) ~ (020) 7357 7173 ~ Children welcome ~ Dogs allowed in bar ~ Open 11-11; 12-9 Sun; closed bank holidays

Recommended by Mayur Shah, Andy Lickfold, Mike and Sue Loseby, Susan and John Douglas, John Saville, R Anderson, Jeremy King, Comus and Sarah Elliott, the Didler

SOUTH LONDON   Map A

Telegraph ◀

Telegraph Road; ⇌ Putney ⊖ East Putney, Southfields but quite a walk; SW15 3TU

A good summer pub, with plenty of outdoor seats and a rural feel; nicely reworked inside too, with excellent choice of beers, reliable food, and good live blues on Fridays

So verdant is this oasis it's hard to believe you're in London. The outdoor space is the main appeal here, and on fine weekends it can get very busy with families and dogs a big part of the mix. Tables are nicely sheltered under big trees and a pergola, and there are a couple of quirky cow-print sofas under a little verandah by the entrance. The two modernised rooms inside have lots of leather armchairs and sofas and framed period prints and advertisements. The long main bar on the left also has quite a variety of wooden furnishings, including some unusually high tables and stools, and a rather grand dining table at one end; there's a TV for sport, rugs on the polished wooden floor, and an appealing little alcove rather like a private lounge, with a fireplace and a table of newspapers; piped music, TV, board games and occasional quiz and blues nights. The beer range is enterprising – as well as Weltons Semaphore, five regularly changing real ales might be from brewers such as Hammerpots, Sambrooks, St Austell and Tintagel. There's a good wine list too, with about 18 by the glass. The pub is named after the Admiralty telegraph station that used to stand nearby, one of a chain of ten between Chelsea and Portsmouth (on a clear day, a message could be sent between the two in 15 minutes).

🍴 As well as sharing platters, bar food includes mushroom and rocket risotto, chicken, chorizo and halloumi skewers, fish and chips, pie of the day, asian duck salad, burgers, lemon pepper chicken schnitzel, provençale rabbit stew and braised lamb shank with rosemary jus, and daily specials such as bass fillet with thyme jus, and fried salmon with tagliatelle and roast pepper and orange sauce; Sunday roast. *Benchmark main dish: braised lamb shank £15.95. Two-course evening meal £21.00.*

Free house ~ Licensee Jay Cearns ~ Real ale ~ Bar food (12-9(10 Fri, Sat)) ~ Restaurant ~ (020) 8788 2011 ~ Children welcome ~ Dogs welcome ~ Open 12(11 Sat)-11(12 Sat,10.30 Sun)

Recommended by Michael Dandy, Peter Dandy, George Wallace, Colin McKerrow, Tracey and Stephen Groves, Sophie Holborow

---

Virtually all pubs in the *Good Pub Guide* sell wine by the glass. We mention wines if they are a cut above the average.

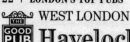

WEST LONDON   Map A

Havelock Tavern ① ♀

Masbro Road; ⊖ ⇄ *Kensington(Olympia); W14 0LS*

Friendly, often vibrant, atmosphere, very good food and well chosen wines

Though it looks pretty ordinary, this blue-tiled corner house is a well regarded gastropub that's very popular for its classy food and laid-back atmosphere. Until 1932 the building was two separate shops and it still has huge shop-front windows. The light and airy L-shaped bar is plain and unfussy with bare boards and long wooden tables that you may end up sharing. A second little room with pews leads to a small paved terrace with benches, a tree and wall climbers. Friendly staff serve Sambrooks Wandle, Sharps Doom Bar and a couple of guests beers like Purity Pure UBU on handpump from the elegant modern bar counter, as well as a good range of well chosen wines with around 19 by the glass; mulled wine in winter and maybe home-made lemonade in summer; board games. More reports please. If you run a tab, they may ask to keep your credit card in a secure box.

The imaginative menu here changes twice a day and everything, from the mayonnaise to ice-cream is home-made. Interesting modern dishes might include pork, duck, prune and pistachio terrine, creamed mushrooms on toast with parmesan and poached egg, warm broccoli, spinach and gorgonzola tart, leg of lamb steak with butternut purée, fillet of bass with mussels, saffron, leek and tomato broth, roast chicken breast with roast garlic, shallot and green peppercorn butter, and smoked ham hock and gruyère with spicy tomato sauce. *Benchmark main dish: bavette steak and chips £14.00. Two-course evening meal £20.00.*

Free house ~ Licensee Andrew Solley ~ Real ale ~ Bar food (12.30-2.30(3 Sun), 7-10(9.30 Sun)) ~ (020) 7603 5374 ~ Children welcome ~ Dogs welcome ~ Open 11-11; 12-10.30 Sun

Recommended by Derek Thomas, Martin and Karen Wake

OUTER LONDON   TQ1769   Map A

Bishop Out of Residence £

Bishop's Hall, down alley off Thames Street; ⇄ *Hampton Wick, Kingston KT1 1PY*

Contemporary pub in a fine Thames spot with plenty of chairs on waterside terrace, lots of space inside, modern décor, real ale and fair-priced food

In fine weather, the many seats on the terrace overlooking the Thames and with views of Kingston Bridge are a real bonus. Inside, the open-plan contemporary bar is split up into more cosy areas with all manner of seating from comfortable sofas facing each other across a chest table, to groups of armchairs beside small circular tables, and yet more tables lining a long curved red wall banquette. There are dark red walls and ornate wallpaper hung with lots of gilt-framed pictures, standard lamps and modern ceiling lights. The upstairs lounge has windows overlooking the water, lots of dining chairs and another long wall banquette by tables on bare boards and trompe l'oeil bookshelves, and a fireplace beside sofas and a chaise longue. Wells & Youngs Bombardier, IPA, Special and a guest on handpump, 27 wines by the glass and various cocktails.

Good modern british cooking includes sandwiches and stone-baked pizzas as well as a weekend brunch, sharing boards, gressingham duck and root vegetable terrine with spiced apple chutney, salmon and haddock fishcake with thyme and lemon butter sauce, bangers and mash with onion gravy, and mushroom, spinach, chestnut and pine nut risotto; prices are fair for the London area. *Benchmark main dish: home-made burger £10.00. Two-course evening meal £15.00.*

Youngs ~ Manager Tanya Tozer ~ Real ale ~ Bar food (12-9.30; 10-10 Sat; 10-9 Sun) ~ (0208) 546 4965 ~ Children and dogs welcome away from upstairs lounge bar ~ Open 11-11(midnight Fri); 10(11 in winter)-midnight Sat; 10(11 in winter)-10.30 Sun

Recommended by Richard Gibbs

OUTER LONDON   TQ0490 Map C

Old Orchard

Off Park Lane; Harefield UB9 6HJ

Wonderful views from the garden in front of this Edwardian house, a good choice of drinks, friendly staff and well liked, interesting food

The stunning view from teak tables and chairs on the terrace in front of this former country house are much prized, so it's best to arrive early if you want to bag one. You look down over the longboats on the canal and on to the lakes that make up a conservation area known as the Colne Valley Regional Park; it's a haven for wildlife. Seats from the gazebo and picnic-sets in the garden have the same amazing view. Inside, the knocked-through open-plan rooms have an attractive mix of cushioned dining chairs around all size and shape of dark wooden tables, lots of prints, maps and pictures covering the walls, books on shelves, old glass bottles on window sills and rugs on wood or parquet flooring. One room is hung with a sizeable rug and some tapestry. There are daily papers to read, three cosy coal fires, big pot plants and fresh flowers. Half a dozen real ales on handpump include Fullers London Pride, Phoenix Brunning & Price, Tring Side Pocket for a Toad, alongside guests from brewers such as Adnams, St Austell and Windsor & Eton; also about two dozen wines by the glass and over 100 whiskies; friendly, helpful staff. The atmosphere is civilised and easy-going.

Popular brasserie-type food (the orders are sent to the kitchen along an unusual vacuum tube) includes interesting sandwiches, light meals and dishes such as roquefort, chestnut and fig tart with caramelised onion salad, spiced cauliflower, sweet potato and coriander bhaji with red pepper and cucumber relish, charcuterie to share, kedgeree with spinach and poached egg, malaysian fish stew, battered haddock, cauliflower, chickpea and almond tagine with apricot and date couscous, chicken, ham and leek pie, and rump steak with watercress and horseradish butter. *Benchmark main dish: sausage and mash £9.95. Two-course evening meal £18.95.*

Brunning & Price ~ Manager Dan Redfern ~ Real ale ~ Bar food (12-10(9.30 Sun)) ~ (01895) 822631 ~ Children welcome ~ Dogs allowed in bar ~ Open 11.30-11; 12-10.30 Sun

Recommended by Richard Gibbs

'Children welcome' means the pub says it lets children inside without any special restriction. If it allows them in, but to restricted areas such as an eating area or family room, we specify this. Places with separate restaurants often let children use them, and hotels usually let them into public areas such as lounges. Some pubs impose an evening time limit – let us know if you find one earlier than 9pm.

THE SOUTH EAST'S TOP PUBS

 ADSTOCK Buckinghamshire

SP7330 Map E

Old Thatched Inn
Main Street, off A413; MK18 2JN

Pretty thatched dining pub with keen landlord, friendly staff, real ales, and enjoyable food

This is a pretty, thatched dining pub in an attractive village and run by an enthusiastic landlord. The pubby front bar has low beams, flagstones, high bar chairs and an open fire and leads on to a dining area with more beams and a mix of pale wooden dining chairs around miscellaneous tables on the stripped wooden floor. There's a modern conservatory restaurant at the back. Fullers London Pride, Hook Norton Hooky Bitter and Timothy Taylors Landlord on handpump, several wines by the glass and 15 malt whiskies served by friendly staff. The sheltered terrace has tables and chairs under a gazebo.

 Making everything in-house including bread and ice-cream, the inventive food includes various appetisers, grilled black pudding and bacon salad with a poached duck egg and grain mustard dressing, asian-spiced cured salmon with sesame oil and bean sprout salad, home-made burger with blue cheese mayonnaise, courgette, lemon, spinach and parmesan risotto, pork fillet with a cider apple cream sauce, and slow-cooked lamb fillet with celeriac purée and a rosemary and redcurrant sauce. *Benchmark main dish: local sausages with onion gravy £11.95. Two-course evening meal £19.95.*

Free house ~ Licensee Andrew Judge ~ Real ale ~ Bar food (12-2.30, 6-9.30; 12-8 Sun) ~ Restaurant ~ (01296) 712584 ~ Children welcome ~ Dogs allowed in bar ~ Open 12-midnight

Recommended by Sue Vincent, Michael Dandy, Richard Inman

ALCISTON Sussex

TQ5005 Map C

Rose Cottage
Village signposted off A27 Polegate—Lewes; BN26 6UW

Old-fashioned cottage with cosy fires and country bric-a-brac, several wines by the glass, well liked food and local beers; bedrooms

This is a smashing old pub with a landlord of some character. It's extremely popular (get there early on Sunday lunchtimes especially) and many of our readers count it among their favourites. There are half a dozen tables with cushioned pews, winter log fires and quite a forest of harness, traps, a thatcher's blade and lots of other black ironware; more bric-a-brac on the shelves above the stripped pine dado or in the etched-glass windows and maybe Jasper the parrot (only at lunchtimes – he gets too noisy in the evenings). The restaurant area has a lunchtime overflow as they don't take bookings in the bar then. Dark Star Hophead, Harveys Best and a guest beer on handpump and several wines by the glass. Piped music, darts and board games. For cooler evenings, there are heaters outside and the small paddock in the garden has ducks and chickens; boules. Nearby fishing and shooting. They take self-catering bedroom bookings for a minimum of two nights. The charming small village (and local church) are certainly worth a look and there are bracing South Downs walks nearby.

🍴 Popular bar food (they also have an evening restaurant menu) includes potted shrimps, farmhouse-style pâté with apple and plum chutney, local sausages with onion gravy, battered local cod, rabbit and bacon pie, lamb tagine with apricots, chickpeas and chilli, and crispy gressingham duck with orange and peppercorn sauce. *Benchmark main dish: fish pie £11.50. Two-course evening meal £18.00.*

Free house ~ Licensee Ian Lewis ~ Real ale ~ Bar food ~ Restaurant ~ (01323) 870377 ~ Children allowed if over 10 ~ Dogs allowed in bar ~ Open 11.30-3, 6.30-11; 12-3, 6.30-10.30 Sun; closed 25 and 26 Dec, evening 1 Jan ~ Bedrooms: /£60S

Recommended by the Didler, PL, Ian and Nita Cooper, Ron and Sheila Corbett, Terry and Nickie Williams, Gene and Tony Freemantle, Simon Watkins, Peter Meister, Phil and Jane Villiers, Alan Franck, R and S Bentley, Mike Gorton, Tracey and Stephen Groves

 ALFRISTON Sussex   TQ5203   Map C

George

High Street; BN26 5SY

Venerable inn in lovely village with comfortable, heavily beamed bars, good wines and several real ales; fine nearby walks; bedrooms

Much enjoyed by our readers, this is an ancient and very well run village inn. The busy long bar has massive hop-hung low beams, appropriately soft lighting and a log fire (or summer flower arrangement) in a huge stone inglenook fireplace that dominates the room, with lots of copper and brass around it. There are settles and chairs around sturdy stripped tables, Greene King IPA and Abbot, Hardys & Hansons Old Trip and a guest like Goddards Fuggle-Dee-Dum on handpump, decent wines including champagne by the glass, board games and piped music; good service. The lounge has comfortable sofas, standing timbers and rugs on the wooden floor and the restaurant is cosy and candlelit. There are seats in the spacious flint-walled garden and two long-distance paths, the South Downs Way and Vanguard Way, cross here; Cuckmere Haven is close by. The beamed bedrooms are comfortable; they don't have a car park but there is parking a couple of minutes away.

🍴 Good, interesting food includes lunchtime sandwiches, rustic sharing boards, grilled field mushrooms with manchego and chorizo, smoked salmon and mackerel terrine, sausage and mash with onion gravy, a changing risotto, game casserole, and corn-fed chicken with a roasted tomato and olive sauce. *Benchmark main dish: seared salmon fillet and prawns with chilli, garlic white wine and cream on pasta £14.50. Two-course evening meal £20.95.*

Greene King ~ Lease Roland and Cate Couch ~ Real ale ~ Bar food (all day) ~ Restaurant ~ (01323) 870319 ~ Children welcome ~ Dogs allowed in bar and bedrooms ~ Open 11-11(midnight Sat) ~ Bedrooms: £70S/£100B

Recommended by Phil Bryant, Andy West, Tracey and Stephen Groves, Ian and Nita Cooper, Phil and Jane Villiers

 ARRETON Isle of Wight   SZ5386   Map D

White Lion £

A3056 Newport—Sandown; PO30 3AA

Friendly local with pubby food

A genuinely warm welcome awaits at this white-painted village house. The neatly kept beamed lounge is comfortably old fashioned and cosy, with dark pink walls or stripped brick above a stained pine dado, gleaming brass and horse tack and lots of cushioned wheelback chairs on the patterned red carpet. The piped music tends to be very quiet, and the public bar has a TV, games machine, darts and board games.Three changing real ales on handpump might be Wells & Youngs Eagle, Sharps Doom Bar and Wadworths 6X and they've a farm cider and draught pear cider. There's also a restaurant (no children in here), family room and stable room. The pleasant garden has a small play area.

Traditional tasty food, served in generous helpings, runs from sandwiches and ploughman's to whitebait and breaded brie with vegetable curry, stews, seasonal local game, fish and seafood as main courses. *Benchmark main dish: pie of the day £9.95. Two-course evening meal £15.45.*

Enterprise ~ Lease Chris and Kate Cole ~ Real ale ~ Bar food (12-9) ~ Restaurant ~ (01983) 528479 ~ Children welcome away from bar ~ Dogs allowed in bar ~ Open 11(12 Sun)-11

Recommended by Simon Collett-Jones, Terry and Nickie Williams

 BANK Hampshire   SU2806   Map D

Oak

Signposted just off A35 SW of Lyndhurst; SO43 7FE

Tucked-away and very busy New Forest pub with well liked food and interesting décor

Given its peaceful and tucked-away location, it's quite a surprise how busy this pub always is; to be sure of a table, it's best to book in advance. On either side of the door in the bay windows of the L-shaped bar are built-in red-cushioned seats, and on the right there are two or three little pine-panelled booths with small built-in tables and bench seats. The rest of the bare-boarded bar has some low beams and joists, candles in individual brass holders on a line of stripped old and newer blond tables set against the wall and all manner of bric-a-brac: fishing rods, spears, a boomerang, old ski poles, brass platters, heavy knives and guns. There are cushioned milk churns along the bar counter and little red lanterns among hop bines above the bar. Fullers London Pride and Gales HSB and Seafarers on handpump; piped music. The pleasant side garden has picnic-sets, long tables and benches by the big yew trees.

Popular bar food includes sandwiches, whole baked camembert with fruit chutney, maple syrup-roasted ham with free-range eggs, pasta parcels filled with cheese and pear in a creamy basil sauce, steak in ale pie, pork chop with five bean rice salad and citrus and sweet chilli sauce, and a steak of the day. *Benchmark main dish: steak in ale pie £10.95. Two-course evening meal £17.00.*

Fullers ~ Manager Martin Sliva ~ Real ale ~ Bar food (12-2.30, 6-9.30; all day weekends) ~ (023) 8028 2350 ~ Children welcome but all under-10s must leave by 6pm ~ Dogs welcome ~ Open 11.30-11; 12-10.30 Sun; 11.30-3, 6-11 weekdays in winter

Recommended by Terry and Nickie Williams, Laurence Smith, the Shiread family, Lois Dyer, Leslie and Barbara Owen, Phyl and Jack Street, Mike and Sue Loseby, Mr and Mrs D Hammond, Peter Meister, Ian and Rose Lock, Mr and Mrs P D Titcomb, Phil and Jane Villiers, N R White, Steven King and Barbara Cameron

---

Please keep sending us reports. We rely on readers for news of new discoveries, and particularly for news of changes – however slight – at the fully described pubs:
feedback@goodguides.com, or (no stamp needed)
The Good Pub Guide, FREEPOST TN1569, Wadhurst, E Sussex TN5 7BR.

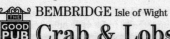

BEMBRIDGE Isle of Wight   SZ6587   Map D

Crab & Lobster

Foreland Fields Road, off Howgate Road (which is off B3395 via Hillway Road); PO35 5TR

Clifftop views from terrace and some bedrooms

Perched on low cliffs within yards of the shore, the relaxed waterside terrace here enjoys terrific Solent views – not surprisingly, it's a very popular summer destination (service can slow down at peak times) and the picnic-sets fill up quickly; the dining area and some of the bedrooms share the same views. Inside it's roomier than you might expect and is done out in an almost parlourish style, with lots of yachting memorabilia, old local photographs and a blazing winter fire; darts, dominoes and cribbage. Goddards Fuggle-Dee-Dum, Greene King IPA and Sharps Doom Bar are on handpump, with a dozen wines by the glass, 16 malt whiskies and good coffee.

As well as curries, lasagne and daily specials, they do seafood dishes including lobster; they may keep your credit card if you run a tab. *Benchmark main dish: crab cakes £10.95. Two-course evening meal £20.90.*

Enterprise ~ Lease Caroline and Ian Quekett ~ Real ale ~ Bar food (12-2.30, 6-9(9.30 Fri, Sat) with limited menu 2.30-5.30 weekends and holidays) ~ Restaurant ~ (01983) 872244 ~ Children welcome ~ Dogs allowed in bar ~ Open 11-11; 12-10.30 Sun ~ Bedrooms: £50S(£55B)/£85S(£90B)

Recommended by Guy Consterdine, Thomas Moore, George Atkinson, Simon Collett-Jones, Paul Humphreys, Tony and Maggie Harwood, Anne and Jeff Peel, Mark Seymour, Jackie Roberts

BENTWORTH Hampshire   SU6740   Map D

Sun

Sun Hill; from the A339 coming from Alton, the first turning takes you there direct; or in village follow Shalden 2¼, Alton 4¼ signpost; GU34 5JT

Smashing choice of real ales and welcoming landlady in popular country pub; nearby walks

Even on a wet and windy winter's day, this bustling 17th-c country pub will be full of chatty customers – all warmly welcomed by the friendly landlady and her helpful staff. The two little traditional communicating rooms have high-backed antique settles, pews and schoolroom chairs, olde-worlde prints and blacksmith's tools on the walls, and bare boards and scrubbed deal tables on the left; three big fireplaces with log fires make it especially snug in winter. An arch leads to a brick-floored room with another open fire. There's a fine choice of seven real ales on handpump: Andwell Resolute Bitter, Bowman Wallops Wood, Fullers London Pride, Hogs Back TEA, Otter Amber, Sharps Doom Bar and Stonehenge Pigswill. There are seats out in front and in the back garden; pleasant nearby walks.

Generous helpings of carefully cooked, good food might include sandwiches, filo prawns with a sweet chilli or garlic mayonnaise dip, chicken curry, avocado and stilton bake, game or steak and mushroom in ale pies, gammon and egg, calves liver and bacon with onion gravy, and chicken in honey and wholegrain mustard sauce. *Benchmark main dish: beer-battered cod £11.95. Two-course evening meal £19.40.*

Free house ~ Licensee Mary Holmes ~ Real ale ~ Bar food ~ (01420) 562338 ~ Children welcome ~ Dogs welcome ~ Open 12-3, 6-11; 12-11 Sun

Recommended by Phyl and Jack Street, Ann and Colin Hunt, Mrs Jill Rich, Neil and Karen Dignan, the Didler, Mr and Mrs D Hammond, Mr and Mrs H J Langley, Martin and Karen Wake, Tony and Jill Radnor, Stephen Saunders, Margaret Grimwood

 BESSELS LEIGH Oxfordshire   SP4501 Map E

 **Greyhound**
A420 Faringdon—Botley; OX13 5PX

400-year-old handsome stone pub with knocked-through rooms, plenty of character and interest, individual furnishings, half a dozen real ales and lots of wines by the glass, good service, and enjoyable food

Dating back 400 years, this is a handsome golden-stone building and a former coaching inn. The knocked-through rooms give plenty of space and interest and the half-panelled walls are covered in all manner of old photographs and pictures. The individually chosen cushioned dining chairs, leather-topped stools and dark wooden tables are grouped on the carpeting or rug-covered floorboards and there are books on shelves, glass and stone bottles on windowsills, big gilt mirrors, three fireplaces (one housing a woodburning stove), and sizeable pot plants dotted about. Wooden bar stools sit against the counter where they serve Adnams Southwold, Brunning & Price Original (brewed for the company by Phoenix), Everards Coppernob, Hook Norton Hooky Bitter, Loose Cannon Pale Ale and White Horse Wayland Smithy on handpump, 15 wines by the glass and 80 malt whiskies, and staff are friendly and helpful. By the back dining extension there's a white picket fence-enclosed garden with picnic-sets under green parasols.

Modern bar food includes good sandwiches and light meals as well as interesting dishes such as pigeon and thyme wellington with celeriac purée and juniper jus, wild mushroom, leek and walnut quiche, venison faggots with bubble and squeak and onion gravy, king prawn, pineapple and cashew nut salad, and chicken, pearl barley and vegetable broth with bacon and thyme dumplings. *Benchmark main dish: steak burger topped with bacon and cheese £10.95. Two-course evening meal £17.70.*

Brunning & Price ~ Manager Emily Waring ~ Real ale ~ Bar food (12-10(9.30 Sun)) ~ (01865) 862110 ~ Children welcome ~ Dogs allowed in bar ~ Open 12-11(10.30 Sun)
Recommended by Jan and Roger Ferris, Derek Goldrei

BIDDENDEN Kent   TQ8238 Map C

Three Chimneys
A262, 1 mile W of village; TN27 8LW
KENT DINING PUB OF THE YEAR

Pubby beamed rooms of considerable individuality, log fires, imaginative food, and pretty garden

The little low-beamed rooms at this appealingly civilised place have a charmingly timeless feel – as one reader put it 'spend more than a couple of pints here and you will cheerfully let slip which decade you are in'. They are simply done out with plain wooden furniture and old settles on flagstones and coir matting, some harness and sporting prints on the stripped-brick walls and good log fires. The public bar on the left is quite down-to-earth, with darts, dominoes and cribbage. Adnams Best, St Austell Tribute and a guest tapped straight from casks racked behind the counter, several wines by the glass, local Biddenden cider and apple juice and several malt whiskies. But don't be misled into thinking this place is in any way old fashioned. In fact, the candlelit bare-boards restaurant though rurally rustic in its decor is chatty and alive with customers and the style of dining is completely up to date. French windows open from the restaurant to a conservatory and garden. Sissinghurst Gardens are nearby.

Excellent (if not cheap) food changes daily but might include french onion soup, smoked haddock, creamed leek and bacon tart, baked mushrooms topped with caramelised red onions, duck leg confit, sun-dried tomato couscous with potato wedge, and grilled brie with balsamic roast vegetables. *Benchmark main dish: smoked haddock with creamed leeks and chive velouté £18.95. Two-course evening meal £23.70.*

Free house ~ Licensee Craig Smith ~ Real ale ~ Bar food (12-2(2.30 Sat, Sun), 6.30-9 (9.30 Sat)) ~ (01580) 291472 ~ Children welcome ~ Dogs allowed in bar ~ Open 11.30-3.30, 5.30-11; 12-4, 6-11.30 Sun

Recommended by Robert Kibble, A and H Piper, Jill and Julian Tasker, John and Enid Morris, Colin and Louise English, Cathryn and Richard Hicks, the Didler, Mrs J Ekins-Daukes, Bill Adie, Anthony Longden, Gordon and Margaret Ormondroyd, Malcolm and Barbara Southwell, Derek Thomas

BLINDLEY HEATH Surrey   TQ3645 Map C

Red Barn ♀

Tandridge Lane, just off B2029, which is off A22; RH7 6LL

Splendidly converted spacious farmhouse and barn with plenty of character, food all day starting with breakfast

The chief glory at this 300-year-old farmhouse is its huge raftered barn conversion that features a central glassed woodburning stove with a chimney that soars up into the roof timbers. Contemporary décor with bright red and green splashes of colour works well against a plethora of stripped beams and timbers. Funky round modern lights and a large model plane hang from the elevated rafters and one wall is dominated by shelves of books stretching high above a window and a wall hung with antlers. An eclectic mix of modern furnishings includes everything from leather or wicker chairs to cow-print pouffes. Clever partitioning creates cosier areas too, each with their own character and comfortably intimate feel. A lighter farmhouse-style room that they call the pantry has big wooden tables and a red cooking range; it's where they serve breakfast. Efficient smartly dressed staff take your order at the table, but this is very much a pub, with bar billiards and a pile of board games in the adjacent bar, along with sofas by another sizeable fireplace; piped music. Two real ales might be from Adnams, Harveys or Sharps and there's a good wine list. A big farmer's market is held here the first Saturday morning of each month and they may also have summer barbecues and hold various foodie events. Out on the lawn, you'll find solid granite tables.

Well presented bar food relies on fresh local ingredients, which, from a daily changing menu, might include filled baguettes, ham hock and parsley terrine, roast courgette and dried tomato tart, black pudding salad with hard-boiled egg, battered haddock, chicken caesar salad, pea, broad bean and mint risotto, cumberland sausage and mash, fried bream with tomato salsa and white wine sauce, and steak, Guinness and mushroom pie. *Benchmark main dish: home-made burger £10.75. Two-course evening meal £20.00.*

Geronimo Inns ~ Manager Sacha Dickinson ~ Real ale ~ Bar food (12-3, 6-9.30(10 Fri, Sat); 12-8 Sun; breakfast 9.30am-11am Sat, Sun) ~ Restaurant ~ (01342) 830820 ~ Children welcome ~ Dogs allowed in bar ~ Live music last Fri of month ~ Open 10-11; 9.30-11 Sat; 9.30-11 Sun

Recommended by Derek Thomas, John Branston, Grahame Brooks

BOUGH BEECH Kent   TQ4846   Map C

Wheatsheaf ♀ ◀

B2027, S of reservoir; TN8 7NU

Former hunting lodge with lots to look at, fine range of local drinks, popular food, and plenty of seats in appealing garden

Said to have been built as a medieval royal hunting lodge, this ancient ivy-clad building is full of characterful features and historic detail. Its neat central bar and long front bar (which has an attractive old settle carved with wheatsheaves) have unusually high ceilings with lofty oak timbers, a screen of standing timbers and a revealed king post. Divided from the central bar by two more rows of standing timbers – one formerly an outside wall to the building – are the snug and another bar. On the walls and above the massive stone fireplaces, there are quite a few horns and heads as well as african masks, a sword from Fiji, crocodiles, stuffed birds, swordfish spears and a matapee. Look out, too, for the piece of 1607 graffiti, 'Foxy Holamby', who is thought to have been a whimsical local squire. Thoughtful touches include piles of smart magazines, board games, tasty nibbles and winter chestnuts to roast. Harveys Best, Westerham Brewery Grasshopper and a guest are on handpump and they've three ciders (including one from local Biddenden), a decent wine list, several malt whiskies, summer Pimms and winter mulled wine. Outside is appealing too, with plenty of seats, flowerbeds and fruit trees in the sheltered side and back gardens. Shrubs help divide the garden into various areas, so it doesn't feel too crowded even when it's full.

Bar food (there may be a wait at busy times) might include breaded whiting with sweet chilli sauce, lamb kofta kebab with chickpea and feta salad and minted yoghurt, potted crab and brown shrimps with harissa, battered whiting, chicken fillet in honey and wholegrain mustard sauce, mexican bean burger with spicy tomato sauce, and fried rump of lamb with sweet potatoes and redcurrant and mint gravy. *Benchmark main dish: shepherd's pie £12.95. Two-course evening meal £18.75.*

Enterprise ~ Lease Liz and David Currie ~ Real ale ~ Bar food (10-12) ~ (01732) 700254 ~ Children welcome in one area of bar ~ Dogs welcome ~ Folk night monthly ~ Open 11-11

Recommended by David and Sue Atkinson, Mrs B Forster, Bob and Margaret Holder, D P and M A Miles, Andrea Rampley, John Branston, Nigel and Jean Eames, Kevin Thomas, Nina Randall

BOVINGDON GREEN Buckinghamshire   SU8386   Map D

Royal Oak ⑪ ♀

0.75 miles N of Marlow, on back road to Frieth signposted off West Street (A4155) in centre; SL7 2JF

BUCKINGHAMSHIRE DINING PUB OF THE YEAR

Civilised dining pub with nice little bar, excellent choice of wines by the glass, real ales, good service, and excellent food

This is a smashing all-rounder and much enjoyed by our readers. Of course, much emphasis is placed on the delicious food but the friendly and helpful staff will make you just as welcome if you only want a drink – they keep Rebellion IPA, Mutiny and Smuggler on handpump, 21 wines by the glass (all from Europe), nine pudding wines and a good choice of liqueurs. Locals tend to head for the low-beamed cosy snug, closest to the car park, which has three small tables, a woodburning stove in an exposed brick fireplace, and a big pile of logs. Several attractively decorated areas open off the central bar: the half-panelled walls variously painted in pale blue, green or cream (though the dining room ones are red). Throughout, there's a mix of church chairs, stripped wooden tables and chunky wall seats, with rugs on the partly wooden, partly flagstoned floors, co-ordinated cushions and curtains, and a very bright, airy feel; thoughtful extra touches enhance the tone: a bowl of olives on the bar, carefully laid-out newspapers and fresh flowers or candles on the tables. Board games and piped music. A terrace with good solid tables leads to an appealing garden, and there's a smaller side garden; pétanque. Civilised dining pub with nice little bar, excellent choice of wines by the glass, real ales, good service and excellent food.

Beautifully presented and imaginative, the food includes lunchtime sandwiches, much-liked bubble and squeak with smoked bacon, free-range poached egg and hollandaise, oak-smoked salmon, soused shallot and potato salad and caviar and dill dressing, rabbit, pearl barley and mustard pie with carrot hash, filo-baked sweet potato, celeriac and double gloucester dauphinoise with dandelion and fennel salad, and roast and braised baby chicken with chorizo and vegetable minestrone. *Benchmark main dish: coley fillet with ham hock and pea risotto and lemon mascarpone £13.75. Two-course evening meal £20.00.*

Salisbury Pubs ~ Lease James Penlington ~ Real ale ~ Bar food (12-2.30(3 Sat, 4 Sun), 6.30-9.30(10 Fri, Sat)) ~ Restaurant ~ (01628) 488611 ~ Children welcome ~ Dogs allowed in bar ~ Open 11-11; 12-10.30 Sun; closed 25 and 26 Dec

Recommended by Serkan Ibrahim, Chris Smith, Jeff and Wendy Williams, Tracey and Stephen Groves, C and R Bromage, Doug Kennedy, Neil and Karen Dignan, Martin and Karen Wake, Gordon Maddocks, Jonathan Holloway, Neil and Anne McDougall

BRAMLEY Surrey   TQ0044   Map C

Jolly Farmer

High Street; GU5 0HB

Relaxed village inn near Surrey hills with great selection of beers

The eight handpumps at this family-owned free house serve Hogsback HBB and Sharps Doom Bar alongside half a dozen guests – they can go through up to 20 different ales a week – typically from brewers such as Ballards, Milestone and Vale. They also keep three changing belgian draught beers and a dozen wines by the glass. The traditional interior is filled with a miscellany of homely wooden tables and chairs, with various collections of plates, enamel advertising signs, sewing machines, antique bottles, prints and old tools filling the walls and surfaces. Timbered semi-partitions, a mixture of brick and timbering and an open fireplace give it a snug cosy feel; piped music, TV (which can be loud), dominoes and board games. There are tables out by the car park and the village is handy for Winkworth Arboretum and walks up St Martha's Hill.

As well as lunchtime sandwiches, bar food includes whitebait, smoked haddock fishcakes, ploughman's, home-made burger, fried cod fillet with citrus and saffron butter, pie of the day, with daily specials such as fried calves liver with red wine jus, fried duck breast with port and redcurrant sauce, mushroom risotto, and baked trout with lemon and dill. *Benchmark main dish: fish and chips £10.00. Two-course evening meal £20.50.*

Free house ~ Licensees Steve and Chris Hardstone ~ Real ale ~ Bar food (12-2.30, 6.30(7 Sun)-9.30) ~ Restaurant ~ (01483) 893355 ~ Children welcome ~ Dogs allowed in bar and bedrooms ~ Open 11-11; 12-11 Sun ~ Bedrooms: £60S(£65B)/£70S(£75B)

Recommended by Brian and Anna Marsden, Revd R P Tickle, LM, John Branston

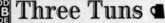 BRANSGORE Hampshire   SZ1997   Map D

Three Tuns ◀

Village signposted off A35 and off B3347 N of Christchurch; Ringwood Road, opposite church; BH23 8JH

Interesting food in pretty thatched pub with proper old-fashioned bar and good beers, as well as a civilised main dining area

In summer, this 17th-c thatched pub with its lovely hanging baskets looks quite charming and there's an attractive, extensive shrub-sheltered terrace with picnic-sets on its brick pavers; beyond that are more tables out on the grass looking over pony paddocks. But whatever time of year, you can be sure of a friendly welcome from the cheerful landlord and his staff and there are always plenty of happy customers. The roomy low-ceilinged and carpeted main area has a fireside 'codgers' corner', as well as a good mix of comfortably cushioned low chairs around a variety of dining tables. On the right is a separate traditional regulars' bar that seems almost taller than it is wide, with an impressive log-effect stove in a stripped brick hearth, some shiny black panelling and individualistic pubby furnishings. Ringwood Best and Fortyniner and Timothy Taylors Landlord and guests like Otter Bitter and Sharps Doom Bar on handpump and a good choice of wines by the glass. The pub is on the edge of the New Forest Country Park. The Grade II listed barn is popular for parties.

Using local produce and making everything in-house, the wide choice of popular food includes lunchtime sandwiches, dorset snails in garlic and tarragon butter, foie gras terrine with crab apple jam, truffle risotto, bangers and mash, rabbit pie, and rack of lamb with aubergine moussaka. *Benchmark main dish: bass with asparagus, tomatoes, shaved fennel and a lemon fish sauce £14.95. Two-course evening meal £20.25.*

Enterprise ~ Lease Nigel Glenister ~ Real ale ~ Bar food (12-2.15, 6-9.15; all day weekends) ~ Restaurant ~ (01425) 672232 ~ Children welcome ~ Dogs allowed in bar ~ Open 11(11.30 Sat)-11.30; 12-11 Sun

Recommended by Laurence Smith, Phyl and Jack Street, N R White, Terry and Nickie Williams, Henry Fryer, Caz Brant, Roger Baynes

BRAY Berkshire   SU9079   Map D

Crown ⑪ ♀

1.75 miles from M4 junction 9; A308 towards Windsor, then left at Bray signpost on to B3028; High Street; SL6 2AH

Low-beamed pub with refurbished, knocked-through rooms, surprisingly pubby food (given the owner), real ales and plenty of outside seating

Now that this 16th-c pub is owned by Heston Blumenthal, many customers are here for the good, surprisingly pubby food. But drinkers drop in, too, and they keep Courage Best and Directors and Sharps Doom Bar on handpump and several wines by the glass. The partly panelled main bar has heavy old beams – some so low you may have to mind your head – plenty of timbers handily left at elbow height where walls have been knocked through, three winter log fires and newly upholstered dining chairs and cushioned settles. There are modern slatted chairs and tables in the courtyard with plenty of picnic-sets in the large, enclosed back garden.

Popular food now includes lunchtime sandwiches, potted duck with grilled bread, moules marinière, macaroni with leeks and chanterelle mushrooms, steak burger with fries, steak in ale suet pie and lemon sole with potted shrimps, cucumber and dill; vegetables are extra which bumps the price up. *Benchmark main dish: hereford sirloin steak with marrowbone sauce £19.50. Two-course evening meal £21.75.*

Scottish Courage ~ Manager Tony Carson ~ Real ale ~ Bar food (12-2.30(3 weekends), 6(7 Sun)-9.30(6.30-10 Fri and Sat)) ~ Restaurant ~ (01628) 621936 ~ Children welcome ~ Dogs welcome ~ Open 11-11; 12-10.30 Sun; closed 25-27 Dec

Recommended by Ron and Sheila Corbett, Hunter and Christine Wright

 **BRAY** Berkshire   SU9079 Map D

Hinds Head 🍴 ♉

High Street; car park opposite (exit rather tricky); SL6 2AB

BERKSHIRE DINING PUB OF THE YEAR

Top-notch gastropub with excellent food, traditional surroundings and a fine choice of drinks

Under the same ownership as the nearby Crown and the renowned Fat Duck restaurant, this handsome old pub is exceedingly popular for its excellent food. They do keep Rebellion IPA and Smuggler and Windsor & Eton Guardsman on handpump, 14 wines by the glass from an extensive list and quite a few malt whiskies, but there's no doubt that most customers are here to eat. The thoroughly traditional L-shaped bar has dark beams and panelling, polished oak parquet, blazing log fires, red-cushioned built-in wall seats and studded leather carving chairs around small round tables, and latticed windows.

First class, if not cheap, food might include devils on horseback, ham hock and foie gras terrine with piccalilli, venison cheeseburger, chicken, smoked guinea fowl and mushroom pie, fillet of bream with wild garlic and mussel broth and steak with bone marrow sauce. *Benchmark main dish: oxtail and kidney pudding £17.50. Two-course evening meal £25.45.*

Free house ~ Licensee Kevin Love ~ Real ale ~ Bar food (12-2.30, 6.30-9.30; 12-4 Sun; not Sun evening) ~ Restaurant ~ (01628) 626151 ~ Children welcome ~ Dogs allowed in bar ~ Open 11-11; 12-10.30 Sun

Recommended by Les Scott-Maynard, John Urquhart, Graham Oddey, Hunter and Christine Wright, Simon Collett-Jones

---

If a pub tries to make you leave a credit card behind the bar, be on your guard. The credit card firms and banks that issue them condemn this practice. After all, the publican who asks you to do this is in effect saying: 'I don't trust you'. Have you any more reason to trust his staff? If your card is used fraudulently while you have let it be kept out of your sight, the card company could say you've been negligent yourself – and refuse to make good your losses. So say that they can 'swipe' your card instead, but must hand it back to you. Please let us know if a pub does try to keep your card.

BRIGHTWELL BALDWIN Oxfordshire   SU6594 Map E

Lord Nelson 🍴 ♀

Off B480 Chalgrove—Watlington, or B4009 Benson—Watlington; OX49 5NP

Attractive inn with several different character bars, real ales, good wines by the glass and enjoyable food; bedrooms

Most customers come to this busy 300-year-old inn to enjoy the interesting food but they do keep Adnams Bitter, Black Sheep Best and Brakspears Bitter on handpump and around 14 wines by the glass. There are wheelback and other dining chairs around a mix of dark tables, candles and fresh flowers, wine bottles on window sills, horsebrasses on standing timbers, lots of paintings on the white or red walls and a big brick inglenook fireplace. One cosy room has cushions on comfortable sofas, little lamps on dark furniture, ornate mirrors and portraits in gilt frames; piped music. There are seats on the back terrace with more in the willow-draped garden and the pub is prettily placed on a quiet lane opposite the church.

 As well as sandwiches, the well thought-of food includes coarse pâté with home-made chutney, thai fishcakes with sesame and lime dipping sauce, asparagus, mint and lemon risotto, beer-battered fresh haddock with triple-cooked chips, calves liver with onion rings and red wine sauce, and half a slow-roasted duck with spiced plum sauce. *Benchmark main dish: local free-range pork sausages with onion gravy £12.95. Two-course evening meal £21.20.*

Free house ~ Licensees Roger and Carole Shippey ~ Real ale ~ Bar food (12-2.30, 6-10) ~ Restaurant ~ (01491) 612497 ~ Children welcome ~ Dogs allowed in bar ~ Open 12-3, 6-11; 12-10.30 Sun ~ Bedrooms: £70B/£90B

Recommended by Hugh Roberts, Neil and Karen Dignan, D and M T Ayres-Regan, Roy Hoing

BROOKLAND Kent   TQ9825 Map C

Royal Oak 🍴 🛏

Just off A259 Rye—New Romney; High Street; TN29 9QR

Lovely old building with gently modernised rooms, comfortable atmosphere, delicious food, and seats in garden; bedrooms

Such are the sensitive alterations at this welcoming 17th-c inn on Romney Marsh that it retains an attractive timeless feel. The bar is light and airy with big windows, one nice old pew and leather upholstered chairs around oak tables on flagstones, oak boards and bricks. Locals pop in to sit on the high bar chairs by the granite-topped counter for a chat and a pint: Adnams Best, Harveys and Woodfordes Wherry on handpump, 17 wines by the glass. The friendly landlord knows a lot about the local area and his equestrian interests are manifest in a lovely set of racing watercolours and a couple of signed photographs on the lime white wall panelling in the bar and in a rather special set of Cecil Aldin prints displayed in the beamed restaurant (with its well spaced tables and big inglenook fireplace). French windows from here open on to a terrace with metal chairs and there are picnic-sets in the narrow garden beyond and quaint views of the ancient church and graveyard next door; piped music and a woodburning stove.

Though we don't usually mention it in the text, most pubs now provide coffee or tea – so it's always worth asking.

🍴 Lovingly sourced and prepared food includes filled baps, ploughman's, chargrilled beefburger, fish and chips, and specials such as seared wood pigeon breasts with rhubarb compote, grilled mackerel with chilli jam glaze and wild garlic mash, chicken breast wrapped in air-dried ham and stuffed with mozzarella and basil and roast pork chop with crumbled black pudding and celeriac and apple mash; they do spit roasts in the inglenook on Wednesday evenings. *Benchmark main dish: grilled rump of lamb £15.95. Two-course evening meal £20.00.*

Enterprise ~ Lease David Rhys Jones ~ Real ale ~ Bar food (12-2(2.30 Fri-Sun), 6.30-9) ~ Restaurant ~ (01797) 344215 ~ No children under 12 in evening restaurant ~ Dogs allowed in bar ~ Open 12-3, 6-11; closed Sun and Mon evenings ~ Bedrooms: /£75(£95B)

Recommended by Sue Fincham, Colin and Louise English, Sara Fulton, Roger Baker, V Brogden, B and M Kendall, John Peppitt, Kevin Thomas, Nina Randall

BROOKLAND Kent   TQ9724 Map C

Woolpack £

On A259 from Rye, about 1 mile before Brookland, take the first right turn signposted Midley where the main road bends sharp left, just after the expanse of Walland Marsh; OS Sheet 189 map reference 977244; TN29 9TJ

15th-c pub with simple furnishings, massive inglenook fireplace, big helpings of tasty food and large garden

Steeped in the atmosphere of days gone by, this crooked early 15th-c cottage is said to have been the haunt of local smugglers. Its ancient entrance lobby has an uneven brick floor and black-painted pine-panelled walls, and to the right, the simple quarry-tiled main bar has basic cushioned plank seats in the massive inglenook fireplace and a painted wood-effect bar counter hung with lots of water jugs. Low-beamed ceilings include some very early ships' timbers (maybe 12th c) thought to be from local shipwrecks. A long elm table has shove-ha'penny carved into one end and there are other old and newer wall benches, chairs at mixed tables with flowers and candles and photographs of locals on the walls. The two pub cats, Liquorice and Charlie Girl, are often toasting themselves around the log fire. To the left of the lobby is a sparsely furnished little room and an open-plan family room; piped music. Shepherd Neame Master Brew, Spitfire and two seasonal brews on handpump. In summer, the award-winning hanging baskets are really quite a sight and there are plenty of picnic-sets under parasols in the garden with its barbecue area; it's all nicely lit up in the evenings.

🍴 Reasonably priced, the pubby food includes sandwiches and baguettes, filled baked potatoes, ploughman's, soup, steak pie, stilton and vegetable bake, battered cod, generous moules marinière and mixed grill. *Benchmark main dish: mixed grill £13.95. Two-course evening meal £15.45.*

Shepherd Neame ~ Tenant Scott Balcomb ~ Real ale ~ Bar food (12-2.30, 7-9; all day Sat, Sun) ~ Restaurant ~ (01797) 344321 ~ Children in family room ~ Dogs welcome ~ Open 11-3, 6-11; 12-11 Sat, Sun

Recommended by Colin and Louise English, John Prescott, Mr and Mrs Price

---

'Children welcome' means the pub says it lets children inside without any special restriction. If it allows them in, but to restricted areas such as an eating area or family room, we specify this. Places with separate restaurants often let children use them, and hotels usually let them into public areas such as lounges. Some pubs impose an evening time limit – let us know if you find one earlier than 9pm.

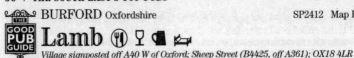

BURFORD Oxfordshire   SP2412   Map E

Lamb

Village signposted off A40 W of Oxford; Sheep Street (B4425, off A361); OX18 4LR

Proper pubby bar in civilised inn, real ales and an extensive wine list, interesting bar and restaurant food, and pretty gardens; bedrooms

This is a lovely 15th-c inn, very much enjoyed by our readers for its civilised but friendly and relaxed atmosphere and its genuine mix of customers – hotel guests, diners and chatty locals. The cosy bar remains the heart of the place with high-backed settles and old chairs on flagstones in front of the log fire, Hook Norton Bitter and Old Hooky on handpump and an extensive wine list with 16 by the glass; board games. The roomy beamed main lounge is charmingly traditional, with distinguished old seats including a chintzy high-winged settle, ancient cushioned wooden armchairs, seats built into its stone-mullioned windows and fresh flowers on polished oak and elm tables; also, rugs on the wide flagstones and polished oak floorboards, a winter log fire under its fine mantelpiece and plenty of antiques and other decorations including a grandfather clock. Service is impeccable. A pretty terrace with teak furniture leads down to small neatly kept lawns surrounded by flowers, shrubs and small trees, and the garden itself is a real suntrap, enclosed as it is by the warm stone of the surrounding buildings.

 Under the new licensee, the good, often interesting food might include open sandwiches, sharing deli boards (charcuterie, fish or antipasti), crayfish and chive risotto, lamb burger with mint sauce and chips, confit duck leg with plum chutney, braised pig's trotter with ham and morels with potato truffle purée and apple and black pudding salad, and salmon and scallops with aubergine caviar, sundried tomato purée and pesto dressing; they offer a two- and three-course set evening menu. *Benchmark main dish: lamb burger with home-made mint sauce £12.50. Two-course evening meal £20.45.*

Cotswold Inns & Hotels ~ Manager Bill Ramsay ~ Real ale ~ Bar food (12-2.30(3 Sun), 6.30-9.30) ~ Restaurant ~ (01993) 823155 ~ Children welcome ~ Dogs welcome ~ Open 12-11(midnight weekends) ~ Bedrooms: £120B/£155B

Recommended by MDN, David and Sue Smith, the Didler, Eithne Dandy, Michael Dandy, Peter Dandy, Graham Oddey, Malcolm Greening, George Atkinson, David Glynne-Jones, Simon Collett-Jones

CAULCOTT Oxfordshire   SP5024   Map E

Horse & Groom

Lower Heyford Road (B4030); OX25 4ND

Bustling and friendly with an obliging licensee, enjoyable bar food, and changing beers

The attentive french chef/patron of this thatched 16th-c cottage keeps everything running smoothly and with genuine friendliness. It's not a huge place: an L-shaped red-carpeted room angles around the servery, with plush-cushioned settles, chairs and stools around a few dark tables at the low-ceilinged bar end and a blazing fire in the big inglenook, with brassware along its long bressumer beam; shove-ha'penny and board games. The far end, up a shallow step, is set for dining with lots of decorative jugs hanging on black joists, some decorative plates and attractive watercolours and original drawings. Hook Norton Hooky Bitter and three changing guests such as Sharps Special, Slaters Why Knot and

White Horse Epona on handpump and decent house wines. There's a small side sun lounge and picnic-sets under cocktail parasols on a neat lawn.

As well as ten different types of speciality sausages, the lunchtime bar food includes filled baguettes, croque monsieur, ham and egg, and home-made burgers with bacon and cheese, with evening choices like pâté with baby onion chutney, fresh pasta with goats cheese, asparagus, artichokes and roasted peppers and olives, steak and mushroom pie, and a proper paella. *Benchmark main dish: moules marinière £12.50. Two-course evening meal £20.00.*

Free house ~ Licensee Jerome Prigent ~ Real ale ~ Bar food (not Sun evening or Mon) ~ Restaurant ~ (01869) 343257 ~ Children must be over 7 and well behaved ~ Open 12-3, 6-11; 12-3, 7-10.30 Sun

Recommended by Jane Hudson, Roger and Anne Newbury, Ian Herdman, David Lamb

CHARLTON Sussex   SU8812   Map D

Fox Goes Free

Village signposted off A286 Chichester—Midhurst in Singleton, also from Chichester—Petworth via East Dean; PO18 0HU

Comfortable old pub with beamed bars, popular food and drink, and big garden; bedrooms

Handy for the Weald and Downland Open Air Museum, West Dean Gardens and Goodwood, this bustling pub is also usefully open all day. The bar is the first of the dark and cosy series of separate rooms: old irish settles, tables and chapel chairs and an open fire. Standing timbers divide a larger beamed bar which has a huge brick fireplace with a woodburning stove and old local photographs on the walls. A dining area with hunting prints looks over the garden. The family extension is a clever conversion from horse boxes and the stables where the 1926 Goodwood winner was housed; darts, games machine and piped music. Ballards Best, a beer named for the pub brewed by Arundel and a guest such as Harveys Best or Sharps Doom Bar on handpump and several wines by the glass. You can sit at one of the picnic-sets under the apple trees in the attractive back garden with the downs as a backdrop and there are rustic benches and tables on the gravelled front terrace, too. There are good surrounding walks including one up to the prehistoric earthworks on the Trundle.

Bar food includes lunchtime filled baguettes (not Sunday), whole roast camembert with toasted fingers, roasted garlic and quince jelly, wild mushroom risotto, honey-roast ham and egg, salmon fillet with pea purée and tomato coulis, a pie of the day, and crispy confit duck leg with hoisin jus. *Benchmark main dish: steak and kidney pie £10.95. Two-course evening meal £22.00.*

Free house ~ Licensee David Coxon ~ Real ale ~ Bar food (12-2.30, 6.30-9.30; all day weekends) ~ Restaurant ~ (01243) 811461 ~ Children welcome ~ Dogs allowed in bar ~ Live music Weds evenings ~ Open 11-11(11.30 Sat); 12-10.30 Sun ~ Bedrooms: £65S/£90S
Recommended by Nick Lawless, Bernard Stradling, Helen and Brian Edgeley, Miss A E Dare

CHENIES Buckinghamshire   TQ0298   Map C

Red Lion ★

2 miles from M25 junction 18; A404 towards Amersham, then village signposted on right; Chesham Road; WD3 6ED

Delightful pub with long-serving licensees, a bustling atmosphere, real ales, and good food

Extremely popular locally – always a good sign – but with a genuine welcome for visitors too, this white-painted brick pub has now been run by the same friendly licensees for 25 years. The L-shaped bar is very traditional and unpretentious (no games machines or piped music) and has comfortable built-in wall benches by the front windows, other straightforward seats and tables, and original photographs of the village and traction engines. There's also a small back snug and a neat dining extension with more modern décor. Well kept Lion Pride is brewed for the pub by Rebellion and served on handpump alongside Vale Best Bitter and a changing guest and Wadworths 6X, and they have up to ten wines by the glass and some nice malt whiskies. The hanging baskets and window boxes are pretty in summer, there are picnic-sets on a small side terrace, and good local walks. No children.

A good range of well liked bar food includes sandwiches, field mushrooms with garlic, mint and chilli, home-made pâté, pasta with sunblush tomatoes, feta, olives and parmesan, their famous pies (lamb is the favourite), mixed seafood in a creamy white sauce with a crumble topping, a changing curry, and lamb with a red wine and rosemary gravy. *Benchmark main dish: lamb pie £11.00. Two-course evening meal £16.60.*

Free house ~ Licensee Mike Norris ~ Real ale ~ Bar food (12-2,7-10; 12-8 Sun) ~ Restaurant ~ (01923) 282722 ~ Dogs allowed in bar ~ Open 11-2.30, 5.30-11; 12-10.30 Sun

Recommended by Roy Hoing, J V Dadswell, John and Victoria Fairley, LM, William Ruxton, Ian Phillips, Peter and Giff Bennett, N J Roberts, Val and Alan Green

CHIPPING NORTON Oxfordshire   SP3127 Map E

Chequers ★ ♀ ◖

Goddards Lane; OX7 5NP

Busy, friendly town pub open all day with several real ales, popular bar food, a cheerful mix of customers and simple bars

Much enjoyed for its efficiently served pre-theatre suppers (the theatre is next door) and for its six well kept real ales, this tucked-away pub has a cheerful and relaxed atmosphere. There's a mix of both locals and visitors and the three softly lit beamed rooms have no frills, but are clean and comfortable with low ochre ceilings, lots of character, and a blazing log fire. Quick staff serve Fullers Chiswick, London Pride, ESB and two guest beers on handpump, and they have good house wines – 15 by the glass. The conservatory restaurant is light and airy and used for more formal dining.

Popular bar food includes sandwiches, pork and rabbit terrine with pear and star anise chutney, chicken caesar salad, local sausages of the day with onion gravy, honey and cider roast gammon and eggs, pumpkin, sundried tomato and olive risotto, and chicken breast in a mushroom and white wine velouté. *Benchmark main dish: home-made pies £9.95. Two-course evening meal £15.45.*

Fullers ~ Lease Jim Hopcroft ~ Real ale ~ Bar food (12-2.30, 6-9.30; 12-4 Sun; not Sun evening) ~ Restaurant ~ (01608) 644717 ~ Children welcome ~ Dogs allowed in bar ~ Live music monthly and Sun evening quiz ~ Open 11(11.30 Sun)-11(midnight Sat)

Recommended by Stuart Turner, Derek and Sylvia Stephenson, Chris Glasson, MP, Barry Collett, the Didler, Steve Whalley, Richard Tilbrook

---

Stars after the name of a pub show exceptional character and appeal. They don't mean extra comfort. And they are nothing to do with food quality, for which there's a separate knife-and-fork symbol. Even quite a basic pub can win stars, if it's individual enough.

COLESHILL Buckinghamshire   SU9594 Map E

Harte & Magpies

E of village on A355 Amersham—Beaconsfield, by junction with Magpie Lane; HP7 0LU

Friendly, professionally run roadside dining pub with enjoyable food all day, well kept local ales, and seats in big garden

Just the place to end a walk across the Chiltern Hills, this is well run and enjoyable for both a drink or a meal. It's big and open-plan but its rambling collection of miscellaneous pews, high-backed booths and some quite distinctive tables and chairs and cosy boltholes over to the right give it a pleasantly snug feel. There's a profusion of vigorously patriotic antique prints, candles in bottles and Scrumpy Jack the self-possessed young labrador who adds a relaxed country touch – as does the jar of dog treats. Brakspears Bitter, Chiltern Ale and Rebellion Smuggler on handpump and a good choice of other drinks, too; service is friendly and civilised. Outside, a terrace has picnic-sets by a tree picturesquely draped with wisteria and a big sloping informal garden has more trees and more tables on wood chippings.

As well as filled baguettes and an all-day breakfast, the tasty food includes pork terrine with red onion marmalade, gammon and eggs, shepherd's pie, vegetable risotto, rare-breed burger and chips, and steak and kidney pudding. *Benchmark main dish: fish and chips £12.50. Two-course evening meal £16.50.*

Free house ~ Licensee Stephen Lever ~ Real ale ~ Bar food (10-9.45; 12-8 Sun) ~ (01494) 726754 ~ Children welcome ~ Dogs welcome ~ Live music Sat evening ~ Open 10am-11pm; 11-10 Sun

Recommended by Tracey and Stephen Groves, Mrs Ann Gray, Phil Harrison

CRANLEIGH Surrey   TQ0539 Map C

Richard Onslow ◀

High Street; GU6 8AU

Well run pub with a good mix of customers in several bar rooms, friendly, efficient staff, real ales, and interesting all-day food

As this pub is right in the middle of a large village and usefully open all day for breakfast (from 9am), morning coffee, lunch and afternoon tea, it's always packed with a wide mix of customers. There's a busy little public bar with stools by the counter, leather tub chairs and a built-in sofa and a slate-floored drinking area where efficient and friendly staff serve Surrey Hills Shere Drop, Wells & Youngs Bombardier and a guest like Dark Star Hophead on handpump, several wines by the glass from a shortish list and home-made summer lemonade and fresh lime soda. Two dining rooms off here have a mix of tartan tub chairs around wooden tables, a rather fine long leather-cushioned church pew, local photographs on mainly pale paintwork and a couple of open fires – one in a nice brick fireplace. The sizeable restaurant, with pale tables and chairs on the wooden floor and modern flowery wallpaper, has big windows overlooking the street; piped music and board games. There are a few tables and chairs on the front pavement. By the time this edition is published, they will have opened eight bedrooms and created some parking space – nearby parking is currently restricted.

A wide choice of interesting food using free-range meat might include sandwiches, chicken and spring onion terrine with apple chutney, deli or veggie boards, leek, pea and dill pancake with gruyère sauce, sausages with onion gravy, fishcakes with lemon butter sauce, chicken with crispy parma ham and roast garlic and basil tagliatelle, and pork tenderloin with potato and beetroot salad. *Benchmark main dish: sustainable yellowfin tuna, cucumber, mooli and edamame bean with soy and sesame dressing £14.50. Two-course evening meal £18.50.*

Peach Pub Company ~ Licensee John Taylor ~ Real ale ~ Bar food (all day from 9am) ~ Restaurant ~ (01483) 274922 ~ Children welcome ~ Dogs allowed in bar ~ Open 9-11
Recommended by Phil Bryant

 DANEHILL Sussex   TQ4128 Map C

Coach & Horses ¶ ♀

Off A275, via School Lane towards Chelwood Common; RH17 7JF

Country dining pub with bustling bars, welcoming staff, enjoyable food and ales, and a big garden

You can be sure of a warm welcome from the friendly staff in this cottagey dining pub. There's a little bar to the right with half-panelled walls, simple furniture on polished floorboards, a small woodburner in the brick fireplace and a big hatch to the bar counter: Harveys Best, Kings Horsham Best and a guest from Hepworth or Hammerpot on handpump and several wines by the glass including prosecco and champagne. A couple of steps lead down to a half-panelled area with a mix of dining chairs around characterful wooden tables (set with flowers and candles) on the fine brick floor and some large Victorian prints. Down another step to a dining area with stone walls, beams, flagstones and a woodburning stove. There's an adult-only terrace under a huge maple tree and picnic-sets and a children's play area in the big garden which has fine views of the South Downs.

Using local meat and game, the interesting food includes sandwiches, welsh rarebit, guinea fowl gateau with redcurrant glaze, courgette croquettes with roasted onion aioli and rocket and courgette frites, beer-battered fish, duck breast with roast cherries and balsamic jus, and soy and honey-glazed salmon fillet with pickled mooli. *Benchmark main dish: crisp pork belly with bramley boulangère £13.75. Two-course evening meal £21.00.*

Free house ~ Licensee Ian Philpots ~ Real ale ~ Bar food (12-2(2.30 Sat, 3 Sun), 7-9(9.30 Sat); not Sun evening) ~ Restaurant ~ (01825) 740369 ~ Well behaved children welcome but not on adult terrace ~ Dogs allowed in bar ~ Open 12-3, 6-11.30; 12-11.30(10.30 Sun) Sat
Recommended by Mr and Mrs R A Bradbrook, Rebecca Gould, Peter Gartrell

 DENHAM Buckinghamshire   TQ0487 Map C

Swan ¶ ♀

Village signed from M25 junction 16; UB9 5BH

Handsome and civilised dining pub in pretty village; stylish furnishings in several bars, open fires, interesting food, and fine choice of drinks

Handsome, Georgian pub in a pretty village and particularly popular for its fresh, interesting bar food. The rooms are stylishly furnished with a nice mix of antique and old-fashioned chairs and solid tables, individually chosen pictures on the cream and warm green walls, rich heavily draped curtains, inviting open fires, newspapers to read and fresh flowers. Courage Best, Rebellion IPA, and Wadworths 6X on handpump, 21 european wines by the glass, plus nine pudding wines and a good choice of liqueurs; piped music. The extensive garden is floodlit at night, and leads from a sheltered terrace with tables to a more spacious lawn; the wisteria is lovely in May. It can get busy at weekends and parking may be not be easy then.

🍴 Impressive bar food using seasonal produce includes rabbit rillettes with home-baked rosemary focaccia, duck livers and hearts with crispy bacon and dandelion and gooseberry salad, beer-battered haddock, free-range chicken tagine with fig couscous and toasted almonds, and gurnard fillet with flageolet bean, chorizo and roast tomato cassoulet. *Benchmark main dish: pork loin chop with braised baby gem and cider cream sauce £14.75. Two-course evening meal £20.00.*

Salisbury Pubs ~ Lease Mark Littlewood ~ Real ale ~ Bar food (12-2.30(3 Sat, 4 Sun), 6.30-9.30(10 Fri and Sat)) ~ Restaurant ~ (01895) 832085 ~ Children welcome ~ Dogs allowed in bar ~ Open 11-11; 12-10.30 Sun; closed 25 and 26 Dec
Recommended by Brian Glozier

DIAL POST Sussex   TQ1519   Map C

Crown

Worthing Road (off A24 S of Horsham); RH13 8NH

Extended village pub with good food, real ales and plenty of space in the bar and two dining rooms; bedrooms

It's the interesting food cooked by the landlord that draws in most customers here – though the bar is a friendly and relaxing place if you just want a drink and a chat. It's a beamed room with a couple of standing timbers, brown squashy sofas and pine tables and chairs on the stone floor, a small woodburning stove in the brick fireplace, and Dark Star Best and Harveys Best and a Harveys guest beer on handpump from the attractive herringbone brick counter. The pub dog is called Chops. The straightforwardly furnished dining conservatory, facing the village green, is light and airy; board games and shove-ha'penny. To the right of the bar, the restaurant (with more beams) has an ornamental woodburner in a brick fireplace, a few photographs on the walls, chunky pine tables, chairs and a couple of cushioned pews on the patterned carpet, and a shelf of books; steps lead down to a further dining room. The bedrooms are in the converted stables and there are picnic-sets on grass behind the pub.

🍴 Using carefully sourced produce, the highly thought-of food might include sandwiches, potted brown shrimps and crayfish with rosemary crostini, beer-battered fish and chips, home-made steak burger with spicy relish and coleslaw, a changing pie and salmon fillet on roasted mediterranean vegetables with pesto; there's also an early bird menu. *Benchmark main dish: crispy local pork belly £15.00. Two-course evening meal £21.00.*

Free house ~ Licensees James and Penny Middleton-Burn ~ Real ale ~ Bar food (12-2(2.30 Sun), 6-9(9.30 Fri and Sat); not Sun evening) ~ Restaurant ~ (01403) 710902 ~ Children welcome but must be dining after 7pm ~ Dogs welcome ~ Open 11.30-3, 6(5.30 Fri)-11; 12-4 Sun; closed Sun evening ~ Bedrooms: £50S/£60S
Recommended by David and Sharon Collison

'Children welcome' means the pub says it lets children inside without any special restriction. If it allows them in, but to restricted areas such as an eating area or family room, we specify this. Places with separate restaurants often let children use them, and hotels usually let them into public areas such as lounges. Some pubs impose an evening time limit – let us know if you find one earlier than 9pm.

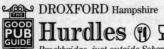 DROXFORD Hampshire   SU6118   Map D

Hurdles

*Brockbridge, just outside Soberton; from A32 just N of Droxford take B2150
towards Denmead; SO32 3QT*

**Roomy smartly updated country dining pub, food interesting and
good value**

Surprisingly grand for such a tucked-away country pub, this handsome
brick building is a reminder that the Meon Valley has long had quite a
touch of class. It's been brought very suitably up to date inside, from the
dark grey leather chesterfield and armchairs by the log fire in one room
with elegant columnar lamps in its big windows, to the dining areas on
the right, with their stylish figured wallpaper, toning stripy chairs around
shiny modern tables, and glittering mirrors. There are high ceilings and
stripped boards throughout. Service by attentive young staff is prompt,
and they have decent wines by the glass, good coffee, and Bowmans
Wallops Wood and a guest beer such as Otter on handpump; unobtrusive
piped pop music. It's a peaceful spot, with wood and metal tables on neat
terraces (one covered and heated), and a long flight of steps up to picnic-
sets on a sloping lawn by tall trees.

Good interesting food includes filled baguettes, potted crab pâté with orange,
basil and red onion, burger with smoked applewood cheese, beetroot and
horseradish chutney, hake fillet wrapped in parma ham with basil, sunblush tomato
and mozzarella risotto, burger with smoked applewood cheese, beetroot and
horseradish chutney, chicken breast with wild mushroom and pancetta tagliatelle
carbonara, and lamb rump with mint pea purée, honey carrots and red wine jus; they
also offer a two- and three-course set menu (Mon-Fri lunchtimes and Mon-Thurs
evenings 6-7pm) and cream teas. *Benchmark main dish: hake fillet wrapped in
parma ham and basil with a sunblush tomato and mozzarella risotto £14.95. Two-
course evening meal £19.45.*

Enterprise ~ Lease Gareth and Sarah Cole ~ Real ale ~ Bar food (12-3, 6-9.30; 12-8 Sun)
~ Restaurant ~ (01489) 877451 ~ Children welcome ~ Dogs allowed in bar ~ Open 11-11;
12-10.30 Sun

Recommended by Phyl and Jack Street, Roger and Anne Mallard, Susan Robinson

---

DUNCTON Sussex   SU9517   Map C

Cricketers

Set back from A285; GU28 0LB

**Charming old coaching inn with friendly licensees, real ales, popular
food, and suntrap back garden**

Doing particularly well under its present licensees, this is a pretty
16th-c coaching inn close to Goodwood. The friendly, traditional bar
has a few standing timbers, simple seating, cricketing memorabilia and an
open woodburning stove in the inglenook fireplace. Steps lead down to
the dining room with wooden tables and chairs. Dark Star Hophead, King
Horsham Best Bitter and Skinners Betty Stogs on handpump, several
wines by the glass and Thatcher's cider. There are some picnic-sets out in
front beneath the flowering window boxes and more on decked areas and
under parasols on the grass in the back garden.

Enjoyable food includes lunchtime sandwiches, crab, prawn and leek gratin,
cheese risotto topped with a poached egg, toad in the hole with onion gravy, a
pie of the day, beer-battered fresh haddock, steak and kidney pudding, and chicken

stuffed with brie and wrapped in pancetta. *Benchmark main dish: steak and mushroom in ale pie £10.95. Two-course evening meal £17.20.*

Inn Company ~ Lease Martin Boult ~ Real ale ~ Bar food (12-2.30, 6-9 (some hot snacks in afternoon); 12-9 weekends) ~ Restaurant ~ (01798) 342473 ~ Children welcome ~ Dogs welcome ~ Open 11-11; 12-10.30 Sun

Recommended by Bruce Bird, Derek and Maggie Washington

 EASINGTON Buckinghamshire   SP6810 Map E

Mole & Chicken 🍽 ♀ 🛏

From B4011 in Long Crendon follow Chearsley, Waddesdon signpost into Carters Lane opposite indian restaurant, then turn left into Chilton Road; HP18 9EY

Country views from decking and garden, an inviting interior, real ales, and much emphasis on restauranty food; nice bedrooms

This is a lovely place to stay in cosy and comfortable bedrooms and the breakfasts are good, too. It's very much a dining pub with upmarket food and prices to match but they do still keep Hook Norton Bitter and Vale Best Bitter on handpump, lots of wines by the glass and quite a few malt whiskies. The opened-up interior is arranged so that its different parts seem quite snug and self-contained without being cut off from the relaxed sociable atmosphere. The beamed bar curves around the serving counter in a sort of S-shape, and there are cream-cushioned chairs and high-backed leather dining chairs at oak and pine tables on flagstones or tiles, a couple of dark leather sofas, and fabric swatches stylishly hung as decorations on creamy walls, lit candles and good winter log fires; piped music. The attractive raised terrace, with views over fine rolling countryside, is a lovely place for a summer's lunch or sunset drink.

🍽 As well as lunchtime sandwiches, ham and free-range eggs and pork and leek sausages, there's a good value two- or three-course set menu as well as chilli fried squid with garlic and lemon, liver, maple-cured bacon, kidneys, grilled onions and mash, gnocchi with butternut squash, feta, pine nuts and balsamic, and lamb shank with bubble and squeak. *Benchmark main dish: duck salad with thai herbs and cashew nuts £9.50. Two-course evening meal £22.00.*

Free house ~ Licensees Alan Heather and Steve Bush ~ Real ale ~ Bar food ~ (01844) 208387 ~ Children welcome ~ Dogs allowed in bar ~ Occasional jazz evenings ~ Open 12-2.30(4 Sun), 6-9.30(9 Sun) ~ Bedrooms: £70B/£95B

Recommended by Richard and Sissel Harris, John Wheeler, David and Lexi Young, Di and Mike Gillam, Karen Eliot

 EAST CHILTINGTON Sussex   TQ3715 Map C

Jolly Sportsman 🍽 ♀

2 miles N of B2116; Chapel Lane – follow sign to 13th-c church; BN7 3BA

SUSSEX DINING PUB OF THE YEAR

Excellent modern food in civilised, rather smart place, small bar for drinkers, contemporary furnishings, fine wine list, and huge range of malt whiskies; nice garden

Extremely well run and a favourite with many of our readers, this is a civilised dining pub with first-class food. The bar may be small but it's full of character and has a roaring winter fire, a mix of furniture on the stripped wood floors and Dark Star Hophead and Harveys Best tapped from the cask. They also have a remarkably good wine list with around a dozen by the glass, over 100 malt whiskies, an extensive list of cognacs, armagnacs and grappa and quite a choice of bottled belgian beers; well trained, charming staff. The larger restaurant is smart but informal with contemporary light wood furniture and modern landscapes on coffee-coloured walls; there's also a new garden room. The cottagey front garden is pretty with rustic tables and benches under gnarled trees, on the terrace and on the front bricked area, and there are more on a large back lawn, a children's play area and views towards the downs; good walks and cycle rides nearby.

As well as good value two- and three-course set menus, the exceptional food might include lunchtime sandwiches, venison carpaccio with horseradish aioli and pickled onion, pike and trout terrine with prawn sauce, chicken breast with chorizo, chickpea and vegetable ragu, beef cheek bourguignon, sea bream fillet with coriander rice, pak choi and black bean salsa, and 28-day-aged rib-eye steak with béarnaise sauce. *Benchmark main dish: rump of local lamb with minted peas and beans £16.85. Two-course evening meal £22.50.*

Free house ~ Licensee Bruce Wass ~ Real ale ~ Bar food (12-2.30(3.30 Sun), 6.30-10) ~ Restaurant ~ (01273) 890400 ~ Children welcome ~ Dogs allowed in bar ~ Open 12-11(10.30 Sun); 12-3, 6-11 weekdays in winter; closed winter Sun evening

Recommended by Susan and John Douglas, Nick Lawless, John Redfern, Terry and Nickie Williams, David Sizer, Laurence Smith, Kelvin Meade, N R White

EAST DEAN Sussex
Tiger ♀ ⇖

TV5597 Map C

Off A259 Eastbourne—Seaford; BN20 0DA

Charming old pub by cottage-lined village green, two little bars and a dining room, and an informal and friendly atmosphere; bedrooms

This is a lovely pub and as popular with drinkers as it is with diners so the atmosphere is always chatty and relaxed. The focal point of the little beamed main bar is the open woodburning stove in its brick inglenook surrounded by polished horsebrasses, and there are just a few rustic tables with benches, simple wooden chairs, a window seat and a long cushioned wall bench. The walls are hung with fish prints and a stuffed tiger's head, there are a couple of hunting horns above the long bar counter, Harveys Best and Old and their own-brewed Beachy Head Legless Rambler and Original on handpump and several wines by the glass. Down a step on the right is a second small room with an exceptionally fine high-backed curved settle and a couple of other old settles, nice old chairs and wooden tables on the coir carpeting, and an ancient map of Eastbourne and Beachy Head and photographs of the pub on the walls. The dining room to the left of the main bar has a cream woodburner and hunting prints. With such a premium on space, it does pay to get here early if you want a seat. There are picnic-sets on the terrace among the window boxes and flowering climbers or you can sit on the delightful cottage-lined village green. The South Downs Way is close by so the pub is naturally popular with walkers, and the lane leads on down to a fine stretch of coast culminating in Beachy Head. The bedrooms are comfortable and the breakfasts good.

As well as lunchtime sandwiches, the much-liked food includes a meat, seafood or cheese platter, chicken or king prawn caesar salad, braised lamb shoulder with fennel and spring onion and a chilli, ginger and anise jus, salmon fillet on minted pea and spinach risotto with a yellow pepper and lemon coulis, and slow-roast pork belly with bubble and squeak and a mustard, cream and bramley apple dressing. *Benchmark main dish: home-made burger with bacon and cheese £8.95. Two-course evening meal £17.45.*

Free house ~ Licensee Jo Staveley ~ Real ale ~ Bar food (12-3, 6-9) ~ (01323) 423209 ~ Children welcome ~ Dogs allowed in bar ~ Open 11-11(10.30 Sun) ~ Bedrooms: /£95S

Recommended by Kevin Thorpe, B and M Kendall

 EAST GARSTON Berkshire   SU3676   Map D

 # Queens Arms 🍷 🛏

3.5 miles from M4 junction 14; A338 and village signposted Gt Shefford; RG17 7ET

Smart but chatty dining pub with good food and friendly country bar

Right at the heart of racehorse-training country, this busy pub is especially popular locally and much of the chat will be to do with horse racing. The roomy opened-up bar has plenty of antique prints (many featuring jockeys), daily papers on a corner table (the most prominent being the *Racing Post*), wheelbacks and other dining chairs around well spaced tables on the wooden floor, Wadworths IPA and 6X and a changing local guest on handpump, several wines by the glass and a fair choice of whiskies. Friendly staff, piped music and live horse-racing on TV. Opening off on the right is a lighter dining area with bigger horse and country prints and a pleasing mix of furniture. There are seats on a sheltered terrace. The bedrooms are attractive, the breakfasts tasty and they can arrange fly fishing and shooting; plenty of surrounding downland walks.

Using seasonal local produce, the enjoyable food might include lunchtime sandwiches, pigeon breast with bacon, black pudding and lentils, goats cheese and roast beetroot salad with pine nuts, croutons and balsamic, bass fillet with creamed black cabbage and caper jus, and rare roast loin of venison with red wine jus. *Benchmark main dish: bass fillet with chorizo £14.50. Two-course evening meal £21.00.*

Free house ~ Licensee Adam Liddiard ~ Real ale ~ Bar food (12-2.30(3 Sun), 6.30-9.30(7-9 Sun)) ~ Restaurant ~ (01488) 648757 ~ Children welcome ~ Dogs welcome ~ Open 11-11(10.30 Sun) ~ Bedrooms: /£90S

Recommended by Phyl and Jack Street

 EAST HENDRED Oxfordshire   SU4588   Map D

Eyston Arms 🍴

Village signposted off A417 E of Wantage; High Street; OX12 8JY

Attractive bar areas with low beams, flagstones, log fires and candles, imaginative food, and helpful service

Always busy and welcoming, this is a well run and pleasant dining pub – although locals do pop in for a drink and a chat. There are several separate-seeming areas with contemporary paintwork and modern country-style furnishings: low ceilings and beams, stripped timbers, the odd standing timber, an inglenook fireplace, nice tables and chairs on the flagstones and carpet, some cushioned wall seats, candlelight and a piano; piped music. Cheerful staff serve Fullers London Pride and Wadworths 6X on handpump and several wines by the glass. Picnic-sets outside overlook the pretty lane and there are seats in the back courtyard garden.

As well as lunchtime sandwiches, the imaginative food includes bruschetta of foie gras, madeira, wild mushrooms and shallots, meat or fish antipasti, trio of local hog (loin, belly and black pudding) with apple mash and cider jus, broad bean, pea and mint risotto, tandoori lamb with shredded mango and cucumber and a yoghurt and lime dressing, and corn-fed chicken with sage and lemon butter and butternut squash. *Benchmark main dish: seafood linguine £16.50. Two-course evening meal £22.20.*

Free house ~ Licensees George Dailey and Daisy Barton ~ Real ale ~ Bar food (not Sun evening) ~ Restaurant ~ (01235) 833320 ~ Children welcome but must be well behaved ~ Dogs allowed in bar ~ Open 11-3, 6-11; 11-7 Sun; closed Sun evening

Recommended by Robert Lorimer, William Goodhart, Jane Hudson, Barry Jackson, Bob and Margaret Holder

 EAST STRATTON Hampshire   SU5339   Map D

Northbrook Arms

Brown sign to pub off A33 4 miles S of A303 junction; SO21 3DU

Easy-going camaraderie in nicely placed village pub; good all round

Just as welcoming if you want a meal or a chatty drink, this is a pleasantly unassuming pub with polite, hard-working staff. There's a relaxed traditional tiled-floor bar on the right, with Flower Pots Perridge Pale, Otter Bitter and maybe a guest like Bowman Swift One on handpump and ten wines by the glass; also, a mix of pubby chairs around sturdy stripped-top tables, a collection of regulars' snapshots, reference books and bric-a-brac on the sills of the big windows and a log fire. Piped pop music is not too obtrusive. On the left, it's carpeted, and progressively rather more formal, ending in a proper dining room beyond a little central hall. There are picnic-sets out on the green across the quiet village road, with more in the good-sized back courtyard – which has a skittle alley, as well as the gents', on the far side. There are fine walks nearby. This is owned by the same good people as the Yew Tree at Lower Wield.

As well as a good value two- and three-course set lunch menu, the enjoyable bar food includes sandwiches, chilli crab soufflé with parmesan cream, a risotto of the day, a proper burger with cheddar or stilton and onion marmalade, fish and chips, bacon steak with egg and chips, and confit of duck with an orange and rosemary jus. *Benchmark main dish: pie of the day £11.95. Two-course evening meal £17.00.*

Free house ~ Licensees Tim Gray and Wendy Nichols ~ Real ale ~ Bar food (not Sun evening or Mon) ~ Restaurant ~ (01962) 774150 ~ Children welcome ~ Dogs allowed in bar and bedrooms ~ Open 12-3, 6-11; 12-10.30 Sun; closed Mon and winter Sun evening from 4pm ~ Bedrooms: £60S/£65S

Recommended by Ann and Colin Hunt

EASTON Hampshire   SU5132   Map D

Chestnut Horse 🍺 ⧓

3.6 miles from M3 junction 9: A33 towards Kings Worthy, then B3047 towards Itchen Abbas; Easton then signposted on right – bear left in village; SO21 1EG

Cosy dining pub with log fires, fresh flowers and candles, deservedly popular food and friendly staff; Itchen Valley walks nearby

Run by a professional, hands-on landlady, this is a smart 16th-c dining pub and the hub of this pretty village of thatched cottages. The open-plan interior manages to have a pleasantly rustic and intimate feel with a series of cosily separate areas, and the snug décor takes in candles and fresh flowers on the tables, log fires in cottagey fireplaces and comfortable furnishings. The black beams and joists are hung with all sorts of jugs, mugs and chamber-pots, and there are lots of attractive pictures of wildlife and the local area. Badger K&B and Hopping Hare on handpump, several wines by the glass and 30 malt whiskies. There are seats and tables out on a smallish sheltered decked area with colourful flower tubs and baskets, and some picnic-sets in front; plenty of nearby walks in the Itchen Valley.

As well as a good value two-course set lunch (not Sunday), the sensibly short choice of interesting food might include lunchtime sandwiches, ham hock terrine, tian of crab and crayfish tails, thai green vegetable curry, sausage and mash with onion gravy, irish stew with Guinness bread, and pork tenderloin with apple and black pudding. *Benchmark main dish: beer-battered fresh cod and chips £12.00. Two-course evening meal £20.00.*

Badger ~ Tenant Karen Wells ~ Real ale ~ Bar food (12-2.30, 6-9.30; 12-8 Sun (not winter)) ~ Restaurant ~ (01962) 779257 ~ Children welcome ~ Dogs allowed in bar ~ Open 12-3.30, 5.30-11; 12-11(10 Sun) Sat; closed winter Sun evening

Recommended by Ann and Colin Hunt, Gene and Tony Freemantle, Neil and Karen Dignan, Helen and Brian Edgeley, Phyl and Jack Street, A M Falconer

ELSTEAD Surrey   SU9044   Map D

Mill at Elstead

Farnham Road (B3001 just W of village, which is itself between Farnham and Milford); GU8 6LE

Fascinating building, big attractive waterside garden, Fullers beers

Inside this largely 18th-c four-storey watermill you'll see the great internal waterwheel turning and hear the gentle rush of the stream running below your feet. Big windows throughout make the most of the charming setting above the prettily banked River Wey. The building has been sensitively converted, with a series of rambling linked bar areas on the spacious ground floor, and a restaurant upstairs, that change in mood from one part to the next. You'll find brown leather armchairs and antique engravings by a longcase clock, neat modern tables and dining chairs on dark woodstrip flooring, big country tables on broad ceramic tiles, iron pillars and stripped masonry, and a log fire in a huge inglenook. They have four Fullers beers on handpump, and a good range of wines by the glass; piped music, board games. Outside there are plenty of picnic-sets dotted around by the water, with its lovely millpond, swans and weeping willows, and the entire scene is well floodlit at night.

The menu here includes sautéed king prawns, welsh rarebit, chicken caesar salad, duck leg confit with raspberry sauce, battered cod, rabbit stew with herb dumplings, smoked haddock and pea risotto, breaded scampi, sausage and mash and well hung sirloin steak; Sunday and Wednesday evening carvery from autumn through to spring. *Benchmark main dish: bass fillet with roast peppers, garlic and tomato £13.50. Two-course evening meal £17.00.*

Fullers ~ Managers Kate and Richard Williams ~ Real ale ~ Bar food (12-9.30(8 Sun, 9 winter Mon-Thurs)) ~ Restaurant ~ (01252) 703333 ~ Children welcome ~ Dogs allowed in bar ~ Open 11-11; 11.30-10.30 Sun

Recommended by Ian Wilson, Ian Herdman, Rosemary and Mike Fielder, Gordon Stevenson

ERIDGE GREEN Sussex

TQ5535 Map C

Nevill Crest & Gun ♀

A26 Tunbridge Wells—Crowborough; TN3 9JR

Handsome 500-year-old building with lots of character, beams and standing timbers, hundreds of pictures and photographs, three real ales, enjoyable modern food, and friendly, efficient staff

This is a fine former farmhouse – around 500 years old – adorned by the crest of the Nevill family on whose estate the building stands. There's plenty of interesting history and it's been carefully and cleverly opened up inside with standing timbers and doorways keeping some sense of separate rooms. Throughout there are heavy beams (some carved), panelling, rugs on wooden floors, woodburning stoves and an open fire in three fireplaces (the linenfold carved bressumer above one is worth seeking out), all manner of individual dining chairs around dark wood or copper-topped tables and lots of pictures, maps and photographs, many of them local to the area. The window sills are full of toby jugs, stone and glass bottles and plants, there are daily papers, board games and a happy mix of customers of all ages; the atmosphere is civilised but informal. Beers from Tunbridge Wells, Westerham and Phoenix Brunning & Price on handpump and good wines by the glass; efficient, friendly staff. In front of the building are a few picnic-sets with teak furniture on a back terrace beside the new dining extension (light oak rafters, beams and coir flooring).

With something for every taste, the modern brasserie food might include roquefort and spring onion fritter with beetroot relish, charcuterie, ploughman's, bouillabaisse, good moroccan-style lamb with apricot and date salad and chickpea cakes, braised pig's cheek with apples, bacon, sage and celeriac mash, tempting puddings and a british cheeseboard. *Benchmark main dish: battered haddock and chips £11.95. Two-course evening meal £18.60.*

Brunning & Price ~ Manager Jamie Rose ~ Real ale ~ Bar food (12-10(9 Sun)) ~ (01892) 864209 ~ Children welcome ~ Dogs allowed in bar ~ Open 11.30-11; 12-10.30 Sun

Recommended by Alan Franck

ESHER Surrey

TQ1566 Map C

Marneys £

Alma Road (one-way only), Weston Green; heading N on A309 from A307 roundabout, after Lamb & Star pub turn left into Lime Tree Avenue (signposted to All Saints Parish Church), then left at T junction into Chestnut Avenue; KT10 8JN

Country feeling pub with good value food and attractive garden

Just a mile from Hampton Court Palace and a surprisingly rural haven for this area, this cottagey little place consists of just two rooms. The small snug bar has a low-beamed ceiling, Fullers London Pride, Youngs and a guest such as Twickenham Original on handpump, about a dozen wines by the glass and perhaps horseracing on the unobtrusive corner TV. To the left, past a little cast-iron woodburning stove, a dining area has big pine tables, pews, pale country kitchen chairs and cottagey blue-curtained windows; piped music. The front terrace has wooden tables with table lighting and views over the rural-feeling wooded common, village church and duck pond, and the pleasantly planted sheltered garden has a decked area.

🍴 As well as sandwiches, the very reasonably priced traditional bar food might include whitebait, thai prawns, goats cheese tart, liver and bacon, vegetable lasagne, chicken curry, and fresh fish. *Benchmark main dish: steak and ale pie £8.95. Two-course evening meal £13.90.*

Free house ~ Licensee Thomas Duxberry ~ Real ale ~ Bar food (12-2.30(3 Sun), 6-9; not Fri-Sun evenings) ~ (020) 8398 4444 ~ Children welcome away from bar ~ Dogs welcome ~ Open 11-11; 12-10.30 Sun

Recommended by C and R Bromage, LM, Ian Phillips

EWHURST GREEN Sussex   TQ7924   Map C

White Dog

Turn off A21 to Bodiam at S end of Hurst Green, cross B2244, pass Bodiam Castle, cross river then bear left uphill at Ewhurst Green sign; TN32 5TD

Comfortable pub with a nice little bar, several real ales and popular food

The garden behind this partly 17th-c pub has lots of picnic-sets and a new children's play area and looks over to Bodiam Castle. The bar on the left has a proper pubby feel with a fine inglenook fireplace, hop-draped beams, wood-panelled walls, farm implements and horsebrasses, just a few tables with high-backed, rush-seated dining chairs and red plush-topped bar stools on the old brick or flagstoned floor. There's also a high-backed cushioned settle by the counter and Dark Star Hophead, Harveys Best and Skinners Betty Stogs on handpump and several wines by the glass. To the right of the door is the busy but fairly plain dining room with more big flagstones, the same tables and chairs as the bar, fresh flowers, black joists and hops, paintings by local artists for sale, and again, one high-backed settle by the bar; piped music. There's also a games room with darts, pool and a games machine.

🍴 Well liked bar food includes sandwiches, scallops with cauliflower purée and bacon, duck terrine, tempura prawns with dipping sauce, lunchtime burgers and sausage and mash, bass with crab and spring onion mash and a sun-dried tomato sauce, and pork tenderloin wrapped in pancetta and sage. *Benchmark main dish: fish and chips £10.95. Two-course evening meal £18.00.*

Free house ~ Licensee Mrs Danni Page ~ Real ale ~ Bar food (12-2.30, 6.30-9; 12-4; not Sun or Mon evenings) ~ Restaurant ~ (01580) 830264 ~ Children welcome ~ Dogs allowed in bar ~ Open 12-3, 5.30-11; 12-11.30 Sat; 12-6 Sun; closed Sun and Mon evenings ~ Bedrooms: /£75B

Recommended by Philip and Cheryl Hill, Dr Martin Owton, Leslie and Barbara Owen, V Brogden, Michael Butler, Arthur Pickering

FERNHAM Oxfordshire   SU2991   Map E

Woodman

A420 SW of Oxford, then left into B4508 after about 11 miles; village a further 6 miles on; SN7 7NX

A good choice of real ales and interesting bar food in a charming old-world country pub

With consistently good food, several real ales and a genuine welcome from attentive staff, this smashing pub, not surprisingly, remains as popular as ever. The heavily beamed main rooms have the most character and are full of an amazing assortment of old objects like clay pipes, milkmaids' yokes, leather tack, coach horns, an old screw press, some

original oil paintings and good black and white photographs of horses.
Comfortable seating includes cushioned benches, pews and windsor
chairs, and the candlelit tables are simply made from old casks; a big
wood fire, too. As well as some comfortable newer areas, there's a large
room for Sunday lunches. Greene King Old Speckled Hen, Oakham JHB,
Timothy Taylors Landlord and Wadworths 6X tapped from the cask and
several wines by the glass; piped music. There are seats outside on the
terrace. Disabled lavatories.

Highly thought-of food includes filled baguettes, duck liver and orange pâté,
rosemary-studded baked camembert, local sausages with red wine onion gravy,
a curry of the day, pasta with wild mushroom and white wine sauce, crispy duck with
stir-fried vegetables, noodles and plum sauce, and bass fillets with tomatoes, capers
and chives. *Benchmark main dish: lamb shank with redcurrant mint jus £16.95.
Two-course evening meal £20.90.*

Free house ~ Licensee Steven Whiting ~ Real ale ~ Bar food (12-2, 6.30-9.30) ~
Restaurant ~ (01367) 820643 ~ Children welcome ~ Dogs welcome ~ Open 11-11
(10.30 Sun)

Recommended by William Goodhart, Lesley and Peter Barrett, Mary Rayner

 FLETCHING Sussex   TQ4223   Map C

Griffin 🍴 ♟ 🛏

Village signposted off A272 W of Uckfield; TN22 3SS

**Busy, gently upmarket inn with a fine wine list, bistro-style bar food,
real ales, and big garden with far-reaching views; bedrooms**

There's a genuinely warm welcome for all – children and dogs, too – in
this civilised and very well run inn. The beamed and quaintly panelled
bar rooms have blazing log fires, old photographs and hunting prints,
straightforward close-set furniture including some captain's chairs and
china on a delft shelf. There's a small bare-boarded serving area off to one
side and a snug separate bar with sofas and a TV. Harveys Best,
Hepworths Iron Horse, Hogs Back TEA and Kings Horsham Best on
handpump, a fine wine list with 16 (including champagne and sweet wine)
by the glass and farm cider. The very spacious two-acre back garden has
plenty of seats on the sandstone terrace and on the grass and lovely views
of rolling countryside. The bedrooms are comfortable and the breakfasts
particularly good and the pub is handy for Glyndebourne. There are
ramps for wheelchairs.

Using carefully sourced local produce, the imaginative and extremely good – if
not cheap – food might include scallops with aubergine caviar, crispy pancetta
and truffle oil, slow-braised oxtail ravioli with red wine jus, wild garlic and brie
risotto with toasted hazelnuts, organic chicken and ham hock pie, confit duck leg
with tomato, rosemary and chickpea stew, and crab linguine with chilli, garlic, white
wine and parsley; summer barbecues. *Benchmark main dish: cod and chips with pea
and mint purée £13.00. Two-course evening meal £22.50.*

Free house ~ Licensees James Pullan, J Gatti and Emma Barlow ~ Real ale ~ Bar food
(12-2.30(3 weekends), 7-9.30) ~ Restaurant ~ (01825) 722890 ~ Children welcome ~
Dogs allowed in bar ~ Open 12am-midnight (1am Sat, 11 Sun) ~ Bedrooms:
£80B/£85S(£95B)

*Recommended by Hugh Roberts, Charles Kingsley Evans, Ann and Colin Hunt, Sheila Topham,
Michael Pelham, Charles Gibbs, Simon and Mandy King, David and Jenny Reed, Grahame Brooks,
Alan Franck, Harriet Tarnoy, John Ralph*

FORTY GREEN Buckinghamshire   SU9291 Map D

Royal Standard of England

3.5 miles from M40 junction 2, via A40 to Beaconsfield, then follow sign to Forty Green, off B474 0.75 miles N of New Beaconsfield; keep going through village; HP9 1XT

Ancient place with fascinating antiques in rambling rooms, and good choice of drinks and food

Often used for filming programmes such as *Midsomer Murders*, this fine old place has been trading for nearly 900 years; they have an interesting leaflet documenting the pub's history. It's a favourite with many of our readers who come back on a regular basis and you can always be sure of a friendly welcome. The rambling rooms have huge black ship's timbers, lovely worn floors, finely carved old oak panelling, roaring winter fires with handsomely decorated iron firebacks and cluttered mantelpieces, and there's a massive settle apparently built to fit the curved transom of an Elizabethan ship. Nooks and crannies are filled with a fascinating collection of antiques, including rifles, powder-flasks and bugles, ancient pewter and pottery tankards, lots of tarnished brass and copper, needlework samplers and richly coloured stained glass. Brakspears, Chiltern Ale and Beechwood Bitter, Rebellion IPA and Mild and Theakstons Old Peculier on handpump, a carefully annotated list of bottled beers and malt whiskies, farm ciders, perry, somerset brandy and around a dozen wines by the glass; board games. You can sit outside in a neatly hedged front rose garden or under the shade of a tree.

Traditional, popular bar food includes lunchtime sandwiches, devilled lamb kidneys on fried toast, chicken caesar salad, vegetable risotto, fish pie, steak and kidney pudding, seasonal game dishes, and pork belly with bubble and squeak with apple sauce. They still ask to keep your card behind the bar. *Benchmark main dish: fish and chips £12.50. Two-course evening meal £17.00.*

Free house ~ Licensee Matthew O'Keeffe ~ Real ale ~ Bar food (12-10) ~ Restaurant ~ (01494) 673382 ~ Children welcome ~ Dogs welcome ~ Open 11-11; 12-10.30 Sun

Recommended by Paul Humphreys, D and M T Ayres-Regan, June and Robin Savage, Tracey and Stephen Groves, the Didler, Richard and Liz Thorne, Roy Hoing, Susan and John Douglas, Anthony Longden, Mark Wilson

FRESHWATER Isle of Wight   SZ3487 Map D

Red Lion ♀

Church Place; from A3055 at E end of village by Freshwater Garage mini-roundabout follow Yarmouth signpost, then take first real right turn signed to Parish Church; PO40 9BP

Good mix of locals and visiting diners, decent food, and composed atmosphere

Steady and reliable, this civilised place is a longstanding stalwart of the *Guide*. The not over-done but comfortably furnished open-plan bar has fires, low grey sofas and sturdy country-kitchen-style furnishings on mainly flagstoned floors and bare boards. Although the food is quite a draw, chatting locals, occupying stools along the counter and enjoying the Flowers Original, Goddards, Shepherd Neame Spitfire and Wadworths 6X, maintain the grown-up pubby atmosphere. Outside, there are tables (some under cover) in a carefully tended garden and beside the kitchen's herb and vegetable garden. A couple of picnic-sets in a quiet square at the front have pleasant views of the church. The pub is virtually on the Freshwater Way footpath that connects Yarmouth with the southern coast at Freshwater Bay.

🍴 Food, listed on blackboards behind the bar, includes a sensible cross-section of dishes from lunchtime filled baguettes and ploughman's to crab and avocado cocktail, sausage and mash, salmon fillet with dill sauce, goats cheese nut roast and several pies; they also do takeaways. *Benchmark main dish: fishcakes £11.50. Two-course evening meal £18.90.*

Enterprise ~ Lease Michael Mence ~ Real ale ~ Bar food (12-2, 6.30-9 (not every Sun evening Jan-March)) ~ (01983) 754925 ~ Children over 10 ~ Dogs welcome ~ Open 11.30-3, 5.30-11; 11.30-4, 6-11 Sat; 12-3, 7-10.30 Sun

Recommended by Stuart Paulley, Paul Humphreys, Geoff and Linda Payne, Denise Bowes, D M and B K Moores

FRILSHAM Berkshire SU5573 Map D

Pot Kiln 🍴 ◀

From Yattendon take turning S, opposite church, follow first Frilsham signpost, but just after crossing motorway go straight on towards Bucklebury ignoring Frilsham signposted right; pub on right after about half a mile; RG18 0XX

Country dining pub, bustling little bar, local beers, and imaginative bar and restaurant dishes; suntrap garden and nearby walks

With plenty of walks in the nearby woods and seats in a big suntrap garden looking across the valley, this particularly well run country pub is very popular in fine weather. But on colder days, too, there are lots of locals and visitors who crowd inside, keen to enjoy the good, interesting food served by warmly friendly staff. The little bar has West Berkshire Brick Kiln Bitter, Mr Chubbs Lunchtime Bitter and Maggs Magnificent Mild, and a weekly changing guest beer on handpump, wines by the glass and a couple of ciders. The main bar area has dark wooden tables and chairs on bare boards, and a winter log fire and the extended lounge is open-plan at the back and leads into a large, pretty dining room with a nice jumble of old tables and chairs, and an old-looking stone fireplace; darts and board games.

🍴 Using home-made bread, some home-grown vegetables, and venison shot by the landlord, the food includes lunchtime sandwiches, venison burger and pork and leek sausages with onion marmalade, with imaginative restaurant choices like ragoût of muntjac with pasta and aged parmesan, wild mushroom risotto with a pheasant egg salad, pork belly with pearl barley broth and wild garlic leaves, and bass with braised gem lettuce, asparagus and saffron sauce. *Benchmark main dish: venison steak sandwich £8.95. Two-course evening meal £22.45.*

Free house ~ Licensees Mr and Mrs Michael Robinson ~ Real ale ~ Bar food (12-2.30, 6.30-8.30; not Tues) ~ Restaurant ~ (01635) 201366 ~ Children welcome ~ Dogs allowed in bar ~ Open 12-2.30, 6-11; 12-11 Sat; 12-10.30 Sun; closed Tues

Recommended by Graham and Toni Sanders, Robert Watt, the Didler, Neil and Karen Dignan, Angela Crum Ewing, Peter Chapman, Dick and Madeleine Brown

---

Please keep sending us reports. We rely on readers for news of new discoveries, and particularly for news of changes – however slight – at the fully described pubs: **feedback@goodguides.com**, or (no stamp needed) The Good Pub Guide, FREEPOST TN1569, Wadhurst, E Sussex TN5 7BR.

FULMER Buckinghamshire   SU9985   Map D

Black Horse 🍴 ♍

Village signposted off A40 in Gerrards Cross, W of its junction with A413;
Windmill Road; SL3 6HD

Appealingly reworked dining pub, friendly and relaxed, with enjoyable up-to-date food, exemplary service, and pleasant garden

Right at the heart of a charming conservation village, this is a bustling dining pub with a warm welcome for drinkers, too. There's a proper bar area on the left – three smallish rooms with low black beams, parquet floor or a rug on bare boards, very mixed tables and chairs, Greene King IPA and Old Speckled Hen and a changing guest beer on handpump, 21 european wines by the glass, nine pudding wines and a good range of liqueurs; service is prompt, friendly and efficient. The main area on the right is set for dining with comfortable, modern dining chairs on a beige carpet and the rest of the pub has a warm, relaxed and contented atmosphere; piped music. The good-sized back terrace, below the church, has teak and wrought-iron tables and chairs, with picnic-sets on the sheltered grass beyond.

 Interesting food includes sandwiches, ham hock terrine with pineapple relish, cornish crab with a watercress and pea shoot salad and crab fritter, pork tenderloin with minestrone, chorizo and crispy salt and pepper squid, corn-fed chicken stuffed with fontina on a tomato, fennel and roast garlic stew with parmesan crackling, and whole lemon sole with a sorrel cream sauce. *Benchmark main dish: slow-roast rabbit with black pudding ravioli, celeriac purée and crispy nettles £13.50. Two-course evening meal £20.25.*

Salisbury Pubs ~ Lease Richard Coletta ~ Real ale ~ Bar food (12-2.30(3 Sat, 4 Sun), 6.30-9.30(10 Fri and Sat)) ~ Restaurant ~ (01753) 663183 ~ Children welcome ~ Dogs allowed in bar ~ Open 11-11; 12-10.30 Sun; closed 25 and 26 Dec

Recommended by Richard Gibbs

 GREAT MISSENDEN Buckinghamshire   SP9000   Map E

Nags Head 🍴 🛏

Old London Road, E – beyond Abbey; HP16 0DG

Well run and pretty inn with beamed bars, an open fire, a good range of drinks and good modern cooking; comfortable bedrooms

Roald Dahl used this pretty brick and flint inn – once three cottages – as his local and the Roald Dahl Museum and Story Centre is just a stroll away. It's quietly civilised and neatly kept with a low beamed area on the left, a loftier part on the right, a mix of small pews, dining chairs and tables on the carpet, Quentin Blake prints on the cream walls and a log fire in a handsome fireplace. Fullers London Pride, Rebellion IPA and Tring Monks Gold on handpump from the unusual bar counter (the windows behind face the road) and a dozen wines by the glass from an extensive list. There's a new outside dining area under a pergola and seats on the extensive back lawn. The beamed bedrooms are well equipped and attractive.

Skilfully cooked modern food includes blinis with crab, home-smoked salmon and a chive cream sauce, wild mushroom, leek and pea risotto, steamed haddock with a chardonnay and tarragon sauce, coq au vin-style cockerel leg with beetroot coulis, sausages of the day with red wine gravy and breast of barbary duck with confit onion mash and dry sherry jus; they also have a two- and three-course set menu. *Benchmark main dish: sliced leg of lamb with shredded shoulder on a rosemary stick with ratatouille £18.95. Two-course evening meal £21.90.*

Free house ~ Licensee Adam Michaels ~ Real ale ~ Bar food (12-2.30(3.30 Sun), 6.30-
9.30(8.30 Sun)) ~ (01494) 862200 ~ Children welcome ~ Dogs allowed in bar ~ Open
12-11(midnight Fri and Sat); 12-10.30 Sun ~ Bedrooms: /£95B

Recommended by Tracey and Stephen Groves, D and M T Ayres-Regan

 GROVE Buckinghamshire   SP9122   Map E

Grove Lock  £

*Pub signed off B488, on left just S of A505 roundabout (S of Leighton
Buzzard); LU7 0QU*

**By Grand Union Canal Lock 28, with plenty of room inside, fair value
food and real ales, and lots of seats overlooking the water**

In fine weather, the seats and picnic-sets in the terraced garden and on the
canopied decking overlooking the Grand Union Canal here are much
prized. Inside, it's open-plan and the bar has a lofty high-raftered pitched
roof, terracotta and wallpapered walls, squashy brown leather sofas on
diagonal oak floor boarding, an eclectic mix of tables and chairs, a couple
of butcher's block tables by the bar, a big open-standing winter log fire and
canal-themed artwork. Steps take you up to the original lock-keeper's
cottage (now a three-room restaurant area) which is partly flagstoned, has
more winter log fires and looks down on the narrow canal lock. Fullers
London Pride and a couple of Fullers seasonal beers on handpump, several
wines by the glass, and friendly staff; piped music and newspapers.

Fair value bar food includes sandwiches, wraps and baps, lamb kofta with
tzatziki dip, leek, cheese and white wine risotto, ham hash with a poached egg
and bloody mary ketchup, beer-battered cod and a steak burger with bacon and
cheese. *Benchmark main dish: treacle-glazed ham £9.95. Two-course evening meal
£15.00.*

Fullers ~ Managers Gregg and Angela Worrall ~ Real ale ~ Bar food (12-9(7 Sun)) ~
(01525) 380940 ~ Children welcome ~ Open 11-11; 12-10.30 Sun

Recommended by Mr and Mrs John Taylor, Tony and Wendy Hobden

 HARE HATCH Berkshire   SU8077   Map D

Horse & Groom

A4 Bath Road W of Maidenhead; RG10 9SB

Spreading pub, very well refurbished recently, good staff, good all round

One of the newest – and biggest – in the small Brunning & Price group:
their typical style, spacious linked areas with a pleasing variety of
well spread tables and chairs on mahogany-stained boards, plenty of
oriental rugs and some carpet to soften the acoustics, open fires in
attractive tiled fireplaces, and a profusion of mainly old or antique prints.
The long bar counter has a splendid choice of drinks, including a good
changing range of wines by the glass, Brakspears Bitter and Oxford Gold,
Marstons and a couple of changing specials on handpump, 15 wines by
the glass, two Weston's farm ciders, lots of spirits including malts of the
week, and good coffees; also several different daily papers. Busy well
trained staff are kind and friendly. A sheltered back terrace has teak
tables under square canvas parasols.

As well as sandwiches, the interesting modern food includes duck liver pâté
with rhubarb chutney, beetroot and chickpea fritters with moroccan coleslaw

and minted yoghurt, potato, thyme and parmesan gnocchi with roast pumpkin, figs, spinach and sage velouté, pork and leek sausages with onion gravy, salad of slow-roasted duck leg with toulouse sausage, butter beans and red wine dressing, and braised lamb shoulder with dauphinoise potatoes. *Benchmark main dish: battered haddock and chips £11.95. Two-course evening meal £17.70.*

Brunning & Price ~ Manager Paul Boden ~ Real ale ~ Bar food (12-10(9.30 Sun)) ~ (0118) 940 3136 ~ Children welcome ~ Dogs allowed in bar ~ Open 11-11(10.30 Sun)
Recommended by Danny Thompson

HEADINGTON Oxfordshire   SP5407 Map E

Black Boy

Old High Street/St Andrews Road; off A420 at traffic lights opposite B4495; OX3 9HT

Stylish and enterprising modern dining pub with good, enjoyable food, and useful summer garden

Black leather seating on dark parquet, big mirrors, silvery patterned wallpaper, nightlights in fat opaque cylinders and glittering bottles behind the long bar counter add up to a cool contemporary look for this friendly place, its neat young black-aproned staff well schooled by the charming landlady. It's all light and airy, particularly for the two tables in the big bay window; just to the side is an open fire, with lower softer seats by it. Crisp white tablecloths and bold black and white wallpaper lend the area on the left a touch of formality. Behind is an appealing terrace, with picnic-sets under alternating black and white parasols on smart pale stone chippings, and a central seat encircling an ash tree. They have Greene King London Glory and Roosters Leghorn on handpump, good coffee and tea, and a good choice of wines by the glass; one enterprising programme is the Sunday morning kitchen class, adults and children alternate weeks.

Using only local produce and making their own bread and ice-cream, the interesting food might include a grazing menu, prawn and cod fishcake with a soy, mirin and lime dressing, gnocchi with fresh basil pesto, a proper burger with cheese, onion and gherkins, beer-battered fish and chips with a pea and mint purée, and confit gressingham duck leg with beetroot, radicchio and an orange and chilli gastrique (a vinegar and sugar caramelised reduction). *Benchmark main dish: roast pork belly with garlic mash and cider jus £12.95. Two-course evening meal £16.75.*

Greene King ~ Lease Abi Rose and Chris Bentham ~ Real ale ~ Bar food (12-2.45, 6-9.15) ~ (01865) 741137 ~ Children welcome ~ Open 12-3, 5-11; 12-10 Sun
Recommended by Richard Gibbs

HEDGERLEY Buckinghamshire   SU9687 Map D

White Horse ★ ◖ £

2.4 miles from M40 junction 2; at exit roundabout take Slough turn-off following alongside M40; after 1.5 miles turn right at T junction into Village Lane; SL2 3UY

Old-fashioned drinkers' pub with lots of beers tapped straight from the cask, regular beer festivals, and a cheery mix of customers

Locals and visitors mix happily in this smashing little pub – all drawn in by the friendly welcome and marvellous choice of real ales. As well as Rebellion IPA they keep up to seven daily changing guests, sourced from all over the country and tapped straight from casks kept in a room behind the tiny hatch counter. Their Easter, May, Spring and August bank holiday beer festivals (they can get through about 130 beers during the May one) are a highlight of the local calendar. This fine range of drinks extends to three farm ciders, still apple juice, a perry, belgian beers, ten or so wines by the glass and winter mulled wine. The cottagey main bar has plenty of unspoilt character, with lots of beams, brasses and exposed brickwork, low wooden tables, standing timbers, jugs, ballcocks and other bric-a-brac, a log fire, and a good few leaflets and notices about village events. A little flagstoned public bar on the left has darts and board games. A canopy extension leads out to the garden where there are tables and occasional barbecues, and there are lots of hanging baskets and a couple more tables in front of the building overlooking the quiet road. Good walks nearby, and the pub is handy for the Church Wood RSPB reserve and popular with walkers and cyclists; it can get crowded at weekends.

Lunchtime bar food such as sandwiches, cold meats and quiches, and changing straightforward hot dishes (their steak and mushroom pie is popular). *Benchmark main dish: steak and mushroom pie £7.25.*

Free house ~ Licensees Doris Hobbs and Kevin Brooker ~ Real ale ~ Bar food (lunchtime only) ~ (01753) 643225 ~ Children in canopy extension area ~ Dogs allowed in bar ~ Open 11-2.30, 5-11; 11-11 Sat; 12-10.30 Sun; closed evenings 25 and 26 Dec

Recommended by D and M T Ayres-Regan, Tracey and Stephen Groves, Nigel and Sue Foster, Gavin Robinson, the Didler, LM, Roy Hoing, N R White, Susan and John Douglas, Kevin Thomas, Nina Randall, Anthony Longden, Dave Braisted, Mark Wilson, Ian and Jane Irving

---

 HENLEY Berkshire   SU7682 Map D

Little Angel ⒲ ⒴

Remenham Lane (A4130, just over bridge E of Henley); RG9 2LS

Relaxed linked contemporary areas plus attractive conservatory, modern bar and restaurant food, helpful service, real ales, and several wines by the glass

After a smart refurbishment, this civilised place is more popular than ever and the genuine mix of customers keeps the atmosphere informal and chatty. The rooms are more or less open plan but with quite distinct seating areas. There are bare boards throughout and the little bar has leather cube stools, some tub and farmhouse chairs and a squashy sofa, high chairs beside the panelled, carved counter and a woodburning stove. Elsewhere, there are all sorts of dining chairs and tables, quite a bit of artwork on Farrow & Ball paintwork and an airy conservatory. Brakspears Bitter and Special, lots of wines (and champagne) by the glass, unobtrusive piped music and board games; helpful, friendly staff. A sheltered floodlit back terrace has tables under cocktail parasols looking over to the local cricket ground.

As well as sharing plates and daily specials, the particularly good food might include lunchtime sandwiches, salt and pepper squid with tomato, red onion and lime and dill salsa, smoked chicken, spring onion and pine nut terrine with avocado cream, creamy wild mushrooms topped with a herb and brioche crumble, confit duck hash with a free-range egg, and maize-fed chicken on spring greens with a red wine jus. *Benchmark main dish: steak burger £11.25. Two-course evening meal £20.00.*

There are report forms at the back of the book.

Brakspears ~ Lease Douglas and Lolly Green ~ Real ale ~ Bar food (12-3, 7-9; all day weekends) ~ Restaurant ~ (01491) 411008 ~ Children allowed but must be well behaved ~ Dogs allowed in bar ~ Open 11-11(midnight Fri and Sat); 12-10 Sun

Recommended by Simon Collett-Jones, Neil and Karen Dignan, Chris Glasson, Tom and Ruth Rees, Kim Upton

HIGHMOOR Oxfordshire

SU6984 Map D

Rising Sun

Witheridge Hill, signposted off B481; OS Sheet 175 map reference 697841; RG9 5PF

Thoughtfully run, pretty pub with a mix of diners and drinkers

This pretty black and cream village pub is usually packed out with cheerful customers but the friendly licensees and their pleasant staff are sure to make you welcome – no matter how busy they are. The two front rooms are for those just wanting a drink as the rest of the place is laid out for dining. On the right by the bar, there are wooden tables and chairs and a sofa on the stripped wooden floors, cream and terracotta walls and an open fire in the big brick inglenook fireplace. The main area spreading back from here has shiny bare boards and a swathe of carpeting with well spaced tables and attractive pictures on the walls. Brakspears Bitter and Oxford Gold on handpump, ten wines by the glass and Weston's cider; piped music and board games. There are seats and tables in the pleasant back garden; boules. As this is the heart of the Chilterns, there are plenty of surrounding walks.

Well liked bar food includes sandwiches, crab and prawn tartlet with tomato coulis, honey-roast gammon and poached egg salad with croûtons, pasta with a creamy courgette sauce and parmesan, pork and leek sausages with onion jus, venison casserole and bass with sweet potato and sticky red onion and tomato dressing. *Benchmark main dish: slow-cooked pork belly with black pudding mash £11.50. Two-course evening meal £18.25.*

Brakspears ~ Tenant Simon Duffy ~ Real ale ~ Bar food (not Sun evening) ~ Restaurant ~ (01491) 640856 ~ Children allowed under strict supervision in dining areas only ~ Dogs allowed in bar ~ Open 12-3, 5.30-11; 12-11(7 Sun) Sat; closed Sun evening

Recommended by Martin and Karen Wake, John Roots, Roy and Jean Russell, Bob and Margaret Holder

HOOK Hampshire

SU7153 Map D

Hogget

1.1 miles from M3 junction 5; A287 N, at junction with A30 (car park just before traffic lights); RG27 9JJ

Well run and accommodating, a proper pub moving with the times and giving good value

On a Friday morning this bustling place opens from 7.30 for breakfast – so helpful for travellers wanting early morning refreshment. Locally popular and chatty, the rooms ramble right round the central servery. The lighting, wallpaper and carpet pattern, and the leather sofas and tub chairs over on the right at the back, give a friendly and homely feel, as does the way it provides several smallish distinct areas. They have well kept Jennings Cumberland and Marstons Best and EPA on handpump, decent wines by the glass, and plenty of staff in neat but informal black uniforms. A sizeable terrace had sturdy tables and chairs, with some in a heated covered area.

Good food using local ingredients and including fair value lunchtime deals includes sandwiches, antipasti boards for sharing, crispy baby squid on crunchy salad with chilli, lime and mango dressing, chicken caesar salad, ham and free-range eggs, home-made burger with bacon and cheese, wild mushroom risotto and slow-roast pork belly with sun-dried tomato mash and a tangy tomato salad. *Benchmark main dish: local sausages with colcannon £10.00. Two-course evening meal £20.90.*

Marstons ~ Lease Tom Faulkner ~ Real ale ~ Bar food (12-2.30, 6.30-9; all day Sat; 12-6 Sun; not Sun evening) ~ Restaurant ~ (01256) 763009 ~ Children welcome ~ Dogs allowed in bar ~ Open 12-3, 5-11; 12-11(10.30 Sun) Sat

Recommended by David and Sue Smith, Jennifer Banks

HORSELL Surrey SU9959 Map D

Red Lion
High Street; GU21 4SS

Contemporary and popular with good food

Plenty of upholstered and leather sofas and chairs give this pleasantly spruced-up place a comfortable relaxed atmosphere. Lots of polished light wood, flowers and plants and cream-painted walls with clusters of pictures keep it feeling light and airy. The long solid wood counter (topped off by a row of metal café lights) serves Courage Best, Fullers London Pride and a guest such as Sharps Doom Bar and a dozen wines by the glass – bar chairs lined up here keep the place feeling pubby. Feeling just special enough, the big dining room has old church pews, exposed brickwork and food listed on blackboards. Outside, the attractive terrace is particularly inviting, with its good quality furnishings, smart umbrellas and big shady tree in the middle; piped music, TV and board games.

As well as sandwiches, the bistro-style food includes potato gnocchi with mushroom, pesto and parmesan, fish and chips, goats cheese, sweet potato and spring onion tart, well hung ribeye steak, and daily specials such as fish pie, grilled mackerel fillets with herb couscous and harissa dressing, fried duck breast with oriental vegetables and teriyaki sauce, and free-range pork chop with black pudding and apple sauce. *Benchmark main dish: rotisserie chicken with pancetta and mushroom sauce £12.95. Two-course evening meal £18.50.*

S&N ~ Licensee Richard Brown ~ Real ale ~ Bar food (12-9.30(10 Fri, Sat)) ~ Restaurant ~ (01483) 768497 ~ Seated children welcome in bar till 6pm and restaurant till 7.30pm ~ Open 11-11(11.30 Sat); 12-10.30 Sun

Recommended by Ian Phillips

HORSHAM Sussex TQ1730 Map C

Black Jug ♀
North Street; RH12 1RJ

Bustling town pub with wide choice of drinks, efficient staff, and good bar food

Always busy with a wide mix of customers, this is a well run town pub with friendly, knowledgeable staff. The one large open-plan, turn-of-the-century room has a large central bar, a nice collection of sizeable dark wood tables and comfortable chairs on the stripped-wood floor, board games and interesting old prints and photographs above a dark wood panelled dado on the cream walls. A spacious conservatory has similar furniture and lots of hanging baskets. Caledonian Deuchars IPA, Harveys

Best, Jennings Cumberland, Theakstons Old Peculier and Thwaites Wainwright on handpump, 20 wines by the glass, around 100 malt whiskies and Weston's cider. The pretty flower-filled back terrace has plenty of garden furniture. The small car park is for staff and deliveries only but you can park next door in the council car park.

🍴 Good, bistro-style food includes sandwiches, ham hock terrine with piccalilli, a charcuterie plate (for two), smoked haddock and salmon fishcakes, lamb, leek and potato hash with a fried egg, potato, thyme and parmesan gnocchi with roast pumpkin, figs, spinach and sage velouté, and venison steak with braised chicory and a blueberry and star anise jus. *Benchmark main dish: beer-battered fish and chips £11.95. Two-course evening meal £17.70.*

Brunning & Price ~ Tenant Alastair Craig ~ Real ale ~ Bar food (12-10(9.30 Sun)) ~ (01403) 253526 ~ Children welcome ~ Dogs allowed in bar ~ Open 11.30-11; 12-10.30 Sun

Recommended by Derek and Maggie Washington, Mike and Eleanor Anderson

 HUNGERFORD Berkshire   SU3368 Map D

Plume of Feathers 🍴 ♀
High Street; street parking opposite; RG17 0NB

Right at the heart of a bustling little town with well liked bar food and a relaxed family atmosphere

Since it's in an appealing small town, there's always a happy mix of both visitors and locals here. It's all open-plan and stretches from its smallish bow-windowed façade around the island bar to an open fire in the stripped fireplace right at the back. There are armchairs and a black leather sofa around low tables under lowish beams on the left at the front and a mix of tables with padded chairs or cushioned small pews on the bare boards elsewhere. They have a fair choice of wines by the glass alongside Greene King IPA and Ruddles Best on handpump and good coffee, and the scottish landlord and his staff are friendly and helpful. The sheltered back courtyard isn't large but is well worth knowing on a warm day: prettily planted, and with a swing seat as well as green-painted metal tables and chairs.

🍴 Well liked food includes lunchtime filled panini, black pudding fritters with apple sauce, brie in filo pastry with red wine and cranberry sauce, ham and free-range eggs, beer-battered haddock, portobello mushroom, spring onion and parmesan risotto, and venison stew with herb dumplings. *Benchmark main dish: beer-battered fresh haddock £11.20. Two-course evening meal £17.00.*

Greene King ~ Lease Haley and James Weir ~ Real ale ~ Bar food (12-2.30(4 Sun), 7-9; not Sun evening) ~ (01488) 682154 ~ Children welcome ~ Dogs welcome ~ Open 11-3, 5.30(6 Sat)-11(midnight Fri); 12-4 Sun; closed Sun evening; 25 and 26 Dec

Recommended by I D Barnett, Chris and Martin Taylor, Richard Tilbrook, Clive and Fran Dutson, Mike and Mary Carter

 **HURST GREEN** Sussex   TQ7326   Map C

White Horse ♀

Silverhill (A21); TN19 7PU

Friendly, well run pub with relaxed bar, elegant dining room, enjoyable food, and seats in garden

---

A former Georgian farmhouse, this is a friendly and civilised place for a drink or a meal. The relaxed bare-boards bar has a few leather armchairs and white-painted dining chairs around various wooden tables (laid with nightlights and wooden candlesticks), game trophies, prints and photographs on the walls, fresh flowers and an open fire. Harveys Best on handpump and 14 nice wines by the glass; piped music. An open doorway leads through to a second bar room with built-in leather wall seats and similar tables and then through again to the dining room. This is an elegant but informal room with similar furniture, oil paintings and ornate mirrors on modern paintwork, chandeliers and some panelling. Outside, there's a sizeable terrace with attractive white metal tables and chairs looking across a lawn and over the Weald.

Enjoyable bar food includes sandwiches, chicken terrine with home-made chutney, tempura prawns with sweet chilli jam, beef and bacon in ale pie, chicken breast wrapped in pancetta with a caper and beurre blanc sauce, open mushroom ravioli with truffle oil, and pork medallions with mustard sauce and garlic-sautéed potatoes. *Benchmark main dish: confit duck with cranberry jus £15.50. Two-course evening meal £21.00.*

Free house ~ Licensee Anthony Panic ~ Real ale ~ Bar food (12-3, 6-10) ~ Restaurant ~ (01580) 860235 ~ Children welcome ~ Dogs allowed in bar ~ Live jazz last Fri of month ~ Open 12-3, 6-11; 12-8 Sun

Recommended by David and Jenny Reed, Richard Mason

ICKHAM Kent   TR2258   Map C

Duke William

Off A257 E of Canterbury; The Street; CT3 1QP

Relaxing family-owned village pub with airy bar, dining conservatory, enjoyable bar food, and plenty of seats outside; bedrooms

---

The big spreading bar at this friendly village pub has huge new oak beams and stripped joists, a fine mix of seats from settles to high-backed cushioned dining chairs, dark wheelback and bentwood chairs around all sorts of wooden tables on the stripped wooden floor, a log fire with a couple of settles and a low barrel table in front of it, a central bar counter with high stools and brass coat hooks and a snug little area with one long table, black leather high-backed dining chairs, a flat-screen TV and a computer if you need it; daily papers, quiet piped music, cheerful modern paintings and large hop bines. Adnams, Harveys and Shepherd Neame Master Brew are on handpump alongside some decent wines and Happy Hour is 4-6pm. Staff are chatty and attentive. A low-ceilinged dining room leads off to the left with dark wood chairs, tables and more cushioned settles, with paintings and mirrors on the walls. At the back of the pub, there's a light dining conservatory with all manner of interesting paintings, prints and heraldry on the walls and similar furniture on the stone floor. Doors lead from here to a big terrace with a covered area to one side, plenty of wooden and metal tables and chairs, and a lawn with picnic-table sets, some swings and a slide.

Tasty bar food includes filled baguettes, chicken liver pâté, whitebait, field mushroom topped with goats cheese and prawns, steak and ale pie, calves liver and bacon, slow-roasted belly of pork with cider and apple sauce, and chicken with tarragon and mushrooms; there's also a good value two-course lunch menu and Sunday roasts (booking advised). *Benchmark main dish: beef and ale pie £11.50. Two-course evening meal £20.80.*

Free house ~ Licensee Louise White ~ Real ale ~ Bar food (12-3, 6-9.30) ~ Restaurant ~ (01227) 721308 ~ Children welcome ~ Dogs allowed in bar ~ Open 11-11(midnight Sat, 10 Sun) ~ Bedrooms: /£65S

Recommended by David Heath, Dr Kevan Tucker

IGHTHAM COMMON Kent   TQ5855   Map C

Harrow ⑪ ♀

Signposted off A25 just W of Ightham; pub sign may be hard to spot; TN15 9EB

Emphasis on good food in friendly, smart dining pub, fresh flowers and candles; pretty back terrace

The amiable landlord and his attentive staff extend a warm welcome at this comfortably genial pub and while most customers visit to enjoy the particularly good food, there's a tiny bar inside the door. The larger relaxed-feeling bar area to the right, painted a cheerful sunny yellow above the wood-panelled dado, is attractively finished with fresh flowers and candles on tables, smart dining chairs on the herringbone-patterned wood floor and there's a winter fire. There's a charming little antiquated conservatory and a more formal dining room; piped music. Gravesend Shrimpers and Loddon Hoppit are on handpump and they offer several wines by the glass. There are tables and chairs out on a pretty little pergola-enclosed back terrace and the pub is handily placed for Ightham Mote (National Trust).

 Good, popular food includes pork sausages with onion gravy, home-baked ham and eggs, risotto verde, thai-style prawn curry, salmon and chive fishcake with citrus cream sauce, goats cheese and caramelised red onion tart with grape salad, duck suprême with dauphinoise potatoes and plum tarte tatin, king scallops wrapped in pancetta with a garlic and herb dressing, and seasonal game like venison or pheasant; Sunday roasts. *Benchmark main dish: fishcakes £13.50. Two-course evening meal £19.00.*

Free house ~ Licensees John Elton and Claire Butler ~ Real ale ~ Bar food (12-2, 6-9) ~ Restaurant ~ (01732) 885912 ~ Children welcome but not in dining room on Sat evening ~ Open 12-3, 6-11; 12-4 Sun; closed Sun evening and all day Mon

Recommended by Derek Thomas, Nick and Carolyn Carter

INKPEN Berkshire   SU3764   Map D

Crown & Garter ◀ 🛏

Inkpen Common: Inkpen signposted with Kintbury off A4; in Kintbury turn left into Inkpen Road, then keep on into Inkpen Common; RG17 9QR

Remote-feeling pub with appealing layout, lovely garden and nearby walks, local ales, nicely lit bars, and especially friendly landlady

Tucked away up a country lane, this is an attractive 16th-c pub run by a friendly and helpful landlady. The low-ceilinged and relaxed panelled bar has West Berkshire Good Old Boy and a guest such as Fullers London

Pride on handpump, decent wines by the glass and several malt whiskies.
Three areas radiate from here; our pick is the parquet-floored part by the
raised woodburning stove which has a couple of substantial old tables
and a huge old-fashioned slightly curved settle. Other parts are slate and
wood with a good mix of well spaced tables and chairs, and nice lighting.
There's a front terrace for outside eating, a lovely long side garden with
picnic-sets, and plenty of good downland walks nearby. In a separate
single-storey building, the bedrooms (many have been redecorated
recently) form an L around a pretty garden. James II is reputed to have
used the pub on his way to visit his mistress who lived locally.

From a varied menu, the choice of food might include sandwiches, twice-baked
natural smoked haddock and cheese soufflé, poached pear, walnut and stilton
salad, chicken curry with an onion bhaji, leek and goats cheese tart, steak and
kidney pudding, and venison casserole with dumplings. *Benchmark main dish: steak
and kidney pudding £11.25. Two-course evening meal £18.20.*

Free house ~ Licensee Gill Hern ~ Real ale ~ Bar food (not Sun evening or Mon and Tues
lunchtimes) ~ Restaurant ~ (01488) 668325 ~ Children allowed in bar only but must be
over 7 evenings and in bedrooms ~ Dogs allowed in bar ~ Open 12-3, 5.30-11;
12-5.30, 7-10.30 Sun; closed Mon and Tues lunchtimes ~ Bedrooms: £79.50B/£99B

*Recommended by I H G Busby, Julia and Richard Tredgett, Mr and Mrs H J Langley,
Mr and Mrs P R Thomas, N R White*

INKPEN Berkshire   SU3564   Map D

THE GOOD PUB GUIDE

Swan

*Lower Inkpen; coming from A338 in Hungerford, take Park Street (first left
after railway bridge, coming from A4); RG17 9DX*

**Extended country pub with rambling rooms, traditional décor, friendly
staff, real ales and plenty of seats outside; bedrooms**

This is a much-extended country pub with a 17th-c heart. The rambling
beamed rooms have cosy corners, traditional pubby furniture, eclectic
bric-a-brac and three log fires and there's a flagstoned games area and a
cosy restaurant, too; piped music. Friendly helpful staff serve Butts and
West Berkshire ales on handpump and local farm cider. There are picnic-
sets outside on tiered front terraces overlooking a footpath; the quiet
bedrooms are set away from the pub in a courtyard. The interesting farm
shop next door sells their own organic beef and ready-made meals, as
well as groceries, dairy products and so forth.

Popular bar food using their own farmed organic produce and home-made
bread and pasta includes sandwiches, beef ravioli with basil tomato sauce and
parmesan, brie and beetroot tatin with caramelised red onion, various home-made
sausages, chicken in a creamy mushroom sauce, lamb shoulder in red wine and
orange, and mixed seafood risotto. *Benchmark main dish: beef curry £12.95. Two-
course evening meal £19.45.*

Free house ~ Licensees Mary and Bernard Harris ~ Real ale ~ Bar food (12-2(4 Sun),
7-9; not Sun evening or winter Mon) ~ Restaurant ~ (01488) 668326 ~ Children welcome
~ Open 12-2.30, 6-11; 12-11(4.30 Sun) Sat; closed Sun evening and winter Mon ~
Bedrooms: £70S/£90S

Recommended by John Robertson, CP

The ⟨🍴⟩ symbol distinguishes pubs where the food is
of exceptional quality.

KINGHAM Oxfordshire   SP2624 Map E

Plough 🍴 ♀ 🛏

Village signposted off B4450 E of Bledington; or turn S off A436 at staggered crossroads a mile SW of A44 junction – or take signed Daylesford turn off A436 and keep on; The Green; OX7 6YD

Friendly dining pub combining an informal pub atmosphere with upmarket food; bedrooms

---

More of a restaurant-with-rooms than a straightforward pub, this busy place continues to draw in plenty of cheerful customers. But despite the emphasis on dining, there's a properly pubby bar with some nice old high-backed settles, as well as brightly cushioned chapel chairs on its broad dark boards, candles on stripped tables and cheerful farmyard animal and country prints; at one end there's a big log fire and at the other (by an unusual cricket table), a woodburning stove. There's a piano in one corner and a snug separate one-table area opposite the servery which has Goffs Jouster and Hook Norton Hooky Bitter on handpump and good wines by the glass. The fairly spacious and raftered two-part dining room is up a few steps. If you stay, the breakfast is good. The heated smokers' shelter is at the back of the building.

Ambitious and inventive food might include scotched quails eggs, duck terrine with duck liver parfait and rhubarb toast, wild vegetable and potato casserole with a green pastry wafer, cock-a-leekie pie with mash, lemon sole with razor clams, tomatoes and potato pancake, and pork loin with crispy trotters, onion tart and sage and onion; interesting local cheeses. *Benchmark main dish: hereford beef with triple-cooked chips and horseradish butter £23.00. Two-course evening meal £22.00.*

Free house ~ Licensees Emily Watkins and Miles Lampson ~ Real ale ~ Bar food (all day) ~ Restaurant ~ (01608) 658327 ~ Children welcome ~ Dogs allowed in bar and bedrooms ~ Open 12-11(10.30 Sun) ~ Bedrooms: /£90S(£130B)

Recommended by Keith and Sue Ward, Myra Joyce, Richard Tilbrook, Anthony and Pam Stamer, George Atkinson, Richard Greaves, Edward Mirzoeff, Anthony Longden, Michael Doswell, David Glynne-Jones, Dr Martin Owton

---

KINGSTON LISLE Oxfordshire   SU3287 Map E

Blowing Stone 🍴 ♀ 🍺

Village signposted off B4507 W of Wantage; OX12 9QL

OXFORDSHIRE DINING PUB OF THE YEAR

Easy-going chatty country pub with up-to-date blend of simple comfort, good food and drink

---

The Tuckers delighted us and our readers at their previous pub, the White Horse over at Woolstone, and have brought the same winning mix of easy country informality with good food and drink to this friendly village pub. Its heart is the central bar, where broad tiles by the log fire suit the muddy riding boots of the cheerful young people in from nearby training stables. They have the *Racing Post* alongside other daily papers, and most of the photographs on the pale sage walls are of racehorses, often spectacularly coming to grief over jumps. Several separate areas radiate off, most of them carpeted, quite small and snug, though a back dining conservatory is more spacious. Apart from a couple of high-backed winged settles, most of the furniture is an unfussy mix of country dining tables each with its own set of matching chairs, either padded or generously cushioned. Decent wines by the glass and Greene King

Morland Original, Hook Norton Hooky Bitter, Ringwood Fortyniner and perhaps a White Horse ale named after the pub; service is quick and friendly and there may be unobtrusive piped music. The pretty front terrace has a couple of picnic-sets under cocktail parasols with more on the back lawn by a rockery; the Ridgeway and Uffington White Horse are both nearby. Many years ago one of your editors, in his teens, was proud of being able to 'sound' the blowing stone itself, a hole-filled boulder outside a cottage down just beyond the crossroads, which can be induced to produce a spine-tingling far-carrying horn blast. Alas, on his re-visit this year, he seemed to have lost the knack – or perhaps he'd just lunched too well here!

Sturdy lunchtime bar food (not Sunday) includes home-baked baguettes with soup or chips, generous ham and eggs and kedgeree, with more elaborate main menu choices like mixed game and foie gras terrine with rosemary toast and chutney, salami with cheeses, home-made sausages, vegetable wellington, spicy monkfish and king prawn curry with aubergine bhaji, and pork cassoulet with confit of duck, toulouse sausages and haricot beans; there's also a good value two-course Tuesday evening menu. *Benchmark main dish: chicken kiev with greek salad £13.50. Two-course evening meal £22.00.*

Free house ~ Licensees Angus and Steph Tucker ~ Real ale ~ Bar food (not Sun evening) ~ Restaurant ~ (01367) 820288 ~ Children welcome ~ Dogs allowed in bar ~ Open 12-11

Recommended by Michael Sissons, Mrs J M Robinson

KIRTLINGTON Oxfordshire   SP4919   Map E

Oxford Arms 🍴 🍷

Troy Lane, junction with A4095 W of Bicester; OX5 3HA

Civilised and friendly stripped-stone pub with enjoyable food and good wine choice

A long line of linked rooms are divided by a central stone hearth with a great round stove – and by the servery itself, with Brakspears and Hook Norton Old Hooky on handpump, an interesting range of wines in two glass sizes, and a good choice of soft drinks. The chef/landlord and his charming young staff ensure a genial atmosphere, helped by the tables' fat church candles and flower bunches. Past the bar area with its cushioned wall pews, creaky beamed ceiling and age-darkened flooring tiles, dining tables on parquet have neat red chairs, and beyond that leather sofas cluster round an end log fire; there is stripped stone throughout. A sheltered back terrace has teak tables under giant parasols with heaters, and beyond are picnic-sets on pale gravel.

Hearty well prepared food using good local ingredients, especially from Kelmscott, includes lunchtime sandwiches, wild garlic and goats cheese tart, salmon and prawn fishcakes, ham and eggs, a risotto of the day, venison burgers with triple-cooked chips, barbary duck leg confit with sweet chilli sauce, and well aged steaks; good cheeses, too. *Benchmark main dish: wild mushroom tagliatelle with parmesan and truffle oil £12.00. Two-course evening meal £18.50.*

Punch ~ Lease Bryn Jones ~ Real ale ~ Bar food (12-2.30, 6.30-9.30) ~ (01869) 350208 ~ Well behaved children welcome ~ Dogs allowed in bar ~ Open 12-3, 6-11; 12-3 Sun; closed Sun evening

Recommended by D C T and E A Frewer, Oxana Mishina, Veronica Hall

> If we know a pub has an outdoor play area for children, we mention it.

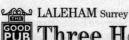 **LALEHAM** Surrey   TQ0568   Map C

Three Horseshoes
Shepperton Road (B376); TW18 1SE

Contemporary styling in aged pub with popular food

Rich deep blue paintwork on the front of the long counter, on some table pedestals and on the dado lends a striking contrast to the white walls at this much freshened-up extending pub. Good natural light and clever lighting keep it airy and spacious while bare boards and a nice mix of farmhouse furniture give a relaxed and pubby feel. Efficient bar staff serve Sharps Doom Bar and a couple of guests such as Hogs Back TEA and Ringwood Best from handpumps and over a dozen wines by the glass; piped music. The dining areas are a little smarter with their grey woodwork and caramel leather chairs. There are tables out on a flagstoned terrace and picnic-sets on grass.

Bar food includes sandwiches with chips or soup, smoked haddock and spinach tart with cheese sauce, caesar salad, duck liver and pistachio terrine with onion marmalade, devilled lambs kidneys, roast butternut and broad bean risotto, crispy duck with peppercorn sauce, lemon and thyme rotisserie chicken with mushroom and pancetta sauce, and well hung fillet steak. *Benchmark main dish: fish and chips £12.50. Two-course evening meal £19.50.*

Unique (Enterprise) ~ Lease Richard Brown ~ Real ale ~ Bar food (12-9.30(10 Fri, Sat)) ~ Restaurant ~ (01784) 455014 ~ Children welcome till 7.30pm ~ Open 11-11(11.30 Fri, Sat, 10.30 Sun)
Recommended by Susan and Neil McLean, M Ross-Thomas

 LANGFORD Oxfordshire   SP2402   Map E

Bell ♀ ◖
Village signposted off A361 N of Lechlade, then pub signed; GL7 3LF

Civilised pub with beams, flagstones, a good log fire, well chosen wines and beer, and quite a choice of bar food

In a quiet and charming village, this country dining pub is tucked away near the church. It's a friendly place with an informal country atmosphere and the simple low-key furnishings and décor add to the appeal. The main bar has just six sanded and sealed mixed tables on grass matting, a variety of chairs, three nice cushioned window seats, an attractive carved oak settle, polished broad flagstones by a big stone inglenook fireplace with a good log fire, low beams and butter-coloured walls with two or three antique engravings. A second even smaller room on the right is similar in character; daily papers on a little corner table. Hook Norton Hooky Bitter, Sharps Doom Bar and St Austell Tribute on handpump and a dozen wines by the glass. The bearded collie is called Madison. There are two or three picnic-sets out in the small garden with a play house; aunt sally.

As well as fish specials such as crab and leek risotto and calamari with a parmesan crust and garlic and lemon mayonnaise, the well liked food might include sandwiches, eggs benedict, beefburger in a rustic roll, nut roast with tomato and basil sauce, thai green chicken curry, steak and kidney pie and rump of lamb on honey-roasted root vegetables with a red wine jus. *Benchmark main dish: seared king scallops with chorizo and rocket and parmesan salad £15.95. Two-course evening meal £20.00.*

Free house ~ Licensees Paul and Jackie Wynne ~ Real ale ~ Bar food (12-1.45, 7-9; not Sun evening or Mon) ~ Restaurant ~ (01367) 860249 ~ Children welcome but no under-4s after 7pm ~ Dogs allowed in bar ~ Open 12-3, 7-11(midnight Fri, 11.30 Sat); 12-3.30 Sun; closed Sun evening, all day Mon

Recommended by Mrs L James, P and J Shapley, Grahame and Myra Williams, Henry Midwinter, Phil and Jane Hodson, Mrs Jean Lewis, KN-R, R K Phillips, Neil and Diane Williams, Graham Oddey, Jennifer and Patrick O'Dell

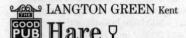 LANGTON GREEN Kent   TQ5439   Map C

Hare ♀

A264 W of Tunbridge Wells; TN3 0JA

Interestingly decorated Edwardian pub with a fine choice of drinks and popular food

With Kent now boasting three Brunning and Price pubs, this roomy mock-Tudor former hotel, dating from 1901, was one of the first in this much-liked chain to open in the South East. Inside, it's high-ceilinged and the rooms have been knocked through, with plenty of light flooding through large windows, especially in the front bar where drinkers tend to gather. Décor, more or less in period with the building, runs from dark-painted dados below light walls, 1930s oak furniture, light brown carpet and turkish-style rugs on stained wooden floors to old romantic pastels and a huge collection of chamber-pots hanging from beams. Greene King IPA, Abbot, Morland Original and Ruddles, alongside a couple of guests on handpump, lots of wines by the glass, over 100 whiskies and a fine choice of vodkas and other spirits; board games. French windows open on to a big terrace with picnic-sets and pleasant views of the tree-ringed village green. Parking is limited.

From a frequently changing menu, interesting modern bistro-style food might include devilled whitebait with lemon and caper mayonnaise, fried scallops with chorizo and chickpeas, sandwiches, steak, venison and mushroom suet pudding, wild mushroom and lentil pie with sweet potato mash, and fried bass with teriyaki noodles. *Benchmark main dish: steak, Guinness and stilton pie £11.95. Two-course evening meal £18.50.*

Brunning & Price ~ Manager Rob Broadbent ~ Real ale ~ Bar food (12-9.30(10 Fri, Sat; 9 Sun)) ~ Restaurant ~ (01892) 862419 ~ Children welcome (away from bar after 6pm) ~ Dogs allowed in bar ~ Open 12-11(midnight Fri and Sat, 10.30 Sun)

Recommended by B J Harding, Vernon Rowe, Ian Phillips

 LEIGH Surrey   TQ2147   Map C

Seven Stars ♀

Dawes Green, S of A25 Dorking—Reigate; RH2 8NP

Popular country dining pub with enjoyable food and good wines

Many readers enjoy the child-free atmosphere (no piped music or games either) at this tile-hung 17th-c tavern. What's more, it's beautifully kept, welcoming, serves well kept beer and jolly good food. The comfortable saloon bar has a 1633 inglenook fireback showing a royal coat of arms, and there's a plainer public bar. The sympathetically done restaurant extension at the side incorporates 17th-c floor timbers imported from a granary. Greene King Old Speckled Hen, Fullers London Pride and Wells & Youngs Bitter are served from handpump, alongside decent wines with about a dozen by the glass. Outside, there's plenty of room in the beer garden at the front, on the terrace and in the side garden.

🍴 The nicely varied menu includes lunchtime ciabattas, breaded whitebait with caper and lemon mayonnaise, pheasant pâté, mushroom, leek and stilton risotto, curry and rice, porcini ravioli in creamy parmesan sauce with mushrooms, leeks and peas, home-smoked hickory ribs, roast chicken stuffed with brie, and confit duck leg with parsley mash. They do two sittings for Sunday lunch and it's advisable to book at all times. *Benchmark main dish: ham, egg and chips £10.95. Two-course evening meal £19.75.*

Punch ~ Lease David and Rebecca Pellen ~ Real ale ~ Bar food (12-2.30(4 Sun), 6-9(6.30-9.30 Fri, Sat); not Sun evening) ~ Restaurant ~ (01306) 611254 ~ Dogs allowed in bar ~ Open 12-10(11 Sat, 8 Sun)

Recommended by Michael and Margaret Cross, Tony and Jill Radnor, Ian and Barbara Rankin, J R Osborne, Mr and Mrs Price, Nick Lawless, M G Hart, Peter Loader, Simon and Mandy King

 LEY HILL Buckinghamshire SP9901 Map E

Swan

Village signposted off A416 in Chesham; HP5 1UT

Charming, old-fashioned pub with chatty customers, four real ales, and quite a choice of popular food

The professional and friendly licensees run a tight ship here and you can be sure of attentive, helpful service and good food and beer. It's all kept spic and span – not easy given the antiquity of the interior – and the atmosphere is chatty and relaxed. The main bar is cosily old fashioned with black beams (mind your head) and standing timbers, an old range, a log fire, a nice mix of old furniture and a collection of old local photographs. Brakspears Bitter, Greene King Old Speckled Hen, St Austell Tribute and Timothy Taylors Landlord on handpump and several wines by the glass. The dining area is light and airy with a raftered ceiling, cream walls and curtains and a mix of old tables and chairs on timber floors. It's worth wandering over the common (where there's a cricket pitch and a nine-hole golf course) opposite this little timbered 16th-c pub to turn back and take a look at the very pretty picture it makes, with its picnic-sets among flower tubs and hanging baskets (there are more in the large back garden).

🍴 Good, enjoyable food includes lunchtime sandwiches, black pudding with bubble and squeak, a poached egg and hollandaise, home-made burger with cheese and mustard mayonnaise, pork and leek sausages with onion gravy, bass with a sun-dried tomato, crayfish and herb sauce, and slow-cooked and crackled pork belly with apple purée and jus. *Benchmark main dish: seafood casserole £13.50. Two-course evening meal £20.50.*

Free house ~ Licensee Nigel Byatt ~ Real ale ~ Bar food (12-2.30(3 Sun), 6.30-9.30; not Sun or Mon evenings) ~ Restaurant ~ (01494) 783075 ~ Live music twice a month ~ Open 12-3, 5.30-11; 12-10.30 Sun; closed Mon evening

Recommended by Roy Hoing, LM, Ashley Frost, Peter and Giff Bennett, Jennifer Beeston and Julian Browne, Tracey and Stephen Groves, John Holroyd

 LISS Hampshire   SU7826 Map D

Jolly Drover
London Road, Hill Brow; B2070 S of town, near B3006 junction; GU33 7QL

Particularly well run traditional pub, comfortable and friendly, with real ales and pubby food; good bedrooms

Smiling quick service and generous helpings of traditional bar food continue to draw customers into this well run pub. The neatly carpeted low-beamed bar includes leather tub chairs and a couple of sofas in front of the inglenook log fire and they keep Bowman Swift One, Fullers London Pride and Sharps Doom Bar on handpump; daily papers, a silenced games machine in one alcove and board games. Several areas, with a gentle décor mainly in muted terracotta or pale ochre, include two back dining areas, one of which opens on to a sheltered terrace with teak furniture, and a lawn with picnic-sets beyond. The neat bedrooms are in a barn conversion.

Generous helpings of well liked pubby food include sandwiches, pollack goujons with tartare sauce, vegetable lasagne, steak and kidney in ale pie, sausages and mash, chicken curry, and a mixed grill. *Benchmark main dish: steak and kidney pie £10.50. Two-course evening meal £17.00.*

Enterprise ~ Lease Barry and Anne Coe ~ Real ale ~ Bar food (12-2(2.30 Sun), 7-9.30; not Sun evening) ~ Restaurant ~ (01730) 893137 ~ Children welcome ~ Open 11-2.30, 6-11; 12-4 Sun; closed Sun evening ~ Bedrooms: £70S/£80S

Recommended by Neil and Pippa King, Tony and Wendy Hobden, Tony and Jill Radnor

LITTLE MARLOW Buckinghamshire   SU8787 Map D

Queens Head ⑪
Village signposted off A4155 E of Marlow near Kings Head; bear right into Pound Lane cul-de-sac; SL7 3SR

Charmingly tucked away, with good food and beers, and an appealing garden

Thoroughly enjoyable all round, this is an unpretentious country pub that our readers like very much. The main bar, with a table of magazines by the door, has simple but comfortable furniture on its polished boards and leads back to a sizeable squarish carpeted dining extension with good solid tables. Throughout are old local photographs on the cream or maroon walls, panelled dados painted brown or sage, and lighted candles. On the right is a small, quite separate, low-ceilinged public bar with Brakspears Bitter, Fullers London Pride and a weekly changing guest on handpump, several wines by the glass, quite a range of whiskies and good coffee; neatly dressed efficient staff and unobtrusive piped music. On a summer's day, the garden of this pretty tiled cottage – though not large – is a decided plus, sheltered and neatly planted, with some teak tables, some quite close-set picnic-sets, and some white-painted metal furniture in a little wickerwork bower.

Bedroom prices normally include full english breakfast, VAT and any inclusive service charge that we know of. Prices before the '/' are for single rooms, after the '/' for two people in a double or twin (B includes a private bath, S a private shower). If there is no '/', the prices are only for twin or double rooms (as far as we know there are no singles). If there is no B or S, as far as we know no rooms have private facilities.

Enjoyable bar food includes lunchtime sandwiches, potted rabbit and pheasant pâté with home-made chutney, roast artichoke and red pepper lasagne, stuffed corn-fed chicken with leek and potato hash with pearl onion, pancetta and jus, and seafood casserole with rouille and gruyère croûton. *Benchmark main dish: fish and chips £10.95. Two-course evening meal £20.45.*

Punch ~ Lease Daniel O'Sullivan and Chris Rising ~ Real ale ~ Bar food (12-2.30 (4 weekends), 6.30-9.30) ~ Restaurant ~ (01628) 482927 ~ Children welcome ~ Open 12-11(10 Sun); closed 24-26 Dec

Recommended by D and M T Ayres-Regan, Doug Kennedy, Martin and Karen Wake, Roy Hoing, Tracey and Stephen Groves, Betsy and Peter Little, Mrs Shirley Hughes, Jamie and Sue May, Samantha Baxendale

 LITTLE MISSENDEN Buckinghamshire   SU9298 Map E

Crown 🍺 £

Crown Lane, SE end of village, which is signposted off A413 W of Amersham; HP7 0RD

Long-serving licensees and pubby feel in little brick cottage, with several real ales and traditional food; attractive garden

Sadly, it's rare nowadays to find a classic Chilterns local like this small brick cottage – which makes coming here all the more special. It's been in the same family for over 90 years and the friendly landlord keeps it spotless and deliberately traditional. There are old red flooring tiles on the left, oak parquet on the right, built-in wall seats, studded red leatherette chairs and a few small tables and a winter fire. A good mix of customers, including a loyal bunch of regulars, adds to the cheerfully chatty atmosphere. Adnams Bitter, Hook Norton Bitter, St Austell Tribute, and a guest or two such as Hogs Back Hop Garden Gold or Sharps Doom Bar on handpump or tapped from the cask, farm cider, summer Pimms and several malt whiskies; darts, bar billiards and board games. The large attractive sheltered garden behind has picnic-sets and other tables, and there are also seats out in front. The interesting church in the pretty village is well worth a visit. Bedrooms are in a converted barn (continental breakfasts in your room only).

 Straightforward lunchtime bar food such as good fresh sandwiches, soup, buck's bite (a special home-made pizza-like dish), filled baked potatoes, ploughman's, and steak and kidney pie. *Benchmark main dish: buck's bite £5.50.*

Free house ~ Licensees Trevor and Carolyn How ~ Real ale ~ Bar food (12-2; not evenings, not Sun) ~ (01494) 862571 ~ Open 11-2.30(3 Sat), 6-11; 12-3, 7-11 Sun ~ Bedrooms: £65S/£75S

Recommended by Patrick and Daphne Darley, Anthony Longden, Tracey and Stephen Groves, Roy Hoing, Peter and Lois McDonald

LODSWORTH Sussex   SU9321 Map D

Halfway Bridge Inn 🍴 🍷 🛏

Just before village, on A272 Midhurst—Petworth; GU28 9BP

Restauranty coaching inn with contemporary décor in several dining areas, log fires, local real ales and modern food; lovely bedrooms

There's no doubt that most customers are here to eat and, although the tables are set for dining, there are regulars who do pop in for a chat and a pint. It's a smart place and the various bar rooms have plenty of intimate little corners and are carefully furnished with good oak chairs and an individual mix of tables; one of the log fires is a well polished kitchen range. The interconnecting restaurant rooms have beams, wooden floors and a cosy atmosphere. Sharps Doom Bar, Skinners Betty Stogs and Triple fff Moondance on handpump and 14 wines by the glass; piped music. At the back, there are seats on a small terrace. The bedrooms in the former stable yard are extremely stylish and comfortable.

Well presented – if not particularly cheap – the interesting food includes lunchtime filled ciabattas, spiced crab and crayfish gateaux with avocado salad and dill dressing, honey-roasted root vegetable tagine with chargrilled polenta, chicken and smoked ham pie, venison steak with bitter chocolate jus and sweet potato fondant, and jerk and herb-crusted lamb loin with minted and chilli couscous and mango relish. *Benchmark main dish: chicken and ham pie £13.75. Two-course evening meal £21.00.*

Free house ~ Licensee Paul Carter ~ Real ale ~ Bar food (12-2.30, 6.30-9.15) ~ Restaurant ~ (01798) 861281 ~ Children welcome ~ Dogs allowed in bar ~ Open 11-11; 12-10.30 Sun ~ Bedrooms: £85B/£120B

Recommended by Colin McKerrow, Tracey and Stephen Groves, Ian Wilson, Mrs Lorna Walsingham, Martin and Karen Wake

LONG CRENDON Buckinghamshire   SP6908   Map E

Eight Bells £

High Street, off B4011 N of Thame; car park entrance off Chearsley Road, not 'Village roads only'; HP18 9AL

Good beers and sensibly priced pubby food in nicely traditional village pub with charming garden

This pub's unchanging character fits well with the interesting old village, known to many from TV's *Midsomer Murders*. The little bareboards bar on the left has two cool well kept regular beers on handpump, Hel's Bells (brewed for the pub) and Wadworths IPA, and two or three changing guests tapped from the cask such as Tring Jack o' Legs and Vale P&Q; they also have a decent choice of wines by the glass. A bigger low-ceilinged room on the right has a log fire, daily papers, darts, and a pleasantly haphazard mix of tables and simple seats on its ancient red and black tiles; one snug little hidey-hole with just three tables is devoted to the local morris men – frequent visitors. Service is cheerful, and full marks to the landlady not just for the excellent quality of her beers but for the way she's preserved the pub's unassuming and welcoming style in an area where pressure to move upmarket is so strong. The quiet garden behind is a particular joy in summer: well spaced picnic-sets among a colourful variety of shrubs and flowers; they play aunt sally.

Enjoyable modestly priced home-made pubby food includes lunchtime sandwiches, lemon and garlic field mushrooms with a rich tomato sauce and mozzarella, corned beef hash with a duck egg, beef or vegetarian lasagne, steak burger topped with cheddar or stilton, pork ribs in barbecue sauce, and chicken enchilada with salsa, guacamole and sour cream. *Benchmark main dish: home-made pie £9.25. Two-course evening meal £13.90.*

Free house ~ Licensee Helen Copleston ~ Real ale ~ Bar food (12-2(2.30 Sun), 6-9; not Sun evening or all day Mon) ~ (01844) 208244 ~ Children welcome ~ Dogs allowed in bar ~ Open 12-3, 5.30-11; 12-11 Sat and Sun; closed Mon lunchtime

Recommended by Doug Kennedy, David Lamb

LONG HANBOROUGH Oxfordshire   SP4214   Map E

George & Dragon
A4095 Bladon—Witney; Main Road; OX29 8JX

Substantial well organised pub, something for everyone

This is almost best thought-of as two separate places – even three, if you count the peaceful back garden, with cream-painted picnic-sets among attractive shrubs, tables under a big dark canopy on a separate sheltered terrace, and further areas where you'll find rabbits and guinea-pigs. The original two-room bar, 17th-c or older, is all stripped stone, low beams, soft lighting, two stoves (one very elaborate), and a thoroughly traditional pubby feel with furnishings to suit. It then forms an L with a roomy thatched restaurant extension, which has comfortably padded dining chairs around the sturdy tables on its boards, plenty of pictures on deep pink walls, and decorative plates on the beams. Neat black-uniformed staff are friendly and efficient; they have well kept Courage Directors and Wells & Youngs Bombardier and Eagle on handpump, Weston's farm cider and a good range of wines; there may be soft piped music.

A very wide choice of good generous food (best to book at weekends) includes plenty of sandwiches and baguettes, duck and orange pâté, a brunch, cottage pie, a full rack of barbecue ribs, cherry tomato and mixed vegetable tarte tatin topped with cheese, lambs liver and bacon with onion gravy, and half a duck with creamy apple and calvados sauce; they also offer a two-course set menu on Monday and Tuesday and for OAPs at lunchtime on Wednesday and Thursday. *Benchmark main dish: steak in ale pie £12.95. Two-course evening meal £20.45.*

Charles Wells ~ Lease Mr A and Mrs J Wright ~ Real ale ~ Bar food (12-2(3 Sun), 6.30-9 (9.30 Fri and Sat); not Sun evening) ~ Restaurant ~ (01993) 881362 ~ Children welcome ~ Dogs allowed in bar ~ Open 12-3, 6-midnight; 12-4, 6.30-11 Sun
Recommended by Peter Grant, P M Newsome

LONGSTOCK Hampshire   SU3537   Map D

Peat Spade 🍴 ♧
Off A30 on W edge of Stockbridge; SO20 6DR

Former coaching inn with boldly painted rooms, shooting and fishing themed décor, imaginative food and real ales; stylish bedrooms

In a pretty village and right by the River Test, this is well run pub where locals, diners and residents all mix easily together. There's quite a sporting feel – they arrange fishing and shooting – and there are stuffed fish, lots of hunting pictures and prints on the dark red or green walls and even a little fishing shop at the end of the garden. Both the bar and dining room have pretty windows, an interesting mix of dining chairs around miscellaneous tables on bare boards, standard lamps and candlelight, wine bottles, old stone bottles and soda siphons, a nice show of toby jugs and shelves of books. The atmosphere is chatty and informal. There's also an upstairs room with comfortable sofas and armchairs. Ringwood Best and local Flack Manor Double Drop on handpump and several wines by the glass; piped music. The terrace and garden have plenty of seats and there are lots of surrounding walks. The contemporary bedrooms are stylish and comfortable.

Highly thought-of food includes lunchtime sandwiches, earl grey smoked duck with pea shoots, honeycomb and shaved radish, chicken liver and foie gras parfait with plum compote, various sharing boards and platters, pumpkin and herb risotto, gammon with a fried duck egg, and bass with scallops, samphire and a brown shrimp and dill butter. *Benchmark main dish: trio of lamb £18.50. Two-course evening meal £21.00.*

Free house ~ Licensee Tracy Levett ~ Real ale ~ Bar food (12-2.30(4 Sun), 6-9.30) ~ Restaurant ~ (01264) 810612 ~ Well behaved children welcome ~ Dogs allowed in bar ~ Open 11-11 ~ Bedrooms: /£145S

Recommended by Phyl and Jack Street, David and Nicola Stout, Ann and Colin Hunt

LONGWORTH Oxfordshire   SU3899 Map E

Blue Boar 🍴

Tucks Lane; OX13 5ET

Smashing old pub with a friendly welcome for all, good wines and beer, and fairly priced good food; Thames-side walks nearby

Mr Dailey has been running this 17th-c thatched stone pub for 32 years now (though his friendly staff tend to be more in evidence) and the atmosphere remains bustling and relaxed – helped by the genuine mix of both diners and chatty locals. The three low-beamed, characterful little rooms are warmly traditional with well worn fixtures and furnishings and two blazing log fires, one beside a fine old settle. Brasses, hops and assorted knick-knacks like skis and an old clocking-in machine line the ceilings and walls, there are fresh flowers on the bar and scrubbed wooden tables, and faded rugs on the tiled floor; benches are firmly wooden rather than upholstered. The main eating area is the red-painted room at the end and there's a quieter restaurant extension, too. Brakspears Bitter, Fullers London Pride and a guest like Prescott Hill Climb on handpump, 20 malt whiskies, nine wines by the glass, summer Pimms and quite a few brandies and ports. There are tables in front and on the back terrace, and the Thames is a short walk away.

🍴 As well as pizzas served all day, the reliably good food includes sandwiches, a changing terrine with home-made chutney, szechuan pepper and ginger squid, potato and rocket salad, beefburger with bacon, cheese and aioli, steak and kidney pudding, seasonal risotto with parmesan, roast wild salmon with wild mushrooms and a red wine sauce, and malaysian prawn or chicken curry. *Benchmark main dish: beer-battered fresh fish and chips £10.50. Two-course evening meal £18.45.*

Free house ~ Licensee Paul Dailey ~ Real ale ~ Bar food (12-2.30(3 Sun), 7-9; pizzas all day) ~ Restaurant ~ (01865) 820494 ~ Children welcome ~ Dogs allowed in bar ~ Open 11.30-11(midnight Sat)

Recommended by Tina and David Woods-Taylor, R K Phillips, Jennifer and Patrick O'Dell, Dick and Madeleine Brown

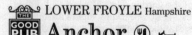

LOWER FROYLE Hampshire   SU7643 Map D

Anchor 🍴 ⇌

Village signposted N of A31 W of Bentley; GU34 4NA

HAMPSHIRE DINING PUB OF THE YEAR

Civilised pub, lots to look at, real ales, good wines and imaginative bar food; comfortable bedrooms

There's always a really good mix of customers in this civilised but informal old pub – locals (often with their dogs) enjoying a pint and a chat and groups of friends, families and couples appreciating the particularly good food; all are made welcome by the friendly and efficient staff. There are low beams and standing timbers, flagstones in the bar and wood stripped floors elsewhere, sofas and armchairs dotted here and there, a mix of nice old tables and dining chairs, lit candles in candlesticks, an open fire and high bar chairs at the counter. Throughout there are all sorts of interesting knick-knacks, books, lots of copper, horsebrasses, photographs (several of Charterhouse School) and all manner of pictures and prints; paint colours are fashionable, values are traditional and they keep Andwells King John and Triple fff Altons Pride and Pale Ale on handpump, nine wines by the glass (including fizz) and interesting pressés. The bedrooms are stylish and breakfasts are good.

Imaginative and highly thought-of food might include sandwiches, pork and sage pâté with rhubarb chutney, hand-picked crab mayonnaise with chilli and lime, avocado purée and brown crab pâté on toast, wild mushroom risotto with parmesan and tarragon butter, local sausages with colcannon, free-range chicken kiev with haricot beans and chorizo, and halibut fillet with lentils, ham hock and spinach gnocchi. *Benchmark main dish: pork five ways £17.50. Two-course evening meal £22.00.*

Free house ~ Licensee Tracy Levett ~ Real ale ~ Bar food (12-2.30(3 Sat), 6.30-9.30 (10 Fri and Sat); 12-4, 7-9 Sun) ~ Restaurant ~ (01420) 23261 ~ Children welcome ~ Dogs allowed in bar and bedrooms ~ Open 11-11(midnight Sat; 10.30 Sun) ~ Bedrooms: £100S/£120S

Recommended by Martin and Karen Wake, John Branston, Tony and Jill Radnor, Dave Braisted

LOWER WIELD Hampshire   SU6339 Map D

Yew Tree ⊕ ♀ £

Turn off A339 NW of Alton at Medstead, Bentworth 1 signpost, then follow village signposts; or off B3046 S of Basingstoke, signposted from Preston Candover; SO24 9RX

Bustling country pub with smashing landlord, relaxed atmosphere and super choice of wines and good food; sizeable garden and nearby walks

As always, the enthusiastic Mr Gray and his friendly staff will give you a genuinely warm welcome here – whether you want just a drink and a chat or a full meal. There's a small flagstoned bar area on the left with pictures above its stripped-brick dado, a steadily ticking clock and a log fire. Around to the right of the serving counter – which has a couple of stylish wrought-iron bar chairs – it's carpeted; throughout there is a mix of tables, including some quite small ones for two, and miscellaneous chairs. Twelve wines by the glass from a well chosen list which may include summer rosé and Louis Jadot burgundies from a shipper based just along the lane. Bowman Eldorado and a beer from Triple fff named after the pub on handpump. There are solid tables and chunky seats out on the front terrace, picnic-sets in a sizeable side garden, pleasant views and a cricket field across the quiet lane; nearby walks.

Top quality food from an interesting menu includes sandwiches, smoked duck breast and pear salad with a beetroot and apricot compote, thyme and blue cheese creamy mushrooms on herbed toast, sausages of the week with spring onion and parsley mash and onion gravy, thai red chicken and baby corn curry, pork belly on caramelised apple with a calvados and apple sauce, and whole bass dressed with orange, fennel and rosemary. *Benchmark main dish: honey-roasted haddock with leeks and parsley sauce £10.50. Two-course evening meal £16.45.*

Free house ~ Licensee Tim Gray ~ Real ale ~ Bar food (not Mon) ~ Restaurant ~ (01256) 389224 ~ Children welcome ~ Dogs allowed in bar ~ Quiz night first Weds of month in winter ~ Open 12-3, 6-11; 12-10.30 Sun; closed Mon; first two weeks in Jan

Recommended by Margaret Ball, Darryl and Lindy Hemsley, Phyl and Jack Street, Ian Herdman, Tony and Jill Radnor, Richard and Stephanie Foskett, Martin and Karen Wake, John Walker, Philip and June Caunt, Stevie Joy, Glen and Nola Armstrong, Margaret Grimwood

LURGASHALL Sussex   SU9327   Map D

Noahs Ark

Off A283 N of Petworth; GU28 9ET

Busy old pub in nice spot with neatly kept rooms, real ales and pleasing food

The position of this 15th-c tile-hung pub is charming as it overlooks the village green and cricket pitch; picnic-sets make the most of this and there are more in the large side garden. The simple, traditional bar is popular locally and has leather-topped bar stools by the counter where they serve Greene King IPA and Abbot and a guest such as Thwaites Wainwright on handpump, several wines by the glass, farm cider and a special bloody mary; also, beams, a mix of wooden chairs and tables on the parquet flooring and an inglenook fireplace. Open right up to its apex, the dining room is spacious and airy with church candles and fresh flowers on light wood tables; a couple of comfortable sofas face each other in front of an open woodburning stove. The pub border terrier is called Gillie and visiting dogs may get a dog biscuit.

To be sure of a meal, it's best to book a table beforehand: sandwiches (not Sunday), home-cured beetroot gravadlax with horseradish mousse, an antipasti plate, burger with cheese and bacon, shrimp, clam and smoked haddock risotto, free-range chicken caesar salad, and seared tuna steak with niçoise salad. *Benchmark main dish: home-made burger £9.95. Two-course evening meal £17.75.*

Greene King ~ Lease Henry Coghlan and Amy Whitmore ~ Real ale ~ Bar food (12-2.30, 7-9.30; 12-3.30 Sun; not Sun evening) ~ Restaurant ~ (01428) 707346 ~ Children allowed but not in bar after 7pm ~ Dogs allowed in bar ~ Open 11-11(midnight Sat); 12-10 Sun; 11-3.30, 5.30-11 in winter

Recommended by Ann and Colin Hunt

MARLOW Buckinghamshire   SU8586   Map D

Two Brewers

St Peter Street, first right off Station Road from double roundabout; SL7 1NQ

Bustling, neatly kept pub close to the Thames with plenty of seating areas, quite an emphasis on dining, real ales and decent wines, and seats outside

As well as being right on the Thames Path, cheerfully painted picnic-sets at the front of this bustling pub have a glimpse of the river; there's also a sheltered back courtyard with more seats and tables – and a covered area, too. Inside, the interesting layout has low beams, shiny black woodwork, a nice mix of wooden tables and chairs on bare floorboards, nautical pictures and gleaming brassware. The River View Room and Cellar are set for dining. Brakspears Bitter, Fullers London Pride and Rebellion IPA and Mutiny on handpump, nice wines and coffee and good friendly service.

Enjoyable food includes lunchtime sandwiches, duck liver parfait with red onion chutney, fresh crab in lemon mayonnaise with red pepper coulis, wild mushroom risotto, a pie of the day, free-range chicken with potato and leek sauté and smoked salmon and prawn fishcake with chive butter sauce; they offer a two- and three-course set menu and may have summer Sunday barbecues. *Benchmark main dish: roast lamb £17.95. Two-course evening meal £20.90.*

Enterprise ~ Lease Anthony Burnham ~ Real ale ~ Bar food (12-3, 6.30-9.30; all day Sat; 12-4 Sun; not Sun evening) ~ Restaurant ~ (01628) 484140 ~ Children welcome ~ Dogs allowed in bar ~ Open 11-11(midnight Fri and Sat, 10.30 Sun)

Recommended by Robert Kibble

MILFORD Surrey   SU9542   Map D

Refectory ♀
Portsmouth Road; GU8 5HJ

Handsome building with plenty of interest inside, beams, timbering, fine stone fireplaces and so forth, plenty of room, real ales, and well liked food

The frontage of this interesting building is most appealing with its golden stone and timbering and it's thought to have been a former cattle barn, and a tea and antique shop. There are teak tables and chairs in the back courtyard by the newer extension and adjacent to the characterful pigeonry. Inside, it's L-shaped and mainly open-plan and throughout there are heavy beams and timbering, exposed stone walls, stalling and standing timbers creating separate seating areas and a couple of big log fires in handsome stone fireplaces. A two-tiered and balconied part at one end has a wall covered with huge brass platters and the rest of the walls are hung with some nice old photographs and various paintings. Individual dining chairs and dark wooden tables are grouped on the wood, quarry-tiled or carpeted flooring and there are rugs, bookshelves, big pot plants, stone bottles on window sills and fresh flowers. High wooden bar stools line the long counter where they serve Hogsback TEA, Phoenix Brunning & Price and four guests from brewers such as Adnams, Andwell and Hammerpot on handpump, around 16 wines by the glass and over 80 malt whiskies.

As well as a good range of sandwiches and light meals, the popular food might include carrot and coriander soup, cracked wheat and chickpea cake with moroccan coleslaw and cinnamon yoghurt, star anise poached chicken with blood orange and toasted fennel salad, crab linguine, battered haddock, black cardamom braised beef with tropical fruit curry, red wine braised cuttlefish and calamari with poached garlic risotto, and spinach and onion pie. *Benchmark main dish: ham, egg and chips £9.95. Two-course evening meal £17.75.*

Brunning & Price ~ Manager Benjamin Redwood ~ Real ale ~ Bar food (12-10) ~ (01483) 413820 ~ Children welcome ~ Dogs welcome ~ Open 11.30-11; 12-10.30 Sun

Recommended by Richard Gibbs

MINSTER LOVELL Oxfordshire   SP3211   Map E

Old Swan & Minster Mill

Just N of B4047 Witney—Burford; OX29 0RN

Carefully restored ancient inn with old-fashioned bar, lots of beamed, comfortable antique-filled rooms, real ales, a thoughtful wine list and acres of gardens and grounds with fishing; exceptional bedrooms

Civilised and rather lovely, this newly restored old inn – with a history going back 600 years – is back in the *Guide* after a break. Of course, much emphasis is placed on the hotel and restaurant side but at its heart is the restful and unchanging small bar with stools by the ancient wooden counter; Brakspears Bitter, Oxford Gold and a guest beer on handpump and several wines by the glass from a fine list. Leading off here is a myriad of attractive low-beamed rooms with big log fires in huge fireplaces, red and green leather tub chairs, all manner of comfortable armchairs, sofas, dining chairs and wooden tables, rugs on bare boards or ancient flagstones, antiques and prints and lots of horsebrasses, bed-warming pans, swords, hunting horns and even a suit of armour; fresh flowers everywhere. Seats are dotted around the 65 acres of grounds (the white metal ones beside the water are much prized) and they have a mile of fishing on the River Windrush, tennis courts, boules and croquet. The bedrooms have a lot of character and some are luxurious.

Using produce from their kitchen garden and other local, seasonal ingredients, the excellent food might include sandwiches, home-baked ham hock, crab apple and mustard seed terrine with home-made piccalilli, roast pumpkin risotto with truffle oil, steak in ale pie, fresh crab with celeriac and fennel rémoulade and cucumber spaghetti, coq au vin, and slow-roasted pork belly with white pudding and cider apple jus. *Benchmark main dish: 28-day-aged hung rib-eye steak £21.95. Two-course evening meal £22.45.*

Free house ~ Licensee Ian Solkin ~ Real ale ~ Bar food (12(12.30 weekends)-3, 6.30-9) ~ (01993) 774441 ~ Children welcome ~ Dogs allowed in bar and bedrooms ~ Open 12(12.30 weekends)-11(10.30 Sun) ~ Bedrooms: £145S/£165S

Recommended by Richard Gibbs

NORTH WALTHAM Hampshire   SU5645   Map D

Fox £

3 miles from M3 junction 7: A30 southwards, then turn right at second North Waltham turn, just after Wheatsheaf; pub also signed from village centre; RG25 2BE

Traditional flint country pub, very well run, with good food and drink, nice garden

Relaxed and chatty, the low-ceilinged bar on the left has lots of bottled ciders as well as Thatcher's on draught, and a well kept guest beer such as Saxon Archer along with Brakspears, Ringwood Best and West Berkshire Good Old Boy at attractive prices on handpump; ten wines by the glass, 22 malt whiskies and quite a collection of miniatures. The big woodburning stove, parquet floor, simple padded country-kitchen chairs, and poultry and 'Beer is Best' prints above the dark dado, all give a comfortably old-fashioned feel – in which perhaps the vital ingredient is the polite and friendly efficiency of the hands-on landlord. There may be very faint piped music. The separate dining room, with high-backed leather chairs on a blue tartan carpet, is rather larger. The garden, colourful in summer with its pergola walkway up from the gate on the lane, and with immaculate flower boxes and baskets, has picnic-sets under cocktail parasols in three separate areas, and overlooks rolling farmland (with a glimpse of the distant M3). Walks include a nice one to Jane Austen's church at Steventon.

Good home-made food includes a bargain bacon butty and other sandwiches, good value bar meals such as ham and eggs, a pie of the day or their speciality cheese soufflé, and restaurant dishes (which you can also eat in the bar) such as ham hock terrine with home-made chutney, gressingham duck breast with a black cherry and red wine sauce and local venison with a port glaze, shallots, field mushrooms, spinach and creamed swede; it's best to book for their Sunday roasts. Benchmark main dish: cheese soufflé £12.50. Two-course evening meal £20.75.

Free house ~ Licensees Rob and Izzy MacKenzie ~ Real ale ~ Bar food (12-2.30(3 Sun), 6.30-9.30(9 Sun)) ~ Restaurant ~ (01256) 397288 ~ Children welcome ~ Dogs allowed in bar ~ Open 11-11(midnight Sat)

Recommended by Patrick Spence, John Branston

NORTH WARNBOROUGH Hampshire   SU7352   Map D

Mill House 🍴 ♀ ◖

A mile from M3 junction 5: A287 towards Farnham, then right (brown sign to pub) on to B3349 Hook Road; RG29 1ET

Attractive layout, lovely waterside terraces, good food and drink

Newly done out in the Brunning & Price fashion – lots of well spaced tables in a variety of sizes and styles, rugs on polished boards or beige carpet, coal-effect gas fires in pretty fireplaces, a profusion of often interesting pictures – this old heavy-beamed and raftered mill building has several linked areas on its main upper floor. A section of glass floor shows the rushing water and mill wheel below, and a galleried part on the left looks down into a dining room on that level, given a more formal feel by its panelling. In warm weather a very big plus is the extensive garden, attractively landscaped around a sizeable millpond, with plenty of solid tables and chairs on various terraces; there are swings on a neatly kept stretch of grass. The well stocked bar has an interesting changing range of malt whiskies, a good choice of wines, and well kept B&P Original (the house beer, brewed by Phoenix), Andwells King John, Saxon Archer, Skinners Porthleven and Stonehenge Heel Stone and Pigswill on handpump; the young staff are cheerful and effective, and the atmosphere is relaxed and comfortable.

Good modern food includes sandwiches, duck liver pâté with rhubarb chutney, ham and free-range eggs, aubergine, lentil and chestnut mushroom moussaka, chicken, pearl barley and vegetable broth with tarragon dumplings, citrus-cured bass, scallop and prawn salad, crispy wasabi rice balls and pickled ginger, and venison rump with venison faggot, bubble and squeak and juniper jus. *Benchmark main dish: braised lamb shoulder with dauphinoise potatoes £16.95. Two-course evening meal £17.70.*

Brunning & Price ~ Lease Ashley Harlow ~ Real ale ~ Bar food (all day) ~ Restaurant ~ (01256) 702953 ~ Children welcome ~ Dogs allowed in bar ~ Open 12-11.30(10.30 Sun)

Recommended by Richard Gibbs

OXFORD Oxfordshire   SP5106   Map E

Bear ◖

Alfred Street/Wheatsheaf Alley; OX1 4EH

Delightful pub with friendly staff, two cosy rooms, six real ales, and well liked bar food

Just off the busy High Street, this charming little pub is the oldest in the city. There are two small low-ceilinged, beamed and partly panelled ancient rooms, not over-smart and often packed with students, with a bustling chatty atmosphere, winter coal fires, thousands of vintage ties on walls and up to six real ales from handpump on the fine pewter bar counter: Fullers Chiswick, ESB, Gales HSB and London Pride and a couple of guests beers such as Butcombe Bitter and Prospect Gold Rush. Staff are friendly and helpful. There are seats under parasols in the back terraced garden where they hold summer barbecues.

🍴 Bar food includes sandwiches, nibbles like olives and hummus with local bread, a proper ploughman's, various burgers including a vegetarian one, fish and chips, garlic tiger prawns, sausage and colcannon mash and belly of pork, and steak in ale pie. *Benchmark main dish: battered fish and chips £9.75. Two-course evening meal £15.00.*

Fullers ~ Manager Stuart Scott ~ Real ale ~ Bar food (all day) ~ (01865) 728164 ~ Children allowed in back room ~ Open 11-11(midnight Fri and Sat, 10.30 Sun)

Recommended by Andrea Rampley, Gordon Stevenson, Tim Williams, Pippa Manley, the Didler, Michael Dandy, Alasdair Mackay

 OXFORD Oxfordshire   SP5107   Map E

Rose & Crown

North Parade Avenue; very narrow, so best to park in a nearby street; OX2 6LX

Long-serving licensees in this lively friendly local, a good mix of customers, fine choice of drinks, and proper home cooking

Well behaved customers (no children or dogs) are still warmly welcomed by the sharp-witted Mr Hall and his wife – who have now run this straightforward local for 28 years – and there's always a good mix of undergraduates and more mature customers. The front door opens into a passage by the bar counter and the panelled back room, with traditional pub furnishings, is slightly bigger with reference books for crossword buffs; no mobile phones, piped music or noisy games machines, but they do have board games. Adnams Bitter, Hook Norton Old Hooky and a couple of guest beers on handpump, 26 malt whiskies and 14 wines by the glass. The pleasant walled and heated backyard can be covered with a huge awning; at the far end is a 12-seater dining/meeting room. The lavatories are pretty basic.

🍴 Traditional but enjoyable food includes interesting sandwiches and baguettes, omelettes, sausage and mash, all-day breakfast, and a hot dish of the day such as honeyed chicken or beef stew with herb dumplings. *Benchmark main dish: sausage and mash £7.00. Two-course evening meal £14.00.*

Free house ~ Licensees Andrew and Debbie Hall ~ Real ale ~ Bar food (12-2.15, 6-9) ~ No credit cards ~ (01865) 510551 ~ Open 11-midnight

Recommended by Robert Lorimer, Tony and Jill Radnor, the Didler, Chris Glasson

 OXFORD Oxfordshire   SP5106   Map E

Turf Tavern 🍴 £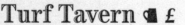

Tavern Bath Place; via St Helen's Passage, between Holywell Street and New College Lane; OX1 3SU

Interesting character pub hidden away behind high walls, with a dozen ales, regular beer festivals, nice food, and knowledgeable staff

Hidden behind the high stone walls of some of the city's oldest buildings, this is arguably Oxford's most characterful pub. It's certainly one of the city's busiest but the helpful, knowledgeable young staff manage to deal quickly and efficiently with the wide mix of customers of all ages. The two dark-beamed and low-ceilinged small bars fill up quickly, though many prefer (whatever the time of year) to sit outside in the three attractive walled-in flagstoned or gravelled courtyards (one has its own bar); in winter, they have coal braziers so you can roast chestnuts or toast marshmallows and there are canopies with lights and heaters. Up to a dozen constantly changing real ales on handpump might include Greene King IPA, Abbot, Morlands Old Speckled Hen and Ruddles Best and maybe Black Country Fireside, Great Oakley Wot's Occurring, Rebellion IPA and Mutiny, Thwaites Lancaster Bomber and Wainwright and White Horse Wayland Smithy. They hold a spring and summer beer festival, keep Weston's Old Rosie cider and offer winter mulled wine.

Enjoyable and reasonably priced, the food includes sandwiches, crab cakes in coriander breadcrumbs with red pepper and chilli dipping sauce, various sharing platters, honey-roast ham and free-range eggs, beef in ale pie with chive mash and gravy, beef and vegetarian burgers, and hunter's chicken (cooked with bacon, barbecue sauce and cheese). *Benchmark main dish: battered cod and chips £8.45. Two-course evening meal £12.70.*

Greene King ~ Manager Stella Berry ~ Real ale ~ Bar food (11-9) ~ (01865) 243235 ~ Children welcome ~ Dogs welcome ~ Open 11-11(10.30 Sun); 12-10.30 Sun

Recommended by Colin and Louise English, Andrea Rampley, Michael Dandy, LM, G Jennings, MP, the Didler, David and Sue Smith, Clive and Fran Dutson, Roger and Donna Huggins, Malcolm Greening, Tim and Ann Newell, Barry Collett

PENN Buckinghamshire   SU9093   Map E

Old Queens Head ♀

Hammersley Lane/Church Road, off B474 between Penn and Tylers Green; HP10 8EY

Smartly updated pub with a good choice of drinks, and interesting modern cooking

They've opened up a new sunny terrace here that overlooks the church of St Margaret's and there are picnic-sets on the sheltered L-shaped lawn; just the place to relax after a walk on the nearby common or in the Penn woods. Inside, it's open-plan and decorated in a stylish mix of contemporary and chintz, with well spaced tables in a variety of linked areas, a modicum of old prints, and comfortably varied seating on flagstones or broad dark boards. Stairs take you up to an attractive (and popular) two-level dining room, part carpeted, with stripped rafters. The active bar side has Greene King IPA and Ruddles County on handpump, 21 wines by the glass, nine pudding wines and quite a few liqueurs; the turntable-top bar stools let you swivel to face the log fire in the big nearby fireplace. There are lots of daily papers and well reproduced piped music.

Enjoyable modern food includes weekday lunchtime sandwiches, pigeon breast with thyme rösti and a red wine and shallot dressing, free-range chicken liver parfait with wild mushroom pâté and onion marmalade, goats cheese and sweet potato cannelloni, trout fillet with warm artichoke and griddled fennel stew, and honey-glazed pork belly with black pudding beignets and sage cream. *Benchmark main dish: free-range chicken stuffed with chorizo on roast sweet peppers with wild garlic gnocchi £13.50. Two-course evening meal £20.75.*

Salisbury Pubs ~ Lease Tina Brown ~ Real ale ~ Bar food (12-2.30(3 Sat, 4 Sun), 6.30-9.30(10 Fri, Sat)) ~ Restaurant ~ (01494) 813371 ~ Children welcome ~ Dogs allowed in bar ~ Open 11-11; 12-10.30 Sun; closed 25 and 26 Dec

Recommended by Tracey and Stephen Groves

PENSHURST Kent   TQ5142   Map C

Bottle House ⊕ ♀

Coldharbour Lane; leaving Penshurst SW on B2188 turn right at Smarts Hill signpost, then bear right towards Chiddingstone and Cowden; keep straight on; TN11 8ET

Low-beamed, connected bars in country pub, friendly service, chatty atmosphere, real ales and decent wines, popular bar food and sunny terrace; nearby walks

Plenty of cosy nooks, with standing timbers separating the open-plan rooms into intimate areas, keep this chatty dining pub feeling pubby. There are beams and joists (one or two of the especially low ones are leather padded), an attractive mix of old wheelback and other dining chairs around all sorts of wooden tables, photographs of the pub and local scenes on the walls (some of which are stripped stone), an old brick floor by the copper-topped wooden bar counter with dark wooden boarding elsewhere; the fireplace houses a woodburning stove and most of the tables are set with fresh flowers. Harveys Best and Larkins Traditional on handpump, a local bottled ale, local apple juice and nearly a dozen wines by the glass from a good list; friendly, helpful young service and piped music. The sunny, brick-paved terrace has green-painted picnic-sets under parasols and some olive trees in white pots; parking is limited. Good surrounding walks in this charming area of rolling country.

From a monthly changing seasonal menu featuring local produce and a daily changing specials board, popular bar food might include ploughman's, fried scallops with pea purée and pancetta, duck liver and orange parfait with toasted brioche, poached pear and stilton salad with walnut dressing, chicken breast stuffed with goats cheese, salami and sun-dried tomatoes with spiced tomato and caper sauce, steak and kidney pudding, fillet of cod with spring onion and ginger sauce, roast pork belly with butternut squash and sage mash and apple and cider sauce, and well hung steak *Benchmark main dish: belly of pork £12.50. Two-course evening meal £19.60.*

Free house ~ Licensee Paul Hammond ~ Real ale ~ Bar food (12-10(9 Sun)) ~ Restaurant ~ (01892) 870306 ~ Children welcome ~ Dogs allowed in bar ~ Open 11-11 (10.30 Sun)

Recommended by LM, Bob and Margaret Holder, Tina and David Woods-Taylor, R and S Bentley, Ann and Colin Hunt, Gerry and Rosemary Dobson, Steve Coates, Simon and Helen Barnes, Heather and Dick Martin, Christian Mole, Derek Thomas

PETERSFIELD Hampshire   SU7227   Map D

Trooper ⊕ ◀ ⇦

From A32 (look for staggered crossroads) take turning to Froxfield and Steep; pub 3 miles down on left in big dip; GU32 1BD

Charming landlord, popular food, decent drinks, and little persian knick-knacks and local artists' work; comfortable bedrooms

Our readers enjoy staying in the comfortable bedrooms of this well run pub whilst walking in the area and the warmly friendly Mr Matini is always on hand to ensure things run smoothly. The bar has a mix of cushioned dining chairs around dark wooden tables, old film star photos and paintings by local artists (for sale) on the walls, little persian knick-knacks here and there, quite a few ogival mirrors, lots of lit candles, fresh flowers and a log fire in the stone fireplace; there's a sun room with lovely downland views, carefully chosen piped music and newspapers and magazines to read. Bowman Swift One and Ringwood Best on handpump and several wines by the glass or carafe. The attractive raftered restaurant has french windows to a paved terrace with views across the open countryside, and there are lots of picnic-sets on an upper lawn. The horse rail in the car park is reserved 'for horses, camels and local livestock'.

Good, popular food includes filled lunchtime rolls, warm chicken liver salad, lime and ginger prawns with sweet chilli dip, hazelnut and mushroom parcel with roasted red pepper sauce, cumberland sausages with onion gravy, spicy thai-glazed salmon with sesame noodles, and chicken, pork and chorizo stew; Tuesday is pie day. *Benchmark main dish: lamb shoulder in honey and mint £15.00. Two-course evening meal £20.00.*

Free house ~ Licensee Hassan Matini ~ Real ale ~ Bar food (not Sun evening or Mon lunchtime) ~ Restaurant ~ (01730) 827293 ~ Children must be seated and supervised by an adult ~ Dogs allowed in bar ~ Open 12-3, 6-11; 12-3.30 Sun; closed Sun evening, Mon lunchtime, 25 and 26 Dec, 1 Jan ~ Bedrooms: £69B/£89B

Recommended by Keith and Chris O'Neill, Henry Fryer, Geoff and Linda Payne, Jenny and Peter Lowater, Mike and Mary Carter, John and Jackie Chalcraft, Richard Mason

PETERSFIELD Hampshire   SU7129   Map D

White Horse

Up on an old downs road about halfway between Steep and East Tisted, near Priors Dean – OS Sheet 186 or 197 map reference 715290; GU32 1DA

Unchanging and much-loved old place with a great deal of simple character, a cheerful, relaxed atmosphere, friendly licensees and up to ten real ales

A favourite with a great many of our readers, this remote 17th-c country pub has remained almost unchanged for 30 years. The two charming and idiosyncratic parlour rooms (candlelit at night) have open fires, oak settles and a mix of dark wooden dining chairs, nice old tables (including some drop-leaf ones), various pictures, farm tools, rugs, a longcase clock, a couple of fireside rocking chairs, and so forth. The beamed dining room is smarter with lots more pictures on the white or pink walls. They keep a fantastic range of up to ten real ales on handpump – such as two beers named for the pub, plus Butcombe Bitter, Caledonian Deuchars IPA, Fullers London Pride, Ringwood Best and Fortyniner and guests such as Elgoods Cambridge Bitter and Ossett Yorkshire Blonde, and lots of country wines. They hold a beer festival in June and a cider festival in September. There are some rustic seats outside and they have camping facilities. If trying to find it for the first time, keep your eyes skinned – not for nothing is this known as the Pub With No Name.

Using local produce and free-range meat the well liked food includes sandwiches, steak in ale pie, home-cooked honey-roast ham and free-range eggs, sausages with colcannon and onion gravy, prawn and salmon fishcakes with a mustard cream sauce, and winter game dishes. *Benchmark main dish: beer-battered fish and chips £11.95. Two-course evening meal £16.00.*

Gales (Fullers) ~ Managers Georgie and Paul Stuart ~ Real ale ~ Bar food (12-2.30, 6-9.30; some cold food all day weekdays; all day weekends) ~ Restaurant ~ (01420) 588387 ~ Children welcome ~ Dogs allowed in bar ~ Open 12-11

Recommended by Ann and Colin Hunt, Jack Matthew, Jenny and Peter Lowater, Mike and Eleanor Anderson, the Didler, W A Evershed

PLUCKLEY Kent   TQ9243 Map C

Dering Arms ♀ ⇦

Pluckley Station, which is signposted from B2077; or follow Station Road (left turn off Smarden Road in centre of Pluckley) for about 1.3 miles S, through Pluckley Thorne; TN27 0RR

Fine fish dishes plus other good food in handsome building, stylish main bar, carefully chosen wines, and roaring log fire; comfortable bedrooms

This former hunting lodge, originally part of the Dering Estate, was built in the 1840s as a mini replica of the manor house. Hence its imposing frontage, mullioned arched windows and dutch gables. Though emphasis is very much on the fish and seafood, the bar is characterful and comfortable and they do keep a beer named for the pub from Goachers on handpump as well as a good wine list of around 100 wines, 50 malt whiskies and an occasional local cider. High-ceilinged and stylishly plain, this main bar has a solid country feel with a variety of wooden furniture on the flagstone floors, a roaring log fire in the great fireplace, country prints and some fishing rods. The smaller half-panelled back bar has similar dark wood furnishings, and an extension to this area has a woodburning stove, comfortable armchairs, sofas and a grand piano; board games. Classic car meetings (the long-serving landlord has a couple of classics) are held here on the second Sunday of the month. Readers very much enjoy staying here – and the breakfasts are excellent.

The landlord himself buys fish straight from the boats in Folkestone and oversees the kitchen at all times. Dishes might include half a pint of prawns, oysters, provençale fish soup, pie of the day, whole crab salad, fried scallops with basil spaghetti and saffron sauce, fillet of black bream with marsh samphire and beurre blanc, and guinea fowl casseroled in sherry and tarragon sauce; seafood platter for two (24 hours' notice). *Benchmark main dish: fillet of turbot meunière £18.95. Two-course evening meal £24.90.*

Free house ~ Licensee James Buss ~ Real ale ~ Bar food ~ Restaurant ~ (01233) 840371 ~ Children welcome ~ Dogs allowed in bar ~ Open 11.30(12 Sun)-3.30, 6-11; closed Sun evening ~ Bedrooms: £55(£75S)/£65(£85S)

Recommended by Philip and Cheryl Hill, Patrick Noble, John Prescott, Simon Collett-Jones, Colin and Louise English

PRESTON CANDOVER Hampshire   SU6041 Map D

Purefoy Arms ⑪ ♀

B3046 Basingstoke—Alresford; RG25 2EJ

Good food and wines in gently upmarket village pub

Reopened after refurbishment a couple of years ago, this has two pairs of smallish linked rooms. On the left, the airy front bar has chunky tables, including ones so tall as to need bar stools, and a corner counter serving a fine changing choice of wines, as well as Andwells and Black Sheep Best on handpump; this opens into a jute-floored back area with four dining tables and characterful mixed seats including old settles. The right-hand front room has red leather sofas and armchairs by a log fire, and goes back into a bare-boards area with three or four sturdy pale pine tables. An understated contemporary décor in grey and puce goes nicely with the informal friendliness of the service; there may be unobtrusive piped pop music. The sizeable sloping garden has well spaced picnic-sets, a wendy house and perhaps a big hammock slung between two of its trees; there are teak tables on a terrace sheltered by the pub. This is an attractive village, with nearby snowdrop walks in February.

🍴 Good food changing daily includes lunchtime sandwiches, quality tapas and other inventive dishes such as a crayfish and blood orange salad, ballottine of quail and foie gras with madeira jelly, burgers made with well hung rare-breed steak, butternut squash risotto with sage and aged parmesan, and specials like slow-roasted shoulder of rare-breed pork with white beans and pata negra (cured spanish ham), and whole plaice with cornish crab gratin. *Benchmark main dish: cider-baked ham, duck eggs and proper chips £10.00. Two-course evening meal £18.00.*

Free house ~ Licensees Andres and Marie-Louise Alenany ~ Real ale ~ Bar food (12-3, 6-10; 12-4 Sun; not Sun evening or Mon) ~ Restaurant ~ (01256) 389777 ~ Well behaved children welcome ~ Dogs allowed in bar ~ Open 12-3, 6-11.30; 12-6 Sun; closed Mon

Recommended by Ann and Colin Hunt, Jill Hurley

 PRESTWOOD Buckinghamshire   SP8799   Map E

Polecat
170 Wycombe Road (A4128 N of High Wycombe); HP16 0HJ

Enjoyable food, real ales and a chatty atmosphere in several smallish civilised rooms; attractive sizeable garden

An evening favourite with several of our readers, this smart country pub has a quietly chatty atmosphere and helpful, friendly staff. Several smallish rooms, opening off the low-ceilinged bar, have a slightly chintzy décor: an assortment of tables and chairs, various stuffed birds, stuffed white polecats in one big cabinet, small country pictures, rugs on bare boards or red tiles, and a couple of antique housekeeper's chairs by a good open fire. Brakspears Bitter, Greene King Old Speckled Hen, Marstons Pedigree and Ringwood Best on handpump, 16 wines by the glass and 20 malt whiskies; may be piped music. The garden is most attractive with lots of spring bulbs and colourful summer hanging baskets and tubs, and herbaceous plants; quite a few picnic-sets under parasols on neat grass out in front beneath a big fairy-lit pear tree, with more on a big well kept back lawn. They don't take bookings at lunchtime (except for tables of six or more) so you do need to arrive promptly at weekends to be sure of a table.

🍴 As well as lunchtime sandwiches, the popular food includes smoked salmon terrine with lime crème fraîche, chicken curry, chickpea, sweet potato and apricot tagine, seafood bake and specials such as ham hock terrine with apple chutney, bass with cherries and kirsch, and pork medallions with caramelised prune and chestnut stuffing and calvados sauce. *Benchmark main dish: steak and kidney pie £10.95. Two-course evening meal £17.00.*

Free house ~ Licensee John Gamble ~ Real ale ~ Bar food (12-2, 6.30-9 (not Sun evening)) ~ (01494) 862253 ~ Children in gallery or drovers' bar only ~ Dogs allowed in bar ~ Open 11.30-2.30, 6-11; 12-3 Sun; closed Sun evening; evenings 24 and 31 Dec, all day 25 and 26 Dec

Recommended by Simon Collett-Jones, Gordon Tong, Tracey and Stephen Groves, Roy Hoing, Peter and Jan Humphreys, Mel Smith

---

Please keep sending us reports. We rely on readers for news of new discoveries, and particularly for news of changes – however slight – at the fully described pubs:
feedback@goodguides.com, or (no stamp needed)
The Good Pub Guide, FREEPOST TN1569, Wadhurst, E Sussex TN5 7BR.

RAMSDEN Oxfordshire   SP3515 Map E

Royal Oak 🍴 ♔ ◀

Village signposted off B4022 Witney—Charlbury; OX7 3AU

Busy pub with long-serving licensees, large helpings of varied food, a carefully chosen wine list, and seats outside; bedrooms

Facing the church and the war memorial in a peaceful village, this 17th-c Cotswold stone pub's unpretentious rooms have a mix of wooden tables, chairs and settles, cushioned window seats, exposed stone walls, fresh flowers, bookcases with old and new copies of *Country Life* and, when the weather gets cold, a cheerful log fire. Hook Norton Hooky Bitter, Wye Valley HPA and a guest from breweries like Stonehenge and Wickwar on handpump, and ten wines by the glass from a carefully chosen list. There are tables and chairs out in front and on the terrace behind the restaurant (folding back doors give easy access). The bedrooms are in separate cottages and there are some fine surrounding walks.

Quite a choice of food served in large helpings includes lunchtime sandwiches (if they are not too busy), baked baby brie with a tomato and herb crust, pasta with a wild mushroom and truffle sauce, home-made burgers with cheese or bacon, a pie of the week, a sri lankan curry, and daily specials like gloucester old spot sausages with haricot beans and onion gravy and pot-roasted local pheasant. *Benchmark main dish: fillet steak with peppercorn sauce £24.00. Two-course evening meal £18.25.*

Free house ~ Licensee Jon Oldham ~ Real ale ~ Bar food (12-2, 7-9.45) ~ Restaurant ~ (01993) 868213 ~ Children in restaurant with parents ~ Dogs allowed in bar and bedrooms ~ Open 11.30-3, 6.30-11; 12-3, 7-10.30 Sun ~ Bedrooms: £50S/£70S

Recommended by Dennis and Doreen Haward, Malcolm and Jo Hart, Roy Harding, Jane Hudson, Chris Glasson, Garry and Hannah Mortimer, Richard and Laura Holmes, Phil and Jane Hodson, Rob and Catherine Dunster, Mike and Mary Carter, JJW, CMW, Colin McKerrow

READING Berkshire   SU7173 Map D

Hobgoblin ◀

2 Broad Street; RG1 2BH

No-frills pub with small panelled rooms, cheerful atmosphere, and eight quickly changing ales

With such a fine choice of up to eight real ales on handpump, this cheerfully basic town pub is as popular as ever. As well as three from the West Berkshire Brewery, the constantly changing choice might include Box Steam Tunnel Vision, Cottage Ambassador, Dark Star Summer Meltdown, Windsor & Eton Guardsman and Wooden Hand Cornish Mutiny. Pump clips cover practically every inch of the walls and ceiling of the simple bare-boards bar – a testament to the enormous number of brews that have passed through the pumps over the years (now over 6,378). They've also lots of different bottled beers, czech lager on tap, farm ciders, perry and country wines. Up a step is a small seating area, but the best places to sit are the three or four tiny panelled rooms reached by a narrow corridor leading from the bar; cosy and intimate, each has barely enough space for one table and a few chairs or wall seats, but they're very appealing if you're able to bag one; the biggest also manages to squeeze in a fireplace; piped music and TV.

 No food.

Community Taverns ~ Manager Katrina Fletcher ~ Real ale ~ No credit cards ~ (0118) 950 8119 ~ Children allowed in booths only ~ Open 11-11; 12-10.30 Sun

Recommended by Simon Collett-Jones, Dr and Mrs A K Clarke, the Didler, Nigel and Sue Foster, Paul Humphreys

 RINGMER Sussex   TQ4313   Map C

Cock ◖ £

Uckfield Road – blocked-off section of road off A26 N of village turn-off; BN8 5RX

16th-c country pub with a wide choice of popular bar food, real ales in character bar, and plenty of seats in the garden

Particularly on a chilly evening, the unspoilt bar of this 16th-c weatherboarded pub is a cosy and friendly refuge. There's a log fire in the inglenook fireplace (lit from October to April), traditional pubby furniture on flagstones, heavy beams and Fullers London Pride, Harveys Best and a guest like Hogs Back Spring Ale on handpump, up to a dozen wines by the glass, 12 malt whiskies and Weston's summer cider; piped music. There are three dining areas. Outside on the terrace and in the garden are lots of picnic-sets with views across open fields to the South Downs; the sunsets are pretty. Visiting dogs are offered a bowl of water and a chew, and their own dogs are called Fred and Tally.

From an extensive menu and using local produce, the well liked food might include sandwiches, chicken liver pâté, deep-fried camembert with cranberry sauce, home-cooked ham and free-range eggs, mushroom and red pepper stroganoff, liver and bacon with mash and onion gravy, local venison burger with spicy relish, and chicken breast with a cheese and spinach sauce. *Benchmark main dish: steak in ale pie £10.25. Two-course evening meal £15.70.*

Free house ~ Licensees Ian, Val and Matt Ridley ~ Real ale ~ Bar food (12-2.15(2.30 Sat), 6-9.30; all day Sun) ~ Restaurant ~ (01273) 812040 ~ Well behaved children welcome away from bar ~ Dogs allowed in bar ~ Open 11-3, 6-11.30; 11-11.30 Sun

Recommended by Tony and Shirley Albert, Mike and Eleanor Anderson, Alan Franck

 ROCKBOURNE Hampshire   SU1118   Map D

Rose & Thistle ⊕ ♀

Signed off B3078 Fordingbridge—Cranborne; SP6 3NL

Pretty pub with hands-on landlady and friendly staff, informal bars, real ales, good food, and seats in garden

Kerry Dutton is a first-class, hands-on landlady and runs her 16th-c thatched pub with great efficiency and friendliness. The bar has homely dining chairs, stools and benches around a mix of old pubby tables and there's a two-roomed restaurant with a log fire in each (one is a big brick inglenook), old engravings and cricket prints and an informal and relaxed atmosphere. Fullers London Pride, Palmers Copper Ale and Timothy Taylors Landlord on handpump, a dozen wines (and prosecco) by the glass and Weston's cider. There are benches and tables under the pretty hanging baskets at the front of the building, with picnic-sets under parasols on the grass; good nearby walks. This is a pretty village on the edge of the New Forest.

🍴 Using local, seasonal produce, the reliably good food includes sandwiches, smoked fish platter, lunchtime welsh rarebit and local pork and leek sausages with wholegrain mustard mash and onion gravy, slow-cooked pork belly with bacon, black pudding and apple, confit of duck leg on braised flageolet beans, pancetta and tarragon, and fish and game specials. *Benchmark main dish: steak and kidney pudding £13.95. Two-course evening meal £21.90.*

Free house ~ Licensee Kerry Dutton ~ Real ale ~ Bar food (12-2.30, 7-9.30; 12-3 Sun; not Sun evening) ~ Restaurant ~ (01725) 518236 ~ Children welcome ~ Dogs allowed in bar ~ Open 11-3, 6-11; 11-11 Sat; 12-10.30(8 in winter) Sun

Recommended by Nick Lawless, Peter Barnwell, Mrs J Butler, Mr and Mrs P R Thomas

 ROLVENDEN Kent TQ8431 Map C

Bull

Regent Street; TN17 4PB

Cottagey pub with relaxed bar, friendly atmosphere and bar food

This small tile-hung cottage has a chatty informal main bar with a woodburning stove in the fine old brick ingelnook, dark brown high-backed leather dining chairs around rustic tables on stripped floorboards, some grey-painted built-in panelled wall seats and a few high bar chairs by the counter where they serve Fullers London Pride, Harveys and Larkins on handpump and just under a dozen wines by the glass. There's a flatscreen TV in one corner and plenty of fresh flowers. The dining room – with less character – has similar chairs around pale oak tables and a decorative fireplace. Helpful service and piped music. There are seats in the back garden and a few picnic-sets in front.

🍴 Bar food might include aubergine pâté with roast tomato chutney, ploughman's, sandwiches, steak and stilton pie, roast vegetable tagine, roast salmon fillet in crayfish and sorrel sauce, home-made burger, and rib-eye steak. *Benchmark main dish: chicken and bacon pie £9.95. Two-course evening meal £17.45.*

Free house ~ Licensee Peter Hughes-Smith ~ Real ale ~ Bar food (12-2.30(6 Sun), 6-9; not Sun evening) ~ Restaurant ~ (01580) 241212 ~ Children welcome ~ Dogs allowed in bar ~ Open 11(12 Sun)-11

Recommended by Richard Gibbs

 ROTHERFIELD GREYS Oxfordshire SU7282 Map D

Maltsters Arms ♀

Can be reached off A4155 in Henley, via Greys Road passing Southfields long-stay car park; or follow Greys Church signpost off B481 N of Sonning Common; RG9 4QD

Well run, civilised Chilterns country pub, nice scenery and walks

Friendly helpful staff make you feel quickly at home here, and they have a winter open fire, decent coffee and a dozen wines by the glass as well as well kept Brakspears Bitter and Old and a guest such as Jennings Cumberland on handpump. The maroon-carpeted front room has comfortable wall banquettes and lots of horsebrasses on its black beams; there may be soft piped music. Beyond the serving area, which has hop bines and pewter tankards hanging from its joists, a back room has cricketing prints on dark red walls over a shiny panelled dado, and a mix of furnishings from pink-cushioned pale wooden dining chairs to a pair of leatherette banquettes forming a corner booth. The chocolate labradors have been here as long as the licensees – 13 years. Terrace tables under a big heated canopy are set with linen for meals, and the grass behind has picnic-sets under green parasols, looking out over paddocks to rolling woodland beyond. Greys Court (NT) is not far and two good walks pass close by.

A wide choice of reasonably priced home-made food runs from from paninis through chicken liver mousse, a daily pie, spinach gnocchi on tomato passata, baked smoked haddock florentine with béchamel sauce, crispy belly of pork chinese style and slow-roasted half shoulder of lamb with mint gravy; it's best to book for weekends. *Benchmark main dish: chicken and mushroom pancake £8.95. Two-course evening meal £16.25.*

Brakspears ~ Tenants Peter and Helen Bland ~ Real ale ~ Bar food (12-2.15(2.30 Sun), 6.15-9.15; not Sun evening) ~ Restaurant ~ (01491) 628400 ~ Children welcome ~ Dogs allowed in bar ~ Open 11.45-3, 6-11(midnight Sat); 12-9(5pm in winter) Sun

Recommended by Roy and Jean Russell, Sharon Oldham, Ross Balaam, Roy Hoing, Tony and Gill Powell, Simon Collett-Jones

RUSCOMBE Berkshire   SU7976   Map D

Royal Oak

Ruscombe Lane (B3024 just E of Twyford); RG10 9JN

Wide choice of popular food at welcoming pub with interesting furnishings and paintings, and adjoining antiques and collectables shop

The new Binghams Brewery is just across the road from this welcoming, well run pub (known locally as Buratta's) and the Space Hoppy and Twyford Tipple arrive on a barrow; they also have Fullers London Pride on handpump and stock wines from the Stanlake Park Vineyard (also in the village). The open-plan carpeted interior is well laid out so that each bit is fairly snug, but still manages to keep the overall feel of a lot of people enjoying themselves. A good variety of furniture runs from dark oak tables to big chunky pine ones with mixed seating to match – the two sofas facing one another are popular. Contrasting with the old exposed ceiling joists, mostly unframed modern paintings and prints decorate the walls – mainly dark terracotta over a panelled dado. Picnic-sets are ranged around a venerable central hawthorn in the garden behind (where there are ducks and chickens); summer barbecues. The landlady's antiques and collectables shop is open during pub hours. The pub is on the Henley Arts Trail.

Using their own eggs and some local produce, the good, popular food includes sandwiches, chicken liver pâté with red onion marmalade, feta cheese, sun-dried tomato and olive salad with parma ham, mushroom and leek stroganoff, saddle of rabbit with garlic and mashed potato, beef stroganoff, and salmon and prawn linguine. *Benchmark main dish: black pudding stack £9.95. Two-course evening meal £21.45.*

Enterprise ~ Lease Jenny and Stefano Buratta ~ Real ale ~ Bar food (12-2.30, 6.30-9.30; 12-4 Sun; not Sun or Mon evenings) ~ Restaurant ~ (0118) 934 5190 ~ Children welcome ~ Dogs welcome ~ Open 12-3, 6-11; 12-4 Sun; closed Sun and Mon evenings

Recommended by Paul Humphreys, John Branston, Tracey and Stephen Groves

---

Anyone claiming to arrange or prevent inclusion of a pub in the *Guide* is a fraud. Pubs are included only if recommended by genuine readers and if our own anonymous inspection confirms that they are suitable.

RYE Sussex   TQ9120 Map C

Ship

The Strand, at the foot of Mermaid Street; TN31 7DB

Informal and prettily set old inn with a relaxed atmosphere, straightforward furnishings, local ales, and often inventive food

There's an easy-going atmosphere and a friendly welcome from the pleasant staff in this 16th-c pub. The ground floor is all opened up, from the sunny big-windowed front part to a snugger part at the back, with a log fire in the stripped-brick fireplace below a stuffed boar's head, and a feeling of separate areas is enhanced by the varied flooring: composition, stripped boards, flagstones, a bit of carpet in the armchair corner. There are beams and timbers, a mixed bag of rather second-hand-feeling furnishings – a cosy group of overstuffed leather armchairs and sofa, random stripped or Formica-topped tables and various café chairs – that suit it nicely, as do the utilitarian bulkhead wall lamps. Harveys Best and a couple of local guest beers such as Old Dairy Blue Top and Whitstable Oyster Stout on handpump, local farm cider and perry, and lots of wines by the glass; piped music and board games. Out by the quiet lane are picnic-sets and one or two cheerful oilcloth-covered tables.

Interesting food using local ingredients includes sandwiches, duck, fig and prune terrine with red onion marmalade, smoked haddock fishcake with spinach, a poached egg and grain mustard sauce, rabbit stew, lamb with jerusalem artichoke gratin and quince aioli, and specials like chicken with a pea, broad bean and dill risotto. *Benchmark main dish: toad in the hole £10.75. Two-course evening meal £19.00.*

Enterprise ~ Lease Karen Northcote ~ Real ale ~ Bar food (12-3(3.30 weekends), 6.30-10; they serve breakfast from 8.30am) ~ (01797) 222233 ~ Children welcome ~ Dogs welcome ~ Open 10am-11pm; 12-10.30pm Sun ~ Bedrooms: $80B/$90S($100B)

Recommended by Barry Collett, Mike Gorton, Mike and Eleanor Anderson

 SALEHURST Sussex   TQ7424 Map C

Salehurst Halt

Village signposted from Robertsbridge bypass on A21 Tunbridge Wells—Battle; Church Lane; TN32 5PH

Relaxed small local in quiet hamlet, chatty atmosphere, real ales, well liked bar food, and seats in pretty back garden

Always bustling and friendly, this informal little pub is very much enjoyed by both locals and visitors. To the right of the door, there's a small stone-floored area with a couple of tables, a piano, a settle, TV and an open fire. To the left, there's a nice long scrubbed-pine table with a couple of sofas, a mix of more ordinary pubby tables and wheelback and mate's chairs on the wood-strip floor and may be piped music; board games. Dark Star American Pale Ale, Harveys Best and Old Dairy Silver Top on handpump, several malt whiskies and decent wines by the glass. The back terrace has metal chairs and tiled tables and there are more seats in the landscaped garden with views out over the Rother Valley; outdoor table tennis.

As well as a fair weather wood-fired pizza oven, the popular bar food includes filled baguettes, smashing burgers, faggots and mushy peas, venison sausages, various pies, lemon sole with brown butter, and onglet steaks. *Benchmark main dish: goat curry £10.00. Two-course evening meal £15.00.*

Free house ~ Licensee Andrew Augarde ~ Real ale ~ Bar food (not Mon) ~
(01580) 880620 ~ Children welcome ~ Dogs welcome ~ Open 12-3, 6-11; 12-11 Sat;
closed Mon

Recommended by Geoff and Linda Payne, Tony and Wendy Hobden, Ellie Weld, David London, Robert Mitchell

 SEVENOAKS Kent   TQ5352 Map C

White Hart ♀

Tonbridge Road (A225 S, past Knole); TN13 1SG

**Well run and bustling old coaching inn with a civilised atmosphere in
many bar rooms, a thoughtful choice of drinks, enjoyable modern food
and friendly, helpful staff**

Part of the Brunning & Price group, this sizeable early 18th-c coaching
inn is extremely popular with both drinkers and diners. The many
rooms are interconnected by open doorways and steps and there are
several open fires and woodburning stoves. All manner of nice wooden
dining chairs around tables of every size sit on rugs or varnished bare
floorboards, the cream walls are hung with lots of prints and old
photographs (many of local scenes or schools) and there are fresh
flowers and plants, daily papers to read, board games and a bustling,
chatty atmosphere. Friendly, efficient staff serve Brunning & Price
Original (brewed for the pub by Phoenix), Fullers London Pride, Harveys
Best, Shepherd Neame Spitfire and two or three guests from brewers
such as Adnams and BrewDog, and they keep over 20 good wines by the
glass, a fair choice of ciders and over 60 whiskies. It's all very civilised. At
the front of the building there are picnic-sets under parasols.

Interesting and enjoyable modern bar food includes lamb patty on toasted muffin
with welsh rarebit and carrot relish, crab and horseradish tart, charcuterie,
ploughman's, sandwiches, crab linguine, battered haddock, fried bass with stir-fried
vegetables and noodle salad, rump of lamb with lavender crust, spring vegetable
casserole with wild garlic dumplings and braised beef in port and cranberry.
Benchmark main dish: beef and ale pie £11.50. Two-course evening meal £17.25.

Brunning & Price ~ Manager Chris Little ~ Real ale ~ Bar food (12-10(9.30 Sun)) ~
Restaurant ~ (01732) 452022 ~ Children welcome away from bar until 7pm ~ Dogs
allowed in bar ~ Open 11-11; 12-10.30 Sun

Recommended by Derek Thomas, Richard Green

 SHALFLEET Isle of Wight   SZ4089 Map D

New Inn ⊕ ♀

A3054 Newport—Yarmouth; PO30 4NS

ISLE OF WIGHT DINING PUB OF THE YEAR

Cheerful pub with seafood specialities, good beers and wines, too

Going from strength to strength, this nice old 18th-c former fishermen's
haunt offers a genuinely happy atmosphere, great seafood and well
kept beer. Its rambling rooms have plenty of character with warm fires,
yachting photographs and pictures, boarded ceilings and scrubbed-pine
tables on flagstone, carpet and slate floors. Goddards Fuggle-Dee-Dum,
and Sharps Doom Bar are kept under light blanket pressure, and they
stock over 60 wines; piped music. As it's popular, you will need to book
and there may be double sittings in summer.

Their famous crab sandwich, seafood platter and crab and lobster salads are served alongside a good choice of fish dishes and pubbier options such as sandwiches, ploughman's, steak and ale pie, gnocchi with mushroom, parsley and walnut cream sauce, and various steaks. *Benchmark main dish: seafood platter £27.50. Two-course evening meal £18.30.*

Enterprise ~ Lease Mr Bullock and Mr McDonald ~ Real ale ~ Bar food (12-2.30, 6-9.30) ~ (01983) 531314 ~ Children welcome ~ Dogs allowed in bar ~ Open 12-11(10.30 Sun)

Recommended by Rochelle Seifas, Gareth James, David Glynne-Jones, Mike Tucker, George Atkinson, Paul Humphreys, David Hoult, Bruce and Sharon Eden, Mr and Mrs P D Titcomb, Joshua Fancett, Penny and Peter Keevil, Mrs Joyce Robson

 SHAMLEY GREEN Surrey   TQ0343 Map C

Red Lion
The Green; GU5 0UB

Pleasant dining pub with tasty food and pleasant gardens

The front garden of this prettily positioned pub overlooks the village green and is quite delightful in summer when there's a cricket match underway. Inside, it's fairly traditional with real fires in its two bars, a mix of new and old wooden tables and chairs on bare boards and red carpeting, stripped standing timbers, fresh white walls and deep red ceilings; piped music. They serve well kept Youngs and a couple of guests such as Hogs Back TEA and Sharps Doom Bar and over a dozen wines by the glass. At the back, hand-made rustic tables and benches are closely set on a terrace, and there are more on a lawn beyond.

As well as sandwiches and ploughman's, bar food includes mushrooms stuffed with brie, garlic king prawns, warm bacon and scallop salad, chicken caesar salad, wild mushroom risotto, spiced pork belly with chinese stir-fried vegetables, lamb shank cooked in red wine, sausage and mash, fish and chips, and daily specials such as malaysian chicken curry. *Benchmark main dish: fried bass £13.50. Two-course evening meal £20.00.*

Punch ~ Lease Debbie Ersser ~ Real ale ~ Bar food (12-2.30(3 Sat, Sun), 6.30-9.30(8.30 Sun)) ~ Restaurant ~ (01483) 892202 ~ Children welcome ~ Dogs allowed in bar ~ Open 11.30-11; 12-10.30 Sun; closed Sun evening Christmas-Easter

Recommended by Shirley Mackenzie

 SHANKLIN Isle of Wight   SZ5881 Map D

Fishermans Cottage £
Bottom of Shanklin Chine; PO37 6BN

On the beach at the foot of Shanklin Chine, simple food

Just a few minutes' walk from busy Shanklin's Esplanade, this unchanging thatched cottage, peacefully tucked into the cliffs and quite literally on Appley beach, enjoys one of the nicest and most unusual settings of any pub we know. Tables on the terrace soak up the sun by day and, later, moonlight shimmers on the sea. It's a lovely walk to get here along the zigzagged path down the steep and sinuous chine, the beautiful gorge that was the area's original tourist attraction. Inside, the clean little flagstoned rooms have an eclectic mix of bric-a-brac including skulls hanging from the low beams and navigation lamps in the windows, with photographs, paintings and engravings on the stripped-stone walls. Goddards Fuggle-Dee-Dum and Yates Undercliff are on handpump; piped music and wheelchair access. Do take note that the pub is closed out of season.

🍴 Pubby food includes sandwiches, ploughman's, vegetable lasagne, cottage or fisherman's pie, and scampi. *Benchmark main dish: seafood pancake £10.95. Two-course evening meal £17.90.*

Free house ~ Licensees Ann Springman and Eric Wright ~ Real ale ~ Bar food (11-2, 6-8) ~ (01983) 863882 ~ Children welcome ~ Dogs welcome ~ Live entertainment Tues, Fri, Sat evening ~ Open 11-11; closed end Oct-early Mar

Recommended by anon

SHILTON Oxfordshire   SP2608   Map E

Rose & Crown

Just off B4020 SE of Burford; OX18 4AB

Simple and appealing little village pub, with a relaxed civilised atmosphere, real ales and good food

Unspoilt – but in a subtly upmarket way – this pretty 17th-c stone-built pub is cosy and friendly with a good mix of customers. The small front bar has low beams and timbers, exposed stone walls, a log fire in a big fireplace and half a dozen or so kitchen chairs and tables on the red tiled floor. There are usually a few locals at the planked counter where they serve Hook Norton Old Hooky, Wells & Youngs Bitter and Wye Valley Dorothy Goodbody's Golden Ale on handpump and 10 wines by the glass; big cafetières of coffee. A second room, similar but bigger, is used mainly for eating, with flowers on the tables and another fireplace. At the side, an attractive garden has picnic-sets.

🍴 Cooked by the landlord, the highly thought-of food includes lunchtime filled ciabattas, pigeon terrine with red onion marmalade, aubergine parmigiana baked with mozzarella, steak and mushroom in ale pie, chicken milanese with gremolata, and roast venison with celeriac purée and cumberland sauce. *Benchmark main dish: fish pie £12.50. Two-course evening meal £17.75.*

Free house ~ Licensee Martin Coldicott ~ Real ale ~ Bar food (12-2(2.45 weekends and bank hols), 7-9; maybe not winter Sun evenings) ~ (01993) 842280 ~ Well behaved children welcome until 7pm ~ Dogs allowed in bar ~ Open 11.30-3, 6-11; 11.30-11 Fri and Sat; 12-10 Sun

Recommended by Jean and Douglas Troup, William Goodhart, Anthony Barnes, Martin and Karen Wake, David Lamb, Richard Wyld, Glenwys and Alan Lawrence, R K Phillips, T R Austin, Guy Vowles

SHIPLAKE Oxfordshire   SU7779   Map D

Baskerville 🍴 ♟

Station Road, Lower Shiplake (off A4155 just S of Henley); RG9 3NY

Emphasis on imaginative food though a proper public bar too; real ales, several wines by the glass, interesting sporting memorabilia, and a pretty garden; bedrooms

Although the exterior here is slightly plain looking, it fronts a particularly well run pub which is very much the hub of the village, offering a warm welcome from friendly staff and top quality imaginative food. There are some bar chairs around the light, modern bar counter (used by the chatty locals), a few beams, pale wooden dining chairs and tables on the light wood or patterned carpeted floors, plush red banquettes around the windows and a couple of log fires in brick fireplaces. A fair amount of sporting memorabilia and pictures, especially old rowing photos (the pub is very close to Henley) and signed rugby shirts and photographs (the pub runs its own rugby club), plus some maps of the Thames are hung on the red walls, and there are flowers and large house plants dotted about. It all feels quite homely, but in a smart way, with some chintzy touches such as a shelf of china cow jugs. Fullers London Pride, Loddon Hoppit and Timothy Taylors Landlord on handpump, 40 malt whiskies and a dozen wines by the glass. There's a separate dining room and a small room for private family or business groups. The pretty garden has a proper covered barbecue area, smart teak furniture under huge parasols and some rather fun statues made out of box. There's a timber play frame for children. The bedrooms are well equipped and comfortable. We'd love to hear from readers who have stayed here.

Usefully open for food all day including a fine breakfast from 9.30am, there might be open sandwiches, goats cheese and rosemary panna cotta with a sweet and spicy tomato relish, steak and kidney in ale pie, chicken saltimbocca with spring onion mash and smoked aubergine caponata, rolled, slow-cooked lamb with apricots, paprika and mustard, and scallops and tiger prawns with pasta, garlic, Pernod, cream and herbs; they also offer a two- and three-course set menu. *Benchmark main dish: fish and chips £12.95. Two-course evening meal £21.70.*

Free house ~ Licensee Allan Hannah ~ Real ale ~ Bar food (9.30am-9.30pm) ~ Restaurant ~ (0118) 940 3332 ~ Children welcome but not in restaurant after 7pm Fri and Sat ~ Dogs allowed in bar and bedrooms ~ Open 9.30am-11pm; 12-4.30, 7-10.30 Sun ~ Bedrooms: £77S/£97.50S(£87.50B)

Recommended by Paul Humphreys, Neil and Karen Dignan, David O'Shaughnessy, Mrs Susan Lines, Ian Herdman

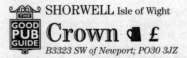

SHORWELL Isle of Wight   SZ4582   Map D

Crown ◑ £

B3323 SW of Newport; PO30 3JZ

Popular pub with appealing streamside garden and play area

They serve a particularly good pint at this pretty inland pub, with their five or six real ales on handpump usually including Adnams Broadside, Goddards Fuggle-Dee-Dum, Ringwood Fortyniner, St Austell Tribute and Sharps Doom Bar. The other main draw here is the appealing tree-sheltered garden with its sweet little stream that broadens into a small trout-filled pool, decent children's play area within easy view of closely spaced picnic-sets and white garden chairs and tables set out on the grass. Inside, four pleasant opened-up rooms spread around a central bar, with either carpet, tiles or flagstones, and chatty regulars lending some local character. The beamed knocked-through lounge has blue and white china on an attractive carved dresser, old country prints on stripped-stone walls and a winter log fire with a fancy tile-work surround. Black pews form bays around tables in a stripped-stone room off to the left with another log fire; piped music and board games.

Pubby bar food runs from starters such as half a pint of prawns and pâté of the day to main courses such as fish and chips, chicken curry, venison curry, nut roast, burgers and pies. *Benchmark main dish: fish and chips £10.25. Two-course evening meal £15.70.*

Enterprise ~ Lease Nigel and Pam Wynn ~ Real ale ~ Bar food (12-9.30) ~ (01983) 740293 ~ Children welcome ~ Dogs welcome ~ Open 10.30(11.30 Sun)-11

Recommended by Quentin and Carol Williamson, Terry and Nickie Williams

SHURLOCK ROW Berkshire   SU8374   Map D

Shurlock Inn ♀ ◖

Just off B3018 SE of Twyford; The Street; RG10 0PS

Comfortable village-owned pub with warm atmosphere, enjoyable food and drinks

Bought and refurbished by a consortium of 17 locals, this has the splendid atmosphere of a place that's run for the sheer enjoyment of doing a good job really well rather than for making pots of money. Décor is simple and clean-cut, with fitted carpet, just a few pictures on plain cream walls, russet curtains, one or two beams in the low ceiling, and a brick hearth with a log-effect gas fire dividing the main area, set for dining, from a small bar. The little corner counter serves three well kept changing ales such as Binghams Brickworks and Marlow Rebellion IPA and Zebedee from handpump, and good wines by the glass; the radio may be on quietly. A side terrace has black metal tables and chairs, with more in a garden with shrubs, sycamore, a big weeping willow, picnic-sets under canvas parasols, and a play area.

Good, interesting food includes lunchtime sandwiches, crab and avocado tian, smoked haddock risotto with a poached egg, a popular burger, sausages of the week with onion gravy, moules marinière, and pork belly with spiced apple, cider and mustard sauce. *Benchmark main dish: sea trout with samphire and new potato chowder £13.95. Two-course evening meal £17.30.*

Free house ~ Licensee Andrew Norman ~ Real ale ~ Bar food (12-2.30, 6-9(9.30 Fri and Sat); 12-8 Sun) ~ Restaurant ~ (0118) 934 9094 ~ Children welcome ~ Dogs allowed in bar ~ Open 12-3, 6-11; 10am-11pm Sat; 10-8 Sun
Recommended by Paul Humphreys

SINGLETON Sussex   SU8713   Map D

Partridge ⑪

Just off A286 Midhurst—Chichester; PO18 0EY

Well run, friendly village pub with daily papers and log fires, real ales, good pubby food, and a pretty walled garden

Handy for the Weald & Downland Open Air Museum and not far from Goodwood, this pretty black and cream 16th-c pub is doing especially well at the moment. It's now run by a former executive head chef of the Ritz and, not surprisingly, the food is extremely good. But despite the emphasis on dining, they keep Ballards Golden Bine, Fullers London Pride and Harveys Best on handpump and several wines by the glass, and there's a friendly, relaxed atmosphere. There are all sorts of light and dark wooden tables and dining chairs on polished wooden floors, flagstones and carpet, daily papers, a woodburning stove and winter log fires, and a modicum of country knick-knacks. Piped music, board games and summer table tennis. Both the terrace and walled garden have plenty of picnic-sets under parasols.

Enjoyable food using local produce includes sandwiches, chicken liver, smoked bacon and port pâté with a berry compote, house-potted brown shrimps, risotto of wild mushrooms with truffle oil, sausage and mash with red onion gravy, steak and mushroom in ale pie, and salmon, smoked haddock and chive fishcakes with lemon mayonnaise. *Benchmark main dish: steak in ale pie £11.95. Two-course evening meal £18.70.*

Enterprise ~ Lease Giles Thompson ~ Real ale ~ Bar food (12-2(3 Sun), 6-9(9.30 Fri and Sat)) ~ Restaurant ~ (01243) 811251 ~ Children welcome ~ Dogs allowed in bar and bedrooms ~ Open 11-11(11.30 Sat); 12-11 Sat

Recommended by G Dobson, Nick Lawless, J A Snell, Tim and Sue Halstead

SKIRMETT Buckinghamshire   SU7790 Map D

 Frog

From A4155 NE of Henley take Hambleden turn and keep on; or from B482 Stokenchurch—Marlow take Turville turn and keep on; RG9 6TG

Bustling pub with modern cooking in a traditional atmosphere, fine choice of drinks, lovely garden, and nearby walks; bedrooms

The long-serving licensees and their friendly staff are sure to make you welcome in this 18th-c coaching inn and although much emphasis is placed on the good, interesting food, the public bar is still very much the heart of the place. There's a winter log fire in the brick fireplace with lots of little framed prints above it, a cushioned sofa and leather-seated bar stools around a low circular table on the wooden floor, and high bar chairs by the counter; piped music. Rebellion IPA and guests like Gales Seafarer and Sharps Atlantic IPA on handpump, a dozen wines by the glass (including champagne) and around two dozen carefully sourced malt whiskies. The two dining rooms are quite different in style – one is light and airy with country kitchen tables and chairs and the other is more formal with dark red walls, smarter dining chairs and tables and candlelight. Outside, a side gate leads to a lovely garden with a large tree in the middle and the unusual five-sided tables are well placed for attractive valley views. Plenty of nearby hikes (Henley is close by) and just down the road is the delightful Ibstone windmill. There's a purpose-built outdoor heated area for smokers. The breakfasts are good (though it might be worth having a room not right above the bar).

Imaginative and extremely good, the food might include grilled mackerel with marinated cucumber and mustard crème fraîche, ham hock terrine with pickled vegetables, a trio of sausages with chive mash and onion gravy, gnocchi with asparagus, sunblush tomatoes and chargrilled peppers in tomato sauce, plaice with brown shrimps and lemon butter sauce, and pork wellington with fruit stuffing wrapped in parma ham and filo pastry. *Benchmark main dish: fish and chips with mushy peas £12.45. Two-course evening meal £18.50.*

Free house ~ Licensees Jim Crowe and Noelle Greene ~ Real ale ~ Bar food (12-2.30, 6.30-9.30; not winter Sun evenings) ~ Restaurant ~ (01491) 638996 ~ Children welcome ~ Dogs allowed in bar ~ Open 11.30-3, 6-11; 12-4, 6-10.30 Sun; closed Sun evening Oct-May ~ Bedrooms: £60B/£80B

Recommended by Martin and Karen Wake, Tracey and Stephen Groves, Richard and Liz Thorne, Ian Wilson, Paul Humphreys, Colin and Louise English, Brian and Anna Marsden, John and Sharon Hancock

SONNING Berkshire   SU7575 Map D

Bull 🛏

Off B478, by church; village signed off A4 E of Reading; RG4 6UP

Pretty timbered inn in attractive spot near Thames, plenty of character in old-fashioned bars, Fullers beers, friendly staff and good food; bedrooms

The two old-fashioned bar rooms in this pretty 16th-c black and white timbered inn have a good bustling atmosphere and plenty of chatty locals. There are low ceilings and heavy beams, cosy alcoves, leather armchairs and sofas, cushioned antique settles and low wooden chairs on bare boards, and open fireplaces. The dining room has a mix of wooden chairs and tables, rugs on parquet flooring and shelves of books. Fullers Chiswick, Discovery, HSB, London Pride and a couple of guests on handpump, served by friendly staff. When the wisteria is flowering, the inn looks especially pretty and the courtyard is bright with tubs of flowers. If you bear left through the ivy-clad churchyard opposite, then turn left along the bank of the River Thames, you come to a very pretty lock.

Good, if not cheap, bar food includes sandwiches, home-made mackerel pâté with gooseberry compote, gratin of smoked haddock, pork and leek sausages with onion gravy, corn-fed chicken with thyme and garlic sweet potatoes and a berry sauce, steak and venison pie, and cinnamon and apple-spiced pork belly with cider gravy and mustard mash. *Benchmark main dish: fish casserole £15.00. Two-course evening meal £22.00.*

Gales (Fullers) ~ Manager Dennis Mason ~ Real ale ~ Bar food (all day) ~ Restaurant ~ (0118) 969 3901 ~ Children welcome ~ Dogs allowed in bar ~ Open 11-11; 12-10.30 Sun ~ Bedrooms: /£99S(£125B)

Recommended by Jennifer Banks, Jack and Sandra Clarfelt, Simon Collett-Jones, Susan and John Douglas, John Saville, David and Sue Atkinson

 SOUTHSEA Hampshire   SZ6499   Map D

Wine Vaults

Albert Road, opposite King's Theatre; PO5 2SF

Bustling pub with a fine choice of real ales and reasonably priced pubby food

The fine range of eight changing real ales continues to pack in the customers at this well run and extremely busy pub. On handpump these might include Fullers London Pride, Discovery, ESB, London Porter and Organic Honey Dew, Gales HSB and guests such as Windsor & Eton Guardsman or Knight of the Garter and Wells & Youngs Bombardier. There are several rooms on different floors – all fairly straightforward and chatty – and the main bar has wood-panelled walls, pubby tables and chairs on the wooden floor, and bar stools by the long plain bar counter; there's a newly smartened-up restaurant area away from the hustle and bustle of the bars. Maybe newspapers to read, piped music and TV for sports events. There's a heated roof terrace for smokers.

Some sort of food is offered all day: sandwiches, garlic mushrooms, champagne pâté with red onion marmalade, beer-battered haddock, vegetable lasagne, steak in ale pie, and minted lamb steak. *Benchmark main dish: beef en croûte £10.95. Two-course evening meal £20.00.*

Fullers ~ Manager Sophie Mannering ~ Real ale ~ Bar food (all day) ~ Restaurant ~ (023) 9286 4712 ~ Children welcome ~ Dogs allowed in bar ~ Open 12-11(1am Fri and Sat; 10.30 Sun)

Recommended by Andy West, the Didler, Ann and Colin Hunt

The letters and figures after the name of each town are its Ordnance Survey map reference. 'Using the *Guide*' explains how it helps you find a pub, in road atlases or on large-scale maps as well as in our own maps.

SPARSHOLT Hampshire   SU4331   Map D

Plough 🍴 ♟

*Village signposted off B3049 (Winchester—Stockbridge), a little W of
Winchester; SO21 2NW*

**Neat, well run dining pub with interesting furnishings, an extensive wine
list, and popular bar food; garden with children's play fort**

Particularly well run by friendly, polite licensees and their well trained
staff, this country pub is always deservedly busy; you must book in
advance to be sure of a table. Of course most customers are here to enjoy
the wide choice of reliably good food but they do keep Wadworths IPA,
6X, Bishops Tipple and Horizon on handpump, and have an extensive
wine list with a fair selection by the glass including champagne and
pudding wine. The main bar has an interesting mix of wooden tables and
chairs with farm tools, scythes and pitchforks attached to the ceiling.
Disabled access and facilities. Outside, there are plenty of seats on the
terrace and lawn and a children's play fort.

Well presented, much-liked food includes lunchtime sandwiches, chicken liver
and bacon in a mushroom cream sauce, grilled mackerel on crostini with a
tomato and garlic compote, beef and mushroom in ale pie with mustard mash,
butternut squash risotto with a pine nut crumb, thai chicken curry, steak burgers
with pepper sauce, and pork loin with stilton sauce, glazed apples and dauphinoise
potatoes. *Benchmark main dish: salmon and crab fishcakes with saffron sauce
£11.95. Two-course evening meal £18.50.*

Wadworths ~ Tenants Richard and Kathryn Crawford ~ Real ale ~ Bar food (12-2, 6-9
(9.30 Fri and Sat)) ~ (01962) 776353 ~ Children welcome except in main bar area ~
Dogs allowed in bar ~ Open 11-3, 6-11

*Recommended by Phyl and Jack Street, John Michelson, Henry Fryer, John and Joan Calvert, Jill
and Julian Tasker, David Jackson, Tony and Jill Radnor*

ST MARGARET'S BAY Kent   TR3744   Map C

Coastguard ♟ ◖

*Off A256 NE of Dover; keep on down through the village to the bottom of the
bay, pub off on right by the beach; CT15 6DY*

Great views, nautical décor, fine range of drinks and well liked food

This terrifically positioned pub in a cosy bay beneath the white cliffs
of Dover has tables out on its prettily planted balcony from where you
can look across the Straits of Dover, and there are more seats down by
the beach. Inside, the warm, carpeted, wood-clad bar has some shipping
memorabilia, Gadds No 5 and Goachers Dark alongside a couple of guests
from brewers such as Fyne and Orkney on handpump, over 40 whiskies,
Weston's cider and a carefully chosen wine list including some from Kent
vineyards; good service even when busy. The restaurant has wooden
dining chairs and tables on a wood-strip floor and more fine views;
piped music.

Well presented bar food typically includes scallops in garlic butter, curried
cauliflower and mediterranean vegetable soup, roast lemon sole, chicken on
blue cheese, bacon and walnut salad, and sirloin steak with garlic butter. *Benchmark
main dish: cod and chips £12.50. Two-course evening meal £18.50.*

Free house ~ Licensee Nigel Wydymus ~ Real ale ~ Bar food (12.30-2.45, 6.30-8.45) ~ Restaurant ~ (01304) 853176 ~ Children welcome away from bar ~ Dogs allowed in bar ~ Open 11-11(10.30 Sun)

Recommended by Christopher Turner, David Jackman, Richard Mason, N R White

 STALISFIELD GREEN Kent   TQ9552   Map C

Plough

Off A252 in Charing; ME13 0HY

Ancient country pub with rambling rooms, open fires, interesting local ales, smashing bar food, and friendly licensees

Perched on the Downs and surrounded by farmland, parts of this ancient country pub are said to date back to 1350. Its several hop-draped rooms, relaxed and easy-going, ramble around, up and down, with open fires in brick fireplaces, interesting pictures on green- or maroon-painted walls, books on shelves, farmhouse and other nice old dining chairs around a mix of pine or dark wood tables on bare boards and the odd milk churn dotted about. Dixie, the pub cat, likes to find a cosy lap to lie on. The cheery, helpful landlord stocks local ales from kentish brewers such as Gadds, Goachers, Old Dairy and Whitstable; he keeps kentish lager as well as local wines, water, fruit juices and cider. Picnic-sets on a simple terrace overlook the village green. They also have a site for caravans.

Using seasonal fruit and vegetables direct from local farms, local meat and game (they hang their own) and making their own sausages, ketchup, bread and ice-creams, the very good food includes sandwiches, walnut and stilton cheesecake with poached pear and a port and redcurrant sauce, steak in ale suet pudding, mackerel fillets with butternut squash, bacon, wilted spinach and paprika roasted potatoes with a cold-smoked butter sauce. *Benchmark main dish: locally reared rump steak £14.95. Two-course evening meal £20.50.*

Free house ~ Licensee Robert and Amy Lloyd ~ Real ale ~ Bar food (12-2, 7-9; 12-9 Sat; 12-4 Sun) ~ Restaurant ~ (01795) 890256 ~ Children welcome on left ~ Dogs allowed in bar ~ Live music Fri monthly ~ Open 12-3, 6-11; 12-12.30(6 Sun) Sat; closed Mon, Tues lunchtime, Sun evening

Recommended by Joan and Alec Lawrence, N R White

 STANFORD DINGLEY Berkshire   SU5771   Map D

Old Boot

Off A340 via Bradfield, coming from A4 just W of M4 junction 12; RG7 6LT

Country furnishings and open fires in welcoming beamed bars, a choice of bar food, real ales, and rural garden views

The beamed bar in this stylish 18th-c pub has two welcoming fires (one in an inglenook) and is just the place for a cosy winter drink. There are fine old pews, settles, old country chairs and polished tables, as well as some striking pictures and hunting prints, boot ornaments and fresh flowers. There's also a conservatory-style restaurant. West Berkshire Good Old Boy and a guest, plus Wadworths 6X on handpump and several wines by the glass. There are seats in the quiet sloping back garden or on the terrace and pleasant rural views; more tables out in front. Please note, they no longer have bedrooms.

Changing bar food includes sandwiches, scallops with celeriac purée, a pie of the week, a proper burger, linguine with cherry tomatoes, pesto and spinach, sesame chicken with a creamy curry sauce, and bass with thai-spiced vegetables. *Benchmark main dish: duck with apple and cider sauce £12.95. Two-course evening meal £20.95.*

Free house ~ Licensee John Haley ~ Real ale ~ Bar food ~ Restaurant ~ (0118) 974 4292 ~ Children welcome ~ Dogs allowed in bar ~ Open 11-3, 6-11; 11-11 Sat and Sun
Recommended by Neil and Karen Dignan

  STANFORD IN THE VALE Oxfordshire   SU3393   Map E

Horse & Jockey ♀

A417 Faringdon—Wantage; Faringdon Road; SN7 8NN

Friendly traditional village local with real character, good value pubby food and a good wine choice

They take trouble with their wines here, serving a fairly priced range in a sensible choice of glass sizes, and have Greene King Morlands Original, Old Speckled Hen and Ruddles County on handpump. Big Alfred Munnings' racecourse prints, Grand National winner-card collections and other horse and jockey pictures reflect not just the pub's name but the fact that this is racehorse training country – which so often seems to guarantee a relaxed and comfortably welcoming atmosphere. The main area, with flagstones, low ochre ceiling and a woodburning stove in its big fireplace, has several old high-backed settles and a couple of bucket armchairs. On the right is a carpeted area with a lofty raftered ceiling, a lattice-windowed inner gallery and some stripped stone, and at the back a spacious bare-boards dining room. Besides the tables out under a heated courtyard canopy, the separate enclosed and informal family garden has a play area; aunt sally. We have not yet heard from readers using the bedrooms here, but would expect an enjoyable stay.

As well as fair value lunchtime choices like sandwiches, sausages with garlic and herb mash and onion gravy, and spinach and ricotta tortellini in white wine and herb cream, the highly thought-of food includes moules marinière, lamb rump with rosemary and redcurrant sauce, bass fillet on spiced potato cake with lobster beurre blanc and slow-roasted pork belly with thyme jus and dauphinoise potatoes. *Benchmark main dish: steak in Guinness casserole £8.95. Two-course evening meal £19.25.*

Greene King ~ Lease Charles and Anna Gaunt ~ Real ale ~ Bar food (12-2.30, 6.30-9(9.30 Fri and Sat)) ~ Restaurant ~ (01367) 710302 ~ Children welcome ~ Dogs allowed in bar ~ Thurs evening quiz and monthly open mike first Weds evening of month ~ Open 11-3, 5-midnight; 11am-12.30am Fri and Sat; midday-midnight Sun ~ Bedrooms: £50S/£60S
Recommended by R K Phillips, Valerie Bone

  STANTON ST JOHN Oxfordshire   SP5709   Map E

Talk House ♀ 🛏

Middle Road/Wheatley Road (B4027 just outside village); OX33 1EX

Attractive thatched dining pub with interesting food from a varied menu in several separate areas, real ales, friendly staff, and seats in a sheltered courtyard; bedrooms

Although the inventive modern food remains the main draw to this partly 16th-c dining pub, they do keep Fullers London Pride, Discovery and Seafarers Ale on handpump, and several wines by the glass; also daily papers. The thatched part, at the front on the left, dates from about 1550, giving a splendid dining area with steeply pitched rafters soaring above stripped-stone walls, a mix of old dining chairs around big stripped tables, and large rugs on flagstones. Most of the rest of the building has been well converted more recently, keeping a similar style – fat candles on stripped tables, massive beams, flagstones or stoneware tiles, log fires below low mantelbeams, and a relaxed and leisurely feel. At the front on the right are dark leather button-back settees and leather-cushioned easy chairs, with two more dining areas at the back. An inner courtyard has comfortable teak tables and chairs, with a few picnic-sets on side grass. The snug ground-floor bedrooms are behind here and they serve good breakfasts.

Using produce from local farms, the well liked food includes sandwiches, smoked salmon roulade, seared scallops with a mustard potato salad and beetroot, gnocchi with asparagus, peas and a salsa verde, battered haddock and chips, steak hash burger with triple-cooked chips and a tomato salsa, and chicken breast stuffed with sunblush tomatoes and a garlic potato rösti. *Benchmark main dish: roasted rump of lamb with red pepper and butternut crush £16.95. Two-course evening meal £19.95.*

Fullers ~ Manager John McKay ~ Real ale ~ Bar food (12-3, 6-9; all day Sat, Sun and bank hols) ~ Restaurant ~ (01865) 351648 ~ Children welcome ~ Dogs allowed in bar ~ Live jazz first Fri of month ~ Open 10am-midnight(1.30am Fri and Sat); 10am-11pm Sun ~ Bedrooms: /£65S

Recommended by Franklyn Roberts

STEEP Hampshire   SU7525   Map D

Harrow ☖ £

Take Midhurst exit from Petersfield bypass, at exit roundabout take first left towards Midhurst, then first turning on left opposite garage, and left again at Sheet church; follow over dual carriageway bridge to pub; GU32 2DA

Unchanging, simple place with long-serving landladies, beers tapped from the cask, unfussy food and a big free-flowering garden; no children inside

There's no pandering to modern methods here – no credit cards, no waitress service, no restaurant, no music and outside lavatories. And our readers love it. The same family have been running it for 82 years now and as a pub it remains quite unchanged and unspoilt. Everything revolves around village chat and the friendly locals who will probably draw you into light-hearted conversation. There are adverts for logs next to calendars of local views being sold in support of local charities and news of various quirky competitions. The cosy public bar has hops and dried flowers hanging from the beams, built-in wall benches on the tiled floor, stripped-pine wallboards, a good log fire in the big inglenook, and wild flowers on the scrubbed deal tables; board games. Ringwood Best and Bowman Swift One are tapped straight from casks behind the counter, and they've local wine, and apple and pear juice; staff are polite and friendly, even when under pressure. The big garden is left free-flowering so that goldfinches can collect thistle seeds from the grass, but there are some seats on paved areas now. The Petersfield bypass doesn't intrude on this idyll, though you will need to follow the directions above to find the pub. No children inside and dogs must be on leads.

Good helpings of unfussy bar food include sandwiches, home-made scotch eggs, hearty ham, split pea and vegetable soup, ploughman's, cottage pie, flans and quiches, and puddings such as treacle tart or seasonal fruit pies. *Benchmark main dish: home-cooked beef ploughman's £5.00.*

Free house ~ Licensees Claire and Denise McCutcheon ~ Real ale ~ Bar food (not Sun evening; limited Mon evening) ~ No credit cards ~ (01730) 262685 ~ Dogs welcome ~ Open 12-2.30, 6-11; 11-3, 6-11 Sat; 12-3, 7-10.30 Sun; closed winter Sun evenings

Recommended by Ian Phillips, David Gunn, Tony and Jill Radnor, Neil and Karen Dignan, the Didler, Phil and Sally Gorton, W A Evershed, Prof James Stevens Curl, John and Anne Mackinnon, John and Jackie Chalcraft

 STOKE MANDEVILLE Buckinghamshire   SP8310   Map E

Woolpack ♀

Risborough Road (A4010 S of Aylesbury); HP22 5UP

Boldy decorated pub with contemporary and stylish bar rooms, imaginative food, a good choice of drinks, and seats outside

Decorated throughout in a thoroughly modern style, this partly thatched pub has plenty of room in its spreading open-plan rooms. Bold red and cream paintwork team up with plenty of contemporary art, high-backed black or beige leather dining chairs around a mix of chunky pale wooden tables on red and beige rugs or stone flooring, high white-seated stools against the bar counter and comfortably cushioned wall seats; there's an open fire in the bar. Brakspears, Purity Pure UBU and Timothy Taylors Landlord on handpump and a good choice of wines by the glass. There are seats and tables in the back garden or on the heated front terrace.

Interesting up-to-date food includes scallops of the day, duck rillettes with rhubarb and ginger chutney, pasta with tiger prawns, crab, chorizo, chilli, tomato and white wine, various pizzas, a proper burger with mustard mayo, curried smoked haddock and leek fishcake with a poached egg, mango salad and hollandaise sauce, and spit-roasted chicken with lemon, garlic and thyme. *Benchmark main dish: crispy duck salad £11.95. Two-course evening meal £17.45.*

Mitchells & Butlers ~ Manager Chloe Godridge ~ Real ale ~ Bar food (12-3, 6-10(10.30 Sun); Sun 12-9) ~ Restaurant ~ (01296) 615970 ~ Well behaved children allowed but not Fri or Sat evenings ~ Open 11-11(midnight Sat;10.30 Sun)

Recommended by John Faircloth, Mel Smith

 STONESFIELD Oxfordshire   SP3917   Map E

White Horse

Village signposted off B4437 Charlbury—Woodstock; Stonesfield Riding; OX29 8EA

Attractively upgraded small country pub with enjoyable food and a relaxed atmosphere

Contemporary artworks, restful colours (grey or near-white in the snug little bar, dark pink over a grey dado in the dining room) and nicely chosen furniture all show that the couple who reopened this in 2009 have a real eye for detail. One of their best touches is the little inner room with just a pair of Sheraton-style chairs around a single mahogany table. Service is cheerful and efficient. The corner bar counter, with padded stools, has White Horse ale on handpump; open fire, daily papers, faint piped pop music. The dining room's french windows open on to a neat walled garden with picnic-sets; there's a skittle alley in the separate stone barn. There are good local walks (the pub is on the Oxfordshire Way) and is handy for the Roman villa (EH) at nearby North Leigh.

Good food cooked by the landlady using carefully sourced local produce includes lunchtime sandwiches, smoked salmon pâté, minted pea risotto, steak and mushroom puff pie, lamb cutlets with pea purée, salmon with a parmesan and parsley crust and a white wine and mushroom sauce, and braised lamb shank with honey and rosemary. *Benchmark main dish: steak and mushroom pie £9.95. Two-course evening meal £14.00.*

Free house ~ Licensees John and Angela Lloyd ~ Real ale ~ Bar food (No food Mon-Thurs (phone to check)) ~ Restaurant ~ (01993) 891063 ~ Children welcome ~ Dogs allowed in bar ~ Open 12-3, 5(6 Fri and Sat)-11; closed Mon; first week Jan

Recommended by Guy Vowles

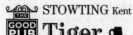 STOWTING Kent   TR1241   Map C

Tiger

3.7 miles from M20 junction 11; B2068 N, then left at Stowting signpost, straight across crossroads, fork left after 0.25 miles and pub is on right; coming from N, follow Brabourne, Wye, Ashford signed to right at fork, then turn left towards Posting and Lyminge at T junction; TN25 6BA

Peaceful pub with friendly staff, traditional furnishings, well liked food, several real ales and open fires; good walking country

Tucked away down leafy lanes, this 17th-c inn is cosily traditional with a happy mix of wooden tables and chairs and built-in cushioned wall seats on wooden floorboards and woodburning stoves at each end of the bar. There's an array of books, board games, candles in bottles, brewery memorabilia and paintings, lots of hops and some faded rugs on the stone floor towards the back of the pub. Fullers London Pride, Harveys Best and Old Dairy Brewery, Shepherd Neame Master Brew and a guest on handpump, lots of malt whiskies, several wines by the glass, local Biddenden cider and local fruit juice. On warmer days you can sit out on the front terrace and there are plenty of nearby walks along the Wye Downs or North Downs Way.

Enjoyable bar food from a daily changing menu, using seasonal local produce, might include items such as sandwiches, caramelised goats cheese with grilled sweet and sour strawberries, steamed asparagus topped with poached egg and lemon hollandaise, red onion, mushroom and gorgonzola tart, dover sole with caper butter, chicken, ham and leek pie, tuna steak niçoise, rack of lamb on courgette provençale with sweet potato dauphinoise, and honey and mustard sausages. *Benchmark main dish: roast pork belly with smoked bacon £15.00. Two-course evening meal £21.00.*

Free house ~ Licensees Emma Oliver and Benn Jarvis ~ Real ale ~ Bar food (12(4 Mon)-9(9.30 Fri, Sat, 8 Sun)) ~ Restaurant ~ (01303) 862130 ~ Children welcome ~ Dogs allowed in bar ~ Jazz every second Mon evening ~ Open 12(4 Mon)-11; 12-11 Sat; 12-10.30 Sun; closed Mon lunchtime, Tues

Recommended by Brian and Anna Marsden, Jill and Julian Tasker, Paul Goldman, N R White, Matthew Lonergan, Michael Butler, Julie and Bill Ryan

SUNBURY Surrey   TQ1068   Map C

Flower Pot

1.6 miles from M3 junction 1; follow Lower Sunbury sign from exit roundabout, then at Thames Street turn right; pub on next corner, with Green Street; TW16 6AA

Appealing contemporary update of small 18th-c inn near the Thames

Though it's not actually on the river, the pub is really just across the road from an attractive reach of the Thames, in quite a villagey area with waterside walks. The building's façade, complete with elegant wrought-iron balconies, makes the bar something of a surprise: modern pale chunky tables on pale boards, a contemporary colour scheme of lavender-grey and deep claret-purple, and round the corner of the horseshoe-shaped bar an aquarium wall. Service, though, is thoroughly old-fashioned in the best helpful sense, and the Brakspears, Jennings Bitter, Ringwood Best and Wychwood Hobgoblin on handpump are kept in fine condition; we particularly liked the comfortable swivelling bar chairs. The atmosphere, suiting the area, is relaxed and uncitified, with a rack of daily papers, unobtrusive piped music, and perhaps locals watching TV racing. We have not yet heard from readers staying here, but would expect good value.

As well as lunchtime sandwiches and filled panini, good value food, changing monthly, might include tempura prawns with sweet chilli dip, baked goats cheese with honey and mustard dressing with smoked salmon and walnut salad, breaded cheese platter with dips, salmon fishcakes, thai fish curry, pie of the day, penne carbonara, chicken caesar salad, mushroom stroganoff, and well hung steak. *Benchmark main dish: fish and chips £9.95. Two-course evening meal £15.00.*

Brakspears ~ Tenant Faye Wood ~ Real ale ~ Bar food (12-2.30(5.30 Sun), 6-9; not Sun evening) ~ Restaurant ~ (01932) 780741 ~ Children welcome ~ Dogs welcome ~ Open 12-11(11.30 Fri, Sat) ~ Bedrooms: £55B/£70B

Recommended by Edward Mirzoeff, Gerry and Rosemary Dobson

SWALLOWFIELD Berkshire

SU7364 Map D

George & Dragon ♀

Church Road, towards Farley Hill; RG7 1TJ

Busy country pub with good nearby walks, enjoyable bar food, real ales, friendly service, and seats outside

Run by long-serving licensees, this popular pub is just the place to head for after enjoying one of the nearby walks. The various interconnected rooms have a thriving atmosphere and plenty of character – as well as beams and standing timbers, ladder-back chairs and stools around individual wooden tables, rugs on flagstones, lit candles, a big log fire and country prints on the red walls; piped music. Bingham Brewery Twyford Tipple, Fullers London Pride and Itchen Valley Pure Gold on handpump and quite a few wines by the glass served by friendly staff. There are picnic-sets on gravel or paving in the garden.

Well liked bistro-style bar food includes sandwiches, flambéed devilled kidneys, battered fish and chips, burger with bacon, guacamole and smoked paprika mayonnaise, tagliatelle with roast garlic mushrooms, creamed leeks and stilton, gressingham duck breast with noodles, crispy seaweed and plum sauce, and veal chop with mustard butter or red wine jus. *Benchmark main dish: slow-cooked lamb shoulder with ratatouille £14.50. Two-course evening meal £20.45.*

Free house ~ Licensee Paul Dailey ~ Real ale ~ Bar food (12-2.30(3 Sun), 7-9.30 (9 Sun)) ~ Restaurant ~ (0118) 9884432 ~ Well behaved children welcome ~ Dogs allowed in bar ~ Open 12-11(10 Sun)

Recommended by Dr and Mrs R E S Tanner, Veryan Young

The price we give for a two-course evening meal in the featured top pub entries is the mean (average of cheapest and most expensive) price of a starter and a main course – no drinks.

SWERFORD Oxfordshire   SP3830 Map E

Masons Arms ⑪ ♀

A361 Banbury—Chipping Norton; OX7 4AP

Attractive dining pub with imaginative food, a fair choice of drinks, a relaxed atmosphere, and country views from outside tables

As we went to press we heard that this popular dining pub had been taken over by new licensees, but early reader reports suggest that things are running as smoothly as ever. Many customers come here to enjoy the interesting food but they do keep Brakspears Bitter and Wychwood Hobgoblin on handpump, lots of wines by the glass, Weston's organic cider and home-made spicy tomato juice. The dining extension is light and airy and the bar has rugs on pale wooden floors, a carefully illuminated stone fireplace, thoughtful spotlighting, and beige and red armchairs around big circular wooden tables. Doors open on to a small terrace with a couple of stylish tables, while steps lead down into a cream-painted room with chunky tables and contemporary pictures. Round the other side of the bar is another roomy dining room with great views by day, candles at night and a civilised feel. Behind is a neat square lawn with picnic-sets and views over the Oxfordshire countryside.

Interesting food includes antipasti, vegetarian or seafood platters (to share), confit duck leg, puy lentils and fig jus, crab and leek fishcakes with caper mayonnaise, home-baked ham and duck egg, venison and juniper pie, gloucester old spot pork loin braised in milk, lemon, rosemary and sage, and mini shoulder of lamb pot-roasted in honey, soy, spring onions, chilli and garlic. *Benchmark main dish: changing scallop dish £18.00. Two-course evening meal £20.00.*

Free house ~ Licensees Jude and Vicky Kelly ~ Real ale ~ Bar food (12-2, 7-9; 12-6 Sun) ~ Restaurant ~ (01608) 683212 ~ Children welcome ~ Open 10-3, 6-11; 11-8 (6 in winter) Sun

Recommended by Michael Dandy, George Atkinson, Sir Nigel Foulkes, David and Lexi Young, Charlie Mcgrath, P and J Shapley

SWINBROOK Oxfordshire   SP2812 Map E

Swan ⑪ ♀ 🛏

Back road a mile N of A40, 2 miles E of Burford; OX18 4DY

Rather smart old pub with handsome oak garden rooms, antique-filled bars, local beers and contemporary food; bedrooms

Handy for the A40, this civilised 17th-c pub is in a lovely spot by a bridge over the River Windrush and seats by the fuchsia hedge make the best of the view. It's owned by the Dowager Duchess of Devonshire (the last of the Mitford sisters who grew up in the village) and has lots of interesting old Mitford family photographs blown up on the walls. There's a little bar with simple antique furnishings, settles and benches, an open fire, and (in an alcove) a stuffed swan; locals do still drop in here for a pint and a chat. The small dining room to the right of the entrance opens into this room and there are two green oak garden rooms with high-backed beige and green dining chairs around pale wood tables, and views over the garden and orchard. Hook Norton Hooky Bitter and a couple of guests from breweries like Arkells and Sharps on handpump, several wines by the glass and Weston's organic cider. The bedrooms are in a smartly converted stone barn beside the pub.

🍴 Inventive food using beef from the family farm includes lunchtime sandwiches, foie gras and chicken liver parfait with quince jelly, chilli cheeseburger, smoked haddock, spinach, poached egg and hollandaise sauce, wild mushroom, leek and ricotta cannelloni, duck leg confit with thai noodle broth, and red mullet fillet with tagliatelle, artichokes, peas and brown shrimps. *Benchmark main dish: lamb chump with bubble and squeak, black pudding and red wine jus £17.50. Two-course evening meal £22.00.*

Free house ~ Licensees Archie and Nicola Orr-Ewing ~ Real ale ~ Bar food (12-2 (3 weekends), 7-9(9.30 Fri and Sat) ~ (01993) 823339 ~ Children welcome ~ Dogs allowed in bar ~ Open 11-11(10.30 Sun); 11-3, 6-11 in winter ~ Bedrooms: £70B/£120B

Recommended by Richard Tilbrook, MDN, Brian Glozier, Henry Midwinter, Myra Joyce, Malcolm and Jo Hart, Bruce and Sharon Eden, Anthony and Pam Stamer, Bernard Stradling, Mrs Blethyn Elliott, David Glynne-Jones, John and Enid Morris, Richard Wyld, Jeff and Wendy Williams, Richard Greaves, David and Lexi Young, Tim and Sue Halstead, Graham Oddey, Malcolm Greening

TADPOLE BRIDGE Oxfordshire   SP3200 Map E

Trout 🍷 🛏

Back road Bampton—Buckland, 4 miles NE of Faringdon; SN7 8RF

Busy country inn by the River Thames with a fine choice of drinks, popular modern food, and seats in the waterside garden; bedrooms

This is a lovely place to stay and the refurbished bedrooms are extremely comfortable; breakfasts are plentiful and enjoyable, too. It's all very civilised and friendly and the L-shaped bar has attractive pink and cream checked chairs around a mix of nice wooden tables, some rugs on the flagstones, green paintwork behind a modern wooden bar counter, fresh flowers, two woodburning stoves and a large stuffed trout. The airy restaurant is appealingly candlelit in the evenings. Ramsbury Bitter, Wells & Youngs Bitter and a couple of guests like Loose Cannon Abingdon Bridge and White Horse Village Idiot on handpump, 14 wines by the glass from a wide-ranging and carefully chosen list, some fine sherries and several malt whiskies. This is a peaceful and picturesque spot by the Thames and there are good quality teak chairs and tables under blue parasols in the pretty garden; it can get pretty packed on a fine day, so it's best to arrive early then. You can hire punts with champagne hampers and there are moorings for six boats – if you book in advance.

🍴 Enjoyable – if not cheap – food includes lunchtime sandwiches, ham hock terrine with rhubarb and red pepper salsa, yellowfin tuna tartare with ginger cucumber spaghetti, loin of wild rabbit with red lentils and coriander, slow-roasted suckling pig with braised apple and black pudding, and cutlet of rose veal with sweet potato gnocchi and cherry tomato confit. *Benchmark main dish: trout pie £12.95. Two-course evening meal £22.22.*

Free house ~ Licensees Gareth and Helen Pugh ~ Real ale ~ Bar food (not winter Sun evening) ~ Restaurant ~ (01367) 870382 ~ Children welcome ~ Dogs welcome ~ Open 11.30-3(4 Sat), 6-11; 12-4.30, 6.30-11 Sat; closed winter Sun evening ~ Bedrooms: £80B/£120B

Recommended by Mr and Mrs J C Cetti, Suzy Miller, Bob and Angela Brooks, Charles Gysin, Martin Cawley, Bruce and Sharon Eden, Bob and Margaret Holder, Glenwys and Alan Lawrence, Colin McKerrow, David and Diane Young, Eleanor Dandy, Tim Gray, Jennifer and Patrick O'Dell, Mary Rayner

We say if we know a pub has piped music.

THURSLEY Surrey   SU9039   Map D

Three Horseshoes 🍴
Dye House Road, just off A3 SW of Godalming; GU8 6QD

SURREY DINING PUB OF THE YEAR

Civilised country village pub with a broad range of good food

For many readers this pretty tile-hung village pub ticks all the boxes. It's family run and is jointly owned by a consortium of villagers who rescued it from closure, and with its good food and drink, lovely staff and friendly clientele it has the feel of a gently upmarket country local. The convivial beamed front bar has a winter log fire, Hogs Back TEA and a guest such as Fullers London Pride on handpump, a farm cider and perry; piped music. Tables in the attractive two-acre garden take in pleasant views over Thursley Common and the 1,000-year-old Saxon church. The terrace has smart comfortable chairs around tables with parasols. A separate area has a big play fort, a barbecue and a charcoal spit-roast area which they use on bank holidays. It's well placed for heathland walks – ask at the bar for a walking map. Lucky visiting dogs and horses get a biscuit or carrot.

🍴 Great care goes into the food here, with breads, ice-creams, parsnip crisps and so forth all made in house. Bar food takes in chicken liver parfait, beetroot cured salmon, ploughman's, sausage and mash with cavolo nero, toad in the hole, confit duck leg with goose fat beans, and steak and kidney pudding. In the evening there might be fried squid with guacamole, tempura soft shell crab, roast butternut ravioli, and beef cheeks braised in red wine; Sunday roast. *Benchmark main dish: sausages and mash £9.50. Two-course evening meal £16.40.*

Free house ~ Licensees David Alders and Sandra Proni ~ Real ale ~ Bar food (12.30-2.15, 7-9.15; 12-3 Sun; not Sun evening) ~ Restaurant ~ (01252) 703268 ~ Children welcome ~ Dogs allowed in bar ~ Open 12-3, 5.30-11; 12-11 Sat; 12-10.30 Sun

Recommended by Ian Herdman, Conor McGaughey, Tony and Jill Radnor, Ellie Weld, David London, Richard Williams, Arthur Snell, Hunter and Christine Wright, John Branston, Martin and Karen Wake, Kate Funnell

TUNBRIDGE WELLS Kent   TQ5839   Map C

Sankeys 🍴 ♀
Mount Ephraim (A26 just N of junction with A267); TN4 8AA

Pubby street-level bar, informal downstairs brasserie, real ales and good wines, chatty atmosphere, and super fish dishes

The street level bar at this laid-back Tunbridge Wells institution is light and airy with comfortably worn, informal leather sofas and pews around all sorts of tables on bare wooden boards. The walls are covered with a fine collection of rare enamel signs and antique brewery mirrors as well as old prints, framed cigarette cards and lots of old wine bottles and soda siphons. They keep a couple of beers from Goachers and Westerham Brewery on handpump, fruit beers, american and british craft beers and several wines by the glass from a good list; big flat-screen TV for sports (not football) and piped music. Steps by the entrance take you down to the flagstoned restaurant which enjoys a fine reputation for its fresh fish and has an oyster bar and lobster tank on display. As in the bar, the atmosphere is chatty and informal. Unfussy décor includes big mirrors on rustic stripped-brick walls, pews or chairs around sturdy tables. French windows open on to an inviting suntrap deck with wicker and chrome chairs and wooden tables. More reports please.

¶¶ Very good value pubby food at lunchtime in the upstairs bar includes sandwiches, filo prawns, fish and chips, sausage and mash, pie of the day, greek salad and thai beef salad. Downstairs, the emphasis is on fish: oysters, pickled cockles, fresh anchovies, potted shrimps, local lemon sole, plaice, john dory, black bream, lobster and huge cornish cock crabs. Sunday roasts and summer barbecues. *Benchmark main dish: dressed cornish crab £16.95. Two-course evening meal £22.00.*

Free house ~ Licensee Matthew Sankey ~ Real ale ~ Bar food (12-3, 6-11) ~ Restaurant ~ (01892) 511422 ~ Children welcome in restaurant and till 6pm in bar ~ Dogs allowed in bar ~ Open 12-1am (3am Sat)

Recommended by Bob and Margaret Holder, Conor McGaughey, Laurence Smith, Alan Franck, Gerry and Rosemary Dobson

ULCOMBE Kent   TQ8550   Map C

Pepper Box £

Fairbourne Heath; signposted from A20 in Harrietsham, or follow Ulcombe signpost from A20, then turn left at crossroads with sign to pub, then right at next minor crossroads; ME17 1LP

Friendly country pub with lovely log fire, well liked food, fair choice of drinks, and seats in a pretty garden

This rural pub is very well run by friendly licensees. The homely bar has standing timbers and a few low beams (some hung with hops), copper kettles and pans on window sills and two leather sofas by the splendid inglenook fireplace (nice horsebrasses on the bressumer beam) with its lovely log fire. A side area, more functionally furnished for eating, extends into the opened-up beamed dining room with a range in another inglenook and more horsebrasses. Shepherd Neame Master Brew, Spitfire and a seasonal beer are on handpump, with local apple juice and several wines by the glass; piped music. The two cats are called Murphy and Jim. There's a hop-covered terrace and a garden with shrubs has delightful views of the Weald. The name of the pub refers to the pepperbox pistol – an early type of revolver with numerous barrels; the village church is worth a look and the Greensand Way footpath runs close by.

¶¶ As well as lunchtime sandwiches, filled baguettes and ploughman's, the well liked bar food could include tiger prawns, sautéed lambs liver and chorizo with sherry glaze, chilli, scampi, roast duck breast with honey and chinese spices, slow-roasted pork belly with cider, apples and thyme, beef stroganoff, and walnut and gorgonzola cannelloni with spinach and provençale sauce. *Benchmark main dish: steak and kidney pudding £11.00. Two-course evening meal £19.00.*

Shepherd Neame ~ Tenant Sarah Pemble ~ Real ale ~ Bar food (12-2.15(3 Sun), 6.30-9.30) ~ Restaurant ~ (01622) 842558 ~ Dogs allowed in bar ~ Open 11-3, 6-midnight; 11-11 Sat; 12-5 Sun; closed Sun evening and Sat afternoon in winter

Recommended by Philip and Cheryl Hill, Michael Tack, Nick Lawless, N R White, Alec and Joan Laurence, Malcolm and Barbara Southwell, Kevin Thomas, Nina Randall

---

If a service charge is mentioned prominently on a menu or accommodation terms, you must pay it if service was satisfactory. If service is really bad, you are legally entitled to refuse to pay some or all of the service charge as compensation for not getting the service you might reasonably have expected.

UPPER BASILDON Berkshire   SU5976 Map D

Red Lion

Off A329 NW of Pangbourne; Aldworth Road; RG8 8NG

Laid-back country pub with friendly family atmosphere, inventive food, and a good choice of drinks

Although many customers come to this well run and friendly country pub for the interesting food, this by no means dominates and there is still a relaxed and informal atmosphere and plenty of chatty drinkers (and maybe their dogs, too). There are chapel chairs, a few pews and miscellaneous stripped tables on the bare boards, a green leather chesterfield and armchair, and pale blue-grey paintwork throughout – even on the beams, ceiling and some of the top-stripped tables. Beyond a double-sided woodburning stove, a pitched-ceiling area has much the same furniture on cord carpet, but a big cut-glass chandelier and large mirror give it a slightly more formal dining feel. Brakspears Bitter, Otter Bitter, West Berkshire Good Old Boy and a weekly changing guest on handpump and an extensive wine list; the *Independent* and *Racing Post* are available, occasional piped music and regular live music – usually jazz-related. There are sturdy picnic-sets in the sizeable enclosed garden, where they have summer barbecues and hog roasts.

Enjoyable food, using local produce, includes sandwiches, a tapas plate, pork terrine with piccalilli, home-cooked ham and free-range duck egg, home-made burger with bacon and cheese, mozzarella, mascarpone and parmesan risotto with confit tomatoes and basil oil, thyme and lemon chicken with aioli, and halibut fillet with prawn and caper butter. *Benchmark main dish: cornish seafood pasta £14.50. Two-course evening meal £17.50.*

Enterprise ~ Lease Alison Green ~ Real ale ~ Bar food (12-2.30, 6-9.30; 12-3, 6-9 Sun) ~ Restaurant ~ (01491) 671234 ~ Children welcome ~ Dogs allowed in bar ~ Open 11-3, 5-11; all day weekends

Recommended by Julia and Richard Tredgett, I H G Busby, Gene and Kitty Rankin, Ian Herdman

WEST END Surrey   SU9461 Map D

Inn at West End

Just under 2.5 miles from M3 junction 3; A322 S, on right; GU24 9PW

Clean-cut dining pub, with prompt friendly service; excellent food and wines, and terrace

The licensee at this immaculately run place is passionate about wine. He holds regular tastings and has recently opened a wine shop here. Needless to say, the wine list is fabulous, with around 20 by the glass – sensibly in a good range of sizes – and includes several sherries and dessert wines, with many from Spain and Portugal. Polished to a shine and well organised, the pub is open-plan and café-like, with bare boards, attractive modern prints on canary-yellow walls above a red dado, and a line of dining tables with crisp white linen over pale yellow tablecloths on the left. The bar counter, with Fullers London Pride and a guest such as Exmoor Ale on handpump, and over 25 malts, is straight ahead as you come in, and is quite a focus, with chatting regulars perched on the comfortable bar stools. The area on the right has a pleasant relaxed atmosphere, with blue-cushioned wall benches and dining chairs around solid pale wood tables, broadsheet daily papers, magazines and a row of reference books on the brick chimneybreast above an open fire. This opens into a garden room, which in turn leads to a grape and clematis pergola-covered terrace and very pleasant garden; boules.

Skilfully prepared using carefully sourced ingredients (some of the herbs and vegetables are grown here), they pluck their own game and use organic meat, the not cheap but very good bar food might include smoked pigeon pâté with beetroot relish, crispy mackerel with sorrel and sweet chilli and passion-fruit sauce, chicken caesar salad, sausage and mash, quails' eggs, onion and broccoli tartlet with tomato sauce, guinea fowl in puff pastry with thyme mousseline, sesame crusted bream with honey and soy and pak choi, and well hung steak; they also do lunchtime sandwiches. *Benchmark main dish: kedgeree £13.95. Two-course evening meal £26.80.*

Enterprise ~ Lease Gerry and Ann Price ~ Real ale ~ Bar food (12-2.30, 6-9.30; 12-3, 6-9 Sun) ~ Restaurant ~ (01276) 858652 ~ Children over 5 welcome if seated and dining ~ Dogs allowed in bar ~ Open 12-3, 5-11; 12-11 Sat; 12-10.30 Sun

Recommended by David M Smith, Edward Mirzoeff, Sheila Topham, Ellie Weld, David London, David and Cathrine Whiting, Ian Phillips, Alan Bowker, Ian Herdman, Rosemary and Mike Fielder, Gerald and Gabrielle Culliford, Sarah May-Miller

 WEST HANNEY Oxfordshire   SU4092 Map D

Plough £

Just off A338 N of Wantage; Church Street; OX12 0LN

Thatched village pub with good choice of drinks, decent food, and plenty of seats outside

Popular locally, this early 16th-c village pub is pretty and neatly thatched. The comfortable simply furnished bar has horsebrasses on beams, some bar stools, wheelback chairs around wooden tables, a log fire in the stone fireplace and lots of photographs of the pub on the walls; there are three pub cats. Loddon Ferryman's Gold, Sharps Doom Bar, Vale Best Bitter and West Berkshire Mr Chubb's Lunchtime Bitter on handpump, several wines by the glass and two farm ciders; separate dining room. There are seats and tables on the back terrace overlooking the walled garden, with plenty of picnic-sets on the grass; aunt sally and a trampoline. Good walks start with a village path right by the pub. More reports please.

Using local farm produce, the bar food includes sandwiches, chicken liver pâté, aberdeen angus burgers with cheese and bacon, toad in the hole, vegetable risotto, and specials like crab claws and battered cod. *Benchmark main dish: lamb Hanney £13.95. Two-course evening meal £14.50.*

Free house ~ Licensee Trevor Cooper ~ Real ale ~ Bar food (12-2, 6-9) ~ Restaurant ~ (01235) 868674 ~ Children welcome ~ Dogs welcome ~ Open 12-3, 6-11; 12-11 (7 Sun) Sat

Recommended by Bob and Angela Brooks

If a pub tries to make you leave a credit card behind the bar, be on your guard. The credit card firms and banks that issue them condemn this practice. After all, the publican who asks you to do this is in effect saying: 'I don't trust you'. Have you any more reason to trust his staff? If your card is used fraudulently while you have let it be kept out of your sight, the card company could say you've been negligent yourself – and refuse to make good your losses. So say that they can 'swipe' your card instead, but must hand it back to you. Please let us know if a pub does try to keep your card.

WEST HOATHLY Sussex   TQ3632   Map C

Cat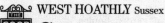

SOUTH EAST PUB OF THE YEAR

Village signposted from A22 and B2028 S of East Grinstead; North Lane; RH19 4PP

Popular 16th-c inn with old-fashioned bar, airy dining rooms, real ales, good food, and seats outside; lovely bedrooms

With hands-on licensees, a genuinely warm welcome for all and highly thought-of food, it's not surprising that so many of our readers like to come back again and again to this bustling 16th-c tile-hung inn. There's a lovely old bar with beams, proper pubby tables and chairs on the old wooden floor, a fine log fire in the inglenook fireplace, Harveys Best and Old and Larkins Traditional Ale on handpump and several wines by the glass; look out for a glass cover over the 75-foot-deep well. The dining rooms are light and airy with a nice mix of wooden dining chairs and tables on the pale wood-strip flooring and throughout there are hops, china platters, brass and copper ornaments and a gently upmarket atmosphere. The contemporary-style garden room has glass doors that open on to a terrace with teak furniture. This is a comfortable and enjoyable place to stay (some of the rooms overlook the church) and the breakfasts are very good. The Bluebell Railway is nearby.

Cooked by one of the landlords, the enjoyable food includes lunchtime sandwiches, vietnamese rare roast beef rolls with coriander and mint salad, smoked chicken and ham hock terrine with celeriac rémoulade, beer-battered fish and chips, root vegetable and parmesan cheese crumble, anchovy-marinated local lamb rump with minted crushed new potatoes, and specials like scallops with soft black pudding and pancetta, and chicken and oyster mushroom suet pudding. *Benchmark main dish: beer-battered fish and chips £12.50. Two-course evening meal £20.00.*

Free house ~ Licensees Ian Huxley and Andrew Russell ~ Real ale ~ Bar food (12-2(2.30 Fri-Sun), 6-9(9.30 Fri and Sat); not Sun evening) ~ (01342) 810369 ~ Children welcome if over 7 ~ Dogs allowed in bar ~ Open 12-3.30, 6-11.30; 12-4 Sun; closed Sun evening ~ Bedrooms: £85B/£100B

Recommended by Peter Meister, Terry Buckland, Nick Lawless, Colin and Louise English, Laurence Evans, Scott Kerr, Chris Bell, Simon and Mandy King

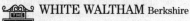

WHITE WALTHAM Berkshire   SU8477   Map D

Beehive

Waltham Road (B3024 W of Maidenhead); SL6 3SH

Enjoyable bar food and welcoming staff at a traditional village pub

This is the sort of pub that once discovered, you tend to come back to again and again. It's a well run country local opposite the village cricket field and you can be sure of a warm welcome from the landlord and his staff. To the right, several comfortably spacious areas have leather chairs around sturdy tables and there's an airy conservatory. The neat bar to the left is brightened up by cheerful scatter cushions on its comfortable built-in wall seats and captain's chairs. Brakspears Bitter, Fullers London Pride, Greene King Abbot and a changing guest from Loddon on handpump, with a good choice of soft drinks; piped music, board games and a quiz evening on the last Thursday of the month. Picnic-sets and teak seats out in front on the terrace take in the pub's rather fine topiary, and there are more seats on a good-sized sheltered back lawn; disabled access and facilities.

Reliably good food includes sandwiches, scallops and shrimps with chorizo, home-baked ham and egg, battered fresh cod, a pie of the day, home-made burgers with cheese, pork tenderloin on puy lentils and red cabbage, and calves liver and bacon with champ and red wine jus. *Benchmark main dish: smoked haddock with spinach and poached egg £12.95. Two-course evening meal £19.90.*

Enterprise ~ Lease Guy Martin ~ Real ale ~ Bar food (12-2.30, 5-9.30; 12-9.30(8.30 Sun) Sat) ~ Restaurant ~ (01628) 822877 ~ Well behaved children welcome ~ Dogs allowed in bar ~ Quiz night last Thurs of month ~ Open 10.30-3, 5-11; 10.30am-midnight Sat; 12-10.30 Sun

Recommended by June and Robin Savage, A Hawkes, J D Franklin, Richard and Liz Thorne, Dr and Mrs A K Clarke, John Pritchard, Roy Hoing

WHITSTABLE Kent  TR1066 Map C

Pearsons Arms

Seawall off Oxford Street, after road splits into one-way system; public parking on left as road divides; CT5 1BT

Seaside pub with an emphasis on interesting food, but serves several ales and has a good mix of customers

Overlooking the pebble beach and with a good mix of both locals and visitors, this weatherboarded pub is doing particularly well under its new landlord. The two front bars are divided by a central chimney and have cushioned settles, captain's chairs and leather armchairs on the stripped-wood floor, driftwood walls and big modern flower arrangements on the bar counter where they serve Ramsgate Gadds No 5, St Austell Tribute, Sharps Doom Bar and Timothy Taylors Landlord on handpump; piped music. A cosy lower room has trompe l'oeil bookshelves and a couple of big chesterfields and dining chairs around plain tables on the stone floor. Up a couple of flights of stairs, the restaurant has sea views, mushroom paintwork, contemporary wallpaper, more driftwood, and church chairs and pine tables on nice wide floorboards.

Quite a choice of interesting food using locally sourced produce might include ham hock ballottine with piccalilli and toasted sour dough, diver-caught scallops with ginger cream sauce, wild boar and apple sausages with caramelised onion gravy, beer-battered cod, steak in ale pie, and slow-roasted pork belly with black pudding and grain mustard sauce. *Benchmark main dish: fish and chips £14.50. Two-course evening meal £21.45.*

Free house ~ Licensee Richard Phillips ~ Real ale ~ Bar food (12-3.30, 6.30-10; not Mon) ~ Restaurant ~ (01227) 272005 ~ Children welcome ~ Dogs welcome ~ Open 12-midnight

Recommended by Mary McSweeney, Richard Mason

WINCHESTER Hampshire 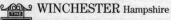 SU4829 Map D

Wykeham Arms ♀

Kingsgate Street (Kingsgate Arch and College Street are now closed to traffic; there is access via Canon Street); SO23 9PE

Tucked-away pub with lots to look at, several real ales and lots of wines by the glass; no children inside

The series of bustling rooms in this tucked-away old pub have all sorts of interesting collections dotted about and three log fires. Also,19th-c oak desks retired from nearby Winchester College, a redundant pew from the same source, kitchen chairs and candlelit deal tables and big windows with swagged curtains. A snug room at the back, known as the Jameson Room (after the late landlord Graeme Jameson), is decorated with a set of Ronald Searle 'Winespeak' prints and a second one is panelled. Fullers London Pride, Seafarers and Gales HSB and a couple of guest beers like Flowerpots Goodens Gold and Perridge Pale on handpump, lots of wines by the glass and several malt whiskies. There are tables on a covered back terrace with more on a small courtyard.

Good, if not cheap, the food includes sandwiches, corn-fed chicken and foie gras terrine with spiced pear purée, crab cake with a caper, tomato, red onion and lemon salsa, mushroom risotto with a poached egg and parmesan, roast lamb rump with sweetbreads and trompette mushrooms, and pork tenderloin with black pudding hash and grain mustard jus. *Benchmark main dish: beer-battered haddock £12.50. Two-course evening meal £20.50.*

Fullers ~ Manager Jon Howard ~ Real ale ~ Bar food (12-3, 6-9.30) ~ Restaurant ~ (01962) 853834 ~ Children over 10 allowed in restaurant, younger children at landlord's discretion ~ Dogs allowed in bar and bedrooms ~ Open 11-11(10.30 Sun) ~ Bedrooms: £72S/£135S(£145B)

Recommended by Mrs C Roe, David Bangert, Martin and Karen Wake, Chris Glasson, the Didler, Franzi Florack, Ann and Colin Hunt

 WINEHAM Sussex   TQ2320   Map C

Royal Oak
Village signposted from A272 and B2116; BN5 9AY

Splendidly old-fashioned local with interesting bric-a-brac in simple rooms, attentive staff, real ales, and well liked food

This is an unspoilt, traditional local and popular with both regulars (and their dogs) and visitors. As well as a blazing log fire in an enormous inglenook fireplace with its cast-iron Royal Oak fireback, there's a collection of cigarette boxes, a stuffed stoat and crocodile and some jugs and ancient corkscrews on the very low beams above the serving counter. Other bits of bric-a-brac too, views of quiet countryside from the back parlour and a bearded collie called Bella. Harveys Best and a couple of guests such as Dark Star Hophead and Old Chestnut tapped from the cask in a still room and quite a few wines by the glass. There are some picnic-sets outside.

Good, seasonally changing food includes good value sandwiches, soup, soft herring roes on toast, asparagus, peas and broad bean risotto, breaded veal escalope with lemon and rocket, cottage pie, local sausages with cider and onion gravy, and rump of lamb with wild mushrooms and red wine jus. *Benchmark main dish: home-made pie £10.00. Two-course evening meal £18.00.*

Punch ~ Managers Sharon and Michael Bailey ~ Real ale ~ Bar food (12-2.30, 7-9; not Sun evening) ~ (01444) 881252 ~ Children welcome away from bar area ~ Dogs welcome ~ Open 11-3(4 Sat), 5.30(6 Sat)-11; 12-4, 7-10.30 Sun; closed evenings 25 and 26 Dec and 1 Jan

Recommended by David and Pam Wilcox, Conor McGaughey, the Didler, Terry Buckland, John Redfern, N R White, Kevin and Maggie Balchin

WINTERBOURNE Berkshire   SU4572 Map D

Winterbourne Arms ♀

3.7 miles from M4 junction 13; at A34 turn into Chieveley Services and follow Donnington signs to Arlington Lane, then follow Winterbourne signs; RG20 8BB

Bustling village pub with quite a choice of bar food, real ales, lots of wines by the glass, and a large landscaped garden

Handy for the M4, this is a pretty black and white village pub. The traditionally furnished bars have stools along the counter, a mix of pine dining chairs and tables, a collection of old irons around the big fireplace and early prints and old photographs of the village on the pale washed or exposed stone walls; piped music. Big windows take in peaceful views over rolling fields. Ramsbury Gold and a beer brewed by them for the pub called Winterbourne Whistle Wetter on handpump and 20 wines by the glass including sparkling and sweet wines. There are seats outside in the large landscaped side garden and pretty flowering tubs and hanging baskets. The surrounding countryside here is lovely, with nearby walks to Snelsmore Common and Donnington Castle.

As well as sandwiches, the varied bar food includes filled baguettes, duckling rillettes with red onion marmalade, a pie of the week, deep-fried fish and chips, mixed mushroom risotto, free-range pork chop on bubble and squeak with a grain mustard sauce, and calves liver and bacon with onion gravy. *Benchmark main dish: sirloin steak £17.95. Two-course evening meal £21.90.*

Free house ~ Licensee Frank Adams ~ Real ale ~ Bar food (12-2.30, 6-10; 12-3, 6-9 Sun) ~ Restaurant ~ (01635) 248200 ~ Children welcome ~ Dogs allowed in bar ~ Open 12-3, 6-11; 12-10.30 Sun

Recommended by Tracey and Stephen Groves, Angela Crum Ewing, Adele Summers, Alan Black, Phyl and Jack Street, Peter Meister, Rob and Catherine Dunster, Dr and Mrs A K Clarke, George and Maureen Roby, N R White, George Atkinson, Mike and Mary Carter, John Pritchard, Pat and Roger Davies

WOOBURN COMMON Buckinghamshire   SU9187 Map D

Chequers

From A4094 N of Maidenhead at junction with A4155 Marlow road keep on A4094 for another 0.75 miles, then at roundabout turn off right towards Wooburn Common and into Kiln Lane; if you find yourself in Honey Hill, Hedsor, turn left into Kiln Lane at the top of the hill; OS Sheet 175 map reference 910870; HP10 0JQ

Busy and friendly hotel with a bustling bar and smart restaurant; comfortable bedrooms

Although this is a bustling hotel, its heart is still in the friendly main bar which continues to thrive as a welcoming local. It feels nicely pubby with low beams, standing timbers and alcoves, characterful rickety furniture and comfortably lived-in sofas on bare boards, a bright log-effect gas fire, pictures, plates, a two-man saw and tankards. In contrast, the bar to the left, with its dark brown leather sofas at low tables on wooden floors, feels plain and modern. They have a good sizeable wine list (with a dozen by the glass), a fair range of malt whiskies and brandies and Greene King IPA and Old Speckled Hen and Rebellion Smuggler on handpump; piped music. The spacious garden, set away from the road, has seats around cast-iron tables and summer barbecues.

As well as sandwiches, the wide choice of popular food might include chicken liver parfait with onion marmalade, salmon, haddock and prawn fishcakes, home-made burger, mushroom risotto, cumberland sausages, corn-fed chicken with stewed tomato, polenta, olives and basil pesto, and navarin of lamb with saffron potatoes and buttered baby vegetables. *Benchmark main dish: fish and chips £10.95. Two-course evening meal £25.00.*

Free house ~ Licensee Peter Roehrig ~ Real ale ~ Bar food (12-2.30, 6-9.30(10 Fri); 12-10(9.30 Sun) Sat) ~ Restaurant ~ (01628) 529575 ~ Children welcome ~ Open 11am-midnight ~ Bedrooms: £99.50B/£107.50B

Recommended by Simon Collett-Jones, Peter and Giff Bennett, D and M T Ayres-Regan

WOODSTOCK Oxfordshire   SP4416 Map E

Kings Arms £ 🛏

Market Street/Park Lane (A44); OX20 1SU

Stylish hotel in centre of attractive town, well liked food, enjoyable atmosphere, and a wide choice of drinks; comfortable bedrooms

Quieter at lunchtime but lively in the evening, the simple and unfussy bar in this stylish town-centre hotel has quite a mix of customers creating a relaxed and informal atmosphere. There are brown leather furnishings on the stripped-wood floor, smart blinds and black and white photographs throughout and at the front, an old wooden settle and interesting little woodburner. In the room leading to the brasserie-style dining room, there's an unusual stained-glass structure used for newspapers and magazines; the restaurant is attractive, with its hanging lights and fine old fireplace. Brakspears Bitter and Oxford Gold on handpump, good coffees, 14 wines plus champagne by the glass and 20 malt whiskies; piped music. Comfortable bedrooms and good breakfasts (available from 7.30-midday for non-residents, too). There are seats and tables on the street outside.

 Fair value lunchtime bar food includes sandwiches, honey and mustard baked ham and free-range eggs, leek, pea and cheese tart and organic beefburger with blue cheese and bacon, with more pricey evening choices like guinea fowl terrine with red onion marmalade, free-range chicken breast with mushroom mousse, braised leeks and tarragon butter sauce, and bass fillet with fennel and spinach and a crab and tomato cream sauce. *Benchmark main dish: pork belly with celeriac purée, caramelised apple and cider sauce £15.50. Two-course evening meal £22.00.*

Free house ~ Licensees David and Sara Sykes ~ Real ale ~ Bar food (12-2.30(3 Sat), 6.30-9(9.30 Sat); all day Sun) ~ Restaurant ~ (01993) 813636 ~ Children welcome in bar and restaurant but no under-12s in bedrooms ~ Open 11-11 ~ Bedrooms: £75S/£140S(£150B)

Recommended by Derek and Sylvia Stephenson, Michael Dandy, Rob and Catherine Dunster, Dave and Jenny Hughes, Martin and Pauline Jennings, John and Sharon Hancock, Pippa Manley, Paul and Mary Walmsley, David and Judy Robison, Graham Oddey

---

Bedroom prices normally include full english breakfast, VAT and any inclusive service charge that we know of. Prices before the '/' are for single rooms, after the '/' for two people in a double or twin (B includes a private bath, S a private shower). If there is no '/', the prices are only for twin or double rooms (as far as we know there are no singles). If there is no B or S, as far as we know no rooms have private facilities.

ALSO WORTH A VISIT IN LONDON

Besides the region's top pubs, we recommend the following. Do tell us
what you think of them: **feedback@goodguides.com**

CENTRAL LONDON

EC1

☆ **Bishops Finger** EC1A 9JR
West Smithfield

Smartly civilised little pub close to Smithfield Market, friendly welcoming atmosphere,
well laid-out bar with cushioned chairs on polished boards, framed market prints on
cream walls, big windows, fresh flowers, Shepherd Neame and seasonal ales, a fine range
of sausages (other dishes too), efficient service, upstairs restaurant; children welcome,
seats outside, closed weekends and bank holidays, otherwise open all day. *Recommended by
Mayur Shah, Ian Phillips, Michael Dandy, Peter Dandy, Colin and Louise English, Derek Thomas*

Butchers Hook & Cleaver EC1A 9DY
West Smithfield

Fullers bank conversion with their full range kept well, all-day pubby food including good
choice of pies, breakfast from 7.30am, friendly helpful staff, daily papers, relaxed
atmosphere, nice mix of chairs including some button-back leather armchairs, wrought-
iron spiral stairs to pleasant mezzanine; piped music, big-screen sports TV; open all day,
closed weekends. *Recommended by DC, Peter Dandy, Michael Dandy, Colin and Louise English*

☆ **Eagle** EC1R 3AL
Farringdon Road

Original gastropub and still popular – you must arrive early as dishes run out or change
quickly; open-plan room dominated by a giant range and all too busy, noisy and scruffy for
some, basic well worn school chairs, assortment of tables, a couple of sofas on bare
boards, modern art (gallery upstairs too), Wells & Youngs, good wines by the glass, decent
coffee; piped music sometimes loud, not ideal for a quiet dinner (weekends quieter);
children and dogs welcome, closed Sun evening, bank holidays and for a week at
Christmas, otherwise open all day. *Recommended by Dr and Mrs A K Clarke*

Gunmakers EC1R 5ET
Eyre Street Hill

Two-room Victorian pub with four well kept changing ales, friendly knowledgeable staff,
enjoyable traditional food with a few twists; dogs welcome, open all day weekdays, closed
weekends. *Recommended by Barbarrick, John and Gloria Isaacs*

☆ **Jerusalem Tavern** EC1M 5UQ
Britton Street

Convincing and atmospheric re-creation of a dark 18th-c tavern (1720 merchant's house
with shopfront added 1810), tiny dimly lit bar, simple wood furnishings on bare boards,
some remarkable old wall tiles, coal fires and candlelight, stairs to a precarious-feeling
(though perfectly secure) balcony, plainer back room, full range of St Peters beers tapped
from casks, good lunchtime food, friendly attentive young staff; can get very crowded at
peak times, no children; dogs welcome, seats out on pavement, open all day during the
week, closed weekends, bank holidays, 24 Dec-2 Jan. *Recommended by Dominic McGonigal,
Mayur Shah, Peter Dandy, Anthony Longden, Giles and Annie Francis, the Didler and others*

Peasant EC1V 4PH
St John Street

Good imaginative food in strikingly furnished upstairs restaurant with a more traditional
menu in welcoming downstairs bar, well kept ales and some reminders of its days as a
more traditional corner house including a tiled picture of St George and the Dragon,
mosaic floor and open fire. *Recommended by Andrew Bosi*

Viaduct
EC1A 7AA
Newgate Street

Opposite Old Bailey on site of Newgate Prison (a couple of cells surviving below), big copper lanterns outside, fine ornate high-ceilinged Victorian interior, three or four snug areas, Fullers ales from horseshoe bar, food from sandwiches up, friendly service; popular with after-work drinkers; open all day, closed Sun. *Recommended by N R White*

EC2

☆ Dirty Dicks
EC2M 4NR
Bishopsgate

Busy re-creation of traditional City tavern, fun for foreign visitors, booths, barrel tables, low beams, interesting old prints, Wells & Youngs ales, enjoyable well priced food from sandwiches up, pleasant service, calmer cellar wine bar with wine racks overhead in brick barrel-vaulted ceiling, further upstairs area too; piped music, games machines and TV; closed weekends. *Recommended by the Didler, Michael Dandy*

☆ Hamilton Hall
EC2M 7PY
Bishopsgate; also entrance from Liverpool Street Station

Showpiece Wetherspoons with flamboyant Victorian baroque décor, plaster nudes and fruit mouldings, chandeliers, mirrors, good-sized comfortable mezzanine, reliable food all day, lots of real ales including interesting guests, decent wines and coffee, good prices; silenced machines, can get very crowded after work; good disabled access, tables outside, open all day. *Recommended by Ian Phillips, Jeremy King*

Lord Aberconway
EC2M 1QT
Old Broad Street

Victorian feel with dark panelling and furniture, real ales such as Fullers, Sharps, Timothy Taylors and Woodlands Midnight Stout, reasonably priced food from sandwiches up, wrought-iron railed upper dining gallery; handy for Liverpool Street Station. *Recommended by Michael Dandy, Ian Phillips*

Railway Tavern
EC2M 7NX
Liverpool Street

Light and airy, with high ceilings and vast front windows, Greene King ales and several wines by the glass from a long bar, fairly priced pubby food from sandwiches up including sharing boards, second room upstairs; TVs and machines; pavement tables. *Recommended by Jeremy King, Michael Dandy*

EC3

Chamberlain
EC3N 1NU
Minories

Comfortable high-ceilinged bar in substantial hotel, Fullers ales, sensibly priced bar food from sandwiches up, helpful prompt service, smart back restaurant; handy for the Tower of London, 64 bedrooms. *Recommended by Richard Tilbrook*

East India Arms
EC3M 4BR
Fenchurch Street

Standing-room Victorian pub refurbished by Shepherd Neame, their ales kept well, good service, old local photographs and brewery mirrors, hops; unobtrusive TV; closed weekends. *Recommended by Barbarrick*

Simpsons Tavern
EC3V 9DR
Just off Cornhill

Pleasingly old-fashioned place founded in 1757, rather clubby small panelled bar serving Bass, Harveys and a couple of guests, stairs down to another bar with snacks, traditional chophouse with upright stall seating (expect to share a table) and similar upstairs restaurant, good value food such as braised oxtail stew, steak and kidney pie and lancashire hotpot; open weekday lunchtimes and from 8am Tues-Fri for breakfast. *Recommended by Barbarrick*

Walrus & Carpenter
Monument Street/Lovat Lane   EC3R 8BU

Nicholsons pub with good choice of well kept changing ales, food from sandwiches and pub favourites up; open all day weekdays, closed Sat evening, Sun. *Recommended by anon*

EC4

☆ Black Friar
Queen Victoria Street   EC4V 4EG

An architectural gem (some of the best Edwardian bronze and marble art nouveau work to be found anywhere) and built on the site of a 13th-c Dominican Priory; inner back room (the Grotto) with low vaulted mosaic ceiling, big bas-relief friezes of jolly monks set into richly coloured florentine marble walls, gleaming mirrors, seats built into golden marble recesses, and an opulent pillared inglenook, tongue-in-cheek verbal embellishments such as Silence is Golden and Finery is Foolish, and try to spot the opium-smoking hints modelled into the front room's fireplace, Fullers, Sharps and Timothy Taylors, plenty of wines by the glass, traditional food (all day) including speciality pies, friendly efficient service despite crowds; children welcome if quiet, smart furniture and plenty of standing room on wide forecourt. *Recommended by Dr and Mrs A K Clarke, Dave Braisted, N R White, Barry Collett, the Didler and others*

Old Bell
Fleet Street, near Ludgate Circus   EC4Y 1DH

Dimly lit 17th-c tavern backing on to St Bride's, heavy black beams, flagstones, stained-glass bow window, brass-topped tables, good changing choice of ales from island servery (can try before you buy), friendly efficient young staff, usual food, coal fire, cheerful atmosphere; piped music; covered heated outside area. *Recommended by N R White, the Didler*

☆ Olde Cheshire Cheese
Wine Office Court, off 145 Fleet Street   EC4A 2BU

Best to visit this 17th-c former chophouse outside peak times (early evening especially) when packed and staff can struggle; soaked in history with warmly old-fashioned unpretentious rooms, high beams, bare boards, old built-in black benches, Victorian paintings on dark brown walls, big open fires, tiny snug and steep stone steps down to unexpected series of cosy areas and secluded alcoves, Sam Smiths, all-day pubby food; look out for the famous parrot (now stuffed) who entertained princes and other distinguished guests for over 40 years; children allowed in eating area lunchtime only, closed Sun evening. *Recommended by N R White, John Wooll, Jeremy King, Peter Dandy and others*

SE1

Rake
Winchester Walk   SE1 9AG

Tiny, discreetly modern bar with amazing bottled beer range in wall-wide cooler as well as half a dozen continental lagers on tap and perhaps a couple of rare real ales, good friendly service; fair-sized terrace with decking and heated marquee. *Recommended by Mike and Sue Loseby, Andrew Hobbs, the Didler*

SW1

☆ Buckingham Arms
Petty France   SW1H 9EU

Welcoming and relaxed bow-windowed 18th-c local, good value pubby food from back open kitchen, Wells & Youngs ales and guests from long curved bar, good wines by the glass, elegant mirrors and woodwork, unusual side corridor fitted out with elbow ledge for drinkers; TVs; dogs welcome, handy for Buckingham Palace, Westminster Abbey and St James's Park, open all day, till 6pm weekends. *Recommended by the Didler, N R White*

Cask
SW1V 2EE
Charlwood Street/Tachbrook Street

Modern and spacious with simple comfortable furnishings, Dark Star and great choice of other ales from far and wide, continental beers, decent wine range too, enjoyable generous food served by friendly helpful staff, chatty atmosphere – can get packed in evenings. *Recommended by N R White, David Sizer*

Clarence
SW1A 2HP
Whitehall

Civilised olde-worlde beamed corner pub now taken over by Geronimo (Youngs), well spaced tables and varied seating including tub chairs and banquettes, decent wines by the glass, friendly chatty landlord, popular food all day from snacks up, upstairs dining area; pavement tables. *Recommended by Ian Phillips*

☆ Grenadier
SW1X 7NR
Wilton Row; the turning off Wilton Crescent looks prohibitive, but the barrier and watchman are there to keep out cars

Steps up to cosy old mews pub with lots of character and military history, but not much space (avoid 5-7pm); simple unfussy bar, stools and wooden benches, changing ales such as Fullers, Hook Norton, Timothy Taylors and Wells & Youngs from rare pewter-topped counter, famous bloody marys, may be bar food, intimate back restaurant (best to book), no mobiles or photography; children (over 8) and dogs allowed, sentry box and single table outside, open all day. *Recommended by Lawrence R Cotter, Mike and Sue Loseby, N R White, LM*

Jugged Hare
SW1V 1DX
Vauxhall Bridge Road/Rochester Row

Popular Fullers Ale & Pie pub in former colonnaded bank, pillars, dark wood, balustraded balcony, large chandelier, busts and old London photographs, back dining room, reasonably priced food from sandwiches up including pie range, good friendly service; piped music, TVs, silent fruit machine; open all day. *Recommended by N R White, the Didler, Peter Roberts, Roger and Donna Huggins, Jeremy King*

☆ Loose Box
SW1P 2AA
Horseferry Road

Modern bar-cum-restaurant named after horse-drawn ferry that crossed the Thames, dark tables and chairs on wood flooring, fresh flowers and large plants, relaxed area with comfortable squashy sofas, lots of cartoons on the walls, enjoyable food from breakfast through coffee and pastries to good contemporary dishes, real ales and decent wines by the glass, friendly helpful staff, buzzy atmosphere; TV, seats on front terrace by pavement, open all day. *Recommended by Colin McKerrow*

☆ Lord Moon of the Mall
SW1A 2DY
Whitehall

Wetherspoons bank conversion with elegant main room, big arched windows looking over Whitehall, old prints and a large painting of Tim Martin (founder of the chain), through an arch the style is more recognisably Wetherspoons with neatly tiled areas, bookshelves opposite long bar, up to nine real ales and their good value food; silenced fruit machines, cash machine; children allowed if eating, dogs welcome, open all day from 9am (till midnight Fri, Sat). *Recommended by Ian Phillips, Katrin Schmidt, Jeremy King, Andy Lickfold, Michael Dandy*

☆ Morpeth Arms
SW1P 4RW
Millbank

Sparkling clean Victorian pub facing Thames, roomy and comfortable, some etched and cut glass, old books and prints, photographs, earthenware jars and bottles, well kept Wells & Youngs and a guest, decent choice of wines and of enjoyable good value food (all day), welcoming service even at busy lunchtimes, upstairs room with fine view across river; games machine, may be unobtrusive sports TV (there's also a monitor to check for cellar

ghosts), young evening crowd; seats outside (a lot of traffic), handy for Tate Britain and
Thames Path walkers, open all day. *Recommended by Ros Lawler, N R White, the Didler,
Robert Pattison, Pete Coxon*

Orange
Pimlico Road

SW1W 8NE

Refurbished gastropub with good choice of enjoyable food including wood-fired pizzas,
friendly attentive staff, real ales such as Adnams, linked light and airy rooms with rustic
furniture and relaxed weathered feel; children welcome, four bedrooms, open all day from
8am. *Recommended by Miss Jennifer Harvey, Mr Stuart Brown, Richard Tilbrook*

Red Lion
Parliament Street

SW1A 2NH

Congenial pub by Houses of Parliament, used by Foreign Office staff and MPs, soft
lighting, parliamentary cartoons and prints, Fullers/Gales beers and decent wines from
long bar, good range of food, efficient staff, also cellar bar and small narrow upstairs
dining room, outside seating. *Recommended by Michael Dandy, David Pulford*

☆ Red Lion
Duke of York Street

SW1Y 6JP

Pretty little Victorian pub, remarkably preserved and packed with customers often
spilling out on to pavement by mass of foliage and flowers; series of small rooms with lots
of polished mahogany, a gleaming profusion of mirrors, cut and etched windows and
chandeliers, striking ornamental plaster ceiling, Fullers/Gales beers, simple bar food
(all day weekdays, snacks in evening, diners have priority over a few of the front tables);
no children; dogs welcome, open all day, closed Sun and bank holidays. *Recommended by
N R White, Val and Alan Green, Michael Dandy, Andrea Rampley, the Didler and others*

Speaker
Great Peter Street

SW1P 2HA

Pleasant chatty atmosphere in unpretentious smallish corner pub, well kept Shepherd
Neame Spitfire, Wells & Youngs and quickly changing guests, lots of whiskies, limited
simple food including good sandwiches, friendly helpful staff, panelling, political cartoons
and prints, no mobiles or piped music; open all day, closed Sat, Sun evening.
Recommended by N R White

☆ Star
Belgrave Mews West, behind the German Embassy, off Belgrave Square

SW1X 8HT

Bustling recently smartened up local with astonishing array of summer hanging baskets
and flowering tubs, restful bar, main seating area with polished tables and chairs, Fullers
ales, upstairs dining room (no food weekends), good service; children and dogs welcome,
the Great Train Robbery is said to have been planned here, open all day. *Recommended by
Mike Tucker, Tracey and Stephen Groves, N R White, Lawrence R Cotter, the Didler and others*

Thomas Cubitt
Elizabeth Street

SW1W 9PA

Popular tastefully refurbished dining pub with floor-to-ceiling french doors opening to
street, oak floors, panelling and open fires, enjoyable food in bar or upstairs dining room,
decent wines, good mix of customers. *Recommended by Derek Thomas, Peter Loader*

White Swan
Vauxhall Bridge Road

SW1V 2SA

Roomy corner pub handy for Tate Britain, lots of dark dining tables on three levels in long
room, good value pubby food from sandwiches up, ales such as Adnams Broadside and
Timothy Taylors Landlord, decent wines by the glass, quick helpful uniformed staff; piped
music; open all day. *Recommended by John Wooll*

SW3

Builders Arms
SW3 3TY

Britten Street

Trendy place, relaxed, comfortable and chatty, with good food, ales such as St Austell Tribute from long counter, good choice of wines; pavement tables under awnings, attractive street. *Recommended by anon*

☆ Coopers Arms
SW3 5TB

Flood Street

Newly refurbished and useful bolthole for King's Road shoppers, dark-walled open-plan bar with mix of good-sized tables on floorboards, pre-war sideboard and dresser, railway clock, moose head, Wells & Youngs ales, decent all-day bar food; well behaved children till 7pm, dogs in bar, seats in courtyard garden. *Recommended by anon*

☆ Cross Keys
SW3 5NB

Lawrence Street

Bustling civilised 18th-c pub with roomy high-ceilinged bar, sofas around low tables, settles and dining chairs on flagstones, two open fires, light and airy conservatory-style back restaurant with fully retractable roof, interesting modern bar food, Courage, Sharps and a guest, quite a choice of wines by the glass, attentive young staff; piped music; children welcome, dogs in bar, open all day till midnight, closed bank holidays. *Recommended by LM*

Hour Glass
SW3 2DY

Brompton Road

Small welcoming pub handy for the V&A and other nearby museums, well kept Fullers London Pride and a guest, good value pubby food (not Sun evening); sports TV; pavement benches. *Recommended by LM*

W1

☆ Argyll Arms
W1F 7TP

Argyll Street

Popular and unexpectedly individual pub, three interesting little front cubicle rooms (essentially unchanged since 1860s) with wooden partitions and impressive frosted and engraved glass, mirrored corridor to spacious back room, well liked bar food (all day), Fullers, Greene King, Timothy Taylors and up to four guests, quieter upstairs bar (children welcome here) overlooking pedestrianised street, theatrical photographs, newspapers; piped music, machines; open all day (till midnight Fri, Sat). *Recommended by Peter Dandy, Ian Phillips, Michael Dandy, Barry Collett, Mike and Sue Loseby, Joe Green and others*

☆ Audley
W1K 2RX

Mount Street

Classic late-Victorian Mayfair pub, opulent red plush, mahogany panelling and engraved glass, chandelier and clock hanging in lovely carved wood bracket from ornately corniced ceiling, Fullers London Pride, Greene King IPA, Wells & Youngs Bombardier and guests from long polished bar, good choice of all-day pub food (reasonably priced for the area), friendly efficient service, upstairs panelled dining room; quiet piped music, TV, pool; children till 6pm, pavement tables. *Recommended by Nigel and Jean Eames*

☆ Dog & Duck
W1D 3AJ

Bateman Street/Frith Street

Tiny Soho pub squeezing in bags of character, unusual old tiles and mosaics (the dog with tongue hanging out in hot pursuit of a duck is notable), heavy old advertising mirrors, open fire, cosy upstairs bar/restaurant, four well kept ales including Fullers from unusual little counter, several wines by the glass, food all day, friendly staff, very busy evenings when people spill on to street; piped music; children allowed in dining room, dogs in bar. *Recommended by Richard Endacott, Jeremy King, LM, Lawrence R Cotter, Mike Gorton, Simon Collett-Jones and others*

☆ Grapes

Shepherd Market

W1J 7QQ

Genuinely old-fashioned pub with dimly lit bar, plenty of well worn plush red furnishings, stuffed birds and fish in display cases, wood floors, panelling, coal fire and snug back alcove, Fullers, Sharps and up to four guests, huge choice of thai food (not Sun evening) cooked by thai chefs, lots of customers (especially early evening) often spilling out on to square; children till 6pm weekdays (anytime weekends), open all day. *Recommended by Tracey and Stephen Groves, Ian Phillips, N R White, Lawrence R Cotter, the Didler, Mike Gorton and others*

☆ Guinea

Bruton Place

W1J 6NL

Lovely hanging baskets and chatty customers outside this tiny 17th-c mews pub, standing room only at peak times, appealingly simple with a few cushioned wooden seats and tables tucked to left of entrance, more in snug back area (most people prop themselves against the little side shelf), bare boards, old-fashioned prints, red planked ceiling with raj fans, famous steak and kidney pie, some sandwiches (no food weekends), Wells & Youngs and seasonal brews from striking counter; very easy to walk into the smart Guinea Grill (uniformed doormen will politely redirect you); no children; closed Sat lunchtime, Sun and bank holidays. *Recommended by Michael Dandy, the Didler*

Newman Arms

Rathbone Street/Newman Passage

W1T 1NG

18th-c pub in the same family for three generations, small panelled bar with particularly well kept Fullers London Pride and guests, traditionally redecorated upstairs dining room serving range of home-made pies and suet puddings, pictures and prints reflecting pub's association with George Orwell and director Michael Powell, good friendly staff and old-school character landlord; open all day, closed weekends. *Recommended by Tracey and Stephen Groves*

Running Horse

Corner of Davies Street/Davies Mews

W1K 5JE

Busy 18th-c oak-panelled Mayfair pub, enjoyable food from sandwiches up (highish prices), good service, small fire in tiled fireplace, newspapers, smart upstairs restaurant with linen tablecloths; pavement tables, colourful hanging baskets, open all day, closed Sun. *Recommended by Barry and Anne*

W2

Mad Bishop & Bear

Paddington Station

W2 1HB

Up escalators from concourse, full Fullers range kept well and a guest beer, good wine choice, reasonably priced standard food quickly served including breakfast from 8am (10am Sun), ornate plasterwork, etched mirrors and fancy lamps, parquet, tiles and carpet, booths with leather banquettes, lots of wood and prints, train departures' screen; piped music, TVs, games machine; tables out overlooking concourse, open all day till 11pm (10.30pm Sun). *Recommended by Dr and Mrs A K Clarke, Roger and Donna Huggins, Giles and Annie Francis, Susan and Nigel Wilson, Taff Thomas*

☆ Victoria

Strathearn Place

W2 2NH

Well run pub with lots of Victorian pictures and memorabilia, cast-iron fireplaces, gilded mirrors and mahogany panelling, brass mock-gas lamps above attractive horseshoe bar, bare boards and banquettes, relaxed chatty atmosphere, good friendly service, full Fullers range kept well, good choice of wines by the glass, well priced food counter; upstairs has leather club chairs in small library/snug, and (mostly for private functions now) replica of Gaiety Theatre bar, all gilt and red plush; quiet piped music, TV; pavement picnic-sets, open all day. *Recommended by Ian Herdman, N R White, Dr and Mrs A K Clarke*

WC1

☆ # Cittie of Yorke
High Holborn   WC1V 6BN

Splendid back bar rather like a baronial hall with extraordinarily extended bar counter, 1,000-gallon wine vats resting above gantry, big bulbous lights hanging from soaring raftered roof, intimate ornately carved booths, triangular fireplace with grates on all three sides, smaller comfortable panelled room with lots of little prints of York, cheap Sam Smiths, bar food, lots of students, lawyers and City types but plenty of space to absorb crowds; fruit machine; children welcome, open all day, closed Sun. *Recommended by Ian Phillips, Jeremy King, N R White, Barry Collett, Michael Dandy, Anthony Longden and others*

☆ # Lamb
Lamb's Conduit Street   WC1N 3LZ

Famously unspoilt and unchanging Victorian pub, plenty of character and lots to look at especially the cut-glass swivelling snob-screens, traditional furnishings, sepia photographs of 1890s actresses on ochre panelled walls, snug little back room, up to seven real ales, good choice of whiskies, pubby bar food; children in dining area only till 5pm, seats in small courtyard, Foundling Museum nearby, pub (like street) named after William Lamb who brought fresh water to Holborn in 1577, open all day, till midnight Thurs-Sat. *Recommended by John and Gloria Isaacs, Dr and Mrs A K Clarke, Eddie Edwards, Roy Hoing, the Didler and others*

Mabels
Mabledon Place, just off Euston Road   WC1H 9AZ

Neat open-plan pub on two levels, well kept Shepherd Neame ales, good wine choice, decent reasonably priced pubby food, friendly welcoming staff, bright décor; big-screen TV; pavement tables, open all day. *Recommended by Ross Balaam*

Museum Tavern
Museum Street/Great Russell Street   WC1B 3BA

Traditional high-ceilinged ornate Victorian pub facing British Museum, busy lunchtime and early evening, but can be quite peaceful other times, good choice of well kept beers including some unusual ones, several wines by the glass, good hot drinks, straightforward food from end servery, friendly helpful staff; one or two tables out under gas lamps, open all day. *Recommended by Michael Butler, Pete Coxon, David and Sue Atkinson*

Penderels Oak
High Holborn   WC1V 7HJ

Vast Wetherspoons with attractive décor and woodwork, lots of books, pew seating around central tables, their usual well priced food and huge choice of good value real ales, efficient charming staff; open all day. *Recommended by Tracey and Stephen Groves*

☆ # Princess Louise
High Holborn   WC1V 7EP

Splendid Victorian gin palace with extravagant décor – even the gents' has its own preservation order; gloriously opulent main bar with wood and glass partitions, fine etched and gilt mirrors, brightly coloured and fruity-shaped tiles, slender Portland stone columns soaring towards the lofty and deeply moulded plaster ceiling, open fire, cheap Sam Smiths from long counter, pubby bar food (not Fri-Sun); gets crowded early weekday evenings, no children; open all day. *Recommended by Tim Maddison, Mayur Shah, Ian Phillips, Barry Collett, Eleanor Dandy, Mr and Mrs C F Turner and others*

☆ # Skinners Arms
Judd Street   WC1H 9NT

Richly decorated, with glorious woodwork, marble pillars, high ceilings and ornate windows, lots of London prints, interesting layout including comfortable back seating area, well kept Greene King ales and guests from attractive long bar, efficient staff, bar food; unobtrusive piped music, muted corner TV; pavement picnic-sets, interesting tiled frontage, handy for British Library, open all day, closed Sun. *Recommended by Tracey and Stephen Groves, N R White*

WC2

☆ Chandos
WC2N 4ER
St Martins Lane

Busy bare-boards bar with snug cubicles, lots of theatre memorabilia on stairs up to smarter more comfortable lounge with opera photographs, low wooden tables, panelling, leather sofas, coloured windows; cheap Sam Smiths OBB, prompt cheerful service, bargain food, air conditioning, darts; can get packed early evening, piped music and games machines; note the automaton on the roof (working 10-2 and 4-9); children upstairs till 6pm, open all day from 9am (for breakfast). *Recommended by Ian Phillips, Bruce Bird, Susan and Nigel Wilson, Taff Thomas*

☆ Cross Keys
WC2H 9EB
Endell Street/Betterton Street

Relaxed and friendly, quick service even at busy times, good lunchtime sandwiches and a few bargain hot dishes, Courage Best and Wells & Youngs ales kept well, decent wines by the glass, masses of photographs and posters including Beatles memorabilia, brassware and tasteful bric-a-brac; games machine; gents' downstairs; sheltered picnic-sets out on cobbles, pretty flower tubs, open all day. *Recommended by the Didler, John and Gloria Isaacs*

Edgar Wallace
WC2R 3JE
Essex Street

Simple spacious open-plan pub dating from the 18th c, half a dozen well kept ales including some unusual ones and a beer brewed for them by Nethergate, friendly efficient service, good value all-day food including doorstep sandwiches, half-panelled walls and red ceilings, interesting old London and Edgar Wallace memorabilia (pub renamed 1975 to mark his centenary), friendly chatty atmosphere; a few high tables in side alleyway, open all day, closed weekends. *Recommended by N R White, LM*

George
WC2R 1AP
Strand

Timbered pub near law courts, long narrow bare-boards bar, good choice of changing ales, several wines by the glass including champagne, lunchtime food from open sandwiches and ciabattas to weekday carvery in upstairs bar, separate evening menu, comedy club Fri, Sat nights, open all day. *Recommended by Pete Coxon, Dr Martin Owton*

☆ Lamb & Flag
WC2E 9EB
Rose Street, off Garrick Street

This basic unpretentious tavern is usually packed, spartan front room leading to cosy low-ceilinged bar with open fire and high-backed black settles, half a dozen ales, decent malt whiskies, short choice of simple lunchtime food, friendly efficient service, upstairs Dryden Room often less crowded (children welcome here lunchtime), jazz Sun evening; lots of lively well documented history including Regency bare-knuckle prize-fights when known as the Bucket of Blood, open all day. *Recommended by Roger and Donna Huggins, Anthony Longden, Mike and Sue Loseby, Bruce Bird, the Didler and others*

Lyceum
WC2R 0HS
Strand

Panelling and pleasantly simple furnishings downstairs, several small discreet booths, steps up to a bigger alcove with darts, food in much bigger upstairs panelled lounge with deep button-back leather settees and armchairs, low-priced Sam Smiths beer, civilised atmosphere and efficient service. *Recommended by Mike and Eleanor Anderson, Taff Thomas, Susan and Nigel Wilson*

Marquess of Anglesey
WC2E 7AU
Bow Street/Russell Street

Light and airy, with Wells & Youngs and a guest beer, decent food including interesting specials, friendly staff, a couple of big sofas, more room upstairs. *Recommended by Michael Dandy, Taff Thomas*

☆ Porterhouse
Maiden Lane

WC2E 7NA

Good daytime pub (can be packed in evenings), London outpost of Dublin's Porterhouse microbrewery, their interesting if pricey draught beers including Porter and two Stouts (comprehensive tasting tray), also their TSB real ale and a guest, lots of bottled imports, good choice of wines by the glass, reasonably priced food from soup and open sandwiches up, with some emphasis on rock oysters, shiny three-level labyrinth of stairs (lifts for disabled), galleries and copper ducting and piping, some nice design touches, sonorous openwork clock, neatly cased bottled beer displays; piped music, irish live music, big-screen sports TV (repeated in gents'); tables on front terrace, open all day. *Recommended by Jeremy King, Taff Thomas*

☆ Salisbury
St Martins Lane

WC2N 4AP

Gleaming Victorian pub surviving unchanged in the heart of the West End with enthusiastic landlord, a wealth of cut glass and mahogany, curved upholstered wall seat creating impression of several distinct areas, wonderfully ornate bronze light fittings, lots of mirrors, back room popular with diners and separate small side room, some interesting photographs including Dylan Thomas enjoying a drink here in 1941, lots of theatre posters, up to six well kept ales, hot toddies, summer Pimms, good bar food all day, coffees and helpful staff; children allowed till 5pm, fine details on building exterior, seats in pedestrianised side alley, open till midnight Fri, Sat. *Recommended by Tracey and Stephen Groves, Jeremy King, David and Sue Smith, Roger and Donna Huggins, Mike Gorton, Joe Green and others*

White Lion
James Street

WC2E 8NS

Panelling and bare boards, Fullers London Pride, Timothy Taylors Landlord and guest ales, Nicholsons menu, dining room upstairs; open all day. *Recommended by Michael Dandy*

EAST LONDON

E1

☆ Prospect of Whitby
Wapping Wall

E1W 3SH

Claims to be oldest pub on the Thames dating back to 1520, with a colourful history (Pepys and Dickens used it regularly and Turner came for weeks at a time to study the river views) – tourists love it; L-shaped bar has plenty of beams, bare boards, flagstones and panelling, ales including Fullers, Sharps and Wells & Youngs from 400-year-old pewter counter, good choice of wines by the glass, bar food from sandwiches up, more formal restaurant upstairs; children welcome (only if eating after 5.30pm), unbeatable views towards Docklands from tables on waterfront courtyard, open all day. *Recommended by Bill Adie, Barry and Anne, the Didler, Paul Rampton, Julie Harding and others*

Town of Ramsgate
Wapping High Street

E1W 2PN

Interesting old London Thames-side setting, with restricted but evocative river view from small back floodlit terrace with mock gallows (hanging dock was nearby), long narrow chatty bar with squared oak panelling, ales such as Fullers London Pride and Sharps Doom Bar, friendly helpful service, good choice of generous standard food and daily specials; piped music, Mon quiz; open all day. *Recommended by Bill Adie, N R White*

E3

☆ Crown
Grove Road/Old Ford Road

E3 5SN

Stylish dining pub with relaxed welcoming bar, faux animal hide stools and chunky pine tables on polished boards, big bay window with comfortable scatter-cushion seating area, books and objects on open shelves, well kept Adnams Broadside, Redemption Pale Ale and Sharps Doom Bar, good choice of wines by the glass, friendly chatty young staff, three individually decorated upstairs dining areas overlooking Victoria Park, imaginative food (all day Sun); piped music; children and dogs welcome, open all day. *Recommended by Andy and Claire Barker, Georgina Tacagni*

Eleanor Arms
E3 5JP

Old Ford Road

Traditional two-room Shepherd Neame corner pub, four of their ales kept well, chatty landlord and friendly atmosphere, no food, live jazz Sun, pool and darts in back bar; dogs welcome, open all day. *Recommended by Mick O'Rorke, Tony Hobden*

Palm Tree
E3 5BH

Haverfield Road

Lone survivor of blitzed East End terrace, by Regent's Canal and beside windmill and ecology centre in futuristic-looking Mile End Park; two Edwardian bars around oval servery, a couple of well kept changing ales, lunchtime sandwiches, long serving landlord and good local atmosphere, live music weekends. *Recommended by Tony Hobden*

E11

Birkbeck Tavern
E11 4HL

Langthorne Road

Down-to-earth high-ceilinged two-room local, stained glass and worn-in furnishings, three or four well kept often unusual ales, good value snacks; TV, fruit machine, pool and darts; children allowed in nice garden with plenty of tables. *Recommended by Jeremy King, Andrew Bosi*

E14

 ## Narrow
E14 8DJ

Narrow Street

Popular stylish dining pub with good Thames views from window seats and terrace, simple but smart bar with white walls and dark blue doors, mosaic-tiled fireplaces and colourfully striped armchairs, Adnams, Greene King and a guest, good wines, food from bar snacks to pricier restaurant meals, dining room also white with matching furnishings, local maps and prints, and a boat complete with oars; piped music; children welcome, open all day. *Recommended by John Saville, Andy and Claire Barker, Mike Owen, Ian Phillips*

North Pole
E14 8LG

Manilla Street

Good honest traditional Victorian pub surviving in the high-rise shadow of Canary Wharf, friendly welcome, bargain home-made pub food, well kept Fullers London Pride, Timothy Taylors Landlord and a guest such as Sharps or Wychwood, darts; closed weekends. *Recommended by Barbarrick*

E15

King Edward VII
E15 4BQ

Broadway

Nicely old-fashioned with dark woodwork and etched-glass screens in traditional bar, small lounge area, back dining room with well lit prints above panelled dado, decent food and four changing real ales, daily papers, open fires; piped music, live music Thurs, Sun quiz. *Recommended by Karen Sloan*

Please tell us if the décor, atmosphere, food or drink at a pub is different from our description. We rely on readers' reports to keep us up to date: **feedback@goodguides.com**, or (no stamp needed) The Good Pub Guide, FREEPOST TN1569, Wadhurst, E Sussex TN5 7BR.

NORTH LONDON

N1

Albion
N1 1HW
Thornhill Road

Front bar and spacious dining area, interesting choice of mid-priced home-made food, well kept Black Sheep and Greene King Abbot, prompt cheerful service, Victorian gents'; tables out at front and on back terrace. *Recommended by Nigel and Sue Foster*

Charles Lamb
N1 8DE
Elia Street

Small friendly backstreet pub with well kept Fullers Chiswick, Timothy Taylors Landlord and a guest, some interesting imports on tap or bottled, good choice of wines by the glass, good blackboard food, big windows, polished boards and simple traditional furniture; piped jazz; tables outside. *Recommended by Kevin Booker, Julia Atkins, Jim Slattery*

Compton Arms
N1 2XD
Compton Avenue, off Canonbury Road

Tiny villagey local again under new management, simply furnished unpretentious low-ceilinged rooms, Greene King and guests; sports TV, can be busy Arsenal match days; dogs welcome, tables under big sycamore tree and glass-covered area, open all day.
Recommended by Tim Maddison

Crown
N1 0EB
Cloudesley Road

Good food and bustling atmosphere in Victorian Fullers pub, their ales from impressive island bar with snob-screens, scrubbed boards, plenty of light oak panelling and cut and etched glass, helpful friendly staff; tables out on small railed front terrace. *Recommended by Jim Slattery*

☆ Duke of Cambridge
N1 8JT
St Peters Street

London's first organic pub and a landlady passionate about the environment; organic real ales, lagers, ciders, wines and spirits and interesting bar food using seasonal produce, big busy main room with good mix of customers, chunky wooden tables, pews and benches on bare boards, a couple of big metal vases with colourful flowers, daily papers, corridor past open kitchen to smaller candlelit rooms set for eating, conservatory; children and dogs welcome, open all day. *Recommended by anon*

Fellow
N1 9AA
York Way

Contemporary pub/restaurant, popular and relaxed, with enjoyable unusual food (not cheap and they add a service charge), real ales and good choice of wines, friendly staff coping at busy times, upstairs cocktail bar (DJ nights Thurs, Fri); piped music; roof terrace. *Recommended by Adam Madai, Graham Coult*

Hemingford Arms
N1 1DF
Hemingford Road

Invitingly dark Capital pub filled with bric-a-brac, good choice of real ales from central servery, traditional food alongside good evening thai menu, open fire, upstairs bar, live music and Weds quiz night; sports TV; picnic-sets outside. *Recommended by Immanuel von Bennigsen*

☆ Marquess Tavern
N1 2TB
Canonbury Street/Marquess Road

Surprisingly traditional and fairly plain bar in imposing Victorian building, bare boards, a mix of wooden tables around big, horseshoe servery, old leather sofa and faded pictures, a couple of fireplaces, Wells & Youngs beers, around 30 malt whiskies, traditional food in bar or back dining room; piped music; children and dogs welcome, some picnic-sets out behind front railings, open all day weekends, closed weekday lunchtimes.
Recommended by anon

N4

White Lion of Mortimer
Stroud Green Road

N4 3PX

One of the earliest Wetherspoons, good choice of changing ales kept well, good value food, back conservatory, some character regulars; TVs. *Recommended by Giles and Annie Francis*

N14

Cherry Tree
The Green

N14 6EN

Roomy beamed Vintage Inn (former coaching inn) with good value food all day from breakfast on, wide choice of wines by the glass and reasonably priced beers, good service, mix of big tables, some leather chesterfields; children welcome, tables out behind, bedrooms in adjacent Innkeepers Lodge, open all day. *Recommended by Colin Moore, Darren Shea, David Jackson*

N16

Jolly Butchers
Stoke Newington High Street

N16 7HU

Good range of changing real ales and ciders, bustling atmosphere. *Recommended by Tony and Gill Powell*

NW1

Betjeman Arms
St Pancras Station

NW1 2QL

On upper concourse with outside seating area facing Eurostar trains, good all-rounder with enjoyable food, well kept Sambrooks and a house beer from Sharps, friendly efficient service, modern décor. *Recommended by Derek Thomas, N R White*

Bree Louise
Cobourg Street/Euston Street

NW1 2HH

Partly divided open-plan bar with half a dozen or more interesting real ales, food emphasising pies (Mon-Thurs bargains), basic décor with prints, UK flags, mixed used furnishings; can get very busy early evening; open all day. *Recommended by Joe Green, Jake Lingwood, Jeremy King*

☆ # Chapel
Chapel Street

NW1 5DP

Usually busy evenings (quieter during the day), this dining pub attracts an equal share of drinkers, spacious cream-painted rooms dominated by open kitchen, smart but simple furnishings, sofas at lounge end by big fireplace, Adnams and Greene King ales, good choice of wines by the glass, several coffees and teas, food usually good; children and dogs welcome, picnic-sets in sizeable back garden, more seats on decking under heated parasols, open all day. *Recommended by Phil and Jane Hodson, Kevin Thomas, Nina Randall, Bruce and Sharon Eden*

☆ # Doric Arch
Eversholt Street

NW1 2DN

Virtually part of Euston Station, upstairs from bus terminus with raised back part overlooking it, two well kept Fullers ales and a guest, Weston's cider, friendly prompt service (even when busy), enjoyable well priced pubby food lunchtime and from 4pm weekdays (12-5pm weekends), pleasantly nostalgic atmosphere and some quiet corners, intriguing train and other transport memorabilia including big clock at entrance, downstairs restaurant; discreet sports TV, machines, lavatories on combination lock; open all day. *Recommended by Ian and Helen Stafford, Joe Green, the Didler, Dennis Jones, Dr and Mrs A K Clarke, Jeremy King and others*

☆ **Engineer** NW1 8JH
Gloucester Avenue

Mix of foodies and drinkers in big informal L-shaped bar, lively and popular, with good interesting food (not cheap), St Peters Organic and Wells & Youngs Bombardier, enterprising wine list, good range of spirits, handsome original woodwork and rather unusual décor, individual more ornate candlelit rooms upstairs (may need to book); piped and live music; children welcome, attractive garden, handy for Primrose Hill, open all day from 9am. *Recommended by Jeremy King, Stephen Ogden*

Euston Flyer
NW1 2RA
Euston Road, opposite British Library

Big welcoming open-plan pub, Fullers/Gales beers, good choice of standard food all day, relaxed lunchtime atmosphere, plenty of light wood, mix of furniture on carpet or boarded floors, mirrors, photographs of old London, smaller raised areas and private corners, big doors open to street in warm weather; piped music, Sky TV, silent games machine, can get packed evenings; open all day, till 8.30pm Sun. *Recommended by
Jeremy King, the Didler, N R White, Brian and Janet Ainscough*

Metropolitan
NW1 5LA
Baker Street tube station, Marylebone Road

Wetherspoons in impressively ornate Victorian hall, large with lots of tables on one side, very long bar the other, leather sofas and some elbow tables, good range of well priced ales, good coffee, their usual inexpensive food; silent fruit machine; family area, open all day. *Recommended by Tony Hobden, Jeremy King*

NW3

☆ **Flask** NW3 1HE
Flask Walk

Bustling local (popular haunt of Hampstead artists, actors and local characters), unassuming old-fashioned bar, unique Victorian screen dividing it from cosy lounge with smart banquettes, panelling, lots of little prints and attractive fireplace, Wells & Youngs ales, 30 wines by the glass, well liked bar food (all day Fri-Sun); piped music, TV; children (till 8pm) and dogs welcome, seats and tables in alley, open all day, till midnight Fri, Sat. *Recommended by Tracey and Stephen Groves, John and Gloria Isaacs, the Didler, Stephen Ogden, N R White*

☆ **Holly Bush** NW3 6SG
Holly Mount

Timeless old favourite tucked away in villagey streets, bare-boards bar with dark sagging ceiling, brown and cream panelled walls, old advertisements and hanging plates, partly glazed partitions forming secretive bays, open fires, cosy back room with lots of small prints, panelled and etched-glass alcoves, three Fullers ales and a couple of guests including Harveys, lots of wines by the glass and malt whiskies, food from traditional choices up (all day weekends), upstairs dining room; children (till 7pm) and dogs welcome, pavement benches, open all day. *Recommended by John Wooll, Barry Collett, the Didler, Stephen Ogden, N R White and others*

☆ **Spaniards Inn** NW3 7JJ
Spaniards Lane

Busy 16th-c pub right next to Hampstead Heath with charming big garden split up into areas by careful planting, flagstoned walk amongst roses, side arbour with climbing plants and plenty of seats on crazy-paved terrace (arrive early weekends as popular with dog walkers and families); attractive and characterful low-ceilinged rooms with oak-panelling, antique winged settles, snug alcoves and open fires, half a dozen real ales, two ciders, continental draught lagers and several wines by the glass, enjoyable unfussy food (all day); car park fills fast and nearby parking difficult; children and dogs welcome. *Recommended by Karen Eliot, John Wooll, David Jackson, Mike and Lynn Robinson, Nick Lawless*

NW4

Greyhound
NW4 4JT

Church End

Friendly three-bar Youngs pub with their ales and a guest kept well, decent bar lunches including home-made pizzas (evening meals Thurs, Fri only), plaque commemorating first greyhound track meeting, some live jazz; dogs welcome, open all day (till 1am Fri, Sat).
Recommended by Ross Balaam

NW5

☆ Bull & Last
NW5 1QS

Highgate Road

Traditional décor with a stylish twist and liked by customers of all ages; single room with big windows, colonial-style fans in planked ceiling, collection of tankards, faded map of London, stuffed bulls' heads and pheasants, four changing ales, good wines and own sloe gin, imaginative if not cheap food, takeaway tubs of home-made ice-cream and picnic hampers for Hampstead Heath, friendly staff; quiz Sun evening; children (away from bar) and dogs welcome, hanging baskets and picnic-sets by street, open all day. *Recommended by Richard Greaves*

Junction Tavern
NW5 1AG

Fortress Road

Victorian corner pub with good fresh food including some enterprising dishes in bar and dining room (service charge added), well kept Caledonian Deuchars IPA and three other well kept ales (beer festivals), good choice of wines by the glass, back conservatory; piped music; no children after 7pm, garden tables, open all day Fri-Sun. *Recommended by Nick Angel*

SOUTH LONDON

SE1

Anchor
SE1 9EF

Bankside

In great spot near Thames with river views from upper floors and roof terrace, extensively refurbished with beams, stripped brickwork and old-world corners, well kept Fullers London Pride and Greene King IPA, good choice of wines by the glass, popular fish and chip bar including takeaways, other good value all-day food as well as breakfast and tearoom; piped music; provision for children, disabled access, more tables under big parasols on raised riverside terrace, bedrooms in friendly quiet Premier Inn behind, open all day. *Recommended by Phil and Jane Hodson, Mike and Sue Loseby, Paul Humphreys, Eleanor Dandy, Pete Coxon*

Anchor & Hope
SE1 8LP

The Cut

Busy informal bare-boards gastropub, contrasting reports on food ranging from excellent to rough and ready, prices can be high and service erratic, well kept Wells & Youngs and guests, wine by tumbler or carafe, plain bar with big windows and mix of furniture including elbow tables, curtained-off dining part with small open kitchen, tight-packed scrubbed tables and contemporary art on purple walls; children and dogs welcome, closed Sun evening and Mon lunchtime, otherwise open all day. *Recommended by Ian Phillips, Eleanor Dandy, Mike and Sue Loseby, Susan and John Douglas, Phil Bryant*

Barrow Boy & Banker
SE1 9QQ

Borough High Street, by London Bridge Station

Comfortable civilised bank conversion with roomy upper gallery, full Fullers beer range kept well, decent wines, efficient young staff, no-nonsense food including good pies, music-free; right by Southwark Cathedral. *Recommended by Fergus McDonald, Phil and Jane Villiers*

☆ Fire Station   SE1 8SB
Waterloo Road

Unusual fire station conversion, busy and noisy, with two huge knocked-through tiled rooms, lots of wooden tables and mix of chairs, pews and worn leather armchairs, distinctive box-shaped floral lampshades, sizeable plants, back bar with red fire buckets on shelf, smarter dining room, good modern all-day food including breakfast from 9am, Fullers, Marstons and a guest, good choice of wines and spirits; children welcome, tables out in front, picnic-sets in scruffy side alley, handy for Old Vic theatre, open till midnight. *Recommended by Ian Phillips, Eleanor Dandy, Rob and Catherine Dunster, Tom and Ruth Rees and others*

☆ Founders Arms   SE1 9JH
Hopton Street

Modern building with glass walls in superb location – outstanding terrace views along the Thames and handy for South Bank attractions; plenty of customers (city types, tourists, theatre and gallery goers) spilling on to pavement and river walls, Wells & Youngs and a guest, lots of wines by the glass, good bar food all day (weekend breakfasts from 9am), cheerful service; piped music; children welcome away from bar, open till midnight Fri, Sat. *Recommended by N R White, Jeremy King, John Wooll, Kevin Thomas, Nina Randall, Mike and Sue Loseby and others*

☆ George   SE1 1NH
Off 77 Borough High Street

Tucked-away 16th-c coaching inn (mentioned in *Little Dorrit*), now owned by the National Trust and beautifully preserved; lots of tables in bustling cobbled courtyard with views of the tiered exterior galleries, series of no-frills ground-floor rooms with black beams, square-latticed windows and some panelling, plain oak or elm tables on bare boards, old-fashioned built-in settles, dimpled-glass lanterns and a 1797 Act of Parliament clock, impressive central staircase up to series of dining-rooms and balcony, well kept Greene King ales plus a beer brewed for the pub, good value traditional food all day (not Sun evening), friendly staff; children welcome away from bar, open all day. *Recommended by Mayur Shah, Mike and Sue Loseby, the Didler, Rob and Catherine Dunster, Andy and Claire Barker and others*

Goldsmith   SE1 0EF
Southwark Bridge Road

Pub/dining room with well kept Adnams Best, Wadworths 6X and a guest, imaginative wine list with many by the glass, enjoyable sensibly priced food, friendly service. *Recommended by Mike and Sue Loseby, Oliver Ward*

☆ Hole in the Wall   SE1 8SQ
Mepham Street

Quirky no-frills hideaway in railway arch virtually underneath Waterloo, rumbles and shakes with the trains, fine range of well kept ales, basic bargain food all day, plush red banquettes in small quieter front bar, well worn mix of tables set well back from long bar in larger back room; big-screen sports TV, machines; open all day, closed weekend afternoons. *Recommended by Jason Pound, Ian Phillips*

☆ Horniman   SE1 2HD
Hays Galleria, off Battlebridge Lane

Spacious, bright and airy Thames-side drinking hall with lots of polished wood, comfortable seating including a few sofas, upstairs seating, several real ales with unusual guests (may offer tasters), teas and coffees at good prices, lunchtime bar food from soup and big sandwiches up, snacks other times, efficient service coping with large numbers after work; unobtrusive piped music; fine river views from picnic-sets outside, open all day. *Recommended by Phil and Jane Villiers*

If you stay overnight in an inn or hotel, they are allowed to serve you an alcoholic drink at any hour of the day or night.

☆ Kings Arms
SE1 8TB

Roupell Street

Proper corner local, bustling and friendly, with curved servery dividing traditional bar and lounge, bare boards and attractive local prints, well kept changing ales, good wine and malt whisky choice, welcoming efficient service, enjoyable food from thai dishes to Sun roasts, big back extension with conservatory/courtyard dining area; piped music; open all day. *Recommended by Colin and Louise English, Peter Dandy, Eleanor Dandy*

☆ Market Porter
SE1 9AA

Stoney Street

Properly pubby no-frills place opening at 6am weekdays for workers at neighbouring market, up to ten unusual real ales (over 60 guests a week) often from far-flung brewers, a handful of good value pubby dishes, particularly helpful, friendly service, main part of bar is pretty straightforward with bare boards and open fire, beams with beer barrels balanced on them, simple furnishings, it gets more old-fashioned the further you venture in; piped music; children allowed weekends till 7pm, dogs welcome, drinkers spill out on to street, open all day. *Recommended by Jeremy King, Mayur Shah, Peter Dandy, N R White, Mike Gorton, Mike and Sue Loseby and others*

White Hart
SE1 8TJ

Cornwall Road/Whittlesey Street

Vibrant corner local in upcoming area, friendly bustle, comfortable sofas, stripped boards and so forth, ales such as Brakspears, Fullers London Pride, Purity and Sharps Doom Bar, several belgian beers, good range of ciders and wines, sensibly priced up-to-date blackboard food including pub standards, helpful efficient staff; piped music. *Recommended by Peter Dandy, Eleanor Dandy*

SE8
Dog & Bell
SE8 3JD

Prince Street

Friendly old-fashioned tucked-away local on Thames Path, wood benches around bright cheerfully decorated L-shaped bar, half a dozen well kept changing ales, bottled belgian beers, prompt friendly service, reasonably priced pub food including good sandwiches, dining room; TV; tables in yard, open all day. *Recommended by N R White*

SE9
Park Tavern
SE9 5DA

Passey Place

Traditional Victorian corner pub off Eltham High Street, up to eight well kept ales, log fire, friendly easy-going atmosphere; soft piped music. *Recommended by Michael and Deborah Ethier*

SE10
☆ Cutty Sark
SE10 9PD

Ballast Quay, off Lassell Street

Smashing Thames views from early 19th-c tavern, genuinely unspoilt old-fashioned bar, dark flagstones, simple furnishings, open fires, narrow openings to tiny side snugs, upstairs room (reached by winding staircase) with ship-deck-feel and prized seat in big bow window, up to four changing ales, organic wines, malt whiskies, all-day bar food; piped music; children and dogs welcome, busy riverside terrace across narrow cobbled lane, limited parking (but free if you get a space). *Recommended by John Saville, Susan and John Douglas, the Didler*

☆ Greenwich Union
SE10 8RT

Royal Hill

Friendly, nicely renovated pub with ales from local Meantime and guests, some unusual bottled beers too, long narrow flagstoned room (feels more bar than pub) with simple front area, woodburner, newspapers, other area with brown leather cushioned pews and armchairs under framed editions of *Picture Post*, modern-feeling conservatory, bar food (all day weekends); piped music, TV; children and dogs welcome, appealing terrace with green picnic-sets and fencing painted to resemble poppy or wheat fields, seats in front overlooking street, open all day. *Recommended by D Crook, N R White, Dave Allister, the Didler, Mrs B Billington*

Kings Arms
King William Walk

SE10 9JH

Well placed dark-panelled open-plan pub, shortish choice of enjoyable good value food, Greene King ales, friendly attentive staff; piped music; pleasant shady back terrace. *Recommended by George Atkinson*

☆ Richard I
Royal Hill

SE10 8RT

Friendly refurbished two-bar Youngs local, popular food including enjoyable Sun lunch, carpets and panelling; children welcome, picnic-sets out in front, lots more in pleasant paved back garden with weekend barbecues – busy summer weekends and evenings. *Recommended by the Didler, D Crook, N R White*

SE11

Prince of Wales
Cleaver Square

SE11 4EA

Comfortably traditional little Edwardian pub in smart quiet Georgian square, well kept Shepherd Neame ales, bar food from good sandwiches up, friendly landlord and staff, arch to small saloon; pavement seats, boules available to play in the square. *Recommended by Tim Maddison*

SE16

☆ Mayflower
Rotherhithe Street

SE16 4NF

Unchanging, cosy, old riverside pub in unusual street with lovely early 18th-c church, wide choice of enjoyable generous food all day, black beams, panelling, nautical bric-a-brac, high-backed settles and coal fires, good Thames views from upstairs restaurant (closed Sat lunchtime), Greene King ales, good coffee and good value wines, friendly service; piped music; children welcome, nice jetty/terrace over water, open all day. *Recommended by the Didler, N R White*

SE21

☆ Crown & Greyhound
Dulwich Village

SE21 7BJ

Big, busy (especially evenings), Victorian pub with cosy period interior, traditional upholstered settles and stripped kitchen tables on bare boards, big back dining room, conservatory, Fullers London Pride, Harveys and a couple of guests (Easter beer festival and summer cider festival), just under two dozen wines by the glass, straightforward bar food (all day), popular Sun carvery; piped music; children and dogs welcome, summer barbecues in pleasant back garden, open all day. *Recommended by Bill Adie, Tracey and Stephen Groves, John Saville, Giles and Annie Francis*

SE22

Herne Tavern
Forest Hill Road

SE22 0RR

Smart traditional panelled pub with well kept ales, enjoyable food in separate dining area; children welcome, big garden with play area, open all day. *Recommended by Giles and Annie Francis*

SE24

Florence
Dulwich Road

SE24 0NG

Handsome Victorian pub visibly brewing its own Weasel ale, farm cider, enjoyable food including Sun roasts, friendly busy atmosphere, glossy bar and appealing contemporary décor, comfortable booth seating, open fire, dining conservatory; children welcome, good terrace tables. *Recommended by Greg Bailey, Mark Stafferton*

SE26

☆ Dulwich Wood House
Sydenham Hill

SE26 6RS

Extended well refurbished Youngs pub in Victorian lodge gatehouse complete with turret, nice local atmosphere, friendly service, decent food cooked to order; steps up to entrance (and stiff walk up from station); children welcome, big pleasant back garden with old-fashioned street lamps, summer barbecues, handy for Dulwich Wood. *Recommended by B J Harding, Jake Lingwood*

SW4

Bread & Roses
Clapham Manor Street

SW4 6DZ

Contemporary café-style with two real ales and some unusual continental beers, good wines by the glass, imaginative well priced food; piped music. *Recommended by Tracey and Stephen Groves*

Windmill
Clapham Common South Side

SW4 9DE

Big bustling pub by Clapham Common, contemporary front bar, quite a few original Victorian features, pillared dining room leading through to conservatory-style eating area, good varied choice of food all day, Wells & Youngs ales and decent wines by the glass, piped music; outside satay bar, tables under red umbrellas along front, also seats in side garden area, good bedrooms. *Recommended by anon*

SW8

Canton Arms
South Lambeth Road

SW8 1XP

Large airy corner pub doing well under newish management, good food from huge sharing plates up, good choice of wines. *Recommended by KJ*

SW11

Eagle
Chatham Road

SW11 6HG

Attractive unpretentious backstreet local, good choice of changing ales including southern brewers like Harveys, Surrey Hills and Westerham, welcoming prompt service, worn leather chesterfield in fireside corner of L-shaped bar; big-screen sports TV; dogs welcome, back terrace with heated marquee, small front terrace too. *Recommended by Mitchell Humphreys*

Falcon
St Johns Hill

SW11 1RU

Restored Victorian pub with good choice of well kept beers from remarkably long light oak counter, bargain pub food, friendly service, lively front bar, period partitions, cut glass and mirrors, subdued lighting, quieter back dining area, daily papers; big-screen TV; handy for Clapham Junction station. *Recommended by Tim Loryman, Mike Gorton, Barbarrick*

☆ Fox & Hounds
Latchmere Road

SW11 2JU

Big Victorian local with particularly good mediterranean cooking (all day Sun, not Mon-Thurs lunchtimes), Fullers, Harveys and a guest, several wines by glass, spacious straightforward bar with big windows overlooking street, bare boards, mismatched tables and chairs, photographs on walls, fresh flowers, daily papers, view of kitchen behind, two rooms off; piped music, TV; children (till 7pm) and dogs welcome, garden seats under big parasols, open all day Fri-Sun, closed Mon lunchtime. *Recommended by anon*

SW13

Bridge
Castelnau Gardens

SW13 9DW

Edwardian corner pub fitted out in relaxed bistro-style, raised booth seating at front overlooking road, original bar behind with Adnams and Fullers London Pride, light and airy back part, good variety of moderately priced food with some creative touches from open kitchen; children welcome, tables on decking in back garden, open all day – handy for Thames Path. *Recommended by Simon and Mandy King*

Brown Dog
Cross Street

SW13 0AP

Well renovated with warm relaxed atmosphere, gastropub menu (not cheap), good choice of wines, well kept Sambrooks and Twickenham, friendly helpful staff, subtle lighting and open fires, daily papers; children and dogs welcome (resident labrador called Willow), garden tables, open all day. *Recommended by Jim Jolliffe, C Cooper*

SW14

Victoria
West Temple Sheen

SW14 7RT

Contemporary styling with emphasis on conservatory restaurant, well kept Fullers London Pride and Timothy Taylors Landlord in small wood-floored bar with leather sofas and woodburning stoves, food can be good if not cheap including breakfast Sat and all day Sun, friendly service; piped music; dogs welcome, children's play area in nice garden, comfortable bedrooms, open all day. *Recommended by Noel Ferrin, Richard Morris*

SW15

Dukes Head
Lower Richmond Road, near Putney Bridge

SW15 1JN

Smartly modernised and expanded Victorian pub, comfortable furnishings in knocked-together front bars and trendy downstairs cocktail bar in disused skittle alley (very popular weekends), good range of well presented pubby food all day including sharing platters and snacks, Wells & Youngs ales, lots of wines by the glass, light and airy back dining room with great river views, friendly service, plastic glasses for outside terrace or riverside pavement; children welcome (high chairs and smaller helpings), open all day. *Recommended by Peter Dandy, N R White*

Green Man
Wildcroft Road, Putney Heath

SW15 3NG

Small friendly old local by Putney Heath, nicely redecorated rooms and alcoves, good choice of enjoyable food, well kept Wells & Youngs ales with a guest such as St Austell; TV; attractive good-sized back garden with decking, also some seats out at front near road, open all day. *Recommended by Peter Dandy*

Most pubs with any outside space now have some kind of smokers' shelter. There are regulations about these – for instance, they have to be substantially open to the outside air. The best have heating and lighting and are really quite comfortable.

SW16

Earl Ferrers

SW16 6JF

Ellora Road

Opened-up Streatham corner local, Sambrooks and several other well kept ales like Ascot, Pilgrim and Twickenham (tasters offered), some interesting food as well as pub favourites and Sun roasts, good informal service, mixed tables and chairs, sofas, old photographs; piped music – live music every other Sun, quiz night Weds, pool and darts; children welcome, some tables outside with tractor-seat stools, open all day weekends, from 4pm weekdays. *Recommended by Richard Warrick, LM, Kevin Chamberlain*

SW18

Ship

SW18 1TB

Jews Row

Popular riverside pub by Wandsworth Bridge with light and airy conservatory-style décor, pleasant mix of furnishings on bare boards, basic public bar, well kept Wells & Youngs ales and Caledonian Deuchars IPA, freshly cooked interesting bistro food in extended restaurant with own garden, attractive good-sized terrace with barbecue and outside bar; children and dogs welcome, open all day. *Recommended by Peter Dandy, Mike Bell*

SW19

Fox & Grapes

SW19 4UN

Camp Road

18th-c dining pub by Wimbledon Common recently refurbished under new french chef/owner, modern bistro feel but keeping some original features in the two dining areas (steps between), good adventurous cooking alongside more traditional dishes, cheaper set menus, well chosen wines by the glass, ales such as Hogs Back and Sharps Doom Bar from central servery, relaxed atmosphere; children and dogs welcome, three bedrooms. *Recommended by Paul Bonner, Susan and John Douglas*

SW6

☆ # Atlas

SW6 1RX

Seagrave Road

Busy tucked-away pub with long, simple, knocked-together bar, plenty of panelling and dark wall benches, school chairs and tables, brick fireplaces, enjoyable bar food (all day Sun), Fullers, St Austell, Sharps and a guest, lots of wines by the glass, big mugs of coffee, friendly service; piped music and they may ask to keep a credit card while you run a tab; children (till 7pm) and dogs welcome, seats under awning on heated and attractively planted side terrace, open all day. *Recommended by Nigel and Sue Foster, Evelyn and Derek Walter, Alistair Forsyth, Nick and Elaine Hall*

Harwood Arms

SW6 1QP

Walham Grove

Interesting bare-boards gastropub, good bar snacks as well as enterprising pricey full meals (oyster fritters, pheasant kiev), friendly caring staff, separate eating area, well kept ales such as Fullers London Pride and St Austell Tribute in proper bar area with leather sofas, young lively atmosphere; closed Mon lunchtime. *Recommended by Antony O'Brien, Katharine Cowherd, Richard Tilbrook*

Sands End

SW6 2PR

Stephendale Road

Enterprising seasonal food, real ales such as Black Sheep, Greene King Old Speckled Hen and Hook Norton, simple country furnishings and open fire. *Recommended by Sam West*

Every entry includes a postcode for use in Sat Nav devices.

☆ White Horse
Parsons Green

SW6 4UL

Busy pub with stylishly modernised U-shaped bar, huge windows with wooden blinds, coal and log fires, plenty of sofas and wooden tables, half a dozen changing ales and many more draught continentals, 120 bottled beers, a perry and good interesting wines, imaginative bar food all day from 9.30am, quick friendly service, regular beer festivals; children and dogs welcome, plenty of seats on heated front terrace (popular barbecues), open till midnight Thurs-Sat. *Recommended by Tracey and Stephen Groves, N R White, the Didler, B and M Kendall, C Cooper and others*

SW7

☆ Anglesea Arms
Selwood Terrace

SW7 3QG

Very busy Victorian pub run well by friendly landlady, mix of cast-iron tables on wood-strip floor, central elbow tables, panelling and heavy portraits, large brass chandeliers hanging from dark ceilings, big windows with swagged curtains, several booths at one end with partly glazed screens, half a dozen ales including Adnams, Fullers London Pride and Sambrooks, around 20 malt whiskies and 30 wines by the glass, interesting bar food, steps down to refurbished dining room; children welcome, dogs in bar, heated front terrace, open all day. *Recommended by Barry and Anne, the Didler, Stephen Ogden*

Queens Arms
Queens Gate Mews

SW7 5QL

Victorian corner pub with open-plan bare-boards bar, enjoyable good value home-made pubby food, good wines by the glass, ales including Adnams and Fullers; disabled facilities, handy for the Albert Hall, open all day. *Recommended by LM, Megan and Jen*

WEST LONDON

W4

☆ Bell & Crown
Strand on the Green

W4 3PF

Well run Fullers local, good friendly staff, enjoyable sensibly priced food, panelling and log fire, great Thames views from back bar and conservatory, lots of atmosphere; dogs welcome, terrace and towpath area, good walks, open all day. *Recommended by Bob and Angela Brooks, N R White*

☆ Bulls Head
Strand on the Green

W4 3PQ

Recently renovated old Thames-side pub (served as Cromwell's HQ during Civil War), seats by windows overlooking the water in beamed rooms, steps up and down, ales such as Fullers and Wells & Youngs, several wines by the glass, decent all-day pubby food, friendly helpful service; piped music, games machine; seats outside by river, pretty hanging baskets, part of Chef & Brewer chain. *Recommended by N R White, Tracey and Stephen Groves*

☆ Duke of Sussex
South Parade

W4 5LF

Big bonus for this Victorian local is the large back garden with lots of tables and careful planting; smartly refurbished but simple bar with huge windows, some original etched glass, well kept Fullers and a couple of guests from big horseshoe counter with fresh flowers, enjoyable food (not Mon lunchtime) including some spanish influences, helpful efficient service, nicely restored dining room with wooden furnishings, little booths and splendid skylight framed by colourfully painted cherubs, lots of black and white photographs; well behaved children and dogs welcome, open all day. *Recommended by B and M Kendall, Tracey and Stephen Groves*

Swan
W4 5HH

Evershed Walk, Acton Lane

Cosy, well supported local, enjoyable food including some interesting dishes, friendly staff, good range of wines by the glass, three real ales; dogs very welcome, children till 7.30pm, good spacious garden. *Recommended by Catherine Woodman, Antony O'Brien, Seb Royce*

W6

☆ Anglesea Arms
W6 0UR

Wingate Road

Good interesting food including weekday set lunches in homely bustling pub, welcoming staff, good choice of wines by the glass and of real ales, close-set tables in dining room facing kitchen, roaring fire in simply decorated panelled bar; children welcome, tables out by quiet street, open all day. *Recommended by David Gunn, the Didler, Robert Del Maestro, C Cooper*

Brook
W6 0XF

Goldhawk Road/Stamford Brook Road (formerly Queen of England)

Handsome brick pub with spacious high-ceilinged rooms, Fullers ales, enjoyable modern food, bustling bar with comfortable squashy sofas, leather tub chairs and mix of dining chairs around pine tables on stripped boards, airy dining room with leather wall seats and white-clothed (or plain wood) tables, fresh flowers, helpful, cheerful young staff; terrace. *Recommended by anon*

☆ Dove
W6 9TA

Upper Mall

Lots of history at this 17th-c riverside pub (framed list of writers, actors and artists who have been here), also in *Guinness World Records* book for smallest bar room – front snug is a mere 4ft 2ins by 7ft 10ins with traditional black panelling, red leatherette built-in wall settles and stools around dimpled copper tables, bigger similarly furnished room with old framed advertisements and photographs of the pub, Fullers ales, 20 wines by the glass including champagne, pubby food (all day weekends), live band once a month; dogs welcome, terrace with seats on flagstoned area and on verandah overlooking Thames Reach (much prized so get there early), tiny exclusive area up spiral staircase too (prime spot for watching rowing crews), open all day. *Recommended by Peter Dandy, Dominic McGonigal, the Didler*

Thatched House
W6 0ET

Dalling Road

Traditional open-plan Victorian corner pub – Youngs, their ales and guests from large wooden servery, mixed furniture including leather chesterfields on bare boards, old books and photographs, station clocks, stained-glass windows, open fire, good choice of food and wine, efficient friendly service, back conservatory; two-tier garden, open all day weekends. *Recommended by Dan Stratton*

W7

Viaduct
W7 3TD

Uxbridge Road

Well maintained Fullers pub with railway memorabilia and old photographs of nearby viaduct, decent food from fairly extensive menu, helpful charming service; sports TV in public bar; open all day. *Recommended by Sue and Mike Todd*

W8

☆ Churchill Arms
W8 7LN

Kensington Church Street

Character irish landlord at this bustling old local, welcoming even when crowds spill on to the street, eclectic interior dense with bric-a-brac including Churchill memorabilia, butterfly prints/books (one of the landlord's passions), foxgloves grown in pots, well kept

Fullers ales, two dozen wines by the glass, good reasonably priced thai food (all day) and traditional dishes at lunchtime in spacious and plant-filled dining conservatory, good value Sunday roast; children and dogs welcome, chrome tables and chairs outside, stunning display of window boxes and hanging baskets, open all day. *Recommended by LM and others*

☆ Scarsdale   W8 6HE
Edwardes Square

Busy Georgian pub in lovely leafy square, stripped-wood floors, good coal-effect gas fires, various knick-knacks, well kept Fullers/Gales ales from ornate counter, enjoyable good value pubby food, friendly helpful service; nice tree-shaded front courtyard, open all day. *Recommended by Barbarrick, Jill Bickerton*

☆ Uxbridge Arms   W8 7TQ
Uxbridge Street

Friendly and cottagey backstreet local with three brightly furnished linked areas, well kept Fullers and a guest such as Harveys, good choice of bottled beers, china, prints and photographs; sports TV; open all day. *Recommended by the Didler, Giles and Annie Francis*

☆ Windsor Castle   W8 7AR
Campden Hill Road

One of the city's best pub gardens with high ivy-sheltered walls, summer bar, winter heaters and lots of seats on flagstones; plenty of inside character in three tiny unspoilt rooms (fun trying to navigate the minuscule doors between them), a wealth of dark oak furnishings, high-backed sturdy built-in elm benches, time-smoked ceilings and coal-effect fire, cosy pre-war-style dining room, fair-priced enjoyable food (all day Fri-Sun), Fullers, Timothy Taylors and three guests, summer Pimms and winter mulled wine, friendly staff; children (till 7pm) and dogs welcome, open all day. *Recommended by Tich Critchlow, the Didler, LM, Giles and Annie Francis*

W9

☆ Warrington   W9 1EH
Warrington Crescent

Most are here for the short choice of interesting modern bar food (not Mon-Weds lunchtimes), but it's also worth exploring this carefully refurbished Victorian gin palace with its opulent art nouveau interior, elaborately patterned tiles, ceilings and stained glass, two exquisitely tiled pillars, drawings of nubile young women, small coal fire, four changing real ales from a splendid marble and mahogany bar counter, unusual bottled beers, several wines by the glass; children welcome till 7pm, open all day (till midnight Fri, Sat). *Recommended by Peter Dandy, LM*

W11

☆ Portobello Gold   W11 2QB
Middle of Portobello Road

Cheerful informal atmosphere at this engaging combination of pub, hotel and restaurant; smallish front bar with cushioned banquettes and nice old fireplace, exotic dining room with big tropical plants and sliding roof, impressive wall-to-wall mirror, vocal canaries, wide choice of enjoyable food all day (also cream teas and Sun roasts), Fullers London Pride, Harveys Best and several draught belgian beers, good selection of bottled imports, particularly good wine list with just under two dozen by the glass, cigar menu, board games, monthly art and photographic exhibition; piped music (live music Sun evening), sports TV, internet café; children welcome, street tables, bedrooms and spacious apartment with rooftop terrace and putting green, open all day. *Recommended by Jeremy King, Dave Braisted*

W12

☆ Princess Victoria   W12 9DH
217 Uxbridge Road

Imposing Victorian gin palace with carefully restored rather grand bar, oil paintings on slate-coloured walls, a couple of stuffed animal heads, comfortable leather wall seats, parquet flooring, small fireplace, Fullers and Timothy Taylors, 36 wines by the glass and lots of spirits from handsome marble-topped horseshoe counter, imaginative modern bar food, large dining room with plenty of original features and more paintings, wine and cigar shop; children allowed if eating, dogs in bar, white wrought-iron furniture on pretty terrace, popular Sat artisan market in front, open all day. *Recommended by Sophie Harrowes, Antony O'Brien*

W13

Duke of Kent   W13 8DL
Scotch Common

Large open-plan pub with discrete areas, coal fires and interesting photos of old Ealing, Fullers ales with guests such as Adnams, food from sandwiches up, newspaper and games. *Recommended by Revd R P Tickle*

W14

☆ Colton Arms   W14 9SD
Greyhound Road

Long-serving landlord at this unspoilt and unchanging little pub, U-shaped main bar with log fire, fine collection of carved antique oak furniture, hunting crops and hunting-scene plates, polished brasses, two small back rooms with tiny serving counter (ring bell for service), Fullers, Sharps and a guest, weekday lunchtime sandwiches only; no credit cards – note the old-fashioned brass-bound till; children welcome till 7pm, dogs in bar, charming back terrace, next to Queen's Club tennis courts. *Recommended by Giles and Annie Francis, Barbarrick, Susan and John Douglas, N R White*

OUTER LONDON

BECKENHAM TQ3769   BR3 6NR
Jolly Woodman
Chancery Lane

Welcoming old-fashioned local in conservation area, cosy chatty atmosphere in small bar with larger room off, woodburner, five or so good changing ales such as Harveys and Timothy Taylors Landlord, good value home-made weekday lunchtime food including sandwiches; flower-filled backyard and pavement tables, open all day, closed Mon lunchtime. *Recommended by N R White*

BIGGIN HILL TQ4359   TN16 3AX
☆ Old Jail
Jail Lane; (E off A233 S of airport and industrial estate, towards Berry's Hill and Cudham)

Big family garden with picnic-sets, substantial trees and good play area at this busy country pub (close to the city); traditional beamed and low-ceilinged rooms with RAF memorabilia, two cosy small areas to right divided by timbers, one with big inglenook, the other with cabinet of Battle of Britain plates, Fullers, Harveys and Shepherd Neame, standard fairly priced food (not Sun evening) from sandwiches up, step up to dining room with more wartime prints/plates and small open fire; discreet piped music; dogs welcome, nice hanging baskets, open all day weekends. *Recommended by B and M Kendall*

BROMLEY TQ4069
BR1 3LG
Red Lion
North Road

Chatty well managed backstreet local in conservation area, traditional dimly lit interior with wood floor, tiling, green velvet drapes and shelves of books, well kept Greene King, Harveys and guests, good service; tables out in front, open all day. *Recommended by N R White*

CARSHALTON TQ2764
SM5 3PE
☆ ## Greyhound
High Street

18th-c coaching inn opposite duck ponds in picturesque outer London 'village', comfortable panelled front lounge bar with log fire, dining areas, friendly service, Youngs ales, wide choice of enjoyable food from interesting sandwiches and ciabattas up; TV in large public bar; picnic-sets out by road, bedrooms. *Recommended by Mierion Perring*

CHELSFIELD TQ4864
BR6 7RE
Five Bells
Church Road; just off A224 Orpington bypass

Ancient chatty village local with two separate bars and dining area, friendly staff, well kept ales such as Cottage, Courage and Sharps Doom Bar, well priced food from snacks up (evening food Thurs-Sat only), live music including jazz, Tues quiz; children welcome, picnic-sets among flowers out in front, open all day. *Recommended by Tony Hobden*

HAMPTON TQ1370
TW12 2EA
Bell
Thames Street

Extensive refurbishment under new owners with focus on food (all day weekends), good service; across road from the Thames, open all day. *Recommended by John Soones*

ISLEWORTH TQ1576
TW7 6QJ
Red Lion
Linkfield Road

Friendly unspoilt backstreet local with nine real ales, three ciders and good choice of belgian beers, home-made food (not Sun evening, Mon, Tues) including popular Sun lunch, four annual beer festivals, theatre company, live music including Mon jazz; children and dogs welcome, picnic-sets out at front, garden with smokers' shelter. *Recommended by C Cooper*

KEW TQ1977
TW9 3BH
Coach & Horses
Kew Green

Modernised former coaching inn overlooking green, decent Wells & Youngs ales and a guest, good coffees, fairly standard bar food from sandwiches up, young friendly staff, relaxed open-plan interior with armchairs, sofas and log fire, small restaurant; piped music, sports TV; teak tables on front terrace, nice setting handy for Kew Gardens and the National Archive, 30 refurbished bedrooms. *Recommended by N R White, Geof Cox, Jeremy King*

KEW TQ1976
TW9 3PZ
Railway
Station Parade

Appealing former station buffet, real ales including Adnams, draught ciders and a decent choice of wines by the glass, reasonably priced generous food, mix of comfortable sofas, tall and more regular tables, newspapers; TVs; large covered and heated area outside. *Recommended by David M Smith*

KINGSTON TQ1869   KT2 5AU
Boaters
Canbury Gardens (park in Lower Ham Road if you can)

Family-friendly pub by the Thames, half a dozen real ales, variety of good value food including vegetarian (some themed evenings), efficient staff, comfortable banquettes in quiet charming bar, newspapers, Sun jazz; smart riverside terrace, in small park, ideal for children in summer, open all day. *Recommended by Ian Phillips, David and Sally Frost*

KINGSTON TQ1869   KT2 6LQ
Canbury Arms
Canbury Park Road

Big-windowed bare-boards open-plan pub with simple fresh contemporary décor, relaxed friendly atmosphere, good up-to-date food including breakfast from 9am (10pm Sun), two-for-one deal Tues evening, five well kept ales such as Harveys, Sharps and Timothy Taylors, good wine choice (bargains Mon night), nice coffee, attentive young staff, stone floor in side conservatory, frequent events; children and dogs welcome, tables out at front iunder parasols, open all day. *Recommended by Keith M Long, Charlotte Salaman, Louis Jones*

LONGFORD TQ0576   UB7 0EE
White Horse
Bath Road, off A3044 (and A4)

Brasses on low 17th-c black beams, fireplace between the two spotless areas, comfortable seats, cosy and friendly with pot plants in windows and rustic decorations such as antique rifles and equestrian bronzes, popular food from hearty traditional things to curries and thai dishes (booking advised), good service, three well kept ales; piped music, games machine; flower tubs and picnic-sets outside, one in a little barn, surprisingly villagey surroundings despite the parking meters, open all day. *Recommended by Andy and Jill Kassube, M J Winterton*

☆ ORPINGTON TQ4963   BR6 7QL
Bo-Peep
Hewitts Road, Chelsfield; 1.7 miles from M25 junction 4

Useful M25 country-feel dining pub, old low beams and enormous inglenook in carpeted bar, two cosy candlelit dining rooms, airy side room overlooking lane, Adnams, Courage and Harveys, cheerful service, pubby food (not Sun evening) as well as some more interesting choices, miniature english bull terrier called Milo; piped music; children welcome, dogs in bar, picnic-sets on big brick terrace, open all day. *Recommended by Guy Vowles, N R White, Tony Brace*

☆ OSTERLEY TQ1578   TW7 5PR
Hare & Hounds
Windmill Lane (B454, off A4 – called Syon Lane at that point)

Roomy suburban Fullers dining pub, wide choice of enjoyable food from sandwiches to hearty reasonably priced main dishes, prompt friendly service, pleasant dining extension, local wartime photographs; disabled facilities, spacious terrace and big floodlit mature garden, nice setting opposite beautiful Osterley Park. *Recommended by Ellie Weld, David London, Revd R P Tickle*

RICHMOND TQ1875   TW9 2NQ
Orange Tree
Kew Road

Big open-plan Youngs pub with lots of sofas and other seating, their ales and often a guest, good reasonably priced wine list including some unusual choices, decent pubby food using good quality ingredients, more formal dining part at back, upstairs area (jazz Weds); tables out in front, small covered terrace behind, open all day. *Recommended by Sue and Mike Todd*

RICHMOND TQ1774   TW9 1LX
Princes Head
The Green

Large unspoilt open-plan pub overlooking cricket green near theatre, clean and well run, with low-ceilinged panelled areas off big island bar, full Fullers range in top condition, popular imaginative food, friendly young staff and chatty locals, coal-effect fire; over-21s only, seats outside – fine spot. *Recommended by Ian Phillips, Richard and Sissel Harris, N R White*

RICHMOND TQ1774   TW9 1TJ
Watermans Arms
Water Lane

Friendly old-fashioned Youngs local, well kept beer, open fire, traditional layout, pub games, enjoyable thai food; handy for the Thames. *Recommended by N R White, Claes Mauroy*

RICHMOND TQ1874   TW9 1TH
☆ White Cross
Water Lane

Very pleasant garden with terrific Thames views, seats on paved area, outside bar and boats to Kingston and Hampton Court; two chatty main rooms with hotel feel (which it was), local prints and photographs, three log fires (one unusually below a window), Wells & Youngs and guests from old-fashioned island servery, a dozen wines by the glass, decent bar food all day, bright and airy upstairs room (children welcome here till 6pm) with pretty cast-iron balcony for splendid river view, good mix of customers; piped music, TV; dogs welcome. *Recommended by Thurstan Johnston, Ian Phillips, the Didler, Paul Humphreys, Michael Dandy and others*

RICHMOND TQ1774   TW9 1PG
White Swan
Old Palace Lane

Small cottagey pub, civilised and relaxed, with rustic dark-beamed open-plan bar, good friendly service, well kept ales such as Fullers London Pride, St Austell Tribute and Timothy Taylors Landlord, fresh wholesome bar lunches, coal-effect fires, popular upstairs restaurant; piped music; children allowed in back conservatory, some seats on narrow paved area at front, more in pretty walled back terrace below railway. *Recommended by LM, Jennifer Banks, N R White*

RICHMOND TQ1873   TW10 6RN
Roebuck
Richmond Hill

Comfortable and attractive 18th-c bay-windowed pub with friendly helpful staff, well kept changing ales, enjoyable food including vegetarian choices, stripped-brick alcoves, some substantial bygones, old Thames photographs and prints; children and dogs welcome, terrace over road with fine views of meadows and river, open all day. *Recommended by Jennifer Banks*

TEDDINGTON TQ1671   TW11 9NN
Tide End Cottage
Broom Road/Ferry Road, near bridge at Teddington Lock

Low-ceilinged pub in Victorian cottage terrace next to Teddington Studios, two rooms united by big log-effect gas fire, well kept Greene King ales and a guest, decent low-priced bar food to numbered tables from sandwiches up, lots of river, fishing and rowing memorabilia and photographs, interesting Dunkirk evacuation link, back dining extension; piped music, TV, minimal parking; children (till 7.30pm) and dogs welcome, small terraces front and back, open all day. *Recommended by Clare Carter, Chris Evans, LM*

ALSO WORTH A VISIT IN BERKSHIRE

Besides the region's top pubs, we recommend the following. Do tell us
what you think of them: **feedback@goodguides.com**

ALDWORTH SU5579   RG8 9SE

☆ **Bell**

A329 Reading—Wallingford; left on to B4009 at Streatley

Unspoilt and unchanging (in same family for over 250 years), simply furnished, panelled
rooms, beams in ochre ceiling, ancient one-handed clock, woodburner, glass-panelled
hatch serving Arkells, West Berkshire and a monthly guest, Upton cider, good house
wines, maybe winter mulled wine, good value rolls, ploughman's and winter soup,
traditional pub games, no mobile phones, credit cards, piped music or machines; can
get busy at weekends; well behaved children and dogs welcome, seats in quiet, cottagey
garden by village cricket ground, animals in paddock behind pub, maybe Christmas
mummers and summer morris men, closed Mon (open lunchtime bank holidays).
*Recommended by Richard Endacott, Henry Midwinter, Dick and Madeleine Brown, the Didler, Mr and
Mrs H J Langley, Guy Vowles and others*

ASHMORE GREEN SU4969   RG18 9HF

☆ **Sun in the Wood**

B4009 (Shaw Road) off A339, right to Kiln Road, left to Stoney Lane

---

Cheery family pub with enthusiastic owners, genuine mix of loyal customers, comfortable
unimposing high-beamed front bar, mix of nice old chairs, padded dining chairs and
stripped pews around sturdy tables, big back dining area with candles on tables, some
interesting touches like stripped bank of apothecary's drawers, small conservatory sitting
area by side entrance, Wadworths ales and a guest, several wines by the glass, good
popular food; seats under parasols on heated decked terrace, picnic-sets in big woodside
garden, small child-free area, nine-hole woodland crazy golf pitch, closed Mon, Sun
evening. *Recommended by Douglas and Ann Hare, Ian Herdman, R T and J C Moggridge, Dave Braisted,
Paul Humphreys*

ASTON SU7884   RG9 3DG

☆ **Flower Pot**

Off A4130 Henley—Maidenhead at top of Remenham Hill

Roomy popular country pub with nice local feel, roaring log fire, array of stuffed fish and
fishing prints on dark green walls of attractively done airy country dining area, enjoyable
food from baguettes to fish and game, Brakspears, Hook Norton and Wychwood ales, quick
friendly service, snug traditional bar with more fishing memorabilia; very busy with
walkers and families at weekends; lots of picnic-sets giving quiet country views from nice
big dog-friendly orchard garden, side field with poultry, crocodile on roof, Thames nearby,
bedrooms. *Recommended by Roy Hoing, Susan and John Douglas, Mike and Mary Carter, Mark Hanley*

BEEDON SU4976   RG20 8SD

Coach & Horses

3 miles N of M4 junction 13, via A34

Modernised pub/restaurant with good food from pub staples and pizzas to more
enterprising cooking, lunchtime set deals too, real ales and plenty of wines by the glass
including champagne, friendly attentive service. *Recommended by Sharon Oldham*

BINFIELD SU8471   RG42 5PH

Jack o' Newbury

Terrace Road North

Friendly family-run Victorian pub, good choice of well kept local ales such as West
Berkshire, good value pubby food including vegetarian choices, skittle alley; children
welcome, seats out at front and in garden. *Recommended by Jez*

BRACKNELL SU8566   RG12 7PB
Golden Retriever
Nine Mile Ride (junction A3095/B3430)

Vintage Inn pastiche of olde-worlde beamed, tiled and thatched pub, comfortable farmhouse-style décor in maze of linked rooms, Caledonian Deuchars IPA, Fullers London Pride and Sharps Doom Bar, plenty of wines by the glass, good choice of decent food all day, friendly service, log fires, daily papers; ample seating outside. *Recommended by Jeremy Stephens, Rosemary and Mike Fielder, Mike and Jayne Bastin*

BURCHETTS GREEN SU8381   SL6 6QZ
Crown
Side road from A4 after Knowl Green on left, linking to A404

Popular dining pub under newish management, good interesting country cooking such as braised pig's cheek with crab apple purée, own bread and home-cured salami, good wines from small producers, compact bar for drinkers with well kept Greene King ales, other areas set for eating, rustic furniture and stripped-back décor; picnic-sets out at front, garden with vegetable patch, open all day (no food Sun evening). *Recommended by Susan and John Douglas, Paul Humphreys*

CHIEVELEY SU4773   RG20 8XB
☆ ## Olde Red Lion
Handy for M4 junction 13 via A34 N-bound; Green Lane

Attractive red-brick village pub, friendly landlord and helpful staff, well kept Arkells, nice varied choice of generously served food from good sandwiches and baguettes up, low-beamed carpeted L-shaped bar with panelling and hunting prints, log fire, extended back restaurant; piped music, games machine, TV; wheelchair accessible throughout, small garden, bedrooms in separate old building. *Recommended by Chris and Angela Buckell, Ian Herdman*

COOKHAM SU8985   SL6 9SQ
☆ ## Bel & the Dragon
High Street (B4447)

Smart old dining pub with panelling and heavy Tudor beams, log fires, bare boards and simple country furnishings in two-room front bar and dining area, hand-painted cartoons on pastel walls, more formal back restaurant, helpful friendly staff, interesting well presented food (at prices you might expect for the area), Greene King ales, good choice of wines; children welcome, well kept garden with terrace tables, Stanley Spencer Gallery almost opposite, open all day. *Recommended by N R White, David and Sue Atkinson*

COOKHAM SU8985   SL6 9SN
Ferry
Sutton Road

Splendidly placed riverside pub with relaxing contemporary décor, Rebellion IPA and Timothy Taylors Landlord, some interesting lagers and good wine range, all-day food including fixed-price menu (Mon-Thurs 12-6), light and airy Thames-view dining areas upstairs and down, sofas and coffee tables by fireplace, small servery in beamed core; piped music; children welcome, extensive decking overlooking river. *Recommended by Mrs Ann Gray, David and Sue Atkinson*

COOKHAM SU8985   SL6 9SJ
Kings Arms
High Street

Modernised linked areas behind old façade, most for dining but also comfortably furnished part for drinkers, good range of pubby and more elaborate food at fair prices, ales such as Adnams and Rebellion IPA, good cheerful service; pleasant back garden, open all day. *Recommended by Clive and Fran Dutson, David and Sue Atkinson, Robert Bell*

COOKHAM DEAN SU8785   SL6 9BQ

☆ **Chequers**

Dean Lane; follow signpost Cookham Dean, Marlow

Restauranty dining pub with good interesting food and professional helpful staff, compact beamed bar with comfortable old sofas on flagstones, fresh flowers on dining tables and crisp white linen, area on left with open stove in big brick fireplace, conservatory, Adnams Bitter, Marlow Rebellion IPA and St Austell Tribute, several wines by the glass, ten infused vodkas, single malt whiskies, good coffees and teas; may be piped music; children welcome, picnic-sets on front terrace and in garden behind, closed Sun evening. *Recommended by Hugh Roberts, P Waterman, Angela Crum Ewing, Paul Humphreys, Alan Sutton, Paul Goldman*

COOKHAM DEAN SU8785   SL6 9NT

Uncle Toms Cabin

Off A308 Maidenhead—Marlow; Hills Lane, towards Cookham Rise and Cookham

Welcoming small-roomed local doing well under present licensees, good pubby food from sandwiches and baguettes up, low beams, wood floors and half panelling, open fire; children in eating areas, sheltered sloping back garden. *Recommended by Paul Humphreys*

CRAZIES HILL SU7980   RG10 8LY

Horns

Warren Row Road off A4 towards Cockpole Green, then follow Crazies Hill signs

Comfortable and individual beamed pub, enjoyable generously served food including bargain OAP lunches (Tues-Sat), well kept Brakspears, good wines by the glass, friendly helpful service, stripped furniture and open fires, raftered barn dining room; children welcome, seats in big informal garden with ponies, rabbits and guinea pigs, closed Sun evening, Mon. *Recommended by Paul Humphreys, Roy and Jean Russell and others*

EASTBURY SU3477   RG17 7JN

Plough

Centre of village by stream

Large lively locals' bar, quieter lounge and contemporary restaurant, well kept changing ales, friendly staff, good value enjoyable food from lunchtime snacks and midweek bargains to more ambitious dishes, log fire; children welcome, dogs in public bar, closed Sun evening. *Recommended by Mark and Ruth Brock, Alex Hickson*

HARE HATCH SU8078   RG10 9TA

Queen Victoria

Blakes Lane; just N of A4 Reading—Maidenhead

Cheerful new landlady doing enjoyable good value food from baguettes up, well kept Brakspears, two low-beamed and panelled bars, conservatory; dogs welcome, some tables outside. *Recommended by Paul Humphreys, Tom Chambers*

HOLYPORT SU8977   SL6 2JR

☆ **Belgian Arms**

1.5 miles from M4 junction 8/9 via A308(M), A330; in village turn left on to big green, then left again at war memorial

Bustling village-green pub, well kept Brakspears and Oxford Gold, several wines by the glass, enjoyable food and good friendly service, low-ceilinged bar with well spaced tables on stripped wood, interesting cricketing memorabilia, hot woodburner, old cellar dining area; piped music, TV; children welcome, dogs in bar, terrace overlooking pond, open all day Fri-Sun. *Recommended by Ian Barker, KC*

Virtually all pubs in the *Good Pub Guide* sell wine by the glass. We mention wines
if they are a cut above the average.

HOLYPORT SU8977   SL6 2JL
George
1.5 miles from M4 junction 8/9, via A308(M)/A330; The Green

Attractive old pub with colourful history, open-plan low-beamed interior with nice fireplace, good choice of enjoyable food (some quite expensive), Adnams, Courage Best and Fullers London Pride, friendly helpful service; picnic-sets on attractive terrace, lovely village green. *Recommended by A Hawkes, J D Franklin*

HUNGERFORD SU3468   RG17 0ED
Downgate
Down View, Park Street

Prettily placed and relaxing old country local with friendly licensees, decent well priced food including good Sun roast, well kept Arkells, two compact linked areas overlooking common, small lower room with open fire, coin/currency collection, model aircraft overhead, old tankards; difficult for wheelchairs, picnic-sets out at front. *Recommended by Phil Bryant*

HURLEY SU8281   SL6 6RB
Dew Drop
Small yellow sign to pub off A4130 just W

Flint and brick pub tucked away in nice rustic setting, enjoyable traditional food from sandwiches up, well kept Brakspears, friendly staff; children and dogs welcome, french windows to terrace, landscaped back garden with views, good walks, open all day Sat, closed Sun evening, Mon lunchtime. *Recommended by Paul Humphreys, DHV*

HURLEY SU8283   SL6 5LX
☆ Olde Bell
High Street; off A4130

Handsome hotel with small old-fashioned bar, massive beams, simple seats and rustic tables on quarry tiles, rocking chair and tall farmhouse chairs by log fire, Rebellion IPA, malt whiskies, bistro-style food, dignified communicating lounge with chintz armchairs and sofas, various nooks and crannies; children and dogs welcome, large back terrace with sturdy oak furniture and barbecue, meadow garden with flower-arbour walk, heated dining tent, attractive Thames-side village, bedrooms, open all day. *Recommended by Susan and John Douglas*

HURST SU8074   RG10 0BP
Green Man
Off A321 just outside village

Partly 17th-c pub now run by former head chef, fairly standard menu from sharing plates to steaks, takeaway fish and chips, well kept Brakspears, friendly uniformed staff, old-fashioned bar with dark beams and standing timbers, cosy alcoves, cushioned wall seats and built-in settles, hot little fire in one fireplace, old iron stove in another, dining area with modern sturdy wooden tables and high-backed chairs on solid oak floor; children welcome, sheltered terrace, picnic-sets under big oak trees in large garden with play area, open all day weekends (food all day then, too). *Recommended by Paul Humphreys, DHV*

KINTBURY SU3866   RG17 9UT
☆ Dundas Arms
Station Road

Fine summer pub, with tables out on deck above Kennet & Avon Canal and pleasant walks; well kept Adnams, Ramsbury, West Berkshire and a guest ale, good coffee and wines by the glass, good reasonably priced home-made pub food (not Sun), evening restaurant; they may ask to keep your credit card while you eat outside; children welcome, wheelchair accessible (helpful staff), comfortable bedrooms with own secluded waterside terrace, good breakfast, closed Sun evening. *Recommended by J C Burgis, Jeff and Wendy Williams*

KNOWL HILL SU8178   RG10 9UP

☆ Bird in Hand

A4, handy for M4 junction 8/9

Relaxed, civilised and roomy, with cosy alcoves, heavy beams, panelling and splendid log fire in tartan-carpeted main area with leather chairs, wide choice of popular home-made food even Sun evenings, well kept Brakspears and guests such as Ascot, Binghams and West Berkshire, good choice of other drinks, attentive prompt service, much older side bar, smart restaurant; soft piped music; tables on front terrace and neat garden, Sun summer barbecues, 15 tidy modern bedrooms. *Recommended by Richard Endacott, Susan and John Douglas*

KNOWL HILL SU8279   RG10 9UU

☆ Old Devil

Bath Road (A4)

Roomy and popular beamed roadhouse, leather sofas and chairs in bar, well spaced tables with fresh flowers in dining areas each side, chintzy feel, wide choice of generously served food, Fullers London Pride, good range of wines by the glass, friendly well organised service; pleasant verandah above attractive lawn. *Recommended by Paul Humphreys, A Hawkes, J D Franklin, Andy Beveridge*

LAMBOURN SU3180   RG17 8QN

Malt Shovel

Upper Lambourn

Décor and customers reflecting race-stables surroundings, traditional locals' bar, enjoyable home-made food in smart modern dining extension including good Sun carvery, good choice of wines by the glass, well kept ales, friendly helpful staff; racing TV. *Recommended by Michael Sargent*

LITTLEWICK GREEN SU8379   SL6 3RA

Cricketers

Not far from M4 junction 9; A404(M) then left on to A4 – village signed on left; Coronation Road

Proper old-fashioned welcoming country pub, well kept Badger and Wells & Youngs ales, good choice of wines by the glass, enjoyable reasonably priced food from lunchtime ciabattas to blackboard specials, huge clock above brick fireplace; piped music, can get crowded; charming spot opposite cricket green, bedrooms, open all day weekends. *Recommended by Paul Humphreys, Richard Endacott, Roger and Anne Newbury, Ian Barker and others*

MAIDENHEAD SU8682   SL6 6PR

☆ Robin Hood

Furze Platt Road, Pinkneys Green (A308N)

Well run Greene King dining pub with their ales and good choice of wines by the glass, extensive series of well divided and varied eating areas off oak-boarded bar, enjoyable good value food from sandwiches up, you can pick your own fish/meat (including kangaroo and ostrich) from counter, friendly helpful service, feature fireplace; piped music; round picnic-sets on big front terrace and lawn, sheltered bower with awning, open all day. *Recommended by Ron Clementson, Paul Humphreys, DHV, June and Robin Savage*

MIDGHAM SU5566   RG7 5UX

☆ Coach & Horses

Bath Road (N side)

Comfortable main-road pub with wide choice of good value generous food, cheerful helpful service even when busy, Fullers and West Berkshire ales; garden behind, closed Mon. *Recommended by Penny Royle*

PALEY STREET SU8676   SL6 3JN

☆ **Royal Oak**

B3024 W

Attractively modernised and stylish 17th-c restaurant pub owned by Sir Michael
Parkinson and son Nick, good british cooking (not cheap) and helpful service, Fullers
London Pride, wide choice of wines by the glass including champagne, smallish informal
beamed bar with open fire, leather sofas and cricketing prints, dining room split by brick
pillars and timbering with mix of well spaced wooden tables and leather dining chairs on
bare boards or flagstones; piped jazz; children welcome but no pushchairs in restaurant,
closed Sun evening. *Recommended by David and Sue Smith, Colin Holdsworth, Ray Carter, I D Barnett*

READING SU7272   RG1 2LG

Allied Arms

St Mary's Butts

Cosy old local with two rooms opening off little cobbled passageway, beams and dark
wood, well kept Fullers London Pride, Loddon Hullabaloo and interesting guests, no food,
juke box; nice garden, closed Sun and Mon lunchtime, otherwise open all day. *Recommended
by Daniel Rooms, the Didler*

READING SU7273   RG1 3DW

☆ **Fishermans Cottage**

Kennet Side – easiest to walk from Orts Road, off Kings Road

Nice spot by canal lock and towpath, good value lunches especially sandwiches (very
busy then but service quick and friendly), full Fullers beer range, small choice of wines,
modern furnishings, pleasant stone snug behind woodburning range, light and airy
conservatory, small darts room; influx of regulars in evenings, Sky TV; dogs allowed (not in
garden), waterside tables, lovely big back garden. *Recommended by the Didler, Susan and
John Douglas*

READING SU7174   RG4 7AD

Griffin

Church Road, Caversham

Popular roomy Chef & Brewer in beautiful Thames-side spot overlooking swan sanctuary,
separate areas with log fires, four well kept ales including Wells & Youngs, good value
generously served food all day, cafetière coffee, friendly efficient young staff; soft piped
music and some live jazz; children welcome, tables in attractive heated courtyard, open
all day. *Recommended by Tony Hobden, Chris Coleman*

READING SU7174   RG1 8BB

Moderation

Caversham Road

Modernised airy Victorian pub with some eastern influences, enjoyable reasonably priced
food including thai/indonesian dishes, Greene King IPA and two other well kept ales;
enclosed garden behind. *Recommended by Nigel and Sue Foster*

READING SU7073   RG1 7XD

Nags Head

Russell Street

Friendly local with good mix of customers, a dozen well kept changing ales, weekday
lunchtime baguettes and bargain early evening meal (lunchtime food weekends only
including Sun roasts), open fire, darts and cribbage, live music Sun; sports TV; garden
with hops, open all day. *Recommended by the Didler, Jason Mackriell*

Half pints: by law, a pub should not charge more for half a pint than half the price of
a full pint, unless it shows that half-pint price on its price list.

READING SU7173 RG1 7RD

☆ **Sweeney & Todd**

Castle Street

Pie shop with popular pub/restaurant behind, warren of private little period-feel alcoves and other areas on various levels, good home-made food all day including wide choice of pies such as venison and wild boar, cheery knowledgeable service, small bar with four well kept ales including Wadworths 6X, Weston's cider, good wines, children welcome in restaurant area, open all day (closed Sun and bank holidays). *Recommended by Ewan and Moira McCall, the Didler, Paul Humphreys, Susan and John Douglas, John Pritchard, Chris Coleman and others*

SHEFFORD WOODLANDS SU3673 RG17 7AA

☆ **Pheasant**

Under 0.5 miles from M4 junction 4 – A338 towards Wantage, first left on B4000

Tucked-away white-painted tile-hung pub with four neat communicating room areas, Loddon and Wadworths 6X, decent wines, enjoyable food, friendly attentive service, cut-away cask seats, wall pews and other chairs on carpeting or stone floors, racehorse prints, log fires, separate dining room, pub games; attractive views from garden, bedrooms. *Recommended by Mrs C Roe, Guy Vowles, John and Gloria Isaacs, Phil Bysh*

SHINFIELD SU7367 RG2 9EA

☆ **Magpie & Parrot**

2.6 miles from M4 junction 11, via B3270; A327 just SE of Shinfield on Arborfield Road

Unusual homely little roadside cottage with warm fire, lots of bric-a-brac (miniature and historic bottles, stuffed birds, dozens of model cars, veteran AA badges and automotive instruments), individualistic seats in two cosy spic-and-span bars, Fullers London Pride and Timothy Taylors from small corner counter, weekday lunchtime snacks and evening fish and chips (Thurs, Fri), hospitable landlady; no credit cards; dogs welcome, seats on back terrace and marquee on immaculate lawn, open 12-7.30, closed Sun evening. *Recommended by the Didler, Dr and Mrs A K Clarke, Simon Collett-Jones*

SHINFIELD SU7367 RG2 9EE

Royal Oak

School Green

Small straightforward pub with three well kept ales including Green King Abbot, short choice of good value traditional food from generously filled rolls/baguettes up, friendly service. *Recommended by John Pritchard*

SINDLESHAM SU7769 RG41 5BP

Walter Arms

Signed from B3349 or B3030

Victorian red-brick gabled dining pub, small modern bar with log fire, comfortable sofas and low cushioned stools, eating areas with modern furniture on terracotta tiles or carpet, varied choice of good popular food (all day weekends) including pizzas, well kept real ales, efficient service and warm atmosphere; children welcome, parasoled picnic-sets at front and in side garden with arbour, open all day. *Recommended by David and Sue Smith*

SUNNINGHILL SU9367 SL5 7AQ

Dog & Partridge

Upper Village Road

Modern feel under hard-working owners with emphasis on good reasonably priced home-made food, friendly helpful staff, real ales, good range of wines; piped music; children and dogs welcome, disabled facilities, sunny garden with play area, closed Mon and lunchtimes Tues-Thurs, open all day weekends. *Recommended by Mary McSweeney, Paul Nickson, Ray Carter*

THEALE SU6471   RG7 4BE
☆ Fox & Hounds
2 miles from M4 junction 12; best to bypass restricted-access town centre – take first
left at town-edge roundabout, then at railway turn right into Brunel Road, then left
past station on Station Road; keep on over narrow canal bridge to Sheffield Bottom
S of town

Large neatly kept dining pub, friendly and relaxed, with enjoyable well priced food (all
day Fri-Sat, not Sun evening) from baguettes up, good service, several Wadworths ales,
Weston's cider, decent wines and coffee, L-shaped bar with dividers, traditional mix of
furniture on carpet or bare boards including area with modern sofas and low tables, two
open fires, daily papers, pool and darts, Sun quiz; children and dogs welcome, outside
seating at front and sides, lakeside bird reserve opposite, open all day Fri-Sun.
Recommended by Phil Bryant, John Pritchard

THEALE SU6168   RG7 5JB
Winning Hand
A4 W, opposite Sulhamstead turn; handy for M4 junction 12

Good choice of bar and more pricey restaurant food, friendly efficient service, two
changing real ales, varied wine list, dining room with stripped-pine furniture and church
candles on wrought-iron stands, new restaurant with modern furniture on light wood floor
and contemporary artwork; quiet piped music, no dogs; children welcome, front and back
terrace tables, some picnic-sets on lawned area, three bedrooms, closed Sun evening,
Mon. *Recommended by John Pritchard*

THREE MILE CROSS SU7167   RG7 1AT
Swan
A33 just S of M4 junction 11; Basingstoke Road

Built in the 17th c and later a posting house, genuine friendly welcome, reliable home-
made pubby food including good sandwiches, up to five well kept ales, beams, feature
fireplace with hanging black pots, old prints and some impressive stuffed fish; good
outside seating, near Madejski Stadium (busy on match days), open all day weekdays,
closed Sun evening. *Recommended by John Pritchard, Marita Lowry*

WALTHAM ST LAWRENCE SU8376   RG10 0JJ
☆ Bell
B3024 E of Twyford; The Street

Heavy-beamed and timbered 15th-c village local with cheerful landlord and chatty
regulars, good log fires, efficient service, good home-made food (not Sun evening) from
bar snacks to local game (may ask to keep your credit card while you eat), five well kept
changing local ales such as Binghams, Loddon and West Berkshire (summer beer
festival), real cider, plenty of malt whiskies and good wine, compact panelled lounge,
daily papers; children and dogs welcome, tables in back garden with extended terrace,
open all day weekends. *Recommended by Paul Humphreys*

WASH COMMON SU4563   RG20 0LU
Woodpeckers
Just off A343 S of Newbury, signposted to East Woodhay

Old beamed village pub spruced up under new management, Arkells ales, enjoyable well
priced pub food, modern back dining area. *Recommended by Mr and Mrs H J Langley*

Bedroom prices normally include full english breakfast, VAT and any inclusive service
charge that we know of. Prices before the '/' are for single rooms, after the '/' for
two people in a double or twin (B includes a private bath, S a private shower). If there
is no '/', the prices are only for twin or double rooms (as far as we know there are no
singles). If there is no B or S, as far as we know no rooms have private facilities.

WEST ILSLEY SU4782   RG20 7AR
Harrow
Signed off A34 at E Ilsley slip road

Appealing family-run country pub in peaceful spot overlooking cricket pitch and pond,
Victorian prints in deep-coloured knocked-through bar, some antique furnishings, log fire,
enjoyable pub food including deals, well kept Greene King ales, good choice of wines by
the glass; children in eating areas, dogs allowed in bar, picnic-sets in big garden, more
seats on pleasant terrace, closed Sun evening. *Recommended by Helen and Brian Edgeley,
Dave Snowden*

WINDSOR SU9676   SL4 1PB
☆ Carpenters Arms
Market Street

Town pub ambling around central servery with ales such as Everards, Fullers, Harveys,
Pilgrim and Sharps Doom Bar, good value pubby food all day from sandwiches up
including range of pies, friendly helpful service, good choice of wines by the glass (and
bargain bottles), sturdy pub furnishings and Victorian-style décor with two pretty
fireplaces, family areas up a few steps, also downstairs beside former tunnel entrance
with suits of armour; piped music, no nearby parking, no dogs; tables out on cobbled
pedestrian alley opposite castle, handy for Legoland bus stop, open all day. *Recommended by
Terry Buckland, David and Sue Atkinson*

WOOLHAMPTON SU5766   RG7 5SH
Rowbarge
Station Road

Extended 18th-c canalside pub doing good fresh food all day, helpful friendly service, well
kept West Berkshire and changing guests, plenty of wines by the glass, two woodburners
in neatly modernised beamed bar, panelled side room, large water-view restaurant; light
piped music; dogs and children welcome, tables out by water and in roomy garden, handy
for A4, open all day. *Recommended by Ian Herdman, John Pritchard*

YATTENDON SU5574   RG18 0UG
☆ Royal Oak
*The Square; B4009 NE from Newbury; right at Hampstead Norreys, village signed
on left*

Handsome brick-built old inn with charming rooms, beams and panelling, appealing
choice of wooden dining chairs around interesting tables, some half-panelled wall seating,
rugs on quarry tiles or bare boards, plenty of prints on brick, cream or red walls, lovely
flower arrangements, four log fires, West Berkshire ales and well chosen wines by the
glass, good modern food and friendly service; wicker armchairs under trellising in nice
walled garden, some picnic-sets in front; attractive bedrooms. *Recommended by
the Didler, Ray Carter, Phil Bysh*

ALSO WORTH A VISIT IN BUCKINGHAMSHIRE

Besides the region's top pubs, we recommend the following. Do tell us
what you think of them: **feedback@goodguides.com**

AMERSHAM SU9597   HP7 0DY
Eagle
High Street

Rambling low-beamed pub, Adnams and Fullers London Pride, good choice of wines by
the glass, standard food, friendly helpful staff, simple décor with a few old prints, log fire,
pub games; pleasant streamside walled back garden, hanging baskets. *Recommended by
Peter and Giff Bennett*

☆ ASKETT SP8105   HP27 9LT
Three Crowns
W off A4010 into Letter Box Lane

Handsome, well run pub in small hamlet among Chiltern Hills; main emphasis on
particularly good, interesting food but also real ales from herringbone brick counter, two
contemporary-styled beamed dining rooms with mix of high-backed pale wood or black
leather dining chairs around dark wood tables on light flooring, minimal décor; some
picnic-sets under parasols outside and pretty front flower beds and baskets. *Recommended
by Doug Kennedy, Peter and Jan Humphreys, Mel Smith*

ASTON CLINTON SP8712   HP22 5EU
Oak
Green End Street

Cosy and attractive part-thatched pub under welcoming new licensees, well kept Fullers
ales and an interesting guest, good inexpensive food cooked to order (all day Sat, not Sun
evening), beams and inglenook log fire; garden with plenty of room for kids, open all day.
Recommended by Brian and Barbara Brown, Sean Hayward

AYLESBURY SP8213   HP20 1TX
Bell
Market Square

Newly opened Wetherspoons with linked beamed rooms; children welcome, open all day.
Recommended by Tim and Ann Newell

AYLESBURY SP7510   HP17 8TY
Bottle & Glass
A418 some miles towards Thame, beyond Stone

Rambling low-beamed pub completely renovated after 2003 fire, nice modern layout and
décor, enjoyable food from sandwiches up using local supplies, well kept beer, friendly
efficient staff. *Recommended by Joyce and Norman Bailey*

AYLESBURY SP8114   HP19 9AZ
Hop Pole
Bicester Road

Friendly open-plan pub tied to Vale, their ales and guests, good value food; open all day.
Recommended by Kevin Brown

☆ AYLESBURY SP8113   HP20 2RW
Kings Head
*Kings Head Passage (off Bourbon Street), also entrance off Temple Street; no nearby
parking except for disabled*

Handsome town-centre pub owned by National Trust, some beautiful early Tudor windows
and stunning 15th-c stained glass in former Great Hall and three timeless carefully

restored rooms – stripped boards, cream walls with little decoration, upholidaystered sofas and armchairs, high-backed cushioned settles and some simple modern furniture, all nicely low-key but civilised, Chiltern ales and guests, enjoyable bar food (not Sun-Tues evenings), friendly helpful service; disabled facilities, teak seats in atmospheric medieval cobbled courtyard shared with arts and crafts shop, open all day. *Recommended by Doug Kennedy, Clive and Fran Dutson, Paul Humphreys*

BEACONSFIELD SU9490   HP9 2JH
Royal Saracens
1 mile from M40 junction 2; London End (A40)

Striking timbered façade (former coaching inn), well updated open-plan layout, comfortable chairs around light wood tables, massive beams and timbers in one corner, log fires, welcoming efficient young staff, wide choice of enjoyable food including shared dishes and fixed-price weekday menu (busy weekends when best to book), well kept ales such as Fullers London Pride and Sharps Doom Bar, quite a few wines by the glass, large back restaurant; attractive sheltered courtyard. *Recommended by Neil Hardwick*

BENNETT END SU7897   HP14 4EB
☆ Three Horseshoes
Horseshoe Road; from Radnage on unclassified road towards Princes Risborough, left into Bennett End Road, then right into Horseshoe Road

Nicely converted country pub in lovely quiet spot – seemingly off the beaten track but close to M40; Rebellion IPA and a guest, several wines by the glass, decent choice of food including some traditional things (not cheap and service charge added), smartly uniformed staff, flagstoned softly lit snug bar with log fire in raised fireplace, original brickwork and bread oven, two further sitting areas, one with long winged settle, the other enclosed by standing timbers, stone floor dining room with big windows overlooking garden, red telephone box half submerged in duck pond and unspoilt valley beyond; children welcome till 9pm, dogs in bar, six bedrooms, closed Sun evening, Mon lunchtime. *Recommended by Di and Mike Gillam, Roy Hoing, Simon and Mandy King, Tracey and Stephen Groves, Brian and Anna Marsden, Anthony Lord and others*

BRADENHAM SU8297   HP14 4HF
☆ Red Lion
A4010, by Walters Ash turn-off

Charming, with friendly landlord, well kept Brakspears, enjoyable pubby food from good choice of baguettes up, small simple carpeted bar, good-sized smarter low-beamed dining room; picnic-sets on terrace and neat lawn, pretty village green nearby, closed Sun evening, Mon lunchtime. *Recommended by anon*

BRILL SP6514   HP18 9TG
☆ Pheasant
Windmill Street; off B4011 Bicester—Long Crendon;

More or less open-plan with some beams, chatty bar with smart chairs by counter, leather tub chairs in front of woodburner, Vale BB and a guest, well liked food, dining areas with high-backed leather or dark wooden chairs, attractively framed prints, books on shelves; piped music; children welcome, dogs in bar, seats on decked area and in garden, fine views over post windmill (one of the oldest in working order), bedrooms, open all day. *Recommended by Doug Kennedy, Jeremy Simmonds*

BUTLERS CROSS SP8407   HP17 0TS
Russell Arms
Off A4010 S of Aylesbury, at Nash Lee roundabout; or off A413 in Wendover, passing station; Chalkshire Road

Civilised pub with wide choice of good food in beamed and flagstoned bar and separate modern light and roomy restaurant, real ales, two open fires; small sheltered garden, well placed for Chilterns walks. *Recommended by Sean Hayward*

CADMORE END SU7793   HP14 3PF
Tree
B482 towards Stokenchurch

Stylishly refurbished but keeping beamed rustic character, wide choice of enjoyable good value food including authentic indian and thai dishes, OAP deal Mon, Brakspears, linked rooms with nice mix of old furniture, restaurant, live jazz third Weds of month; some motorway noise; children welcome, modern hotel part with 16 bedrooms, open all day from 8am. *Recommended by Susan and John Douglas, D and M T Ayres-Regan*

CADSDEN SP8204   HP27 0NB
Plough
Cadsden Road

Extended and refurbished former coaching inn with airy open-plan bar/dining area, well spaced tables on flagstones, exposed brick and some faux beams, very popular with families and Chilterns ramblers, good choice of real ales and of hearty home-made food (not Sun evening), cherry pie festival (first Sun in Aug), friendly efficient service; lots of tables in delightful quiet front and back garden, pretty spot on Ridgeway Path, bedrooms, open all day weekends. *Recommended by Doug Kennedy, Roy Hoing, C Galloway, Charles Gysin, N R White*

CHALFONT ST GILES SU9895   HP8 4RS
☆ ## Ivy House
A413 S

Old brick-and-flint beamed coaching inn tied to Fullers, their ales, good food including some interesting choices, good wines by the glass, espresso coffee, friendly young staff, comfortable fireside armchairs in carefully lit and elegantly cosy L-shaped tiled bar, lighter flagstoned dining extension; dogs allowed in bar, pleasant terrace and sloping garden (can be traffic noise), five bedrooms. *Recommended by Mrs Ann Gray, Jonathan Holloway*

CHALFONT ST GILES SU9893   HP8 4LP
White Hart
Three Households, Main Street

Spacious and airy with emphasis on the enjoyable food from interesting sandwiches up including fixed-price menu (Mon-Thurs), good service, well kept Greene King ales, lots of wines by the glass, smart modern furnishings in bar and bare-boards dining room, newspapers; soft piped music; children welcome, picnic-sets on sheltered back terrace and in garden beyond, 11 refurbished bedrooms, open all day. *Recommended by Karen Eliot, Revd R P Tickle*

CHALFONT ST PETER TQ0090   SL9 9RA
Greyhound
High Street

Spacious beamed inn dating from 15th c but opened up in modern style, flagstoned bar with log fire, comfortable restaurant with light wood floor and painted panelling, enjoyable food (some quite pricey) from pubby things up, well kept Fullers London Pride and Greene King Old Speckled Hen, plenty of wines by the glass including champagne, friendly young staff; piped music, TV; small pleasant garden, 12 well equipped bedrooms, open all day. *Recommended by Mark Daniel, Antonia Doggart*

CHALFONT ST PETER SU9990   SL9 9HH
Village Hall
Gold Hill W

Spacious and comfortable with separate bar and restaurant sides, friendly welcome, Fullers London Pride, Timothy Taylors Landlord and a local guest, enjoyable all-day food from pub standards and grills up, lunchtime deals (Mon-Weds) and themed evening menus; Tues quiz, Sat live music, sports TV; children welcome, tables out on decking. *Recommended by D Crook*

CHENIES TQ0198   WD3 6EQ
Bedford Arms
Signed from A404

Country-house hotel with two bars (one doing good pubby food) and more formal oak-panelled restaurant, three ales including Courage Directors and Wells & Youngs Bombardier, efficient service; tables in attractive garden, 18 bedrooms. *Recommended by Ian Phillips*

CHESHAM SP9501   HP5 1JD
Queens Head
Church Street

Welcoming red-brick Fullers corner pub, traditional interior with scrubbed tables, their ales kept well, good authentic thai food plus lunchtime bar snacks, open fires; sports TV; children welcome, tables in small courtyard popular with smokers, next to little River Chess, open all day. *Recommended by Brian Glozier, Chris Hall, N R White*

COLNBROOK TQ0277   SL3 0JZ
Ostrich
1.25 miles from M4 junction 5 via A4/B3378, then 'village only' road; High Street

Spectacular timbered Elizabethan building (with even longer gruesome history) given contemporary makeover, comfortable sofas on stripped wood and a startling red plastic and stainless steel bar counter, blazing log fires, well kept changing ales such as Hogs Back, Hook Norton and Windsor & Eton, good choice of wines by the glass including champagne, enjoyable food from pub favourites up, efficient friendly service, attractive restaurant; soft piped music, comedy and live music nights upstairs; children welcome, open all day Sun. *Recommended by Sally Norman, Terry Buckland, Peter Eyles, Ian Phillips*

CUDDINGTON SP7311   HP18 0BB
☆ Crown
Spurt Street; off A418 Thame—Aylesbury

Convivial thatched cottage with good chatty mix of customers, comfortable pubby furnishings including cushioned settles in two low-beamed linked rooms, log fire in big inglenook, Fullers ales and maybe a guest such as Adnams, around 20 wines by the glass, well liked bar food (not Sun evening), carpeted two-room back area with dark red walls and country-kitchen chairs around nice mix of tables; children welcome; neat side terrace with modern garden furniture and planters, picnic-sets in front. *Recommended by Ian Herdman, Doug Kennedy, Dennis and Doreen Haward, Roy Hoing, Ian Kennedy and others*

DINTON SP7610   HP17 8UL
Seven Stars
signed off A418 Aylesbury—Thame, near Gibraltar turn-off; Stars Lane

Pretty 17th-c family-run pub with inglenook bar, beamed lounge and refurbished dining room, three well kept ales such as Black Sheep, Fullers and Timothy Taylors Landlord, several wines by the glass, good choice of enjoyable home-made food at realistic prices including carvery (Sun till 7pm, Weds evening), friendly service; tables under cocktail parasols in sheltered garden with terrace, pleasant village, open all day weekends. *Recommended by Garth Rodgers*

DORNEY SU9279   SL4 6QW
Palmer Arms
2.7 miles from M4 junction 7, via B3026; Village Road

Modernised extended dining pub in attractive conservation village, popular all-day food from pub favourites up, lots of wines by the glass, Greene King ales, open fires, daily papers, civilised front bar, back dining room; piped music; children welcome, dogs in certain areas, disabled facilities, terrace overlooking mediterranean-feel garden, enclosed play area, good riverside walks nearby, open all day. *Recommended by Simon Collett-Jones, Nigel and Sue Foster, I D Barnett, Susan and John Douglas, Roy and Jean Russell*

DORNEY SU9279   SL4 6QS

☆ **Pineapple**

Lake End Road: 2.4 miles from M4 junction 7; left on A4 then left on B3026

Nicely old-fashioned pub, shiny low Anaglypta ceilings, black-panelled dados, leather
chairs around sturdy country tables (one very long, another in big bow window),
woodburner and pretty little fireplace, china pineapples and other decorations on shelves
in one of three cottagey carpeted linked rooms on left, Black Sheep Bitter, Fullers London
Pride and Marstons Pedigree, up to 1,000 varieties of sandwiches in five different fresh
breads; piped music, games machine; children and dogs welcome, rustic seats on roadside
verandah, round picnic-sets in garden, fairy-lit decking under oak tree, some motorway
noise, open all day. *Recommended by Charles Harvey, Steve and Claire Harvey, Peter Price*

EMBERTON SP8849   MK46 5DH

Bell & Bear

Off A509 Olney—Newport Pagnell; High Street

Old family-run stone-built village pub, good value interesting home-made food (not Mon),
all locally sourced including own bread, well kept ales such as Hopping Mad, Isle of
Purbeck, Silverstone and Vale, farm cider, friendly efficient staff, public bar with fire,
darts, skittles, sports TV and quiz machine; children welcome, garden tables, open all day
Fri, closed Sun evening, Mon lunchtime. *Recommended by Christopher Middleton, Peter Martin*

EVERSHOLT SP9832   MK17 9DU

Green Man

Church End

Contemporary refurbishment of early Victorian country pub with emphasis on eating
(but keeping local feel), stone floor bar and adjacent restaurant, enjoyable food (not
Sun evening) including pub favourites and blackboard specials, Fullers London Pride,
St Austell Tribute and Sharps Doom Bar, friendly service, May Day beer/sausage festival;
piped music; children and dogs welcome, big terrace, picturesque village, open all day
weekends, closed Mon lunchtime. *Recommended by Michael Dandy*

FINGEST SU7791   RG9 6QD

☆ **Chequers**

Off B482 Marlow—Stokenchurch

15th-c pub under new welcoming family, unspoilt public bar with country charm, several
traditional rooms with big open fires, horsebrasses and pewter tankards, Brakspears,
Marstons and maybe a seasonal ale from Ringwood, several wines by the glass, enjoyable
home-made food, smart back dining extension; children and dogs welcome, terrace
picnic-sets, big garden with Hambleden Valley views, good walks, opposite interesting
church with twin-roofed Norman tower, has been closed Sun evening. *Recommended by Susan
and John Douglas, Nick Massey, Roy Hoing*

FORD SP7709   HP17 8XH

☆ **Dinton Hermit**

SW of Aylesbury

Carefully extended 16th-c stone inn in quiet hamlet; bar with scrubbed tables and
comfortable wicker-backed mahogany-look chairs on old black and red tiled floor, white-
painted plaster on thick uneven stone walls, old print of John Bigg (supposed executioner
of King Charles I and later known as the Dinton Hermit), huge inglenook fireplace, back
dining area with similar furniture on quarry tiles, church candles, hundreds of wine
bottles decorating walls and thick oak bar counter, Adnams, Batemans and Brakspears,
decent choice of wines, fair range of bar food; well behaved children allowed, lots of
garden picnic sets, bedrooms, open all day. *Recommended by J A Snell*

FRIETH SU7990   RG9 6PY
Prince Albert
Off B482 SW of High Wycombe

Friendly cottagey Chilterns local with low black beams and joists, high-backed settles, big
black stove in inglenook, log fire in larger area on the right, decent food (mainly
lunchtime) from sandwiches up, well kept Brakspears and Marstons; children and dogs
welcome, nicely planted informal side garden with views of woods and fields, good walks,
open all day. *Recommended by Tracey and Stephen Groves, Peter Dandy, the Didler*

GREAT HAMPDEN SP8401   HP16 9RQ
☆ Hampden Arms
W off A4128

Friendly village pub opposite cricket pitch, good mix of locals and visitors, comfortably
furnished front and back rooms (back one more rustic with big woodburner). Adnams,
Hook Norton and a guest from Vale, several wines by the glass and maybe Addlestone's
cider from small corner bar, good pubby food, cheerful efficient service; children and dogs
welcome, seats in tree-sheltered garden, good Hampden Common walks. *Recommended by
Roy Hoing, Ross Balaam, Paul Humphreys*

GREAT KINGSHILL SU8798   HP15 6EB
☆ Red Lion
A4128 N of High Wycombe

Carefully refurbished pub with contemporary décor, interesting, popular brasserie-style
food, local beers, good wine list, plenty of space in 'lobby' plus cosy little bar with brown
leather sofas and tub armchairs, low tables, log fire, spacious candlelit dining room on
left with flagstones and modern paintings, relaxed atmosphere; well behaved children
welcome, closed Sun evening, Mon. *Recommended by Tracey and Stephen Groves*

GREAT MISSENDEN SP8901   HP16 0AU
☆ Cross Keys
High Street

Relaxed and friendly village pub, unspoilt beamed bar divided by standing timbers,
traditional furnishings including high-backed settle, log-effect gas fire in huge fireplace,
well kept Fullers ales and often an unusual guest, decent food from sandwiches up
including Sun roasts, cheerful helpful staff, spacious beamed restaurant; children and
dogs welcome, back terrace with picnic sets, open all day. *Recommended by Mrs Ann Gray,
Roy Hoing, Tracey and Stephen Groves, Paul Humphreys, Mel Smith*

HAMBLEDEN SU7886   RG9 6RP
☆ Stag & Huntsman
Off A4155 Henley—Marlow

Handsome brick and flint pub in pretty Chilterns village, congenial old-fashioned front
public bar with masses of beer mats, big fireplace in low-ceilinged partly panelled
lounge bar, Loddon Hoppit, Rebellion IPA, Sharps Doom Bar and a guest beer, farm cider
and good wines, friendly efficient staff, good reasonably priced pubby food (not Sun
evening), secluded dining room; darts, TV, piped music; children and dogs welcome, good
garden with some raised areas and decking, summer Sun barbecues, nice walks, three
bedrooms, open all day Fri-Sun; refurbishments planned as we went to press, when
there will be a limited service. *Recommended by Roy Hoing, Simon Collett-Jones, Tracey and
Stephen Groves, DHV*

HAWRIDGE SP9505   HP5 2UG
☆ Rose & Crown
Signed from A416 N of Chesham; The Vale

Roomy open-plan pub dating from 18th c, enjoyable home-made traditional food (not Sun
evening, Mon) from snacks up, well kept local beers, good cider and perry, big log fire,
peaceful country views from upper restaurant area; children and dogs welcome, pretty

hanging baskets, broad terrace with lawn dropping down beyond, play area, open all day Thurs-Sun, closed Mon lunchtime. *Recommended by Taff Thomas*

HAWRIDGE COMMON SP9406   HP5 2UH

☆ **Full Moon**

Hawridge Common; left fork off A416 N of Chesham, follow for 3.5 miles towards Cholesbury

18th-c pub with low-beamed little bar, ancient flagstones and chequered floor tiles, built-in floor-to-ceiling oak settles, hunting prints and inglenook fireplace, Adnams, Bass, Fullers London Pride, Timothy Taylors Landlord and a guest, several wines by the glass, well liked bar food from sandwiches up; piped music; seats in pleasant garden or on heated covered terrace with views over fields and windmill beyond, paddock for hitching horses, walks on common. *Recommended by Ross Balaam, Roy Hoing, John and Victoria Fairley, Susan and John Douglas, John Branston, Peter and Giff Bennett and others*

HUGHENDEN VALLEY SU8697   HP14 4LX

☆ **Harrow**

Warrendene Road, off A4128 N of High Wycombe

Small brick and flint roadside cottage at start of Chilterns valley walks, pubby tiled-floor bar with black beams and joists, wall benches and plush stools round straightforward tables, old country engravings, big fireplace with pewter mugs on high mantelbeam, larger right-hand bar similarly furnished with sizeable dining tables on brick floor, Fullers London Pride, Rebellion and Wells & Youngs, decent pubby food, friendly staff; children welcome, picnic-sets out in front, more on back lawn with swings and slide, side terrace with modern wood and chrome furniture. *Recommended by Tracey and Stephen Groves, Mike and Eleanor Anderson*

ICKFORD SP6407   HP18 9JD

Rising Sun

E of Thame; Worminghall Road

Pretty thatched local with cosy low-beamed bar, friendly staff and regulars, four real ales including Adnams and Black Sheep, good range of simple reasonably priced home-made food with occasional game. *Recommended by David Lamb*

IVINGHOE ASTON SP9518   LU7 9DP

Village Swan

Aston; signed from B489 NE of Ivinghoe

Friendly village-owned pub, enjoyable home-made pubby food including Sun carvery, good choice of real ales; handy for Ivinghoe Beacon and Icknield Way. *Recommended by Ed Sturmer, Jeff and Joan Ward*

LACEY GREEN SP8200   HP27 0QU

Black Horse

Main Road

Friendly mix of customers in this little beamed country local, popular good value home-made food (not Sun evening, Mon), four real ales, good choice of wines by the glass, big open fire; sports TV; picnic-sets in garden with play area, closed Mon lunchtime, open all day Thurs-Sun. *Recommended by Graham Middleton, D and M T Ayres-Regan, Mel Smith*

LACEY GREEN SP8201   HP27 0RJ

☆ **Pink & Lily**

A4010 High Wycombe—Princes Risborough follow Loosley sign, then Great Hampden, Great Missenden one

Modernised dining pub with good mix of customers, reasonably priced generous food from sandwiches up, Brakspears Bitter, Red Squirrel RSB and Tring Royal Poacher, several wines by the glass, airy main bar with pubby furniture, open fire, cosier side areas and conservatory-style extension with big arches, small tap room with built-in wall benches on red tiles, old wooden ham rack hanging from ceiling, broad inglenook with low mantelpiece, framed Rupert Brooke poem (there's a room dedicated to him, too) that begins with a mention of the pub; piped music; children and dogs welcome, lots of tables and pretty hanging baskets in big garden, open all day, till 8pm Sun (4pm winter). *Recommended by Ryta Lyndley, Tim and Ann Newell, Doug Kennedy, the Didler, Roy Hoing, Edward Mirzoeff and others*

LACEY GREEN SP8100   HP27 0PG
Whip
Pink Road

Cheery and attractive local welcoming walkers, mix of simple traditional furnishings in smallish front bar and larger downstairs dining area, usual food from sandwiches up, good choice of interesting well kept/priced ales including local Chiltern, Oct beer festival with jazz, friendly service; fruit machine, TV; tables in sheltered garden looking up to windmill. *Recommended by Brian and Anna Marsden*

LANE END SU8091   HP14 3JG
Grouse & Ale
High Street

Comfortable and welcoming with enjoyable food from standards up, great range of wines by the glass including champagne, well kept changing ales, helpful staff, fresh flowers, newspapers, log fires; soft piped music; children welcome (toys provided), seats outside. *Recommended by Simon Collett-Jones, Mrs Margo Finlay, Jörg Kasprowski*

LITTLE MARLOW SU8788   SL7 3RZ
☆ Kings Head
Church Road; A4155 about 2 miles E of Marlow

Long, flower-covered pub with friendly landlord, open-plan bar with low beams, captain's chairs and other traditional seating around dark wooden tables, cricketing memorabilia, log fire, Adnams, Fullers and Timothy Taylors, enjoyable food from baguettes up, gingham-clothed tables in attractive dining room; modern tables and chairs on terrace in big walled garden. *Recommended by Paul Humphreys, Doug Kennedy, Roy Hoing and others*

LITTLE MISSENDEN SU9298   HP7 0QZ
☆ Red Lion
Off A413 Amersham—Great Missenden

Unchanging pretty 15th-c cottage, small black-beamed bar, plain seats around elm pub tables, piano squashed into big inglenook beside black kitchen range packed with copper pots, kettles and rack of old guns, even smaller country dining room with pheasant décor, well kept Greene King IPA, Marstons Pedigree and Wadworths 6X, fair-priced wines, good coffee, inexpensive pubby food, good friendly service, live music Tues and Sat; children welcome, dogs in bar (there's a friendly pub dog), picnic-sets out in front and on grass behind little wall, more in sheltered back garden by pond with fancy waterfowl, aviaries with more foreign birds in meadow, open all day Fri, Sat. *Recommended by Roy Hoing, Susan and John Douglas, LM, Michael and Deborah Ethier*

LUDGERSHALL SP6617   HP18 9NZ
☆ Bull & Butcher
Off A41 Aylesbury—Bicester; bear left to The Green

Nicely old-fashioned country pub facing village green, bar with low beams in ochre ceiling, wall bench and simple pub furniture on dark tiles or flagstones, inglenook log fire, back dining room, decent bar food, Greene King IPA and Vale VPA, aunt sally and domino teams, quiz (second Sun of month); children welcome, picnic-sets on pleasant front terrace, play area, closed Mon. *Recommended by David Lamb*

You can send reports directly to us at **feedback@goodguides.com**

MARLOW SU8486   SL7 1BA
Chequers
High Street

Attractive bar/restaurant reopened under the Tailor Made Steaks brand, contemporary styling mixing with bare boards and heavy beams, food from pubby things to more expensive restaurant food, counter where you can choose your own steak, ales such as Brakspears and Wychwood Hobgoblin tapped from the cask, good choice of wines by the glass, friendly service, three dining areas including more formal half-panelled grill room with view through to kitchen; piped music; children welcome, pavement tables, open all day (till late Fri, Sat). *Recommended by D and M T Ayres-Regan*

MARLOW BOTTOM SU8588   SL7 3RA
Three Horseshoes
Signed from Handy Cross roundabout, off M40 junction 4

Much-extended beamed pub tied to nearby Rebellion, usually their full range kept well, brewery photographs, knowledgeable helpful staff, extensive choice of popular blackboard food (not Sun evening), good value wines by the glass; open all day Fri-Sat. *Recommended by Tracey and Stephen Groves, Susan and John Douglas*

MARSWORTH SP9114   HP23 4LU
☆ Red Lion
Vicarage Road; off B489 Dunstable—Aylesbury;

Low-beamed partly thatched 18th-c pub close to impressive flight of locks on Grand Union Canal, main quarry-tiled bar with pews and open fire, front snug, steps up to lounge and dining area, Fullers London Pride with guests like Rebellion and Vale, well liked pubby food, cheerful, efficient staff, games room with bar billiards, darts and juke box; children and dogs welcome, picnic-sets in small sheltered back garden with heated smokers' gazebo, more seats at front facing quiet lane. *Recommended by Ross Balaam, Tracey and Stephen Groves, Roy Hoing, Susan and John Douglas*

MEDMENHAM SU8084   SL7 2HE
Dog & Badger
Bockmer (A4155)

Spacious low-beamed pub, nice décor with good mix of old furniture on polished boards, open fire, enjoyable food in bar and restaurant, charming service, Rebellion ales, resident golden retriever; piped and some live music; children welcome, terrace tables, open all day. *Recommended by T A R Curran, Paul Humphreys*

OAKLEY SP6312   HP18 9QB
☆ Chandos Arms
The Turnpike; brown sign to pub off B4011 Thame—Bicester

Friendly 16th-c thatched village local with warmly inclusive atmosphere, two smallish rooms, one for locals and one for diners, low black beams some stripped stone, padded country kitchen chairs on patterned carpet, inglenook housing big basket of books, Courage Best, Greene King IPA and Sharps Doom Bar, sensibly priced pubby food, helpful service, darts; games machine, maybe quiet radio, TV; picnic-sets on terrace and aunt sally. *Recommended by Malcolm Lock, Sharon Oldham, David Lamb, Andy and Maureen Pickering and others*

OLNEY SP8851   MK46 4EA
Bull
Market Place /High Street

Former 18th-c coaching inn smartened up by present licensees, sofas and other seats in three smallish front rooms, big airy eating area on the right, popular food (not Sun evening) from bar snacks up including mussels done in six ways and interesting vegetarian choices, pleasant efficient service, well kept Wells & Youngs and guests (Aug bank holiday beer festival), good coffee, open and log-effect gas fires; children welcome, seats in courtyard and big back garden (no dogs) with climbing frame; start of the famous Shrove Tuesday pancake race; open all day from 10am. *Recommended by George Atkinson*

OLNEY SP8851   MK46 4AA
☆ **Swan**
High Street S

Friendly beamed and timbered linked rooms, wide choice of enjoyable sensibly priced food (not Mon) from sandwiches up, well kept ales such as Shepherd Neame and Wadworths 6X, good choice of wines by the glass, quick helpful service, daily papers, attractive flowers, rather close-set pine tables, log fires, small back bistro dining room (booking advised for this); back courtyard tables, some cover. *Recommended by Gerry and Rosemary Dobson, Michael Sargent, Michael Dandy*

OVING SP7821   HP22 4HN
☆ **Black Boy**
Off A413 N of Aylesbury

Extended 16th-c timbered pub near church, low heavy beams, log fire in enormous inglenook, steps up to snug stripped-stone area, well kept ales such as Batemans, Brakspears and Rebellion, lots of wines by the glass, pubby bar food and more elaborate restaurant menu, modern dining room with good-sized pine tables and picture windows, prompt friendly service; piped music; children and dogs welcome, tables on spacious sloping lawns and terrace (music here on Sun in summer), expansive Vale of Aylesbury views, closed Sun evening, Mon. *Recommended by Dick Vardy, Andy Dobbing, J A Snell, Malcolm Ward*

PENN STREET SU9295   HP7 0PX
☆ **Hit or Miss**
Off A404 SW of Amersham, keep on towards Winchmore Hill

Traditional pub with friendly licensees, heavily-beamed main bar with leather sofas and armchairs on parquet flooring, horsebrasses, open fire, two carpeted rooms with interesting cricket and chair-making memorabilia, more sofas, wheelback and other dining chairs around pine tables, Badger ales (summer beer festivals), interesting if not cheap food; piped music; children welcome, dogs in bar, picnic-sets on terrace overlooking pub's cricket pitch, open all day. *Recommended by H Wainman, Tracey and Stephen Groves, D and M T Ayres-Regan, Mrs Ann Gray, LM and others*

PENN STREET SU9295   HP7 0PX
Squirrel
Off A404 SW of Amersham, opposite the Common

Family-friendly sister pub to nearby Hit or Miss, open-plan bar with flagstones, log fire, comfortable sofas as well as tables and chairs, good value home-made traditional food from baguettes up (not Sun evening), good children's meals, well kept changing ales, free coffee refills, bric-a-brac and cricketing memorabilia, darts; big garden with good play area and village cricket view, lovely walks, open all day weekends. *Recommended by David Lamb, C and R Bromage, Tracey and Stephen Groves*

PRINCES RISBOROUGH SP8104   HP27 0LL
Red Lion
Whiteleaf, off A4010; OS Sheet 165 map reference 817043

Simple comfortably worn-in village pub with welcoming landlady, good generous food at reasonable prices (freshly cooked so can take a while), well kept Greene King Gangly Ghoul and Sharps Doom Bar, log fire, traditional games; garden tables, charming village, good Chilterns walks. *Recommended by Peter Donaghy, Roy Hoing, Brian and Anna Marsden, David Lamb*

All *Guide* inspections are anonymous. Anyone claiming to be a *Good Pub Guide* inspector is a fraud. Please let us know.

QUAINTON SP7420   HP22 4AR
George & Dragon
The Green

Traditional flower-decked pub on village green, well kept Hook Norton, Shepherd Neame,
Wells & Youngs and guests, good choice of enjoyable home-made food (not Sun evening,
Mon lunchtime), friendly efficient staff, split level bar, post office facility Weds afternoon;
tables outside, good view of windmill, open all day in summer. *Recommended by Peter Lee,*
Tony and Wendy Hobden

SEER GREEN   HP9 2YG
Jolly Cricketers
Chalfont Road, opposite the church

Refurbished 19th-c red-brick dining pub doing well under present management, good
original modern cooking featuring fresh fish and game (no food Sun evening, Mon), four
local ales, lots of wines by the glass, cricketing odds and ends, woodburner, live jazz and
beer festivals; children and dogs welcome, picnic-sets in compact garden, good walks,
open all day. *Recommended by anon*

SHERINGTON SP8946   MK16 9PE
White Hart
Off A509; Gun Lane

Good changing ales such as Archers, Greene King, Purity and Rebellion, helpful landlord
and friendly staff, good pub food (not Sun evening) from sandwiches and tapas up, bright
fire, two-room bar, contemporary flagstoned dining room; children and dogs welcome,
picnic-sets in garden with terrace, pretty hanging baskets, bedrooms in adjacent building.
Recommended by Mrs C Roe, Gerry and Rosemary Dobson

ST LEONARDS SP9107   HP23 6NW
White Lion
Jenkins Lane, by Buckland Common; off A4011 Wendover—Tring

Neat open-plan pub, highest in the Chilterns, with old black beams and inglenook, well
kept ales such as Batemans, Greene King and Tring, good value pub food, friendly service;
children and dogs welcome, attractive sheltered garden, good walks. *Recommended by*
Roy Hoing, Susan and John Douglas, David Lamb

STOKE GOLDINGTON SP8348   MK16 8NR
☆ **Lamb**
High Street (B526 Newport Pagnell—Northampton)

Chatty village pub with friendly helpful licensees, up to four interesting changing ales,
Weston's farm cider, good range of wines and soft drinks, good generous home-made food
(all day Sat, not Sun evening) from baguettes to bargain Sun roasts, public bar with table
skittles, quiet lounge with log fire and sheep decorations, two small pleasant dining
rooms; may be soft piped music, TV; dogs welcome, terrace and sheltered garden behind,
open all day weekends. *Recommended by JJW, CMW and others*

STONE SP7912   HP17 8QP
Bugle Horn
Oxford Road, Hartwell (A418 SW of Aylesbury)

Long 17th-c stone-built Vintage Inn (former farmhouse), friendly and comfortable linked
rooms with mix of furniture, good choice of modestly priced food all day, friendly service,
ales from Fullers, Wadworths and Wells & Youngs, lots of wines by the glass, log fires,
conservatory; children welcome, attractive terrace, lovely trees in big garden with
pastures beyond, open all day. *Recommended by Tim and Ann Newell, Phil and Jane Hodson*

Virtually all pubs in the *Good Pub Guide* sell wine by the glass. We mention wines
if they are a cut above the average.

SWANBOURNE SP8027   MK17 0SH
Betsy Wynne
Mursley Road

Popular new pub (part of the Swanbourne Estate) built in traditional timbered style, enjoyable freshly cooked food from landlord/chef using estate and other local produce, good choice of real ales, welcoming efficient staff, spacious layout with plenty of exposed oak beams including raftered dining room, wood or terracotta-tiled floors, woodburner in central brick fireplace; children and dogs welcome, tables on terrace and lawn, play house and old tractor, open all day. *Recommended by Brian Glozier*

TAPLOW SU9182   SL6 0ET
Oak & Saw
Rectory Road

Open-plan bare-boards local opposite attractive village green, clean and unpretentious, with well kept Brakspears, Fullers and guests, plenty of wines by the glass, good choice of reasonably priced decent pubby food (not Sun or Mon evenings), efficient friendly service, interesting pictures; TV; children welcome, terrace and garden tables. *Recommended by Peter Scott*

THE LEE SP8904   HP16 9LZ
☆ Cock & Rabbit
Back roads 2.5 miles N of Great Missenden, E of A413

Stylish place run for 25 years by same friendly italian family, although much emphasis on the good italian cooking they do keep Flowers and a guest ale and are happy to provide lunchtime baps, carefully decorated plush-seated lounge, cosy dining room and larger restaurant; seats outside on verandah, terraces and lawn. *Recommended by Paul Humphreys, Roy Hoing, David Lamb and others*

THE LEE SP8904   HP16 9NU
☆ Old Swan
Swan Bottom, back Road 0.75 miles N of The Lee

Welcoming tucked-away 16th-c dining pub, three attractively furnished linked rooms, low beams and flagstones, cooking-range log fire in inglenook, good choice of enjoyable food, Brakspears; big back garden with play area, good walks. *Recommended by Doug Kennedy, Paul Humphreys*

TURVILLE SU7691   RG9 6QU
☆ Bull & Butcher
Valley road off A4155 Henley—Marlow at Mill End, past Hambleden and Skirmett

Black and white pub in pretty village (famous as film and TV setting), two traditional low-beamed rooms with inglenooks, wall settles in tiled-floor bar, deep well incorporated into glass-topped table, well kept Brakspears and decent wines by the glass, enjoyable if pricey food, friendly welcoming service; piped and monthly live music, TV; children (away from bar) and dogs welcome, seats by fruit trees in attractive garden, good walks, open all day. *Recommended by Simon Collett-Jones, Doug Kennedy, Dr Kevan Tucker, John Saville, Peter Dandy, Stuart and Jasmine Kelly and others*

WEST WYCOMBE SU8394   HP14 3AB
George & Dragon
High Street; A40 W of High Wycombe

Popular rambling hotel bar in preserved Tudor village, massive beams and sloping walls, dim lighting, big log fire, Courage Best, Brakspears, St Austell Tribute and a guest, fairly priced food from sandwiches and baguettes up, good friendly staff, small family dining room; dogs welcome, grassed area with picnic-sets and fenced play area, character bedrooms (magnificent oak staircase), handy for West Wycombe Park, open all day weekends. *Recommended by Doug Kennedy, Paul Humphreys, Edward Mirzoeff, Mel Smith*

WING SP8822   LU7 0NS
Queens Head
High Street

Welcoming 16th-c pub with good freshly cooked food in bar and restaurant, well kept
Courage Directors, Wells & Youngs and a guest like Slaters Queen Bee, decent wines,
afternoon tea with home-made scones, log fires; children welcome, disabled facilities,
garden picnic-sets, open all day. *Recommended by Peter Kirby, Trevor Brown,*
David and Diane Young

WOOBURN MOOR SU9189   HP10 0NA
Falcon
Old Moor Lane; SE edge of Loudwater

Unpretentious little low-beamed local with friendly relaxing atmosphere, three well kept
changing ales, freshly cooked pubby food including Sun roasts, homely lived-in linked
rooms with bare boards, evening candles and coal fires, board games, paperback library,
open-mike and quiz nights; garden. *Recommended by Susan and John Douglas*

ALSO WORTH A VISIT IN HAMPSHIRE

Besides the region's top pubs, we recommend the following. Do tell us
what you think of them: **feedback@goodguides.com**

ALRESFORD SU5832   SO24 9AT
Bell
West Street

Comfortable and welcoming Georgian coaching inn (originally the Market Inn), good
popular food including weekday fixed-price menu, efficient service, well kept local beer
and good choice of wines, spic-and-span interior with bare boards, scrubbed tables, bric-
a-brac and log fire, daily papers, smallish dining room, may be jazz on Sun in summer;
attractive back courtyard, six bedrooms, open all day, closed Sun evening. *Recommended by*
Leon Wise, Ann and Colin Hunt, Val and Alan Green, Phyl and Jack Street

ALRESFORD SU5831   SO24 9LW
Cricketers
Jacklyns Lane

Large comfortable and friendly local with popular food including good value set deals,
real ales, good service, cottagey eating area down steps; children welcome, sizeable
garden with covered terrace and good play area. *Recommended by Tony and Jill Radnor*

ALRESFORD SU5832   SO24 9AD
Swan
West Street

Long narrow oak-panelled red-carpeted bar in 18th-c hotel (former coaching inn),
three ales including Courage Best, decent wines, tea and coffee, good choice of popular
reasonably priced food plus good Sun carvery, two dining rooms; children welcome,
23 bedrooms. *Recommended by Val and Alan Green, Gordon Neighbour, Ann and Colin Hunt*

ALTON SU7138   GU34 1RT
French Horn
The Butts (A339 S of centre, by railway bridge)

Popular and cheery catslide-roof local with well kept Butcombe, Ringwood, Sharps, Triple
fff, Wells & Youngs and a guest, plenty of wines by the glass, wide choice of enjoyable food
including blackboard specials, nice coffee, good service, tankards and whisky-water jugs

on beams, bowler hats and french horn above inglenook log fire, newspapers, partly stripped-brick dining room, separate skittle alley; piped music; children welcome, covered heated smokers' terrace, picnic-sets in two garden areas, play area, bedrooms in adjacent building, next to Watercress Line with occasional steam trains, open all day. *Recommended by LM, Phil and Sally Gorton*

AMPFIELD SU4023   SO51 9BQ
☆ **White Horse**
A3090 Winchester—Romsey

Snug low-beamed front bar with candles and soft lighting, inglenook log fire and comfortable country furnishings, far-spreading beamed dining area behind, well kept Greene King ales and guests, good choice of enjoyable all-day snacks, several wines by the glass, efficient friendly service, locals' bar with another inglenook; piped music; children and dogs welcome, high-hedged garden with plenty of picnic-sets, cricket green beyond, good walks in Ampfield Woods, handy for Hillier Gardens, open all day. *Recommended by Phyl and Jack Street, Matt Cutting*

BALL HILL SU4263   RG20 0NQ
Furze Bush
Leaving Newbury on A343 turn right towards East Woodhay

Clean airy décor, pews and pine tables, log fire, wide choice of good generous food promptly served by friendly staff, several well kept ales including Fullers London Pride, decent wines, reasonable prices, restaurant; children welcome, tables on terrace by good-sized sheltered lawn with fenced play area. *Recommended by Mr and Mrs H J Langley, Ian Herdman, J V Dadswell*

BARTON STACEY SU4341   SO21 3RL
Swan
Village signed off A303

Warm friendly atmosphere in beamed former coaching inn, enjoyable food from pubby things up, well kept ales such as Bowman, Fullers and Otter, good choice of wines, little lounge area between front log-fire bar and cosy dining part, back restaurant; piped music; children and dogs welcome, tables on front lawn and back terrace, open all day Fri, Sat, closed Sun evening. *Recommended by Russell Traynor, Sarah Flynn*

BASING SU6653   RG24 8AE
☆ **Millstone**
Bartons Lane, Old Basing; follow brown signs to Basing House

Well run busy pub with lots of picnic-sets out by River Loddon (ducks and swans) looking across to former viaduct through scrubland, enjoyable freshly cooked food, full Wadworths range kept well, Weston's farm cider, good choice of wines by the glass, dark panelling, old prints and etchings, sturdy pub furnishings; may be faint piped jazz; children and dogs welcome, by ruins of Basing House, open all day. *Recommended by Douglas and Ann Hare, Karen Sloan*

BEAUWORTH SU5624   SO24 0PB
Milbury's
Off A272 Winchester/Petersfield

Attractive old tile-hung pub, beams, panelling and stripped stone, massive 17th-c treadmill for much older incredibly deep well, galleried area, good choice of real ales, straightforward reasonably priced food, good service, skittle alley; children in eating areas, garden with fine downland views, good walks. *Recommended by the Didler, Ann and Colin Hunt, Michael and Maggie Betton, Steve Frampton*

BISHOP'S WALTHAM SU5517   SO32 1AJ

Barleycorn
Lower Basingwell Street

Buoyant 18th-c two-bar local, enjoyable good value generous pub food, friendly efficient service, well kept Greene King ales and a guest, decent wine, beams and some low ceiling panelling, open fires; children and dogs welcome, large garden with back smokers' area, open all day. *Recommended by Robert Lorimer, Henry Fryer, Ann and Colin Hunt, Stephen and Jean Curtis and others*

BISHOP'S WALTHAM SU5517   SO32 1AD

☆ Bunch of Grapes
St Peter's Street – just along from entrance to central car park

Neat civilised little pub in quiet medieval street, smartly furnished keeping individuality and unspoilt feel (run by same family for a century), good chatty landlord and regulars, Courage Best, Goddards and a guest tapped from the cask, no food; charming back terrace garden with own bar, opening times may vary. *Recommended by Henry Fryer, the Didler, Stephen and Jean Curtis, Phil and Jane Villiers*

BOLDRE SZ3198   SO41 8NE

☆ Red Lion
Off A337 N of Lymington

Attractive black-beamed rooms with entertaining collection of bygones, pews and other seats, log fires, attentive friendly staff coping well at busy times, popular food including specials board, well kept Ringwood ales and a guest, great choice of wines by the glass, decent coffee; children and dogs welcome, tables in nice back garden, open all day. *Recommended by Phyl and Jack Street, Mr and Mrs W W Burke, Ann and Colin Hunt, Steve Kent and others*

BRAISHFIELD SU3724   SO51 0QE

Wheatsheaf
Village signposted off A3090 on NW edge of Romsey

Smartened up by newish management (the bric-a-brac collection has gone), well kept Flack Manor, Timothy Taylors Landlord and a guest, huge choice of wines by the glass including champagne, enjoyable seasonal food from sensibly short menu, log fire; piped music; children and dogs welcome, garden with good views, boules, woodland walks nearby, close to Hillier Gardens, open all day Fri-Sun. *Recommended by John Chambers*

BRAMBRIDGE SU4721   SO50 6HZ

☆ Dog & Crook
Near M3 junction 12, via B3335

Cheerful bustling 18th-c pub, traditional home-made food including plenty of fresh fish, cosy dining room, beamed bar with friendly drinking end, Fullers and Ringwood ales, lots of wines by the glass, neat efficient staff; piped music, TV, regular events and summer music nights; dogs welcome, garden with heated decking and arbour, Itchen Way walks nearby. *Recommended by Phyl and Jack Street, Ann and Colin Hunt, Mr and Mrs D G Waller*

BRAMDEAN SU6127   SO24 0LP

☆ Fox
A272 Winchester—Petersfield

Pleasant 17th-c weatherboarded dining pub with long-serving owners, loyal regulars in old-fashioned open-plan bar, black beams, cushioned wall pews and wheelbacks, tall stools with backrests at counter, Greene King Morland Original, standard bar food (not Sun evening) including good crab sandwiches; piped music, no children; dogs in bar if not busy, walled-in terraced area and neatly kept spacious lawn under fruit trees, good surrounding walks, closed Sun evening. *Recommended by Mr and Mrs W W Burke, Colin McKerrow*

BRANSGORE SZ1897 BH23 8AA
Crown
Ringwood Road; off A35 N of Christchurch

Rambling, traditionally done Vintage Inn, popular food from usual pub dishes to venison and guinea fowl, Fullers London Pride, Ringwood and a guest, lots of wines by the glass, log fire; children welcome, picnic-sets in big garden, open all day. *Recommended by Sue and Mike Todd*

BROOK SU2714 SO43 7HE
Bell
B3079/B3078, handy for M27 junction 1

Really a hotel with golf club and plush restaurant, but has neatly kept bar with lovely inglenook fire, good choice of well kept ales including Ringwood and good bar food from sandwiches to steak, helpful friendly uniformed staff; big garden, delightful village, 25 comfortable bedrooms. *Recommended by Phyl and Jack Street*

BROOK SU2713 SO43 7HE
☆ Green Dragon
B3078 NW of Cadnam, just off M27 junction 1

Immaculate thatched New Forest dining pub dating from 15th c, good welcoming service even when busy, enjoyable fresh food including plenty of seasonal game and fish as well as pubby favourites, well kept Fullers and Ringwood, daily papers, bright linked areas with stripped pine and other pubby furnishings; attractive small terrace, garden with paddocks beyond, picturesque village, self-catering apartment. *Recommended by Bob and Angela Brooks, R and M Thomas, PL, Howard G Allen, Mr and Mrs P D Titcomb and others*

BUCKLERS HARD SU4000 SO42 7XB
☆ Master Builders House
M27 junction 2 follow signs to Beaulieu, turn left onto B3056, then left to Bucklers Hard

Smart sizeable hotel with riverside garden (waterside walks) in charming village, two-level bar with heavy beams, mullioned windows, rugs on wood floor and log fire in old brick fireplace, bar stools on quarry tiles by counter serving Marstons and Ringwood, varied bar food; children and dogs welcome, front terrace, bedrooms, open all day. *Recommended by Mrs Ann Gray, Mr and Mrs D Hammond, Steven King and Barbara Cameron, Martin and Karen Wake*

BURGHCLERE SU4660 RG20 9JY
Carpenters Arms
Harts Lane, off A34

Small unpretentious pub under newish local management, well kept Arkells and an occasional guest, sensibly priced home-made food (not Sun evening), helpful staff, good country views from dining extension and terrace picnic-sets, log fire; piped music; children and dogs welcome, handy for Sandham Memorial Chapel (NT) and Highclere Castle, six comfortable annexe bedrooms, open all day. *Recommended by John Quinn, Sean Dunn, Mr and Mrs H J Langley*

BURITON SU7320 GU31 5RX
☆ Five Bells
Off A3 S of Petersfield

Low-beamed 17th-c pub, pleasant staff, fresh pubby food from baguettes up, Badger beers, good wines by the glass, big log fire, daily papers, flowers and church candles, some ancient stripped masonry and woodburner on public side; piped music; children and dogs welcome, nice garden and sheltered terraces, pretty village, good walks, self-catering in converted stables, open all day. *Recommended by W A Evershed, Terry and Eileen Stott*

BURLEY SU2202   BH24 4AZ
White Buck
Bisterne Close; 0.7 miles E, OS Sheet 195 map reference 223028

Popular 19th-c mock-Tudor hotel now owned by Fullers, their ales and a guest in long comfortably divided bar, lots of pictures, log fires each end, pleasant dining room with tables out on decking; children and dogs welcome, front terrace and spacious lawn, lovely New Forest setting, superb walks towards Burley itself and over Mill Lawn, seven bedrooms, open all day. *Recommended by Mrs Joy Griffiths, John and Joan Calvert, Mr and Mrs D Hammond, Sara Fulton, Roger Baker*

BURSLEDON SU4809   SO31 8DE
☆ Fox & Hounds
Hungerford Bottom; 2 miles from M27 junction 8

Popular rambling 16th-c Chef & Brewer of unusual character, ancient beams, flagstones and big log fires, linked by pleasant family conservatory area to ancient back barn with buoyant rustic atmosphere, lantern-lit side stalls, lots of interesting farm equipment, well kept ales such as Adnams and Ringwood, good choice of wines, decent coffee, enjoyable reasonably priced food from sandwiches up including vegetarian choices, cheerful obliging staff, daily papers; children allowed, tables outside. *Recommended by Phyl and Jack Street, Ann and Colin Hunt, Phil and Jane Villiers*

BURSLEDON SU4909   SO31 8DN
☆ Jolly Sailor
Off A27 towards Bursledon Station, Lands End Road; handy for M27 junction 8

Busy efficiently run Badger dining pub in prime spot overlooking yachting inlet, good fairly priced food cooked to order, their usual ales and good wine choice, log fires; open all day. *Recommended by the Didler, Ann and Colin Hunt, Louisa Fleming*

CADNAM SU2913   SO40 2NP
☆ Sir John Barleycorn
Old Romsey Road; by M27 junction 1

Wide choice of good up-to-date food in picturesque low-slung thatched pub extended from cosy beamed and timbered medieval core, good service, Ringwood and a guest ale, two log fires, modern décor and stripped wood flooring; suntrap benches in front and out in colourful garden, open all day. *Recommended by Bob and Angela Brooks, Phyl and Jack Street*

CHALTON SU7316   PO8 0BG
☆ Red Lion
Off A3 Petersfield—Horndean

Largely extended thatched all-day dining pub with interesting 16th-c core around ancient inglenook fireplace, wide range of popular food from good sandwiches up, well kept Fullers/Gales ales and lots of country wines, decent coffee, helpful smart staff, well spaced tables; children and dogs allowed, good disabled access and facilities, nice views from neat rows of picnic-sets on rectangular lawn by large car park, good walks, handy for Queen Elizabeth Country Park, open all day. *Recommended by David M Smith, Ann and Colin Hunt, Conor McGaughey*

CHARTER ALLEY SU5957   RG26 5QA
White Hart
White Hart Lane, off A340 N of Basingstoke

Handsome beamed pub with Bowman, Palmers and Triple fff, continental beers, summer farm cider, decent wines including country ones, good choice of generous well presented food (not Sun evening) from baguettes up, comfortable lounge bar with woodburner in big fireplace, dining area, simple public bar with skittle alley; small garden and water-feature terrace, nine bedrooms, open all day Sun. *Recommended by J V Dadswell, Joan and Michel Hooper-Immins*

CHAWTON SU7037   GU34 1SB
☆ Greyfriar
Off A31/A32 S of Alton; Winchester Road

Popular flower-decked beamed dining pub opposite Jane Austen's house, enjoyable if pricey food (not Sun evening) from good baguettes and sandwiches up, Sun roasts, Fullers ales, decent wines by the glass, good coffees, welcoming relaxed atmosphere and quite a few older midweek lunchers, comfortable seating and sturdy pine tables in neat linked areas, open fire in restaurant end; piped music; dogs in bar, children till 9pm, tables on terrace in small garden, good nearby walks, open all day. *Recommended by Ann and Colin Hunt, Maureen and Keith Gimson, B and F A Hannam, B M Eldridge*

CHERITON SU5828   SO24 0QQ
☆ Flower Pots
Off B3046 towards Beauworth and Winchester; OS Sheet 185 map reference 581282

Unspoilt country local in same family for over 40 years, own-brewed good value beers (brewery tours by arrangement) along with Flowerpots ales tapped from casks, standard food (not Sun evening or bank holiday evenings, and possible restrictions during busy times), popular curry night Weds, extended plain public bar with covered well, another straightforward but homely room with country pictures on striped wallpaper and ornaments over small log fire; no credit cards or children; dogs welcome, seats on pretty front and back lawns, summer marquee, bedrooms. *Recommended by Paul J Robinshaw, Klaus and Elizabeth Leist, Tony and Jill Radnor, N R White, the Didler, Ann and Colin Hunt and others*

CHILWORTH SU4118   SO16 7JZ
☆ Chilworth Arms
Chilworth Road (A27 Southampton—Romsey)

Stylish well run modern dining pub, popular food with some italian-influences from home-made pizzas to more adventurous things, fixed-price lunch/early evening menu Mon-Thurs, good wine choice, ales such as Greene King, Sharps and Wells & Youngs, neat efficient young staff, chunky furniture including quite a lot of leather, log fires, conservatory-style back restaurant, chattier areas too; piped music; children welcome, disabled facilities, large neat garden with terrace, open all day. *Recommended by Phyl and Jack Street, Howard G Allen, Dr and Mrs A K Clarke and others*

COLDEN COMMON SU4821   SO50 7HG
☆ Fishers Pond
Junction B3354/B2177 (Main Road), at Fishers Pond just S

Big Vintage Inn in appealing position by peaceful woodside lake, various different areas and alcoves making the most of waterside views, some painted brickwork, carpet or rugs on aged terracotta, dark leather built-in banquettes, heavy beams and log fires, brighter modern end section, popular all-day bar food, ales such as Ringwood and Sharps Doom Bar; piped music, machines; children welcome, solid teak furniture on heated partly covered lakeside terrace, handy for Marwell Zoo. *Recommended by Joan and Michel Hooper-Immins, Jim Metcalfe, Ann and Colin Hunt, Phyl and Jack Street and others*

CRAWLEY SU4234   SO21 2PR
☆ Fox & Hounds
Village signed from A272 and B3420 NW of Wincludinghester

Mock-Tudor building with jutting upper storeys, pegged structural timbers in neat brickwork and elaborately carved steep gable-ends; civilised neatly kept linked rooms with mix of attractive furniture on polished floors, built-in wall seats in traditional little bar, log fires, reasonably priced popular bar food, Ringwood, Wadworths and Wychwood, friendly licensees and efficient young staff; children welcome, gardens with picnic-sets and play equipment, picturesque village, bedrooms in converted outbuildings, closed Sun evening. *Recommended by Phyl and Jack Street, Brian Johnson and others*

CRONDALL SU7948   GU10 5NT
Plume of Feathers
The Borough

Attractive smallish 15th-c village pub popular for good range of home-made food from
standards to more innovative dishes, friendly helpful staff, well kept Greene King and
some unusual guests, good wines by the glass, beams and dark wood, prints on cream
walls, restaurant with log fire in big brick fireplace (not usually lit lunchtimes); children
welcome, picturesque village. *Recommended by KC*

CROOKHAM SU7952   GU51 5SU
Exchequer
Crondall Road

Welcoming refurbished pub doing enjoyable home-made food (not Sun evening) in bar
and restaurant, three local ales tapped from the cask, bar games and quiz nights; piped
music; near Basingstoke Canal and popular with walkers, open all day Sun till 7.30pm,
closed Mon evening. *Recommended by Jessica Courtney*

CURDRIDGE SU5314   SO32 2BH
Cricketers
Curdridge Lane, off B3035 just under a mile NE of A334 junction

Open-plan low-ceilinged Victorian village pub, sensibly priced food, cheerful efficient
staff, Greene King ales, banquettes in lounge area, traditional public area, rather smart
dining part; soft piped music; tables on front lawn, pleasant walks. *Recommended by
Henry Fryer*

DAMERHAM SU1016   SP6 3HQ
☆ ## Compasses
Signed off B3078 in Fordingbridge, or off A354 via Martin; East End

Appealing old country inn, well kept ales including Ringwood, good choice of wines by the
glass, lots of malt whiskies, good food from sandwiches up, small neat lounge bar divided
by log fire from pleasant dining area with booth seating, pale wood tables and kitchen
chairs, conservatory, separate bar with pool, friendly locals and dogs; children welcome,
long pretty garden by attractive village's cricket ground, high downland walks, nice
bedrooms. *Recommended by N R White, Susanne House*

DENMEAD SU6211   PO7 4QX
Chairmakers Arms
Forest Road

Roomy country pub surrounded by paddocks and farmland, good value quickly served food
from bar snacks up, Sun carvery, Fullers ales, log fires; can get busy; tables in spacious
garden with pergola, nice walks. *Recommended by W A Evershed*

DIBDEN PURLIEU SU4106   SO45 4PU
Heath
Beaulieu Road; B3054/A326 roundabout

Comfortable and welcoming family dining pub, popular and spacious, with bright clean
contemporary linked areas, good choice of enjoyable food all day, friendly efficient young
staff, beers such as Ringwood, Shepherd Neame Spitfire and Wadworths 6X. *Recommended
by Phyl and Jack Street and others*

DROXFORD SU6018   SO32 3PA
☆ ## Bakers Arms
High Street; A32 5 miles N of Wickham

Attractively opened-up pub with dark beams and exposed brickwork, well spaced mix of
tables on carpet or neat bare boards, leather chesterfields, log fire, good changing choice
of interesting home-made food including popular Sun roasts, home-baked bread, Bowman

Swift One and Wallops Wood, Weston's cider, attached post office; children and dogs welcome, picnic-sets outside, closed Sun evening and Mon. *Recommended by Jenny Bolton, Phyl and Jack Street, D and J Ashdown, Ann and Colin Hunt and others*

DUMMER SU5846   RG25 2AD
Queen
Under a mile from M3 junction 7; take Dummer slip road

Comfortable beamed pub well divided with lots of softly lit alcoves, Courage Best, Fullers London Pride, John Smiths and a guest, decent choice of wines by the glass, popular food from lunchtime sandwiches and light dishes up, friendly service, big log fire, Queen and steeplechase prints, no mobile phones, restaurant allowing children; piped music; picnic-sets under parasols on terrace and in extended back garden, attractive village with ancient church. *Recommended by Mrs Ann Gray, Michael and Margaret Cross*

DUNBRIDGE SU3126   SO51 0LF
☆ # Mill Arms
Barley Hill

Much extended 18th-c coaching inn opposite railway station, friendly informal atmosphere in spacious high-ceilinged rooms, scrubbed pine tables and farmhouse chairs on oak or flagstone floors, several sofas, two log fires, Ringwood Best and guests, good bistro-style food (all day weekends), dinning conservatory, two skittle alleys; piped music; children welcome, dogs in bar, big pretty garden, plenty of walks in surrounding Test Valley, bright comfortable bedrooms, open all day weekends (till 4pm winter Sun). *Recommended by Phyl and Jack Street, Ann and Colin Hunt, Dave Braisted, Martin and Karen Wake, Glenwys and Alan Lawrence and others*

DUNDRIDGE SU5718   SO32 1GD
☆ # Hampshire Bowman
Off B3035 towards Droxford, Swanmore, then right at Bishops W signpost

Good chatty mix at this friendly relaxed country tavern, five well kept local ales tapped from casks, summer farm cider, well liked food (all day Fri-Sun) from hearty pub dishes to specials using local produce including own herbs and vegetables, smart stable bar sitting comfortably alongside cosy and unassuming original one, some colourful paintings, Archie the pub dog, no mobile phones (£1 fine in charity box); children (under-14s in stable bar) and dogs welcome, hitching post for horses, heated terrace, peaceful lawn, play equipment, open all day. *Recommended by Robert Lorimer, Henry Fryer, Ann and Colin Hunt, the Didler, Stephen and Jean Curtis, Howard and Margaret Buchanan and others*

DURLEY SU5116   SO32 2BT
Farmers Home
B3354 and B2177; Heathen Street/Curdridge Road

Helpful long-serving landlord in comfortable beamed pub with two-bay dining area and big restaurant, generous reasonably priced food including fresh fish and lovely puddings, good friendly service, well kept Fullers/Gales and Ringwood BB, decent wine, log fire; children welcome, big garden with good play area, nice walks. *Recommended by Phyl and Jack Street, Ann and Colin Hunt*

DURLEY SU5217   SO32 2AA
Robin Hood
Durley Street, just off B2177 Bishops Waltham—Winchester – brown signs to pub

Open-plan beamed pub under newish enthusiastic landlord, Greene King ales and a guest, enjoyable food from varied blackboard menu (order at bar), friendly staff, log fire and leather sofas in bare-boards bar, dining area with stone floors and mix of old pine tables and chairs, bookcase door to lavatories; piped music; children and dogs welcome, disabled facilities, decked terrace with barbecue, garden with play area and nice country views, open all day Sun. *Recommended by Graham, Phyl and Jack Street*

EAST MEON SU6822   GU32 1NH

 ☆ **Olde George**

Church Street; signed off A272 W of Petersfield, and off A32 in West Meon

Relaxing heavy-beamed rustic pub, enjoyable if not cheap bar and restaurant food from
sandwiches up including set lunch, good smartly dressed staff, well kept Badger ales, cosy
areas around central bar counter, inglenook log fires; children and dogs welcome, nice
back terrace, five comfortable bedrooms, pretty village with fine church, good walks, open
all day Sun. *Recommended by E Clark, W A Evershed, Ann and Colin Hunt*

EAST TYTHERLEY SU2927   SO51 0LW

☆ **Star**

B3084 N of Romsey; turn off by railway crossing opposite Mill Arms, Dundridge

Pretty country inn with comfortable sofas and tub chairs mixing with traditional pubby
furniture, rich red walls, bookcase to one side of log fire, ales from Andwell, Cottage and
Itchen Valley, reasonably priced food cooked by licensees' son, formally set restaurant;
piped music – live music Fri evening; children welcome, dogs in bar, tables out at front
and on back terrace by giant chessboard, bedrooms overlooking cricket pitch, good
breakfast, nearby walks, closed Sun evening, Mon. *Recommended by Christopher and Elise Way,
Ann and Colin Hunt, T A R Curran, Phyl and Jack Street, P J Checksfield, JES and others*

EASTON SU5132   SO21 1EJ

Cricketers

Off B3047

Pleasantly smartened-up traditional local, home-made food with some modern touches in
bar and smallish restaurant, good friendly service, Marstons-related ales including
Ringwood, good choice of wines by the glass, dark tables and chairs on carpet, bare-
boards area with darts, shove-ha'penny and other games; piped and some live music,
sports TV; children and dogs welcome, front terrace with heated smokers' shelter, handy
for Itchen Way walks, three bedrooms, open all day summer. *Recommended by
Mrs Margaret Weir, Ann and Colin Hunt, Tony and Jill Radnor*

ELLISFIELD SU6345   RG25 2QW

☆ **Fox**

Green Lane; S of village off Northgate Lane

Simple tucked-away place under new ownership; mixed collection of stripped tables,
country chairs and cushioned wall benches on bare boards and old floor tiles, some
stripped masonry, open fires in plain brick fireplaces, Sharps Doom Bar, Fullers London
Pride and a guest or two, home-made food; outside gents'; children and dogs welcome,
picnic-sets in nice garden, good walking country near snowdrop and bluebell woods, open
all day. *Recommended by anon*

EMERY DOWN SU2808   SO43 7DY

 ☆ **New Forest**

Village signed off A35 just W of Lyndhurst

In one of the best bits of the Forest for walking, well run and popular, with good
reasonably priced food (all day weekends) including local venison, friendly attentive
uniformed staff, ales such as Fullers, Ringwood and Shepherd Neame, real cider, good
choice of wines by the glass, coffee and tea all day, attractive softly lit separate areas on
varying levels, each with its own character, hunting prints, two log fires; piped music;
children and dogs welcome, covered heated terrace, small pleasant three-level garden,
bedrooms, open all day. *Recommended by Mr and Mrs D Hammond, Stephen Moss, Laurie Scott*

EVERSLEY SU7861   RG27 0NB

☆ **Golden Pot**

B3272

Small attractive creeper-covered dining pub with good food from traditional choices up
(small helpings available), well kept changing ales such as Crondall, West Berkshire and

Windsor & Eton, several wines by the glass, friendly landlord and staff, neatly refurbished linked areas, log fire; piped music – live Mon; children welcome, dogs in bar, tables out among colourful flowers, closed Sun evening. *Recommended by Joan and Tony Walker, Mrs Pam Mattinson, KC, G Ridgway, Caz Brant and others*

EVERTON SZ2994   SO41 0JJ
Crown
Old Christchurch Road; pub signed just off A337 W of Lymington

Quietly set New Forest-edge restaurant/pub with enjoyable varied food, good service, Ringwood and guests, reliable wine choice, two attractive dining rooms off tiled-floor bar, log fires; picnic-sets on front terrace and in garden behind. *Recommended by Phyl and Jack Street, Steve Green, David Sizer*

EXTON SU6120   SO32 3NT
 ## Shoe
Village signposted from A32 NE of Bishop's Waltham

Newish licensees for pleasant brick-built country pub on South Downs Way, three linked rooms with log fires (not always lit), good food from traditional favourites to more imaginative restaurant-style dishes using own produce, Wadworths ales and a seasonal guest; children and dogs welcome, disabled facilities, seats under parasols at front, more in garden across lane overlooking River Meon. *Recommended by Henry Fryer, Glenwys and Alan Lawrence, Geoff and Linda Payne*

FACCOMBE SU3958   SP11 0DS
☆ ## Jack Russell
Signed from A343 Newbury—Andover

Light and airy creeper-covered pub in village-green setting opposite pond by flint church, enjoyable fairly priced traditional food (not Sun evening) from snacks to Sun roasts, well kept ales including Greene King IPA and one brewed for the pub, good service, carpeted bar with some old farming tools and other bric-a-brac, log fire, darts, conservatory restaurant (children welcome here); piped music; disabled facilities, lawn by beech trees, three bedrooms, good walks. *Recommended by Mr and Mrs H J Langley, David and Judy Robison*

FAIR OAK SU4919   SO50 7HB
Fox
Winchester Road (A3051)

Popular smartly refurbished pub with enjoyable food (all day Weds-Sun), ales such as Fullers London Pride and Ringwood, nice wines, welcoming bright young staff, clean modern décor in lounge, restaurant, coffee room and conservatory; children welcome, big garden, path to nearby Bishopstoke woods, open all day. *Recommended by Phyl and Jack Street and others*

FAREHAM SU5806   PO16 7AE
Golden Lion
High Street

Clean friendly Fullers pub, their ales and enjoyable food from nice baguettes up; open all day (till 9pm Mon, closed Sun evening). *Recommended by Val and Alan Green*

FARNBOROUGH SU8756   GU14 8AL
☆ ## Prince of Wales
Rectory Road, near station

Up to ten good changing ales in friendly Victorian local, exposed brickwork, carpet or wood floors, open fire, antiquey touches in its three small linked areas, popular lunchtime pubby food (not Sun) including sandwiches, good friendly service; smokers' gazebo, open all day Fri-Sun. *Recommended by Dr Martin Owton, Thurstan Johnston, Joan and Michel Hooper-Immins, Tim Gallagher*

FARRINGDON SU7135   GU34 3ED
☆ Rose & Crown
Off A32 S of Alton; Crows Lane – follow Church, Selborne, Liss signpost

Airy 19th-c village pub with L-shaped log-fire bar, comfortable and well run, several well
kept ales including Adnams, good reasonably priced food (all day Sun) with some
interesting choices and vegetarian options, efficient friendly young staff, formal back
dining room, jazz nights (last Mon of month); well behaved children and dogs welcome,
wide views from attractive back garden, open all day weekends. *Recommended by Ann and
Colin Hunt, Tony and Jill Radnor, Simon Collett-Jones*

FAWLEY SU4603   SO45 1DT
Jolly Sailor
Ashlett Creek

Cottagey waterside pub near small boatyard and sailing club, straightforward good value
bar food, Marstons Pedigree and Ringwood Best, cheerful service, raised log fire, mixed
pubby furnishings on bare boards, second bar with darts and pool; children welcome,
tables outside looking past creek's yachts and boats to busy shipping channel, handy for
Rothschild rhododendron gardens at Exbury. *Recommended by Ann and Colin Hunt*

FINCLUDINGHDEAN SU7312   PO8 0AU
George
Centre of village

Red-brick pub dating from the 18th c, beamed front bar, separate dining area with
conservatory, food (all day weekends) from good value bar menu up, efficient staff, well
kept ales such as Fullers, Sharps and Wells & Youngs, live music; children welcome, dogs
in bar, garden tables, good nearby walks, open all day weekends. *Recommended by Ann and
Colin Hunt, W A Evershed*

FRITHAM SU2314   SO43 7HJ
☆ Royal Oak
Village signed from M27 junction1

Bustling country tavern in rural New Forest and part of working farm (ponies and pigs out
on green), three straightforward but characterful black-beamed rooms, panelling, antique
chairs at solid tables on oak floors, pictures of local characters, two log fires,
up to seven real ales tapped from casks (September beer festival), simple but tasty
lunchtime food, friendly chatty staff; no credit cards; children and dogs welcome,
marquee and pétanque in big neatly kept garden, open all day (closed winter weekday
lunchtimes). *Recommended by Mr and Mrs W W Burke, Simon Watkins, N R White, the Didler, Mr and
Mrs D Hammond, Richard, Anne and Kate Ansell and others*

FROGHAM SU1712   SP6 2JA
☆ Foresters Arms
Abbotswell Road

Friendly chatty New Forest pub, chef/landlord doing good value blackboard food from
sandwiches to very popular Sun lunch (compact dining room fills quickly – they ask to
keep a credit card while you eat), welcoming attentive young staff, well kept Wadworths
ales, good wines by the glass, cosy rustic refurbishment with frog-theme bar; children and
dogs welcome, pleasant garden with pretty front verandah and good play area, small
campsite adjacent, nearby ponies, deer and good walks, closed Tues. *Recommended by
John and Joan Calvert, J Buckby*

GOODWORTH CLATFORD SU3642   SP11 7QY
Royal Oak
Longstock Road

Comfortably modern L-shaped bar with welcoming landlord and obliging staff, good
carefully sourced food from pub staples up, well kept local ales, good choice of wines by

the glass; sheltered and very pretty dell-like garden, large and neatly kept, attractive Test Valley village, good River Anton walks, closed Sun evening. *Recommended by Phyl and Jack Street*

GOSPORT SU6101   PO12 4LQ

☆ ## Jolly Roger
Priory Road, Hardway

Popular old beamed harbour-view pub with enjoyable fairly priced food, real ales such as Adnams, Greene King and Shepherd Neame, decent house wines, lots of bric-a-brac, log fire, attractive eating area including new conservatory; open all day. *Recommended by Ann and Colin Hunt*

GOSPORT SZ6100   PO12 1LG

Queens
Queens Road

Classic bare-boards local, long-serving landlady keeps Ringwood Fortyniner, Roosters, Wells & Youngs Special and two guests in top condition, beer festivals, quick service, three areas off bar with good log fire in interesting carved fireplace, sensibly placed darts, pub dog called Stanley; TV room – children welcome here daytime; closed lunchtimes Mon-Thurs, open all day Sat. *Recommended by Ann and Colin Hunt*

GREYWELL SU7151   RG29 1BY

Fox & Goose
Near M3 junction 5; A287 towards Odiham then first right to village

Traditional two-bar village pub popular with locals and walkers, country-kitchen furniture, home-made food from good lunchtime sandwiches up, well kept Courage Best and a couple of guests, friendly helpful service; dogs welcome, good-sized garden behind, attractive village, Basingstoke Canal walks, open all day Sun (can get very busy lunchtime then). *Recommended by Ann and Colin Hunt, Peter Farman*

HAMBLE SU4806   SO31 4HA

☆ ## Bugle
3 miles from M27 junction 8

Chatty and bustling little 16th-c village pub by River Hamble, beamed and timbered rooms with flagstones and polished boards, church chairs, woodburner in fine brick fireplace, bar stools along herringbone-brick and timbered counter, Bowman Swift One and Ringwood Best, popular food (all day weekends); piped music, TV; children welcome, dogs in bar, seats on the terrace from which you can see the boats), open all day. *Recommended by Bob and Angela Brooks, Phyl and Jack Street*

HAMBLEDON SU6716   PO8 0UB

☆ ## Bat & Ball
Broadhalfpenny Down; about 2 miles E towards Clanfield

Extended dining pub opposite cricket's first-ever pitch (matches most summer Sundays), plenty of cricketing memorabilia, log fires and comfortable modern furnishings in three linked rooms, Fullers ales, enjoyable food from well priced snacks up, good friendly service, panelled restaurant; children welcome, tables on front terrace, garden behind with lovely downs views, good walks, open all day. *Recommendedby W A Evershed, N R White*

HANNINGTON SU5455   RG26 5TX

Vine
Signposted off A339

Spacious 19th-c village pub with light bright décor, comfy leather sofas and woodburner, real ales such as Black Sheep, good wines, fairly priced food using home-grown produce, friendly service, back dining conservatory; children and dogs welcome, big garden with terrace, nice spot up on downs, good walks, closed Sun evening and Mon in winter. *Recommended by Ann and Colin Hunt, N R White*

HAWKLEY SU7429   GU33 6NE
Hawkley Inn
Off B3006 near A3 junction; Pococks Lane

Small pubby village local with splendid range of well kept ales from central bar, farm
ciders, too, including a blackberry one, good mix of customers, open fires, bare boards,
flagstones and well used carpet, old pine tables and assorted chairs; piped music;
children and dogs welcome, terrace tables and nice garden, useful for walkers (on
Hangers Way), bedrooms, open all day weekends. *Recommended by the Didler, Tim Maddison, Ann
and Colin Hunt, Geoff and Linda Payne*

HAYLING ISLAND SU7201   PO11 0PS
Maypole
Havant Road

Sizeable two-bar roadside local well run by friendly couple, parquet floors and polished
panelling, plenty of good seating, well kept Fullers/Gales beers, good choice of generous
reasonably priced pub food including fish on Fri; garden. *Recommended by Terry and
Nickie Williams, Val and Alan Green, Ann and Colin Hunt, Dave Jennings*

HECKFIELD SU7260   RG27 0LE
New Inn
B3349 Hook—Reading (former A32)

Well run rambling open-plan dining pub, good welcoming service, enjoyable food
including good light lunch selection, well kept Badger ales, good choice of wines by the
glass, attractive layout with some traditional furniture in original core, two log fires;
restaurant; good-sized heated terrace, bedrooms in comfortable and well equipped
extension. *Recommended by Peter Sampson*

HERRIARD SS6744   RG25 2PN
Fur & Feathers
Pub signed just off A339 Basingstoke—Alton

Refurbished Victorian pub under newish ownership, three changing ales such as Ballards,
Bowmans and Hogs Back, popular home-made blackboard food, friendly helpful service,
smallish bar area with stools along counter, dining areas either side, pine furniture on
stripped-wood flooring, painted half-panelling, old photographs and farm tools, log fire in
big brick fireplace; piped music; garden behind, open Fri and Sat, closed Sun evening,
Mon. *Recommended by Martin and Karen Wake*

HIGHCLERE SU4359   RG20 9PU
Red House
Andover Road (A343)

Traditional building given fresh contemporary revamp, spacious bar and separate
restaurant, food from pub staples up, Timothy Taylors Landlord and West Berkshire ales,
good choice of wines by the glass, pleasant service; children welcome away from bar, dogs
away from eating areas, open all day Fri, closed Sun evening, Mon. *Recommended by
John Redfern*

HIGHCLERE SU4358   RG20 9SE
Yew Tree
Hollington Cross

Smartly reworked country inn (Marco Pierre White is a major shareholder), good food
(not too expensive) in nicely furnished comfortable low-beamed eating areas, relaxed
civilised atmosphere, serious wine list, welcoming efficient staff, stylish contemporary
bar, big inglenook log fire, attractive lighting and pictures; picnic-sets under cocktail
parasols on pleasant terrace, six good bedrooms. *Recommended by Hunter and Christine Wright*

We say if we know a pub allows dogs.

HOOK SU7354   RG27 9EH
Crooked Billet
A30 about a mile towards London

Comfortably extended and welcoming roadside pub with large dining area, wide choice of
enjoyable food including interesting specials and plenty of fish, swift helpful service, well
kept Courage Best and Directors with guests like Bath and Sharps, reasonably priced
wines, good range of soft drinks, daily papers in area with sofa and log fire; soft piped
music; children welcome, attractive smallish garden by stream with trout and ducks.
Recommended by Mike and Monnie Jefferies, Ian Herdman

HORDLE SZ2996   SO41 6DJ
☆ ## Mill at Gordleton
Silver Street

Charming tucked-away country inn with very special waterside gardens, small relaxed
panelled bar with leather armchairs, Victorian-style mahogany dining chairs, feature
stove and pretty corner china cupboard, cosy lounge overflow and roomy second bar by
sizeable beamed restaurant extension, good food – all home-made including breads and
preserves, Dorset Piddle Cocky Hop and Ringwood Best, nice wines by the glass, daily
papers; comfortable, individual bedrooms, excellent breakfasts, good walks.
Recommended by N R White

HOUGHTON SU3432   SO20 6LH
☆ ## Boot
Village signposted off A30 in Stockbridge

Bustling country local with lots of stuffed creatures in cheery log-fire bar, good local
Andwell ales, food from well filled baguettes up, friendly service, roomy more decorous
lounge/dining room; well behaved children and dogs welcome, spacious tranquil garden
with half a dozen picnic-sets down by lovely (unfenced) stretch of River Test, where they
have fishing; good walks, and opposite Test Way cycle path. *Recommended by Edward Mirzoeff,
Ann and Colin Hunt, N R White*

HURSLEY SU4225   SO21 2JW
Kings Head
A3090 Winchester—Romsey

Substantial early 19th-c coaching inn, good local home-made food, five well kept changing
ales such as Ringwood and Sharps Doom Bar, good choice of ciders, friendly staff,
restaurant, skittle alley; children and dogs welcome, garden tables, eight comfortable
bedrooms, open all day. *Recommended by Chris and Jeanne Downing, Terry Buckland*

KEYHAVEN SZ3091   SO41 0TP
☆ ## Gun
Keyhaven Road

Busy rambling 17th-c pub looking over boatyard and sea to Isle of Wight, low-beamed bar
with nautical bric-a-brac and plenty of character (less in family rooms and conservatory),
good reasonably priced local food including crab, well kept beers tapped from the cask
such as Flowers, Ringwood, Shepherd Neame and Wychwood, Weston's cider, lots of malt
whiskies, helpful young staff, bar billiards; piped music; tables out in front and in big back
garden with swings and fish pond; you can stroll down to small harbour and walk to Hurst
Castle. *Recommended by Norma and David Hardy, N R White, Joshua Fancett* .

KING'S SOMBORNE SU3531   SO20 6PW
Crown
Romsey Road (A3057)

Long low thatched pub opposite village church, friendly relaxed local atmosphere, good
simple well priced home-made food, well kept ales such as Ringwood and Wychwood
Hobgoblin, local cider, good wines and coffee, several linked rooms, comfortable sofas,
fresh flowers; seats out at front and in garden behind, Test Way and Clarendon Way

footpaths nearby. *Recommended by Ian and Rose Lock, Mr and Mrs H J Langley, David and Judy Robison, Mike*

KINGSCLERE SU5258   RG20 5PP
Swan
Swan Street

Old-fashioned 15th-c village inn, lots of beams, welcoming landlord and friendly helpful staff, Theakstons XB and three guests, enjoyable reasonably priced home-made food (not Sun evening); dogs welcome, tables outside, good walks, nine comfortable clean bedrooms. *Recommended by Ann and Colin Hunt, Steven Paine*

 LANGSTONE SU7104   PO9 1RY
Royal Oak
Off A3023 just before Hayling Island bridge; Langstone High Street

Charmingly placed waterside dining pub overlooking tidal inlet and ancient wadeway to Hayling Island, boats at high tide, wading birds when it goes out; four real ales including Greene King, good choice of wines by the glass, reasonably priced food with all-day sandwiches and snacks, smart friendly staff, spacious flagstoned bar and linked dining areas, log fire; children in eating areas, nice garden, good coastal paths nearby, open all day. *Recommended by W A Evershed*

LANGSTONE SU7104   PO9 1RD
Ship
A3023

Busy waterside 18th-c former grain store, lovely views to Hayling Island from roomy softly lit nautical bar with upper deck dining room, Fullers ales, good choice of wines by the glass, log fire, wide range of generous reasonably priced food including local fish and venison; children welcome, plenty of tables on heated terrace by quiet quay, good coast walks, open all day. *Recommended by Andy West, W A Evershed, Glen and Nola Armstrong*

LINWOOD SU1910   BH24 3QY
High Corner
Signed from A338 via Moyles Court, and from A31; keep on

Big rambling pub very popular for its splendid New Forest position up a track, with extensive neatly kept wooded garden and lots for children to do; some character in original upper bar with log fire, big back extensions for the summer crowds, nicely partitioned restaurant, verandah lounge, interesting family rooms, wide choice of generous bar snacks and restaurant-style food, well kept Wadworths; welcomes dogs and horses (stables and paddock available), seven bedrooms, open all day weekends. *Recommended by Dennis and Doreen Haward, J Buckby*

LINWOOD SU1809   BH24 3QT
Red Shoot
Signed from A338 via Moyles Court, and from A31; go on up heath to junction with Toms Lane

Edwardian pub in nice New Forest setting, big picture-window bar with attractive old tables, mixed chairs and rugs on bare boards, country pictures on puce walls, log fire, large back dining area, generous honest good value food (all day weekends), friendly helpful staff, well kept Wadworths and two or three ales brewed at the pub including Muddy Boot (beer festivals Apr and Oct); children, dogs and muddy boots welcome, some disabled access, sheltered side terrace, open all day summer – very touristy then (by big campsite and caravan park). *Recommended by S Harris, Carey Tyler*

☆ LITTLETON SU4532   SO22 6QS
Running Horse
Main Road; village signed off B3049 NW of Winchester

Popular dining pub refurbished in up-to-date style, enjoyable food from pubby to more elaborate dishes including two-course weekday lunch, good service, cushioned metal and wicker chairs at modern tables on polished boards, also some deep leather chairs, good colour photographs of Hampshire scenes, Andwell Resolute and Bowman Wallops Wood from marble and hardwood counter with swish bar stools, log fire, flagstoned back restaurant; piped music; children welcome, dogs in bar, good disabled facilities, nice front and back terraces and garden, bedrooms, open all day. *Recommended by Phyl and Jack Street, Karen Eliot, Mrs Ann Adams and others*

LOCKERLEY SU3025   SO51 0JF
Kings Arms
The Street

Fully refurbished under new management, enjoyable food from bar snacks to restaurant dishes, interesting wine list, well kept ales, good service and thriving local atmosphere. *Recommended by John Chambers*

LOCKS HEATH SU5006   SO31 9JH
☆ Jolly Farmer
Fleet End Road, not far from M27 junction 9

Popular flower-decked pub with relaxing series of softly lit linked rooms, nice old scrubbed tables and masses of interesting bric-a-brac and prints, emphasis on wide choice of enjoyable food (all day weekends) including good value Sun lunch (two-sittings), interesting long-serving landlord and good friendly service, Fullers/Gales ales, decent wines including country ones, coal-effect gas fires; two sheltered terraces (one with play area and children's lavatories), dogs allowed in public bar, nearby walks, five nice bedrooms, good breakfast, open all day. *Recommended by Phyl and Jack Street, Ann and Colin Hunt, David and Gill Carrington*

LONG SUTTON SU7447   RG29 1TA
☆ Four Horseshoes
Signed off B3349 S of Hook

Welcoming open-plan black-beamed country local with two log fires, long-serving landlord cooking bargain pubby food, friendly landlady serving good range of changing ales such as Palmers, decent wines and country wine, no piped music or machines, small glazed-in verandah; disabled access, picnic-sets on grass over road, boules and play area, three good value bedrooms (bunk beds available for cyclist/walkers). *Recommended by Tony and Jill Radnor*

LONGPARISH SU4344   SP11 6PZ
Cricketers
B3048, off A303 just E of Andover

Cheerful homely village pub with good chatty landlady, connecting rooms and cosy corners, woodburner, wide choice of carefully cooked food from light snacks to popular Sun lunch, prompt service, good range of real ales; sizeable back garden; closed Mon. *Recommended by Phyl and Jack Street, Mr and Mrs A Curry*

LONGPARISH SU4244   SP11 6PB
☆ Plough
B3048, off A303 just E of Andover

Bustling open-plan country pub with welcoming staff and comfortably upmarket feel; beams, standing timbers, flagstone and oak floors, contemporary paintwork, high-backed wooden or black leather dining chairs, working fireplaces (one with woodburner), good bar food (all day summer, till 4pm winter), Itchen Valley, Otter and Ringwood; children and dogs welcome, chickens, rabbits and tortoise in garden with plenty of seats on decking, open all day (till 9pm Sun). *Recommended by Edward Mirzoeff, Neil and Karen Dignan, Michael and Jenny Back, Evelyn and Derek Walter and others*

All *Guide* inspections are anonymous. Anyone claiming to be a *Good Pub Guide* inspector is a fraud. Please let us know.

LYMINGTON SZ3295   SO41 3AY
☆ Ship
Quay Road

Lively well run pub with popular quayside deck overlooking harbour, light modern interior with lots of nautical bric-a-brac, including huge flags, blue gingham and leather sofas, raised log fire, Adnams Broadside, Fullers London Pride and Hook Norton Old Hooky (plenty of standing room by counter), enjoyable fair value interesting food (all day), attractive wall-planked restaurant with blue and cream paintwork and driftwood decorations; children and dogs welcome, showers for visiting sailors. *Recommended by John Voos*

LYMINGTON SZ3395   SO41 5SB
Wagon & Horses
Undershore Road; road to IOW ferry

Well run comfortable Wadworths pub, friendly staff, some interesting food, beamed restaurant with leaded windows, games room; terrace tables, handy for IOW ferry. *Recommended by Joan and Michel Hooper-Immins*

LYNDHURST SU2908   SO43 7BG
Fox & Hounds
High Street

Big busy low-beamed Chef & Brewer, comfortable and much-modernised, with good range of food all day including blackboard specials, obliging cheerful staff, Ringwood and several other ales, decent wines, exposed brickwork and standing timbers, back 19th-c barn (moved here from Winchester); children welcome, disabled facilities, outside picnic-sets, bedrooms. *Recommended by John Robertson, Phyl and Jack Street*

MAPLEDURWELL SU6851   RG25 2LU
Gamekeepers
Off A30, not far from M3 junction 6

Dark-beamed dining pub with good upmarket food (not cheap) from interesting baguettes up, welcoming landlord, well kept Badger ales, good coffee, a few sofas by flagstoned and panelled core, well spaced tables in large dining room; piped music, TV; children welcome, terrace and garden, lovely thatched village with duck pond, good walks, open all day. *Recommended by Edward Mirzoeff*

MARCHWOOD SU3809   SO40 4WU
Pilgrim
Hythe Road, off A326 at Twiggs Lane

Popular picturesque thatched pub (originally three cottages), good choice of enjoyable sensibly priced food, efficient friendly service even at busy times, well kept Fullers ales, decent wine, open fires; tree-lined garden with round picnic-sets, 14 stylish bedrooms in building across car park, open all day. *Recommended by Phyl and Jack Street, Ian and Rose Lock and others*

MICHELDEVER SU5142   SO21 3AU
Dove
Micheldever Station, off A33 or A303

Large square pub with several well refurbished interconnecting rooms around central bar, enjoyable food from pub favourites up, Ringwood BB, obliging friendly service, beams, exposed brickwork, woodburner; small side terrace, bedrooms. *Recommended by Edward Mirzoeff, Diana Brumfit*

Half pints: by law, a pub should not charge more for half a pint than half the price of a full pint, unless it shows that half-pint price on its price list.

MINLEY MANOR SU8357   GU17 9UA
Crown & Cushion
A327, just N of M3 junction 4A

Attractive little traditional pub with enjoyable fairly priced food including some unusual
choices, well kept Shepherd Neame ales, coal-effect gas fire; big separate raftered and
flagstoned rustic 'meade hall' behind, very popular weekends (evenings more a young
people's meeting place), with huge log fire, friendly staff cope well when busy; children
in eating area, heated terrace overlooking own cricket pitch. *Recommended by David and
Sue Smith*

MINSTEAD SU2810   SO43 7FY
Trusty Servant
Just off A31, not far from M27 junction 1

Attractive 19th-c building in pretty New Forest hamlet with interesting church,
wandering cattle and ponies, and plenty of easy walks; bright and simple mildly upscale
refurbishment, two-room bar and big dining room, real ales, food from sandwiches up; big
sloping garden, open all day. *Recommended by Bob and Angela Brooks, Henry Fryer, John Redfern*

MONXTON SU3144   SP11 8AW
Black Swan
High Street

Friendly 17th-c rambling pub, enjoyable food including Sun carvery and takeaway fish and
chips, well kept real ales, log fire; car park down street; children welcome, lovely
sheltered garden by stream with ducks, open all day. *Recommended by Chris and Meredith Owen*

NEW CHERITON SU5827   SO24 0NH
☆ Hinton Arms
A272 near B3046 junction

Neatly kept popular country pub with cheerful accommodating landlord, three or four real
ales including Bowman Wallops Wood and one brewed for the pub by Hampshire, decent
wines by the glass, generous food including game specials, sporting pictures and
memorabilia, relaxing atmosphere; TV lounge; terrace, big garden, very handy for Hinton
Ampner House (NT). *Recommended by Phil and Jane Villiers, Ann and Colin Hunt, P J Checksfield*

NEWTOWN SU4763   RG20 9BH
Swan
A339 2 miles S of Newbury, by junction with old A34

Ancient black and white pub refitted in modern style, good nicely presented food, well
kept Badger ales, friendly young staff, flagstones and open fires; children welcome,
terrace and lovely streamside garden. *Recommended by Keith and Margaret Kettell*

NEWTOWN SU6112   PO17 6LL
Travellers Rest
Off A32 N of Wickham

Friendly lived-in country pub gently enlarged but still cosy, one chatty local bar, two
further rooms mainly for food, four well kept ales including Bowman, open fires and
traditional furnishings; children welcome, pretty back garden, caravan park. *Recommended
by Val and Alan Green, Ann and Colin Hunt*

ODIHAM SU7450   RG29 1LY
Bell
The Bury

Simple unspoilt two-bar local in pretty square opposite church and stocks, three well kept
changing ales, good value straightforward food, log fire; plenty of seats outside.
Recommended by Ann and Colin Hunt, Peter Farman

ODIHAM SU7451   RG29 1AL
Water Witch
Colt Hill – quiet no through road signed off main street

Olde-worlde décor in nicely kept Chef & Brewer near picturesque stretch of Basingstoke Canal, big but cosily divided, wide choice of food, friendly staff, real ales; no dogs inside; disabled access, big garden with children's facilities. *Recommended by Chris and Jeanne Downing, Jim and Frances Gowers*

OTTERBOURNE SU4623   SO21 2EE
Old Forge
Main Road

Popular old bistro-style chain pub, welcoming and comfortable, with wide choice of enjoyable food all day, friendly well organised staff, ales such as Everards, Sharps and Timothy Taylors, good choice of wines by the glass, tables spread through linked rooms, cosy nooks and rather individual décor, log fires; children welcome. *Recommended by PL, Henry Fryer, Phyl and Jack Street, Mr and Mrs J J A Davis and others*

OTTERBOURNE SU4522   SO21 2HW
Otter
Boyatt Lane, off Winchester Road

Unpretentious dining pub opposite village green, enjoyable food from sandwiches and snacks up, Ringwood ales and Otter, good service, three-sided bar (one side set for dining), dark oak tables and chairs, banquettes; seats in garden. *Recommended by Mrs Joy Griffiths, M and GR, Val and Alan Green*

OVERTON SU5149   RG25 3HQ
Red Lion
High Street

Smartly refurbished old village pub with emphasis on good imaginative food, well kept ales such as Flowerpots and Triple fff, enthusiastic landlord and friendly efficient staff, wood floors including some parquet, open fires, skittle alley; piped music; terrace and garden, closed Sun evening. *Recommended by Bruce Bird*

PETERSFIELD SU7423   GU31 4AE
Red Lion
College Street

Newly refurbished Wetherspoons in former coaching inn, usual good value food and beers; open all day from 7am. *Recommended by Dom Humphries, Val and Alan Green*

PORTSMOUTH SZ6399   PO1 2JA
abarbistro
White Hart Road

Modern airy bar/restaurant (was the American Bar) with mural of beach huts and deckchair-stripe banquettes giving seaside feel, decent choice of food all day including some pubby things, special diets catered for, well kept ales such as Fullers London Pride, good choice of wines by the glass, friendly staff; terrace and secluded garden, handy for IOW ferry. *Recommended by Ann and Colin Hunt*

PORTSMOUTH SZ6399   PO1 2JJ
Bridge Tavern
East Street, Camber Dock

Flagstones, bare boards and lots of dark wood, comfortable furnishings, maritime theme with good harbour views, Fullers ales, plenty of fish dishes; nice waterside terrace. *Recommended by Ann and Colin Hunt, W A Evershed*

PORTSMOUTH SU6402   PO2 9AA
Fountain
London Road, North End

Unchanging tiled pub with large bar and family room off, nicely polished brass, interesting pictures of local pubs, mirrors each end, unusual ceiling lights, well kept beer including Gales HSB, no food; seats outside. *Recommended by Ann and Colin Hunt*

PORTSMOUTH SZ6399   PO1 3TY
☆ Old Customs House
Vernon Buildings, Gunwharf Quays; follow brown signs to Gunwharf Quays car park

Handsome late 18th-c red-brick building (former customs house) in waterfront development, big-windowed high-ceilinged rooms with bare boards, nautical prints and photographs on pastel walls, coal-effect gas fires, good range of Fullers/Gales ales, well liked good value food all day (breakfast from 9am), good prompt service, stairs up to carpeted more restauranty floor with similar décor; piped music, machines and can get very busy; children allowed until 8pm (welcome upstairs after that), disabled facilities, picnic-sets out by water. *Recommended by Dave Braisted, Maureen Wood, Ann and Colin Hunt, Phil Bryant*

PORTSMOUTH SZ6399   PO1 2NR
Pembroke
Pembroke Road

Buoyant atmosphere in comfortable well run traditional local, unspoilt under long-serving landlord, Bass and Fullers/Gales, fresh rolls, real fire; open all day. *Recommended by Ann and Colin Hunt*

PORTSMOUTH SZ6299   PO1 2JL
Still & West
Bath Square, Old Portsmouth

Great location with superb views of narrow harbour mouth and across to Isle of Wight, especially from glazed-in panoramic upper family area and waterfront terrace with lots of picnic-sets; nautical bar with fireside sofas and cosy colour scheme, Fullers ales, good choice of wines by the glass, food all day including signature fish and chips; piped music may be loud, nearby pay & display; children welcome, handy for Historic Dockyard. *Recommended by Andy West, Ann and Colin Hunt, W A Evershed, J A Snell, B M Eldridge*

ROCKFORD SU1608   BH24 3NA
Alice Lisle
Follow sign on village green

Big well laid-out open-plan family dining pub (a former school) attractively placed on green by New Forest (can get very busy), large conservatory-style eating area, enjoyable varied choice of food (all day weekends) from sandwiches up, Fullers ales, good choice of wines by the glass, good service; baby-changing facilities, dogs welcome, big garden overlooking lake with ponies wandering nearby, play area, handy for Moyles Court, open all day. *Recommended by Mrs J Plante Cleall*

ROMSEY SU3523   SO51 0HB
☆ Dukes Head
A3057 out towards Stockbridge

Attractive 16th-c dining pub with good landlady and friendly staff, small comfortable spic-and-span linked rooms, big log fire, good range of enjoyable food, well kept Ringwood and guests, decent wines and coffee; children welcome, colourful hanging baskets, sheltered back terrace and pleasant garden, open all day. *Recommended by Phyl and Jack Street, J V Dadswell, Ann and Colin Hunt*

ROMSEY SU3520   SO51 8HL
Three Tuns
Middlebridge Street (but car park signed straight off A27 bypass)

Old bow-windowed beamed pub reopened after refurbishment by new owners, well kept
ales such as Bath, traditional pub food; children welcome. *Recommended by John Evans*

ROWLAND'S CASTLE SU7310   PO9 6DA
☆ Castle Inn
Off B2148/B2149 N of Havant; Finchdean Road

Cheerful proper country pub with friendly hands-on tenants, comfortable bar with
enormous log fire and good choice of Fullers/Gales ales, nice coffee, neat staff, two
appealing little dining rooms on left, attractively priced pubby food with more exotic
evening choices; children and dogs welcome, pony paddock by good-sized garden, good
disabled facilities, open all day. *Recommended by Andy West, Ann and Colin Hunt, W A Evershed*

ROWLAND'S CASTLE SU7310   PO9 6AB
Robin Hood
The Green

Nicely refurbished pub on village green, light and airy bar, good choice of enjoyable food,
Badger ales and a guest, efficient service, restaurant; children and dogs welcome,
disabled facilities, picnic-sets on front terrace, six bedrooms, good breakfast, open all day.
Recommended by Tony and Gill Powell

SARISBURY SU5008   SO31 7EL
Bold Forester
Handy for M27 junction 9; Bridge Road (A27), Sarisbury Green

Roomy and well run with good choice of popular food from baguettes and sharing plates
up, friendly attentive staff, four real ales including Ringwood, pictures of this increasingly
built-up area in its strawberry-fields days; children welcome, pretty hanging baskets and
tubs in front, large recently redone garden behind, open all day. *Recommended by
Christine Whitehead*

SELBORNE SU7433   GU34 3JJ
Queens
High Street

Comfortably refurbished under new licensee, interesting local memorabilia, open fires,
well kept Hogs Back TEA and Triple fff Alton Pride, food (not Sun evening) from
sandwiches and pubby things to french country dishes, cream teas, cheerful smartly
dressed staff, occasional jazz; children and dogs welcome, garden picnic-sets, eight
bedrooms, very handy for Gilbert White's house, open all day. *Recommended by Ann and
Colin Hunt*

SHALDEN SU7043   GU34 4DJ
Golden Pot
B3349 Odiham Road N of Alton

Refurbished and under newish management, emphasis on dining but drinkers welcome,
modern airy décor with sage-green walls, bare boards and log fires, enjoyable food
including tapas, friendly service, good choice of wines by the glass, beers such as Andwell
and Otter; tables outside. *Recommended by N R White, Martin and Karen Wake*

SHEDFIELD SU5513   SO32 2JG
Wheatsheaf
A334 Wickham—Botley

Busy friendly no-fuss local, Flowerpots ales tapped from the cask, farm cider, short
sensible choice of bargain bar lunches (evening food Tues-Thurs); dogs welcome, garden,
handy for Wickham Vineyard, open all day. *Recommended by Jenny and Peter Lowater, Val and
Alan Green, Ann and Colin Hunt, Joan and Michel Hooper-Immins*

SHERFIELD ENGLISH SU3022   SO51 6FP
Hatchet
Romsey Road

Beamed and panelled 18th-c pub under new licensees, popular fairly priced generous food including good steaks and fish, Fullers London Pride, Ringwood and guests, good wine choice, friendly hard-working staff, long bar with cosy area down steps, woodburner, steps up to second bar with darts, TV, juke box and machines; children and dogs welcome, outside seating on two levels, garden play area, open all day weekends. *Recommended by Phyl and Jack Street, Steve Cogdell*

SHIRRELL HEATH SU5714   SO32 2JN
Prince of Wales
High Street (B2177)

Refurbished smallish front bar with restaurant behind, good well presented/priced food, real ales, welcoming staff; back garden with terrace and play area. *Recommended by Samuel Fancett, Ann and Colin Hunt, Jenny and Peter Lowater*

SOPLEY SZ1596   BH23 7AX
☆ Woolpack
B3347 N of Christchurch

Pretty thatched dining pub with rambling open-plan low-beamed bar, welcoming helpful staff, good generous traditional food, real ales such as Ringwood Best and Fortyniner, good choice of wines by the glass, modern dining conservatory; they ask to keep a credit card if you're running a tab; children in eating areas, dogs in certain areas, terrace and charming garden with weeping willows, duck stream and footbridges, open all day. *Recommended by Hans Becker, Sue and Mike Todd, Jo Hankins, David Cannings*

SOUTHAMPTON SU4111   SO14 2AH
☆ Duke of Wellington
Bugle Street (or walk along city wall from Bar Gate)

Striking ancient timber-framed building dating from 14th c, cellars even older, heavy beams, great log fire, well kept ales such as Ringwood and Wadworths, good choice of wines by the glass, good value traditional pub food (not Sun evening) from baguettes to nursery puddings, friendly helpful service; piped music in cheery front bar, staider back area welcoming children; handy for Tudor House Museum, sunny streetside picnic-sets, open all day. *Recommended by Val and Alan Green*

SOUTHAMPTON SU4211   SO14 2DF
Standing Order
High Street

Big busy Wetherspoons with up to ten well kept ales, low-priced food, helpful efficient young staff, cosy corners (strange and interesting collection of books in one), civilised atmosphere; open all day. *Recommended by Val and Alan Green*

SOUTHSEA SZ6499   PO5 4BS
Eldon Arms
Eldon Street/Norfolk Street

Rambling backstreet tavern under newish management, Fullers London Pride and four changing guests, Thatcher's cider, simple cheap lunchtime food (not Mon), Sun carvery, flowers on tables, old pictures and advertisements, attractive mirrors, bric-a-brac and shelves of books; piped music, sensibly placed darts, bar billiards, pool, games machine; dogs on leads and children welcome, tables in back garden, open all day. *Recommended by Ann and Colin Hunt*

SOUTHSEA SZ6499   PO5 3BY
☆ Hole in the Wall
Great Southsea Street

Small friendly unspoilt local in old part of town, up to six good changing ales such as Dark Star, Hammerpot, Oakleaf and Tom Woods, Wheal Maiden alcoholic ginger beer, Thatcher's cider, simple good value food including speciality local sausages and meat puddings, nicely worn boards, dark pews and panelling, old photographs and prints, over 700 pump clips on ceiling, little snug behind the bar, daily papers, quiz night Thurs, Oct beer festival; small outside tiled area at front with benches, side garden, closed till 4pm weekdays, open all day Fri-Sun. *Recommended by Andy West, Joan and Michel Hooper-Immins, Ann and Colin Hunt*

SOUTHSEA SZ6499   PO5 4EH
King Street Tavern
King Street

Sympathetically refurbished corner pub in attractive conservation area, spectacular Victorian tiled façade, bare boards and original fittings, four well kept Wadworths ales and guests, real ciders, straightforward home-made food; piped and live music including fortnightly Sat jazz; courtyard tables, closed lunchtimes apart from Sun. *Recommended by Ann and Colin Hunt, Nick Birtley*

STOCKBRIDGE SU3535   SO20 6HB
Three Cups
High Street

Lovely low-beamed building dating from 1500, more restaurant than pub now, lots of smartly set pine tables but still some high-backed settles, country bric-a-brac and four well kept ales such as Ringwood; food can be very good including local trout fishcakes, amiable service, good wines by the glass; children and dogs welcome, vine-covered verandah and charming cottage garden with streamside terrace, bedrooms, open all day. *Recommended by Geoffrey Kemp*

STOCKBRIDGE SU3535   SO20 6HF
☆ White Hart
High Street; A272/A3057 roundabout

Thriving divided beamed bar, attractive décor with antique prints, oak pews and other seats, friendly helpful staff, enjoyable food from snacks to substantial daily specials, well kept Fullers/Gales beers, comfortable restaurant with blazing log fire (children allowed); dogs in bar, disabled facilities, terrace tables and nice garden, 14 good bedrooms, open all day. *Recommended by Phyl and Jack Street, Edward Mirzoeff, Dr and Mrs A K Clarke, Ann and Colin Hunt, Helen and Brian Edgeley and others*

STUBBINGTON SU5402   PO14 3QF
Crofton
Crofton Lane

Modern two-bar estate local, neat and airy, with friendly efficient staff, well kept Sharps Doom Bar and changing guests, good value wines, enjoyable nicely varied food including well liked weekday OAP deals; children and dogs welcome. *Recommended by Sally Matson*

SWANMORE SU5716   SO32 2PA
Brickmakers

Popular family-friendly pub smartly refurbished by current owners, four real ales including Bowman and Otter, good wines, enjoyable reasonably priced fresh food, armchairs and log fire; garden with raised deck. *Recommended by Val and Alan Green*

SWANMORE SU5815   SO32 2PS

☆ **Rising Sun**

Droxford Road; signed off A32 N of Wickham (and B2177 S of Bishops Waltham), at Hillpound E of village centre

Proper country pub (busy Sun) with friendly homely atmosphere, unpretentious furnishings and good log fire in low-beamed carpeted bar, stripped-brick barrel vaulting in one area of pleasant dining area, Adnams, Courage, Otter and Ringwood, well liked bar food including smaller helpings and weekday two-course set menu; piped music; children and dogs welcome, garden with play area, handy for Kings Way long-distance path. *Recommended by Ann and Colin Hunt, Martin and Karen Wake, Howard and Margaret Buchanan, Phyl and Jack Street*

THRUXTON SU2945   SP11 8EE

White Horse

Mullens Pond, just off A303 eastbound

Attractive old thatched pub tucked below A303 embankment, comfortably modernised, with emphasis on fresh food, good friendly service, plenty of wines by the glass, well kept ales such as Greene King, woodburner, a couple of sofas, very low beams, separate dining area; good-sized garden and terrace, four bedrooms, closed Sun evening, Mon. *Recommended by B J Harding*

TICHBORNE SU5730   SO24 0NA

☆ **Tichborne Arms**

Signed off B3047

Traditional thatched pub with latticed windows, panelling, antiques and stuffed animals, interesting changing ales tapped from the cask, food (not Sun evening) from baguettes up, locals bar, darts, board games and shove-ha'penny; children and dogs welcome, big garden in rolling countryside, Wayfarers Walk and Itchen Way pass close by, closed Sun evening. *Recommended by Conor McGaughey, Tony and Jill Radnor, Martin and Karen Wake, Tony and Wendy Hobden, the Didler and others*

TIMSBURY SU3325   SO51 0LB

☆ **Bear & Ragged Staff**

A3057 towards Stockbridge; pub marked on OS Sheet 185 map reference 334254

Reliable roadside dining pub with wide blackboard choice of popular food all day, friendly efficient service, lots of wines by the glass, Greene King IPA, log fire, good-sized beamed interior; children welcome in eating part, tables in extended garden with play area, handy for Mottisfont, good walks. *Recommended by Andrew Shore, Rich Best, Phil and Jane Villiers, Phyl and Jack Street*

TITCHFIELD SU5305   PO14 4AF

Bugle

The Square, off A27 near Fareham

Roomy and comfortable 18th-c coaching inn, popular good value food from light meals up in bar or old barn restaurant behind, friendly attentive service, four well kept ales including Timothy Taylors Landlord, log fires; no dogs; children welcome, attractive village handy for Titchfield Haven nature reserve, fine walk by former canal to coast, eight bedrooms. *Recommended by Val and Alan Green*

TITCHFIELD SU5406   PO15 5RA

☆ **Fishermans Rest**

Mill Lane, off A27 at Titchfield Mill pub

Open-plan pub/restaurant with wide choice of good value fresh food including deals, informal tables throughout, well kept Greene King ales and Ringwood, smartly dressed staff, two log fires, daily papers, trout-theme décor, some cosy nooks; fine riverside position opposite Titchfield Abbey, tables out behind overlooking water, open all day. *Recommended by Ann and Colin Hunt, Phyl and Jack Street*

TOTFORD SU5737   SO24 9TJ
Woolpack
B3046 Basingstoke—Alresford

Nicely refurbished roadside inn, clean and comfortable, with good food from bar snacks to restaurant dishes, Palmers, an ale brewed for the pub and a guest such as Bowman, several wines by the glass including champagne, nice italian coffee, efficient service, raised open fire in bar, smart split-level dining room; pool; round picnic-sets outside on gravel, lovely setting in good walking country, seven bedrooms, open all day. *Recommended by Janet Whittaker, Caroline Mackenzie*

TURGIS GREEN SU6959   RG27 0AX
Jekyll & Hyde
A33 Reading—Basingstoke

Bustling rambling pub with nice mix of furniture and village atmosphere in black-beamed and flagstoned bar, blazing fire, some interesting prints and pithy sayings dotted about, larger stepped-up three-room dining area, Badger ales, enjoyable sensibly priced pubby food all day including children's choices, attentive cheerful service; piped music; dogs welcome, disabled facilities, lots of picnic-sets in good sheltered garden (some traffic noise) with terrace, play area, open all day. *Recommended by Pat and Roger Davies*

TWYFORD SU4824   SO21 1QT
☆ Bugle
B3355/Park Lane

Nicely done modern pub with contemporary furniture, lots of leather, carpet or dark flagstones, good enterprising food, attentive friendly service, well kept ales from Bowman, Flowerpots and Upham, woodburner, highly coloured landscape photographs; piped music; attractive verandah seating area, good walks nearby, open all day. *Recommended by B J Harding, Phyl and Jack Street, Tony Hobden, Henry Fryer*

UPHAM SU5320   SO32 1JJ
☆ Brushmakers Arms
Shoe Lane; village signed from Winchester—Bishops Waltham downs road, and from B2177

Plenty of regulars and weekend dog walkers at this cheery low-beamed village pub, L-shaped bar divided by central woodburner, cushioned settles and chairs around mix of tables, lots of brushes and related paraphernalia, little back snug with games machine and piped music, enjoyable bar food, Fullers, Ringwood and a guest, decent coffee, pub cats (Luna and Baxter); children and dogs welcome, big garden with picnic-sets on sheltered terrace and tree-shaded lawn, open all day Sun. *Recommended by Val and Alan Green, Tony and Jill Radnor, Ann and Colin Hunt, Bruce and Penny Wilkie and others*

WALHAMPTON SZ3396   SO41 5RE
Walhampton Arms
B3054 NE of Lymington; aka Walhampton Inn

Large comfortable Georgian-style family roadhouse with popular food including good value carvery in raftered former stables and two adjoining areas, pleasant lounge, Ringwood ales, cheerful helpful staff; attractive courtyard, good walks, open all day. *Recommended by Phyl and Jack Street and others*

WALTHAM CHASE SU5614   SO32 2LX
Black Dog
Winchester Road

Low-ceilinged two-bar pub covered with lovely hanging baskets, good reasonably priced food including vegetarian choices and weekday lunchtime deals from new french chef/landlord, three well kept Greene King ales, wide choice of wines by the glass, smart interior with big back restaurant extension; no dogs inside; children welcome, tables in good-sized neatly kept garden, open all day weekends. *Recommended by Ann and Colin Hunt*

WELL SU7646   RG29 1TL
Chequers
Off A287 via Crondall, or A31 via Froyle and Lower Froyle

Appealing low-beamed and panelled country pub with welcoming landlord, enjoyable food
including popular Sun lunch, well kept Badger ales, decent wines by the glass, pews and
brocaded stools, 18th-c country-life prints and old sepia photographs, a few GWR carriage
lamps, log fire (not always lit); picnic-sets on vine-covered terrace and in spacious back
garden. *Recommended by Trish Bellamy, Sally Garside, Tony and Jill Radnor*

WEST END SU4514   SO18 3HW
White Swan
Mansbridge Road

Pleasantly refurbished family food pub in nice spot, Itchen Valley and Wells & Youngs ales,
busy carvery restaurant, conservatory; attractive terrace by River Itchen (so liable to
flooding). *Recommended by Phyl and Jack Street and others*

WEST MEON SU6424   GU32 1LN
☆ Thomas Lord
High Street

Friendly bustling village pub named for founder of Lord's cricket ground, individual rustic
style with interesting mix of chairs around candlelit wooden tables, old leather sofa,
stuffed animals in display cabinets, bare boards and log fires, back room lined with books
for sale, imaginative if not cheap food, cask-tapped ales such as Bowman, Ringwood and
Upham, farm cider; children and dogs welcome, attractive formal garden with outdoor
bar, wood-fired pizza oven, chicken run and neat vegetable patch, open all day weekends,
closed Mon except bank holidays. *Recommended by Val and Alan Green, Henry Fryer, Darryl and
Lindy Hemsley, Phyl and Jack Street, Edward Bradley and others*

WEST TYTHERLEY SU2730   SP5 1NF
Black Horse
North Lane

Compact unspoilt village local, welcoming licensees and chatty regulars, traditional bar
with a couple of long tables and big fireplace, nicely set dining area off, three real ales,
enjoyable reasonably priced food including good Sun roasts, takeaway fish and chips
Thurs, skittle alley; dogs welcome. *Recommended by Phyl and Jack Street, Graham Horder, Ann and
Colin Hunt*

WHERWELL SU3839   SO20 6AX
☆ Mayfly
*Testcombe (over by Fullerton, and not in Wherwell itself); A3057 SE of Andover,
between B3420 turn-off and Leckford where road crosses River Test; OS Sheet 185 map
reference 382390*

Well run busy pub with decking and conservatory overlooking River Test, spacious beamed
and carpeted bar with fishing paraphernalia, rustic pub furnishings and woodburner,
Adnams Best, Gales HSB, Hop Back Summer Lightning, Palmers Gold and Wadworths 6X,
lots of wines by the glass, wide range of popular reasonably priced bar food all day (order
from separate counter), good, courteous service; piped music; well behaved children and
dogs on leads welcome. *Recommended by Ian Herdman, Terry and Nickie Williams, Betsy and Peter
Little, Edward Mirzoeff, Mr and Mrs A Curry, Michael and Jenny Back and others*

WHERWELL SU3840   SP11 7JF
White Lion
B3420

Refurbished early 17th-c multi-level beamed village inn, emphasis on dining with good
choice of enjoyable food, Harveys, Hop Back, Ringwood Best and guest such as Sharps
Doom Bar, several wines by the glass, open fire, comfy leather armchairs, dining rooms
either side of bar; piped music; dogs on leads and well behaved children welcome, new

garden area with good quality furniture, Test Way walks, four bedrooms, open all day from 7.30am (breakfast for non-residents). *Recommended by B J Harding, Phyl and Jack Street, Stephen Pacey, Michael and Jenny Back and others*

☆ WICKHAM SU5711   PO17 5JQ
Greens
The Square, at junction with A334

Civilised dining place with clean-cut modern furnishings and décor, small bar with leather sofa and armchairs as well as bar stools, wide wine choice, Bowmans Swift One and another ale, efficient considerate young staff, step down to split-level balustraded dining areas, enjoyable food from typical bar lunches to imaginative specials; pleasant lawn overlooking water meadows, closed Sun evening and Mon. *Recommended by Darryl and Lindy Hemsley, Mrs Joy Griffiths, Phyl and Jack Street*

WICKHAM SU5711   PO17 5JN
Kings Head
The Square

Bustling refurbished village local, open-plan bar with big windows and open fires, well kept Fullers/Gales ales, enjoyable reasonably priced food from sandwiches up including tapas, back dining area up some steps; piped music; tables out on square and in garden behind (former coach yard). *Recommended by Ann and Colin Hunt, Val and Alan Green, Sally Matson*

☆ WINCHESTER SU4828   SO23 9NQ
Black Boy
B3403 off M3 junction 10 towards city then left into Wharf Hill; no nearby daytime parking – 220 metres from car park on B3403

Splendidly eccentric decor at this chatty old-fashioned pub, floor-to-ceiling books, lots of big clocks, mobiles made of wine bottles or spectacles, stuffed animals including a baboon and dachshund, two log fires, orange-painted room with big oriental rugs on red floorboards, barn room with open hayloft, half a dozen often local beers, straightforward food (not Sun evening, Mon, Tues lunchtime), service can be slow, table football and board games; piped music; supervised children and dogs welcome, slate tables out in front and seats on attractive secluded terrace, open all day. *Recommended by Val and Alan Green, Henry Fryer, Ann and Colin Hunt, MJVK and others*

☆ WINCHESTER SU4829   SO23 9EX
Eclipse
The Square, between High Street and cathedral

Chatty licensees in picturesque unspoilt 14th-c local with massive beams and timbers in its two small cheerful rooms, chilled ales including Fullers London Pride and Ringwood, decent choice of wines by the glass, good value lunchtime food from ciabattas to popular Sun roasts, open fire, oak settles, friendly burmese cat; children in back area, seats outside, very handy for cathedral. *Recommended by Ann and Colin Hunt*

WINCHESTER SU4829   SO23 8RZ
Old Gaol House
Jewry Street

Traditional Wetherspoons attracting good mix of customers, ten real ales, decent sensibly priced food all day, nice coffee, walls of books; children welcome. *Recommended by Ann and Colin Hunt, Val and Alan Green*

☆ WINCHESTER SU4829   SO23 9HA
Old Vine
Great Minster Street

Lively big-windowed town bar with well kept ales such as Bowman Swift One, Flowerpots, Ringwood Best and Timothy Taylors Landlord, efficient friendly staff, high beams, worn oak boards, smarter and larger dining side with good up-to-date seasonal food; faint piped music; by cathedral, with sheltered terrace, partly covered and heated, charming bedrooms, open all day. *Recommended by Alastair and Rebecca Lockwood, Glenwys and Alan Lawrence, David and Judy Robison, Richard Mason*

WINCHESTER SU4829   SO23 9EX
William Walker
The Square

Pleasantly refurbished rambling corner pub in Cathedral Close, decent range of food from sandwiches and baguettes up, Ringwood BB and Sharps Doom Bar, quick friendly service. *Recommended by Phil and Jane Villiers, Val and Alan Green, Dave Braisted*

 WINCHESTER SU4829   SO23 8QX
Willow Tree
Durngate Terrace; no adjacent weekday daytime parking, but Durngate car park is around corner in North Walls; a mile from M3 junction 9, by Easton Lane into city

Warmly welcoming and snug, landlord/chef using much local produce for often unusual and enjoyable food (gives cookery lessons, too), big perhaps even over-generous helpings, cheerful efficient young staff, well kept Greene King beers, good wines; long pleasant riverside garden. *Recommended by Ann and Colin Hunt, Geoff and Linda Payne*

WOODLANDS SU3211   SO40 7GH
Gamekeeper
Woodlands Road, just N of A336 Totton—Cadnam

Unspoilt traditional village local by New Forest, friendly landlord, reasonably priced food and beers including Wadworths 6X and one brewed for the pub, good coffee, dining room with conservatory; terrace tables. *Recommended by Phil and Jane Villiers*

ALSO WORTH A VISIT ON THE ISLE OF WIGHT

Besides the region's top pubs, we recommend the following. Do tell us what you think of them: **feedback@goodguides.com**

BEMBRIDGE SZ6488   PO35 5NN
Pilot Boat
Station Road/Kings Road

Small harbourside pub reworked in style of a ship, good food from sandwiches to local seafood, decent choice of ales; tables out overlooking water or in pleasant courtyard behind, well placed for coast walks, open all day. *Recommended by William Goodhart, George and Linda Ozols*

BINSTEAD SZ5792   PO33 3RD
Fleming Arms

Welcoming with wide choice of good reasonably priced food, Ringwood Best and Flowers, attentive service; children and dogs welcome, garden. *Recommended by Keith Widdowson, Paul Baines*

BONCHURCH SZ5778   PO38 1NU
☆ Bonchurch Inn
Bonchurch Shute; from A3055 E of Ventnor turn down to Old Bonchurch; opposite Leconfield Hotel

Quirky former stables with restaurant, owned by Italians, fairly basic family room and congenial bar with narrow-planked ship's decking and old-fashioned steamer-style seats, Courage ales tapped from the cask, bar food and good italian dishes, charming helpful

staff, darts, shove-ha'penny and other games; piped music; dogs welcome, delightful
continental-feeling central courtyard (parking here can be tricky), holiday flat.
*Recommended by J L and J A Johnston, Geoff and Linda Payne, George and Linda Ozols, Guy Vowles,
Mr and Mrs P D Titcomb, Mark Seymour, Jackie Roberts and others*

CARISBROOKE SZ4687   PO30 5SS

☆ **Blacksmiths Arms**
B3401 1.5 miles W

Quiet hillside pub with friendly landlord and staff, Fullers, Shepherd Neame and Yates,
decent wines and cider, food can be good including fresh fish, scrubbed tables in neat
beamed and flagstoned front bars, superb Solent views from airy bare-boards family
dining extension; dogs and walkers welcome, terrace tables and smallish back garden
with same view, play area, open all day. *Recommended by Penny and Peter Keevil, Peter Meister*

COWES SZ5092   PO32 6NB

☆ **Folly**
Folly Lane signed off A3021 just S of Whippingham

Glorious Medina estuary views from bar and waterside terrace of this cheery laid-back
place, timbered ship-like interior with simple wood furnishings, wide range of sensibly
priced hearty food from breakfast on, Greene King Old Speckled Hen, Goddards and
possibly a guest; piped and live music, TV, games machine and pool – can get very lively at
weekends; children and dogs welcome, showers, long-term parking and weather forecasts
for sailors, water taxi, open all day. *Recommended by Quentin and Carol Williamson,
George Atkinson, Simon Collett-Jones, Bruce and Sharon Eden, George and Linda Ozols, Terry and
Nickie Williams and others*

FRESHWATER SZ3485   PO40 9QX

Sandpipers
Coastguard Lane

Victorian hotel's refurbished bar, well kept ales such as Courage Best, Fullers ESB, Island
Yachtsman's and Red Rat Crazy Dog Stout, enjoyable reasonably priced bar food,
comfortable lounge areas with sofas, games room, dining conservatory, weekend music;
children welcome, tables outside, bedrooms (some with sea views). *Recommended by
Joan and Michel Hooper-Immins*

GODSHILL SZ5281   PO38 3HZ

☆ **Taverners**
High Street

Welcoming 17th-c pub with landlord/chef doing good seasonal food with emphasis on
fresh local produce, children's menu and Sun roasts too, very popular at weekends when
booking advised, well kept Fullers London Pride, a house beer from Yates and a guest,
good friendly service, spacious bar and two front dining areas, beams, bare boards and
slate floors, woodburner; dogs welcome, garden with terrace and play area, own shop,
limited parking, open all day, closed Sun evening except bank/school summer holidays.
*Recommended by C and R Bromage, George Atkinson, George and Linda Ozols, Alan Clark, Andy Hogben, the
Farmers*

HULVERSTONE SZ3984   PO30 4EH

☆ **Sun**
B3399

Picture-book thatched country pub in charming peaceful setting with terrific views over
the Channel, low-ceilinged bar with ales such as Adnams, Goddards, Ringwood and
Timothy Taylors, nice mix of old furniture on flagstones and floorboards, brick and stone
walls, horsebrasses and ironwork around fireplace, large windows in traditionally
decorated newer dining area, all-day pubby food including local meat, darts and board
games; piped music – live music Sat evening; children welcome away from bar area, dogs
in bar, secluded split-level cottagey garden, open all day. *Recommended by Stuart Paulley,
Simon Watkins, Paul Humphreys, Peter Meister, Geraldine and James Fradgley and others*

NEWCHURCH SZ5685   PO36 0NN

☆ **Pointer**

High Street

Popular two-room pub under newish management, generous good value food using local produce including good deli boards, well kept Fullers and a guest ale, friendly service; children and dogs welcome, pleasant back garden, boules. *Recommended by Guy Vowles*

NINGWOOD SZ3989   PO30 4NW

☆ **Horse & Groom**

A3054 Newport—Yarmouth, a mile W of Shalfleet

Possibly changing hands but has been roomy friendly pub liked by families; thoughtfully laid-out interior with comfortable leather sofas grouped around low tables, nice mix of sturdy tables and chairs, pale pink walls and old flagstones, Greene King, Goddards and Ringwood, good value standard bar food; piped music, games machine; ample tables in garden with terrific play area – bouncy castle, crazy golf, tyre trails and more. *Recommended by anon*

NITON SZ5075   PO38 2NE

☆ **Buddle**

St Catherine's Road, Undercliff; off A3055 just S of village, towards St Catherine's Point

Old smugglers haunt with views from clifftop sloping lawn and stone terraces, handy for coast path, charmingly timeless heavily black-beamed bar with massive oak mantelbeam over broad stone fireplace, captain's chairs and solid wood tables on big flagstones, pewter mugs, six real ales including local brews, tasty imaginative food, bar billiards and darts; piped music; children in Old Barn, dogs welcome, open all day. *Recommended by David Glynne-Jones, J L and J A Johnston, Geoff and Linda Payne, Bruce and Sharon Eden, George and Linda Ozols*

NORTHWOOD SZ4983   PO31 8LS

Travellers Joy

Off B3325 S of Cowes

Friendly real-ale pub with eight well kept beers including local ones (tasters offered), enjoyable reasonably priced pubby food from sandwiches up, long bar with over 200 pump clips on the walls, conservatory, old pinball machine in games room, Sun quiz; piped radio; children and dogs welcome, garden with pétanque and play area, open all day Fri, Sat. *Recommended by Joan and Michel Hooper-Immins*

SEAVIEW SZ6291   PO34 5EX

☆ **Seaview Hotel**

High Street; off B3330 Ryde—Bembridge

Small gently civilised but relaxed hotel, traditional wood furnishings, seafaring paraphernalia and log fire in pubby bare-boards bar, comfortable more refined front bar with good soft furnishings, Goddards, Yates and a guest, good wine list including some local ones, well presented generous pub food and more elaborate restaurant menu using produce from their farm; they may ask for a credit card if you run a tab, piped music, TV; children welcome, dogs in bar, sea glimpses from tables on tiny front terrace, nice bedrooms (some with sea views), open all day. *Recommended by Thomas Moore, David Glynne-Jones, George Atkinson, Paul Humphreys, Mr and Mrs P D Titcomb, Karen Eliot and others*

VENTNOR SZ5677   PO38 1JX

☆ **Spyglass**

Esplanade, SW end; road down is very steep and twisty, and parking nearby can be difficult – best to use the pay-and-display (free in winter) about 100 yards up the road

Perched above the beach with a fascinating jumble of seafaring bric-a-brac in snug quarry-tiled interior, well kept Ringwood and a couple of guests, generously served food including good crab sandwiches, friendly helpful staff; piped music – live most evenings and Sun lunchtime, can get very busy; children welcome, dogs in bar, terrace tables with lovely sea views, coast walk towards Botanic Garden, heftier hikes on to St Boniface Down and towards the eerie shell of Appuldurcombe House, bedrooms, open all day. *Recommended by Penny and Peter Keevil, Dennis and Doreen Haward, George Atkinson, Tony and Maggie Harwood*

WHITWELL SZ5277   PO38 2PY

☆ **White Horse**
High Street

Popular sympathetically restored old thatched pub, extensive range of good value generous food from pub staples to more innovative dishes and good Sun roasts, several well kept ales including Goddards, good friendly service, large cheery high-ceilinged family dining area with small beamed bar and second area off; may be piped music; picnic-sets in big garden. *Recommended by Terry and Nickie Williams*

ALSO WORTH A VISIT IN KENT

Besides the region's top pubs, we recommend the following. Do tell us what you think of them: **feedback@goodguides.com**

ADDINGTON TQ6559   ME19 5BB

Angel
Just off M20 junction 4; Addington Green

14th-c pub in classic village-green setting, olde-worlde décor with beams, scrubbed tables and big fireplaces, enjoyable food from sandwiches/wraps and traditional things up including weekday set menus, fair choice of beers from barrel-fronted counter, lots of wines by the glass, good friendly service, stables restaurant, live music (Weds, Fri); tables out at front and back, two bedrooms. *Recommended by A N Bance, Gill and Keith Croxton*

APPLEDORE TQ9529   TN26 2BU

Black Lion
The Street

Compact 1930s village pub with bustling atmosphere, very welcoming helpful staff, good generous food all day from simple sandwiches to imaginative dishes, lamb from Romney Marsh and local fish, three or four well kept changing ales, Biddenden farm cider, log fire, partitioned back eating area; piped music; tables out on green, attractive village, good Military Canal walks. *Recommended by Colin and Louise English, Peter Meister*

APPLEDORE TQ9729   TN26 2DF

Railway Hotel
Station Road (B2080 E)

Friendly refurbished red-brick Victorian hotel with rail memorabilia and open fire in big bar, Shepherd Neame master brew and a guest, daily papers, bar billiards, darts and other pub games, interesting food using local and organic ingredients in separate restaurant (closed Mon, Tues); dogs welcome, garden tables, seven bedrooms, open all day. *Recommended by Peter and Jean Hoare*

BEARSTED TQ8055   ME14 4EJ

Oak on the Green
The Street

Two hop-festooned bar areas with bare boards and half-panelling, bustling and friendly, with wide choice of home-made food all day including children's menu, well kept regularly changing ales, restaurant; disabled access, seats out at front under big umbrellas. *Recommended by Michael Tack*

BEKESBOURNE TR1856   CT4 5ED
☆ **Unicorn**
Bekesbourne Hill, off Station Road; village E of Canterbury

Small, friendly pub with just a few scrubbed old pine tables on worn floorboards in simply
furnished bars, ales such as Ramsgate Gadds No. 5, Shepherd Neame Early Bird and
Westerham Grasshopper, Biddenden cider, traditional food (not Sun evening, limited
Mon); piped music, live folk music/acoustic on Sun; children welcome and dogs (not
during food times), prettily planted side terrace, garden with bat and trap, large back car
park reached from small track at end of adjacent terrace of cottages, open all day
weekends, closed Mon in winter. *Recommended by anon*

BENENDEN TQ8032   TN17 4DE
☆ **Bull**
The Street; by village green

Relaxed informal atmosphere in bare-boards or dark terracotta tiled rooms, pleasing mix
of furniture, church candles on tables, hops, fire in brick inglenook, friendly hands-on
licensees, Dark Star Hophead, Harveys Best, Larkins Traditional and a guest from carved
wooden counter, local cider too, smarter dining room with burgundy brocade dining
chairs, enjoyable home-made food (not Sun evening) including OAP menu and popular
Sun roasts, live music most Sun afternoons; piped jazz, unobtrusive TV; children welcome,
dogs in bar, picnic sets by road, open all day except Mon lunchtime. *Recommended by*
Conor McGaughey, Kevin Thomas, Nina Randall

BIRLING TQ6860   ME19 5JW
Nevill Bull
Near M20 junction 4

Under welcoming newish licensees, generous well liked food, Kent Brewery ales, decent
wines, friendly attentive service, cheery fires in beamed bar and dining room. *Recommended*
by John Mitchell

BODSHAM TR1045   TN25 5JQ
☆ **Timber Batts**
Following Bodsham, Wye sign off B2068 keep right at unsigned fork after about
1.5 miles

Charming french owner in cottagey country pub, traditional carpeted bar with Adnams
Bitter, Woodfordes Wherry and a guest, good french wines by the glass (some from
Mr Gross's cousin's vineyard), informally rustic beamed dining area with happy mix of
stripped-pine tables, pews, dark tables and dining chairs on carpet, delicious french food
(not Sun evening, booking advised) cooked by landlord's son using local produce, three-
course lunch menu, some pubby dishes too; children and dogs welcome (pub labrador
called Bounty), lovely views over wide-spreading valley from back garden. *Recommended by*
Jill and Julian Tasker, John and Enid Morris, Derek Thomas, Peter Heaton, Justin and Emma King,
Heather and Dick Martin and others

BOXLEY TQ7758   ME14 3DR
Kings Arms
1.75 miles from M20 junction 7; opposite church

Cosy country dining pub under welcoming newish landlord, largely 16th/17th-c, low
beams, red chesterfield by huge fireplace, well kept Greene King IPA, Harveys Best,
Fullers London Pride, Gales HSB and guests, good choice of food (not Sun evening) from
sandwiches and traditional things up; piped music, some live; children and dogs welcome,
new furniture in appealing garden, pretty village, pleasant walks, open all day.
Recommended by Harry Ramsden

All *Guide* inspections are anonymous. Anyone claiming to be a *Good Pub Guide*
inspector is a fraud. Please let us know.

BOYDEN GATE TR2265   CT3 4EB

☆ Gate Inn

Off A299 Herne Bay—Ramsgate – follow Chislet, Upstreet sign opposite Roman
Gallery; Chislet also signed off A28 Canterbury—Margate at Upstreet – after turning
right into Chislet main street keep right on to Boyden

The long-serving landlord at this delightfully unpretentious rustic pub has retired, but new
licensee intends to keep things the same; comfortably worn traditional quarry-tiled rooms,
flowery-cushioned pews around tables of considerable character, hop-hung beams,
attractively etched windows, inglenook log fire, Shepherd Neame Master Brew, Spitfire and a
couple of guests from tap room casks, interesting bottled beers, pubby food (now lunchtime
and evening); children and dogs welcome, sheltered garden bounded by two streams with
tame ducks and geese. *Recommended by Kevin Thorpe, N R White, Colin and Louise English*

BRABOURNE LEES TR0740   TN25 6QB

Plough

Lees Road

Welcoming beamed 18th-c village local (changed hands 2010), well kept Shepherd
Neame, enjoyable home-made food including good Sun roasts, inglenook log fire, pool,
board games, some live music; garden with bat & trap, nice country views, open all day.
Recommended by James Powell

BRENCHLEY TQ6841   TN12 7AX

Halfway House

Horsmonden Road

Beamed 18th-c coaching inn with attractive olde-worlde mix of rustic and traditional
furnishings on bare boards, old farm tools, two log fires, particularly friendly landlord and
efficient staff, enjoyable home-made food including good fish and popular Sun roasts,
good range of well kept changing ales tapped from the cask such as Goachers, two
tranquil eating areas; children and dogs welcome, picnic-sets and play area in big garden,
summer barbecues and beer festivals, bedrooms, open all day. *Recommended by Jamie and*
Sue May, N R White, Alan Franck, Peter Meister

BROADSTAIRS TR3967   CT10 1AN

Royal Albion

Albion Street

Smartly refurbished 18th-c seafront hotel reputedly used by Dickens; Shepherd Neame
ales, reasonably priced quickly served food from sandwiches up, pleasant conservatory-
style area with modern wicker-backed dining chairs and lovely sea views, restaurant;
stepped mediterranean-theme front terrace, 21 bedrooms, open all day from 8am.
Recommended by John Wooll

BURMARSH TR1032   TN29 0JJ

Shepherd & Crook

Shear Way

Friendly two-bar traditional 16th-c marshside local with smuggling history, well kept
Adnams and a guest beer, Biddenden cider, good straightforward home-made food at low
prices, prompt service, interesting photographs and blow lamp collection, log fire; dogs
welcome, open all day Fri-Sun. *Recommended by N R White*

CANTERBURY TR1458   CT1 2AA

Dolphin

St Radigund's Street

Modernised dining pub with enjoyable home-made pubby food from baguettes up, Sharps
Doom Bar, Timothy Taylors Landlord and a couple of guests such as Gadds and Old Dairy,
country wines, friendly staff, bric-a-brac on delft shelf, board games, flagstoned
conservatory, pianist Sun evening, quiz night first Mon of month; no dogs; children
welcome, disabled access, good-sized back garden with heaters, open all day. *Recommended*
by Rob and Catherine Dunster, John Baker

CHIDDINGSTONE TQ5045   TN8 7AH
Castle Inn
Off B2027 Tonbridge—Edenbridge

Rambling old pub in pretty NT village, handsome beamed bar, settles and sturdy wall benches, attractive mullioned window seat, woodburners, brick-floor snug, Harveys Best and local Larkins including winter Porter (brewed in village), good choice of food with blackboard specials, friendly staff; children and dogs welcome, tables out in front and in nice secluded garden with own bar, circular walks from village, open all day.
Recommended by LM

CHIDDINGSTONE CAUSEWAY TQ5146   TN11 8JJ
Little Brown Jug
B2027

Open-plan Whiting & Hammond pub next to Penshurst station, comfortable bar and big dining extension, enjoyable food at sensible prices from sandwiches and deli plates to full meals, well kept Greene King ales, good wine list, friendly efficient service, log fires; attractive garden with play area, beer and music festivals, open all day weekends.
Recommended by Gerry and Rosemary Dobson, Christian Mole

CHILHAM TR0653   CT4 8BY
☆ White Horse
The Square

Popular 15th-c pub in picturesque village square, fresh modern décor, handsomely carved ceiling beams and massive fireplace with Lancastrian rose carved on mantelbeam, chunky light oak furniture on pale wooden flooring and more traditional pubby furniture on quarry tiles, bright paintings, horsebrasses and a couple of stained-glass panels, well kept changing ales, good popular freshly cooked food (not Sun evening) using local organic produce, home-made cakes and coffee all day; piped music and TV; children welcome, dogs in bar, handy for the castle, open all day. *Recommended by I A and D J Mullins*

CHILHAM TR0753   CT4 8DL
Woolpack
Off A28/A252; The Street

Friendly old inn dating from 15th c, traditional beamed bar with pews and good inglenook, well kept Shepherd Neame ales, enjoyable food including weekday set menu, bay-windowed red-carpeted restaurant; children welcome, courtyard tables, delightful village, 14 bedrooms, open all day. *Recommended by John Baker, I A and D J Mullins*

CHILLENDEN TR2653   CT3 1PS
☆ Griffins Head
SE end of village; 2 miles E of Aylesham

Attractive beamed, timbered and flagstoned 14th-c pub with two bar rooms and back flagstoned dining room, gently upscale local atmosphere, big log fire, full range of Shepherd Neame ales, good choice of enjoyable home-made food, good wine list, friendly attentive service; dogs welcome in some parts, pleasant garden surrounded by wild roses, Sun barbecues, attractive countryside. *Recommended by Philip and Cheryl Hill, Stephen Burke*

CHIPSTEAD TQ4956   TN13 2RZ
Bricklayers Arms
Chevening Road

Attractive pub overlooking lake and green, popular good value food (not Sun evening) served by cheerful helpful staff, full range of Harveys beers kept well and tapped from casks behind long counter, relaxed chatty atmosphere, heavily beamed bar with open fire and fine racehorse painting, unpretentious larger back restaurant; seats out front.
Recommended by Alan Cowell, N R White

CHIPSTEAD TQ5056   TN13 2RW
☆ **George & Dragon**
Near M25 junction 5

Attractive country dining pub under same owners as the George and Dragon at
Speldhurst; heavy black beams and standing timbers, grey-green panelling, old tables and
chapel chairs on bare boards, log fires, good changing food all day using organic local
produce, Westerham ales including Georges Marvellous Medicine brewed for the pub,
good choice of wines by the glass, good service, upstairs restaurant; piped music; children
and dogs welcome, terrace and garden with veg/herbs, play area, open all day.
Recommended by Sophie Broster, Derek Thomas, John Evans

COWDEN TQ4640   TN8 7JG
Fountain
Off A264 and B2026; High Street

Good sensibly priced blackboard food in attractive tile-hung beamed village pub, steep
steps up to unpretentious dark-panelled corner bar, well kept Harveys, decent wines, old
photographs on cream walls, good log fire, mix of tables in adjoining room, woodburner in
small back dining room with one big table; piped music; walkers and dogs welcome,
picnic-sets on small terrace and lawn, pretty village. *Recommended by LM, Gwyn Jones,
R and S Bentley*

CROCKHAM HILL TQ4450   TN8 6RD
Royal Oak
Main Road

Cosy old village pub revamped by Westerham brewery, their ales kept well, popular good
value home-made food, friendly helpful staff, mix of furniture including leather sofas on
stripped-wood floor, original Tottering-by-Gently cartoons, old local photographs, quiz
nights and live folk; dogs and walkers welcome, small garden, handy for Chartwell (NT),
open all day Sat. *Recommended by Gwyn Jones, Stephen Bennett*

DEAL TR3751   CT14 7EQ
Berry
Canada Road

Small no frills local opposite old Royal Marine barracks, welcoming enthusiastic landlord,
L-shaped carpeted bar, well kept Harveys Best and several changing microbrews (tasting
notes on slates, beer festivals), farm cider and perry, no food, coal fire, newspapers, quiz
and darts teams, pool, live music Thurs; small vine-covered terrace, open all day
weekends, closed Tues-Thurs lunchtimes. *Recommended by Kevin Thorpe, Dr Kevan Tucker,
N R White*

DEAL TR3753   CT14 6JZ
Ship
Middle Street

Dimly lit local in historic maritime quarter, five well kept changing ales including
Ramsgate Gadds, friendly landlord, lots of dark woodwork, stripped brick and local ship
and wreck pictures, piano and woodburner in side bar; dogs welcome, small pretty walled
garden, open all day. *Recommended by N R White, Dr Kevan Tucker*

DENTON TR2147   CT4 6QZ
Jackdaw
A260 Canterbury—Folkestone

Imposing old brick-and-flint open-plan pub, welcoming service, enjoyable family food all
day, half a dozen well kept ales, friendly young staff, RAF memorabilia in front area, large
back restaurant; quiet piped music; children welcome, good-sized charming garden,
picturesque village, open all day. *Recommended by Michael and Judy Buckley*

DUNKS GREEN TQ6152   TN11 9RU
☆ Kentish Rifleman
Dunks Green Road

Tudor pub restored in modern rustic style, welcoming helpful staff, well kept ales such as
Harveys and Westerham, enjoyable reasonably priced food (not Sun evening), bar and two
dining areas, rifles on low beams, cosy log fire; children and dogs welcome, tables in
pretty garden with well, good walks, open all day weekends. *Recommended by Mark Sowery,*
Nigel and Jean Eames, Bob and Margaret Holder, Conor McGaughey, B and M Kendall and others

DUNTON GREEN TQ5156   TN13 2DR
☆ Bullfinch
London Road, Riverhead

Huge spreading place with modern décor in linked rooms, pubbier part to left with
contemporary built-in wall benches, dining chairs and wooden tables, bare-boards area
with sofas and brick fireplace, dining rooms with two-way log fire in glass enclosure,
upholidaystered banquettes and wide mix of tables and chairs, popular slightly upmarket
traditional food, pleasant staff, well kept McMullens ales, good choice of wines,
newspapers; TV, fruit machine; children welcome, attractive garden with heated terrace,
open all day weekends. *Recommended by Revd R P Tickle, Derek Thomas*

FARNINGHAM TQ5467   DA4 0DT
Chequers
High Street/Dartford Road, just off A20

Traditional one-bar corner local with good choice of real ales including Fullers and
Timothy Taylors Landlord, unpretentious lunchtime food (not Sun), friendly staff;
benches outside, picturesque village. *Recommended by N R White*

FAVERSHAM TR0161   ME13 7BP
Anchor
Abbey Street

Friendly two-bar character pub, good reasonably priced food from baguettes up, well kept
Shepherd Neame range, simple dimly lit bare-boards bar with log fire, ancient beams and
dark panelling, frosted windows, boat pictures and models, small side room with pub
games and books, restaurant; some live music; dogs welcome, tables in pretty enclosed
garden with bat and trap, attractive 17th-c street near historic quay, open all day.
Recommended by Quentin and Carol Williamson, the Didler, Nick Lawless

FAVERSHAM TR0161   ME13 7BH
Phoenix
Abbey Street

Historic town pub with heavy low beams and stripped stone, well kept beers such as
Greene King, Harveys and Wells & Youngs, good choice of food (all day Fri and Sat, not
Sun evening) from snacks up, afternoon teas, good friendly service, leather chesterfields
by open fire, restaurant, various events including live music and poetry reading; some
pavement tables, open all day. *Recommended by LM*

FAVERSHAM TR0161   ME13 7JE
Sun
West Street

Rambling old-world 15th-c pub in pedestrianised street, good unpretentious atmosphere
with small low-ceilinged partly panelled rooms, big inglenook, well kept Shepherd Neame
beers from nearby brewery, enjoyable bar food including OAP deals, smart restaurant
attached, friendly efficient staff; unobtrusive piped music; wheelchair access possible
(small step), pleasant back courtyard, eight bedrooms, open all day. *Recommended by the*
Didler, LM, Neil Hardwick

FRITTENDEN TQ8141   TN17 2EJ
Bell & Jorrocks
Corner of Biddenden Road/The Street

Welcoming simple 18th-c tile-hung and beamed local includingorporating village post
office, well kept Adnams, Harveys, Woodfords and guests, Weston's and Thatcher's ciders,
good traditional home-made food (not Sun evening, lunchtimes Mon, Tues), open fire with
propeller from crashed plane above, kentish darts; sports TV; children welcome, open all
day. *Recommended by N R White, Donald Bremner*

GOODNESTONE TR2554   CT3 1PJ
Fitzwalter Arms
The Street; NB this is in East Kent NOT the other Goodnestone

Old dimly lit beamed village local with two little rustic bars, Shepherd Neame ales, good
locally sourced food including seasonal game, friendly chatty service, small dining room,
log fires; lovely church next door. *Recommended by N R White, Dr Kevan Tucker*

GOUDHURST TQ7037   TN17 1HA
☆ Green Cross
Station Road (A262 W)

Good generous food with emphasis on fish and seafood, friendly helpful service, well kept
Harveys Best, good wines and own sloe gin, two-room dark-wood bar with country prints
and photographs, large stuffed fish above one fireplace, hop-strewn roomy back
restaurant with stripped-wood floor and timbered walls, flowers on tables, paintings for
sale, log fire; piped music; no dogs; terrace tables, light and airy good value bedrooms.
Recommended by David S Allen, Anthony Longden

GROOMBRIDGE TQ5337   TN3 9QH
☆ Crown
B2110

Charming tile-hung wealden inn with snug low-beamed bar, old tables on worn flagstones,
panelling, bric-a-brac, fire in sizeable brick inglenook, Harveys, Larkins and a guest,
traditional food (not Sun evening), roughly plastered dining area with dark wood pubby
tables; children welcome, dogs in bar, narrow old brick terrace overlooking steep green,
bedrooms, open all day summer Fri-Sun, closed winter Sun evening. *Recommended by Ann
and Colin Hunt, Mrs B Forster, Alan Franck*

HARBLEDOWN TR1358   CT2 9AB
Old Coach & Horses
Church Hill

Modern split-level two-room bistro/bar, airy yet cosy, with log fire in two-way fireplace,
farmhouse chairs around pine tables, cabinet of toy vans and classic-car cigarette cards;
more pubby part with curved cushioned pews, stone flagons and daily newspapers,
interesting well liked food, upstairs restaurant with modern pine furniture, sitting room
with black leather seating; garden picnic-sets, good views, parking on hill (no car park).
Recommended by Andy Towse

HAWKHURST TQ7531   TN18 5EJ
☆ Great House
Gills Green; pub signed off A229 N

Busy stylish white-weatherboarded dining pub, popular food (not cheap, all day
weekends), Harveys Best and a seasonal brew from marble counter, sofas, armchairs and
bright scatter cushions in chatty bar, moving into dark wood dining tables and smartly
upholidaystered chairs on slate floor, gilt-framed pictures on red or green walls, steps
down to light airy dining room with big picture windows, colourful cushions on carved
built-in shabby chic seating, plenty of modern art; piped music, TV; children welcome,
dogs in bar, modern blue furniture on side terrace, open all day, closed Mon in Jan and
Feb. *Recommended by Peter Veness*

HEADCORN TQ8344   TN27 9NL
George & Dragon
High Street

Good atmosphere and service, welcoming landlady, wide range of enjoyable home-made food, local ales and cider, extensive wine list, open fires, separate dining room.
Recommended by Bill Adie, Alec and Joan Laurence, Anna Smith

HEAVERHAM TQ5758   TN15 6NP
Chequers
Watery Lane

Attractive 16th-c beamed pub with friendly locals' bar, decent food (not Sun evening or Mon), Shepherd Neame ales, dining room with inglenook, raftered barn restaurant with resident ghost; children welcome, big pretty garden, open all day, closed Mon.
Recommended by Gordon and Margaret Ormondroyd, Mark Waters

HERNE BAY TR1768   CT6 5HT
Old Ship
Central Parade

Old white weatherboarded pub with window tables looking across road to sea, well kept beers including Bass, food (cheaper lunchtime menu) including Sun roasts; children welcome till 6pm, sea-view deck. *Recommended by John Wooll*

HEVER TQ4743   TN8 7LJ
Greyhound
Uckfield Lane

Well laid-out beamed bar with quiet corners, benches and chairs around scrubbed tables, friendly landlord and staff, reasonably priced bar food from sandwiches up, well kept ales such as Timothy Taylors Landlord, more formal restaurant; no dogs inside; tables on front decking and in garden behind, bedrooms, handy for Hever Castle. *Recommended by R and S Bentley*

HEVER TQ4744   TN8 7NH
Henry VIII
By gates of Hever Castle

Partly 14th-c pub, some fine oak panelling, wide floorboards and heavy beams, inglenook fireplace, Henry VIII décor, well kept Shepherd Neame ales, food from well filled baguettes up, small dining room, friendly efficient staff; no dogs even in garden; tables out on terrace and pondside lawn, bedrooms. *Recommended by Ann and Colin Hunt, LM*

HODSOLL STREET TQ6263   TN15 7LE
☆ Green Man
Signed off A227 S of Meopham; turn right in village

Bustling village pub with neatly arranged traditional furnishings in big airy carpeted rooms, friendly atmosphere, Greene King Old Speckled Hen, Harveys Best, Timothy Taylors Landlord and a guest, well liked pubby food (all day Sun) including good baguettes and popular two-course weekday lunch; piped music – live music second Thurs of month, quiz Mon; children and dogs welcome, tables and climbing frame on well tended lawn, open all day Fri-Sun. *Recommended by Jeremy Hancock, Dr Jennifer Sansom, Gwyn Jones, Jan and Rod Poulter, D P and M A Miles, A N Bance and others*

HOLLINGBOURNE TQ8354   ME17 1TR
☆ Windmill
M20 junction 8: A20 towards Ashford then left into B2163 – Eyhorne Street village

Old coaching inn with pleasant old-world feel and small pubby core but mainly set for dining, several smallish mostly carpeted areas with heavy low black beams, solid pub tables with padded country or library chairs, shelves of books, log fire in huge inglenook, Fullers London Pride, Harveys Best and Shepherd Neame Master Brew, traditional food (all day weekends) including good value two-course menu Mon-Thurs; piped music; children must remain seated in bar, dogs welcome, picnic-sets and play area in neatly kept sunny garden. *Recommended by Michael Doswell, Roger and Pauline Pearce, Charles and Pauline Stride, N R White*

IDE HILL TQ4851
TN14 6JN

Cock

Off B2042 SW of Sevenoaks

Pretty village-green local dating from the 15th c, chatty and friendly with long serving landlord, two dimly lit bars with steps between, Greene King ales, enjoyable traditional food including game (not Sun or Mon evenings, snacks Sun lunchtime), cosy in winter with good inglenook log fire; well behaved children and dogs welcome, picnic-sets out at front, handy for Chartwell (NT) and nearby walks. *Recommended by N R White, Heather and Dick Martin*

IDE HILL TQ4952
TN14 6BU

Woodman

Whitley Row, Goathurst Common; B2042 N

Large roadside pub with good choice of enjoyable food all day including dishes from South Africa (landlord's homeland), well kept beer, decent wine, young well trained staff; piped music and live jazz; nice garden, good walks. *Recommended by Tina and David Woods-Taylor*

IDEN GREEN TQ7437
TN17 2PB

Peacock

A262 E of Goudhurst

Tudor, with blazing inglenook log fire in low-beamed main bar, quarry tiles and old sepia photographs, well priced enjoyable pubby food (all day Sat, not Sun evening) from sandwiches up, very helpful service, well kept Shepherd Neame ales, pastel dining room with cork-studded walls, public bar; TV; well behaved dogs welcome, no muddy boots, good-sized garden, closed Sun evening. *Recommended by Conrad Freezer, Nigel and Jean Eames*

IDEN GREEN TQ8031
TN17 4HT

☆ Woodcock

Not the Iden Green near Goudhurst; village signed off A268 E of Hawkhurst and B2086 at W edge of Benenden; in village follow Standen Street sign, then fork left into Woodcock Lane

Informal friendly little local with a couple of big standing timbers supporting very low-ceilings, chatty regulars on high stools near corner counter, comfortable squashy sofa and low table by inglenook woodburner, concrete floor, brick walls hung with horsebrasses, Greene King Abbot, IPA, Morlands Original and XX Mild, well liked pubby food (not Sun evening), small panelled dining area with pine tables and chairs; children welcome, dogs in bar, back garden, open all day, closed Mon (except bank holidays). *Recommended by A and H Piper, Steve Coates, V Brogden, Gordon and Margaret Ormondroyd*

IGHTHAM TQ5956
TN15 9HH

☆ George & Dragon

A227

Stylishly refurbished ancient timbered pub, good reasonably priced food from generous snacks up (all day till 6.30pm, not Sun), plenty of friendly smartly dressed staff, well kept Shepherd Neame ales, decent wines, sofas among other furnishings in long sociable main bar, heavy-beamed end room, woodburner and open fires, restaurant; children and dogs welcome, back terrace, handy for Ightham Mote (NT), good walks, open all day. *Recommended by Bob and Margaret Holder, Gavin Markwick, Gordon and Margaret Ormondroyd*

IVY HATCH TQ5854   TN15 0NL

☆ Plough

High Cross Road; village signed off A227 N of Tonbridge

Tile-hung 18th-c dining pub, light wood floors with mix of cushioned chairs around wooden tables, large plants, leather chesterfields by open fire, Harveys and a guest ale, local fruit juice, interesting if not cheap food (not Sun evening) using local produce including some home-grown, conservatory restaurant, may be own chutneys and eggs for sale; piped music; children welcome, seats in landscaped garden surrounded by cob trees, handy for Ightham Mote (NT), open all day Sat, closed winter Sun evening. *Recommended by Bob and Margaret Holder, Mr and Mrs J M Sennett, LM, Gordon and Margaret Ormondroyd and others*

LITTLE CHART TQ9446   TN27 0QB

Swan

The Street

Comfortable and substantial 17th-c village local with lots of beams, open fires in simple unspoilt front bar and interesting smarter bar, good-sized dining area, enjoyable straightforward food, real ales and decent wines, friendly staff; dogs welcome, nice riverside garden. *Recommended by Richard Mason*

LOWER HARDRES TR1453   CT4 7AL

☆ Granville

Faussett Hill, Street End; B2068 S of Canterbury

Spacious airy interior with contemporary furnishings, unusual central fire with large conical hood and glimpses of kitchen, proper public bar with farmhouse chairs, settles and woodburner, deservedly popular food (not Sun evening, Mon – booking advised), fine choice of wines from blackboard, Shepherd Neame Master Brew and a seasonal beer, good service, daily papers; piped music; children and dogs welcome, french windows to garden with large spreading tree and small sunny terrace, open all day Sun. *Recommended by Barry and Patricia Wooding, Dr Kevan Tucker*

LUDDESDOWN TQ6667   DA13 0XB

☆ Cock

Henley Street, N of village – OS Sheet 177 map reference 664672; off A227 in Meopham, or A228 in Cuxton

Early 18th-c country pub, friendly long-serving no-nonsense landlord, at least six ales including Adnams, Goachers, Harveys and Shepherd Neame, sensibly priced all-day pubby food (not Sun evening) from wide choice of sandwiches up, rugs on polished boards in pleasant bay-windowed lounge bar, quarry-tiled locals' bar, woodburners, pews and other miscellaneous furnishings, aircraft pictures, masses of beer mats and bric-a-brac like stuffed animals, model cars and beer can collections, bar billiards and darts, back dining conservatory; no children in bar or part-covered heated back terrace; dogs welcome, big secure garden, good walks, open all day. *Recommended by A N Bance, N R White*

MEOPHAM TQ6364   DA13 0QA

Cricketers

Wrotham Road (A227)

Recently refurbished Whiting & Hammond pub (was the Long Hop) in nice spot overlooking cricket green, popular food, friendly staff; garden behind. *Recommended by Geoff Deaves, Christian Mole*

MERSHAM TR0438   TN25 6NU

Farriers Arms

The Forstal/Flood Street

Large community-run beamed pub owned by village and reopened in 2009 after refurbishment, good value fresh food, friendly staff, microbrewery, restaurant; streamside garden behind, pleasant country views. *Recommended by Simon Good*

NEWNHAM TQ9557   ME9 0LL

☆ **George**

The Street; village signed from A2 W of Ospringe, outside Faversham

Old-world village pub under new licensees, series of spreading open-plan rooms, hop-strung beams, stripped brickwork, polished floorboards, candles and lamps on handsome tables, two inglenooks one with woodburner, Shepherd Neame Master Brew and a seasonal beer, locally sourced food (not Sun evening) from lunchtime snacks up; piped and some live music, no dogs inside; children welcome, picnic-sets in spacious tree-sheltered garden, open all day Sun. *Recommended by anon*

NORTHBOURNE TR3352   CT14 0LG

Hare & Hounds

Off A256 or A258 near Dover; The Street

Chatty village pub with several well kept ales including Harveys, good choice of generous popular food (lamb from nearby farm), friendly efficient service, spacious modernised brick and wood interior, log fires; dogs welcome, terrace tables. *Recommended by N R White*

OARE TR0163   ME13 7TU

☆ **Shipwrights Arms**

S shore of Oare Creek, E of village; signed from Oare Road/Ham Road junction in Faversham

Remote and ancient marshland tavern with plenty of character, up to five kentish beers tapped from the cask (pewter tankards over counter), basic food (not Sun evening or Mon), three dark simple little bars separated by standing timbers, wood partitions and narrow door arches, medley of seats from tapestry-cushioned stools to black panelled built-in settles forming booths, flags or boating pennants on ceiling, wind gauge above main door (takes reading from chimney); piped local radio; children welcome away from bar area, dogs in bar, large garden, path along Oare Creek to Swale estuary, lots of surrounding bird life, closed Mon. *Recommended by Conor McGaughey, Colin McKerrow, Tony Brace, N R White, the Didler and others*

OARE TR0063   ME13 0QA

Three Mariners

Church Road

Comfortable simply restored old pub with good reputation for food including fresh fish, Tues-Fri lunch deals, Shepherd Neame ales, log fire; attractive garden overlooking Faversham Creek, open all day Sat, closed Sun evening, Mon (operates then as mid-morning post office). *Recommended by Warren Marsh, Alistair Jones, Ken and Lynda Taylor*

OLD ROMNEY TR0325   TN29 9SQ

Rose & Crown

A259 opposite church

Simple friendly village pub with good value standard food from sandwiches up, well kept Courage, Greene King, Rother Valley and guests, Biddenden cider, helpful staff, old local photographs, dining conservatory; TV; children welcome, pretty garden with boules, chalet bedrooms, open all day. *Recommended by Julia and Richard Tredgett, Colin McKerrow*

PENSHURST TQ5243   TN11 8BT

Leicester Arms

High Street

Country hotel feel with comfortable old bars and meadowland-view dining room up steps, well kept Fullers London Pride, Harveys and Greene King Old Speckled Hen, enjoyable food all day from bar and main menus, friendly polite service; lavatories down steps (disabled one in car park opposite); children and dogs welcome, pretty back garden, seven bedrooms. *Recommended by Peter Meister, Ann and Colin Hunt, Paul Rampton, Julie Harding*

PENSHURST TQ4943   TN8 7BS

☆ # Rock

Hoath Corner, Chiddingstone Hoath, on back road Chiddingstone—Cowden; OS Sheet 188 map reference 497431

Tiny welcoming cottage with undulating brick floor, simple furnishings and woodburner in fine brick inglenook, well kept Larkins ales, enjoyable pub food from good sandwiches up, friendly young staff, large stuffed bull's head for ring the bull, up a step to smaller room with long wooden settle by nice table; dogs welcome (may be a biscuit), picnic-sets in front and on back lawn. *Recommended by Tina and David Woods-Taylor, LM, Grahame Brooks, Anthony Bradbury*

PENSHURST TQ5241   TN11 8EP

☆ # Spotted Dog

Smarts Hill, off B2188 S

Quaint old weatherboarded pub under welcoming newish family, heavy low beams and timbers, attractive moulded panelling, rugs and tiles, antique settles, inglenook log fire, Harveys, Larkins and two guests, local cider, good mostly traditional food (all day weekends) including weekday lunch deals, smart staff; children and dogs welcome, tiered back terrace (they may ask to keep your credit card while you eat here), open all day. *Recommended by John Redfern, Andy Surman, Alan Franck, Heather and Dick Martin*

PETTERIDGE TQ6640   TN12 7NE

Hopbine

Petteridge Lane; NE of village

Small unspoilt cottage in quiet little hamlet, two small rooms with open fire between, traditional pubby furniture on red-patterned carpet, hops and horsebrasses, well kept Badger ales, enjoyable good value home-made food, friendly staff, steps up to simple back part with piano and darts, flagons in brick fireplace; seats in side garden. *Recommended by anon*

PLAXTOL TQ6054   TN15 0PT

☆ # Golding Hop

Sheet Hill (0.5 miles S of Ightham, between A25 and A227)

Secluded traditional country local, simple dimly lit two-level bar with hands-on landlord who can be very welcoming, cask-tapped Adnams, and guests kept well, local farm ciders (sometimes their own), short choice of basic good value bar food (not Mon or Tues evenings), old photographs of the pub, woodburners, bar billiards; portable TV for big sports events; no children inside; suntrap streamside lawn and well fenced play area over lane, good walks, open all day Sat. *Recommended by N R White, Bob and Margaret Holder, Conor McGaughey, the Didler and others*

RYARSH TQ6759   ME19 5LS

Duke of Wellington

Birling Road; not far from M20 junction 4, via Leybourne and Birling

Appealing Tudor bar and bar/restaurant, good blackboard food including weekday deals, several well kept real ales, live jazz Thurs evening; garden with pétanque. *Recommended by David Jackman*

SANDWICH TR3358   CT13 9EF

Bell

Upper Strand Street

Comfortable nicely done Edwardian hotel opposite river, enjoyable bar food including good value lunchtime set menu, well kept Greene King IPA, restaurant; children welcome, seats outside, 34 bedrooms. *Recommended by MDN, John Wooll*

SEASALTER TR0864   CT5 4BP
☆ **Sportsman**
Faversham Road, off B2040

Restauranty dining pub just inside seawall and rather unprepossessing from outside; good imaginative contemporary cooking with plenty of seafood (not Sun evening or Mon, must book and not cheap), home-baked breads, good wine choice including english, well kept Shepherd Neame ales, friendly staff; two plain linked rooms and long conservatory, wooden floor, pine tables, wheelback and basket-weave dining chairs, big film star photographs; plastic glasses for outside; children welcome, open all day Sun. *Recommended by Colin McKerrow, Prof and Mrs J Fletcher, V Brogden, N R White*

SELLING TR0455   ME13 9RY
☆ **Rose & Crown**
Follow Perry Wood signs

Tucked-away 16th-c country pub, hops strung from beams, two inglenook log fires, friendly service, well kept Adnams and Harveys, several ciders, generous food from sandwiches up; piped music; children welcome, dogs on leads in bar, cottagey back garden with play area, closed Sun evening. *Recommended by N R White, the Didler, Jenny Titford*

SELLING TR0356   ME13 9RQ
☆ **White Lion**
Off A251 S of Faversham (or exit roundabout, M2 junction 7); The Street

Comfortable 17th-c pub with well kept Shepherd Neame ales from unusual semicircular bar counter, decent wines, friendly helpful staff, wide blackboard choice of good home-made food, hop-hung main bar, paintings for sale, log fire with working spit, another fire in small lower lounge with comfortable sofas, back restaurant; quiz nights; children welcome, tables out at front and in attractive garden, colourful hanging baskets. *Recommended by Mike Trainer, John Roots, Peter Meister*

SHIPBOURNE TQ5952   TN11 9PE
☆ **Chaser**
Stumble Hill (A227 N of Tonbridge)

Comfortably opened-up with civilised linked rooms converging on large central island, stripped-wood floors, frame-to-frame pictures on deep red and cream walls, pine wainscoting, candles on mix of old solid wood tables, shelves of books, open fires, Greene King ales, good wine and malt whisky choice, good popular food all day (breakfast Thurs, Sat and Sun), dark panelling and high timber-vaulted ceiling in striking chapel-like restaurant; piped music; children welcome, dogs in bar, courtyard and small side garden, Thurs morning farmers' market, open all day. *Recommended by Christian Mole, Tony Brace, Tina and David Woods-Taylor, N R White, David and Sally Cullen and others*

SHOREHAM TQ5162   TN14 7TJ
Crown
High Street

Friendly old-fashioned three-bar village pub, good value food including enjoyable Sun roasts, well kept ales such as Greene King and Westerham, open fires; walkers and dogs welcome. *Recommended by Chris and Carol Kendall*

SHOREHAM TQ5161   TN14 7SJ
Kings Arms
Church Street

Cosy old place serving good honest food and well kept beers, friendly staff, plates and brasses, restaurant; picnic-sets outside, quaint unspoilt village on River Darent, good walks. *Recommended by Richard Mason*

SHOREHAM TQ5261   TN14 7RY
Olde George
Church Street

Refurbished 16th-c pub with low beams, uneven floors and a cosy fire, friendly staff, changing real ales, dining area; children and dogs welcome, picnic sets by road with view of church, picturesque village. *Recommended by N R White*

SHOREHAM TQ5161   TN14 7TD
Two Brewers
High Street

Two softly lit smartly refurbished beamed bars, main emphasis on the popular food but drinkers welcome too, real ales including Adnams, friendly helpful staff; open all day Sun, closed Mon. *Recommended by N R White*

SNARGATE TQ9928   TN29 9UQ
☆ Red Lion
B2080 Appledore—Brenzett

Little changed since 1890 and in the same family for over 100 years, simple old-fashioned charm in three timeless little rooms with original cream wall panelling, heavy beams in sagging ceilings, dark pine Victorian farmhouse chairs on bare boards, an old piano stacked with books, coal fire, local cider and four or five ales including Goachers tapped from casks behind unusual free-standing marble-topped counter, no food, traditional games like toad in the hole, nine men's morris and table skittles; children in family room, dogs in bar, outdoor lavatories, cottage garden. *Recommended by Andrea Rampley, Tim Maddison, the Didler, Phil and Sally Gorton, B and M Kendall and others*

SPELDHURST TQ5541   TN3 0NN
☆ George & Dragon
Village signed from A264 W of Tunbridge Wells

Fine half-timbered building based around medieval manorial hall, main half-panelled bar to right has log fire in huge sandstone fireplace, heavy beams, wheelbacks and other dining chairs around tables on flagstones, horsebrasses, Harveys, Larkins and Westerham ales, several wines by the glass, second similarly furnished dining room with another inglenook, room to left of entrance hall used more for drinking with woodburner, high-winged settles and other seats, enjoyable if not cheap food (not Sun evening), upstairs restaurant; children welcome, dogs in bar, seats in front on nicely planted gravel terrace, more in back covered area and lower terrace (300-year-old yew tree and modern sculpturing), open all day. *Recommended by Simon and Helen Barnes, Derek Thomas, John Redfern, Christian Mole*

STAPLEHURST TQ7846   TN12 0DE
☆ Lord Raglan
About 1.5 miles from town centre towards Maidstone, turn right off A229 into Chart Hill Road opposite Chart Cars; OS Sheet 188 map reference 785472

Well run country pub, cosy chatty area around narrow bar counter, hop-covered low beams, big winter log fire, mixed comfortably worn dark wood furniture, enjoyable food from sandwiches up, Goachers, Harveys and a guest, farm cider and perry, good wine list; children and dogs welcome, reasonable wheelchair access, high-hedged terrace, picnic-sets in side orchard, closed Sun. *Recommended by Joan and Alec Lawrence, Malcolm and Barbara Southwell*

STODMARSH TR2160   CT3 4BA
☆ Red Lion
High Street; off A257 just E of Canterbury

Cheerfully quirky country pub with chatty landlord, all manner of bric-a-brac from life-size Tintin and Snowy to a tiger's head in hop-hung rooms, one wall covered in sheet music, empty wine bottles everywhere, green-painted, cushioned mate's chairs around nice pine tables, candles, big log fire, good interesting food using prime local meat and seasonal produce, Greene King IPA and Harveys Best tapped from casks, nice wine, good summer Pimms and winter mulled wine/cider, dining conservatory; piped jazz; children welcome, dogs in bar, pretty garden with roaming chickens and ducks, bat and trap, handy for Stodmarsh National Nature Reserve, bedrooms (not ensuite). *Recommended by Tony and Jill Radnor, N R White, Andy Towse, Mr D Matharu and others*

STONE IN OXNEY TQ9327   TN30 7JN
☆ Crown
Off B2082 Iden—Tenterden

Smart country pub with friendly landlord and staff, well kept Shepherd Neame and a guest like Larkins tapped from the cask, very good food from landlady/chef including some imaginative cooking, also wood-fired pizzas (takeaways available), light airy open feel with lots of wood, red walls, and big inglenook log fire; no under-12s after 7.30pm, rustic furniture on terrace, two bedrooms. *Recommended by Peter Meister*

STONE IN OXNEY TQ9428   TN30 7JY
☆ Ferry
Appledore Road; N of Stone-cum-Ebony

Attractive 17th-c smugglers' haunt, consistently good popular food including local fish (Rye scallops), welcoming landlord and friendly efficient staff, changing guest ales and a beer brewed for them by Westerham, small plain bar with woodburner and inglenook, bare boards, hops and old maps, steps up to pleasant dining area, games room; seats in garden and sunny front courtyard, lovely setting by marshes. *Recommended by Alec and Joan Laurence, Colin and Louise English, Peter Meister and others*

THURNHAM TQ8057   ME14 3LD
☆ Black Horse
Not far from M20 junction 7; off A249 at Detling

Large olde-worlde dining pub with enjoyable food all day, children's menu, well kept changing ales such as Sharps Doom Bar and Westerham Grasshopper, farm ciders and country wines, friendly efficient uniformed service, bare boards and log fires; dogs and walkers welcome, pleasant garden with partly covered back terrace, nice views, by Pilgrims Way, comfortable modern bedroom block, good breakfast. *Recommended by Brian and Anna Marsden, Alec and Joan Laurence*

TOYS HILL TQ4752   TN16 1QG
☆ Fox & Hounds
Off A25 in Brasted, via Brasted Chart and The Chart

Traditional country pub with plain tables and chairs on dark boards, leather sofa and easy chair by log fire, hunting prints, plates, old photographs, pewter mugs and copper jugs, modern carpeted dining extension with big windows overlooking tree-sheltered garden, enjoyable well presented home-made food (not Sun evening) including some interesting choices, well kept Greene King ales, several wines by the glass, traditional games, no mobile phones; piped music; children and dogs welcome, roadside verandah used by smokers, good local walks and views, handy for Chartwell and Emmetts Garden (both NT), open all day summer, closed Mon evening (and from 8pm Sun in winter).
Recommended by Tina and David Woods-Taylor, N R White, Cathryn and Richard Hicks, LM, C and R Bromage and others

TUDELEY TQ6145   TN11 0PH
☆ Poacher
Hartlake Road

Smart modern bar and restaurant, light and airy, with wide range of good food including daily specials, ales such as Sharps, Shepherd Neame and one brewed for the pub by Kings, good choice of wines by the glass, friendly attentive staff, live music Thurs evening; terrace tables, near interesting church with Chagall stained glass. *Recommended by Nigel and Jean Eames, Peter Eyles, Kellie Williams*

TUNBRIDGE WELLS TQ5638   TN3 9JH
Beacon
Tea Garden Lane, Rusthall Common

Cheery and airy Victorian pub with Harveys Best, Larkins and Timothy Taylors Landlord, lots of wines by the glass, good coffee, fireside sofas, stripped panelling, bare boards and ornate wall units, linked dining areas; children welcome, decking tables with fine view, paths between lakes and springs, three bedrooms, open all day. *Recommended by Alan Franck*

TUNBRIDGE WELLS TQ5839   TN1 1RZ
Black Pig
Grove Hill Road

Refurbished pub under same ownership as George & Dragon at Speldhurst, good food (all day weekends) using local and organic supplies, home-baked bread, Harveys Best, interesting wine list, long narrow front bar, big leather sofas by woodburner, balustraded raised area, elegant mix of dining chairs, decorative fireplace, fresh flowers, Hogarth-style prints, olive-painted panelling, back dining room, open all day. *Recommended by Derek Thomas, Steve and Liz Tilley*

TUNBRIDGE WELLS TQ5837   TN2 5LH
Bull
Frant Road

Friendly refurbished local with two linked areas, neatly set dining part with well spaced pine tables and chunky chairs on stripped wood, similar bar area, corner black sofa, well kept Shepherd Neame ales, decent wine and food, daily papers; piped pop, TV, pool; dogs allowed. *Recommended by Tony Hobden, Steve Halsall, Imogen Cust*

TUNBRIDGE WELLS TQ5941   TN4 9BQ
High Brooms
High Brooms Road

Eccentric local crammed with bric-a-brac and home to the High Brooms Ukulele Group (alternate Mon nights). *Recommended by anon*

TUNBRIDGE WELLS TQ5839   TN1 2BJ
Last Post
Goods Station Road

Former Dog & Duck, reopened late 2010 under new licensees, aiming for relaxed atmosphere in wine-bar environment; no under-30s. *Recommended by anon*

TUNBRIDGE WELLS TQ5739   TN4 8BX
Mount Edgcumbe Hotel
The Common

Nicely updated tile-hung and weatherboarded 18th-c hotel, well kept Harveys Best, Weston's cider, bar and brasserie food including good steaks, unusual grotto-like snug cut into rock, live music Sun evening; children and dogs welcome, tables out under big heated umbrellas, pleasant setting with Common views, barbecues, five refurbished bedrooms, open all day. *Recommended by Tilly Hunt*

WINGHAM TR2457   CT3 1BB
☆ ## Dog
Canterbury Road

Pub/restaurant in Grade II* listed medieval building, log fires, uneven walls, heavy beams, old brickwork and panelling, leather sofas and armchairs on wood floors, conservatory restaurant, enjoyable food including good value set lunch, well kept Courage, Ramsgate and Shepherd Neame, good wines by the glass. *Recommended by Gavin Markwick, Julie and Bill Ryan*

WORTH TR3356   CT14 0DF
☆ **St Crispin**
Signed off A258 S of Sandwich

Dating from 16th c with low beams, stripped brickwork and bare boards, welcoming landlady and friendly attentive staff, popular generous home-made food from good baguettes to some imaginative dishes in bar, restaurant and back conservatory, three changing real ales, belgian beers, local farm cider, well chosen wines, central log fire; good bedrooms (including motel-style extension), charming big garden behind with terrace and barbecue, lovely village position. *Recommended by Dr Kevan Tucker*

WROTHAM TQ6258   TN15 7RR
Moat
London Road

Well refurbished Badger family dining pub in Tudor-style building, flagstones, beams and stripped masonry, wide range of good value food, their usual ales kept well, friendly efficient staff; garden tables, great playground, open all day. *Recommended by Gordon and Margaret Ormondroyd, Christian Mole*

YALDING TQ6950   ME18 6JB
☆ **Walnut Tree**
B2010 SW of Maidstone

Timbered village pub with split-level main bar, fine old settles, a long cushioned mahogany bench and mix of dining chairs on brick or worn carpeted floors, chunky wooden tables with church candles, interesting old photographs on mustard walls, hops, big inglenook, Harveys Best, Sharps Doom Bar and Wychwood Hobgoblin, good bar food and more inventive restaurant menu, attractive raftered dining room with high-backed leather dining chairs on parquet flooring, lots of local events (pumpkin carving and guess the weight on our visit); piped and occasional live music, TV; a few picnic-sets out at front by road, bedrooms. *Recommended by Steve and Claire Harvey*

ALSO WORTH A VISIT IN OXFORDSHIRE

Besides the region's top pubs, we recommend the following. Do tell us what you think of them: **feedback@goodguides.com**

ADDERBURY SP4735   OX17 3NG
☆ **Red Lion**
The Green; off A4260 S of Banbury

Attractive and congenial 17th-c coaching inn, good choice of enjoyable well priced food (all day weekends), helpful friendly staff, Greene King ales and a guest, good wine range and coffee, three linked bar rooms, big inglenook log fire, panelling, high stripped beams and stonework, old books and Victorian/Edwardian pictures, daily papers, games area on left; piped music; children in eating area, picnic-sets out on roadside terrace, 12 character bedrooms, good breakfast, open all day summer. *Recommended by Ian Herdman, George Atkinson*

ALVESCOT SP2704   OX18 2PU
☆ **Plough**
B4020 Carterton—Clanfield, SW of Witney

Comfortable neatly kept bar with aircraft prints and cottagey pictures, china ornaments, big antique case of birds of prey and sundry bric-a-brac, woodburner, Wadworths ales and Weston's cider, straightforward food including good ploughman's, prompt service, proper public bar with TV and darts, skittle alley, pub cats; piped music; children welcome, picnic sets on back terrace (nice hanging baskets), aunt sally and children's play area in garden (and perhaps ornamental pheasants and japanese quail), open all day. *Recommended by Tina and David Woods-Taylor, KN-R, R K Phillips, Guy Vowles*

ASHBURY SU2685   SN6 8NA
Rose & Crown
B4507/B4000; High Street

Roomy open-plan beamed bistro bar, good choice of enjoyable food from pub favourites up, well kept Arkells 2B and 3B, good range of wines by the glass, polished woodwork, traditional pictures, chesterfields and pews, raised section with further oak tables and chairs, games area with pool and darts, separate roomy restaurant; children welcome, disabled facilities, tables out in front and behind, lovely view down pretty village street of thatched cottages, handy for Ridgeway walks, bedrooms. *Recommended by Neil and Karen Dignan*

ASTON TIRROLD SU5586   OX11 9EN
☆ Sweet Olive
aka Chequers; Fullers Road; village signed off A417 Streatley—Wantage

Has atmosphere of rustic french restaurant rather than village pub; main room with wall settles, mate's chairs, a few sturdy tables, grass matting over quarry tiles, small fireplace, good well liked food, nice french wines by the glass (wine box ends decorate the back of the servery), Brakspears and Fullers beers, smaller room more formally set as restaurant with restrained décor; piped music; children welcome, dogs in bar, picnic-sets under parasols in small cottagey garden, aunt sally, closed Sun evening, Weds, all Feb and two weeks in July. *Recommended by Neil and Karen Dignan, Dave Snowden*

BANBURY SP4540   OX16 5NA
☆ Olde Reindeer
Parsons Street, off Market Place

Interesting town pub always full of regulars and shoppers, welcoming front bar with 16th-c beams, broad polished oak boards, traditional solid furnishing and magnificent carved overmantel for one of the two roaring log fires, Hook Norton ales and guests, country wines, winter mulled wine, straightforward reasonably priced lunchtime food including OAP weekday deals, worth looking at the handsomely proportioned Globe Room (used by Cromwell during the Civil War) with its fine 17th-c carved oak panelling, restaurant; children allowed in one area, dogs welcome in bar, seats under parasols in small back courtyard with aunt sally and pretty flowering baskets, open all day, closed Sun. *Recommended by Mick and Cathy Couchman, the Didler, Andy Lickfold, George Atkinson*

BECKLEY SP5611   OX3 9UU
☆ Abingdon Arms
Signed off B4027; High Street

Old dining pub in attractive unspoilt village, comfortably modernised simple lounge, smaller public bar with antique carved settles, open fires, well kept Brakspears and guests, fair range of wines, good choice of enjoyable home-made food including two-course deals (Mon-Thurs) and Sun roasts, good friendly service; piped and some live music; children and dogs welcome, big garden dropping away from floodlit terrace to trees, summer house, superb views over RSPB Otmoor reserve – good walks, open all day weekends. *Recommended by Canon Michael Bourdeaux, Colin McKerrow, Martin and Pauline Jennings, Melanie Court*

BLEWBURY SU5385   OX11 9PQ
Red Lion
Nottingham Fee – narrow turning N from A417

Attractive and popular downland village pub, enjoyable honest food, well kept Brakspears and a guest, good service, beams, tiled floor and big log fire, restaurant; children welcome, terrace tables in back garden, pretty surroundings. *Recommended by Tim and Sue Halstead*

BLOXHAM SP4235   OX15 4LY
☆ **Joiners Arms**
Old Bridge Road, off A361

Golden stone inn with some refurbishment in rambling rooms, plenty of exposed stone, white dining chairs around pale tables on wood floor, open fires, Courage and Theakstons beers, enjoyable traditional food, exposed well in raftered room off bar; children and dogs welcome, pretty window boxes, seats out under parasols on various levels – most popular down steps by stream (play house there, too), open all day. *Recommended by Mr and Mrs John Taylor*

BLOXHAM SP4631   OX15 0SJ
Red Lion
High Street (A361)

Comfortable beamed two-bar pub with open fire, good choice of food and friendly service, Fullers ales, nice coffee; TV; children welcome, sizeable back garden on lower level. *Recommended by Michael Dandy*

BRIGHTWELL SU5890   OX10 0RT
Red Lion
Signed off A4130 2 miles W of Wallingford

Welcoming community-spirited village pub, five well kept local ales, wines from nearby vineyard, enjoyable good value home-made food, two-part bar with snug seating by log fire, unobtrusive dining extension; dogs welcome, tables outside. *Recommended by Anne Worsnop, John Pritchard*

BROUGHTON SP4238   OX15 5ED
☆ **Saye & Sele Arms**
B4035 SW of Banbury

16th-c pub split into three distinct areas, dining room at one end with over 200 colourful water jugs hanging from beams, tiled area by bar counter with cushioned window seats, a few brasses and dark wooden furnishings, and a carpeted room with red walls and big fireplace, good food cooked by landlord, up to four well kept ales, several wines by the glass, friendly service; children allowed if dining, a mix of seats on terrace and lawn, pergola and smokers' shelter, herb garden, aunt sally, handy for Broughton Castle, closed Sun evening. *Recommended by Carolyn Drew, Rob and Catherine Dunster, Kevin Thomas, Nina Randall, Jane Hudson, Clive and Fran Dutson, R K Phillips and others*

BUCKLAND SU3497   SN7 8QN
☆ **Lamb**
Off A420 NE of Faringdon

Smart 18th-c stone-built dining pub with popular food (not Mon) from lunchtime special deals to grander and more expensive evening menus, several ales including local ones, good choice of wines by the glass, lamb motif everywhere, formal restaurant; piped music; children welcome, pleasant tree-shaded garden, good walks nearby, comfortable bedrooms, closed Sun evening and over Christmas and New Year. *Recommended by Graham and Toni Sanders, Henry Midwinter, the Didler, Jennifer and Patrick O'Dell*

BUCKNELL SP5525   OX27 7NE
☆ **Trigger Pond**
Handy for M40 junction 10; Bicester Road

Neatly kept and welcoming stone-built beamed pub opposite the pond, wide choice of good sensibly priced food from baguettes up (must book Sun lunch), helpful friendly service, Wadworths ales including seasonal, good value wines, small bar with dining areas either side, inglenook woodburner, conservatory; colourful terrace and garden. *Recommended by Mr and Mrs R Green, George Atkinson, David Lamb, Lucien Perring*

BURFORD SP2512   OX18 4SN
☆ Angel
Witney Street

Long heavy-beamed dining pub in attractive ancient building, warmly welcoming with good reasonably priced brasserie food, good range of drinks; big secluded garden, three comfortable bedrooms, closed Sun evening, Mon. *Recommended by Leslie and Barbara Owen, David Glynne-Jones, Jennifer and Patrick O'Dell*

BURFORD SP2512   OX18 4LW
Bay Tree
Sheep Street

Attractive old village inn with smart yet informal and comfortable beamed bar, big log fires, cosy armchairs and leaded lights in small front room, second room with tartan seating, polished boards and sets of antlers, Brakspears, good choice of bar food from sandwiches up, friendly helpful staff, more formal restaurant; charming small walled terraced garden, bedrooms. *Recommended by Michael Dandy, N R White*

BURFORD SP2512   OX18 4QA
Golden Pheasant
High Street

Small early 18th-c hotel's flagstoned split-level bar, civilised yet relaxed and pubby, sofas, armchairs, well spaced tables and woodburner, enjoyable food from baguettes to steaks, well kept Greene King ales, good house wines, friendly helpful service, back dining room down steps; children welcome, pleasant terrace behind, bedrooms, open all day. *Recommended by Tim and Joan Wright, Michael Dandy, Malcolm Greening*

BURFORD SP2512   OX18 4RG
☆ Highway
High Street (A361)

Comfortable 15th-c inn with notable windows in bar (each made up of several dozen panes of old float glass); you can sit at long cushioned window seat and look out on High Street, ancient stripped stone mixing with filigree black and pale blue wallpaper, other interesting touches such as stag candlesticks and Cecil Aldin hunting prints, log fire in attractively simple fireplace with old station clock above, second bar with another big window seat, cellar restaurant, Hook Norton and a guest beer, lots of wines by the glass, mixed food reports recently; piped music; children welcome, dogs allowed in bar (resident springers Cassie and Oscar), picnic-sets standing above pavement, bedrooms, open all day, closed first two weeks in Jan. *Recommended by Nigel and Sue Foster, N R White, Graham Oddey*

BURFORD SP2512   OX18 4QF
☆ Mermaid
High Street

Handsome jettied Tudor dining pub with beams, flagstones, panelling, stripped stone and nice log fire, good food at sensible prices including local free-range meat and fresh fish, friendly efficient service, well kept Greene King ales and a guest, bay seating around row of tables on the left, further airy back dining room and upstairs restaurant; piped music (live Fri); children welcome, tables out at front and in courtyard behind, open all day. *Recommended by Michael Dandy, Mike Horgan, Di Wright*

BURFORD SP2512   OX18 4SN
☆ Royal Oak
Witney Street

Relaxed homely 17th-c stripped-stone local, an oasis in this smart village, with long-serving friendly landlord, Wadworths ales and an occasional guest from central servery, simple generous good value food using local produce from filled rolls up, good service, over a thousand beer mugs, steins and jugs hanging from beams, antlers over big log fire (underfloor heating, too), light wood tables, chairs and benches on flagstones, more in carpeted back room with bar billiards; well behaved children and dogs welcome, terrace tables, sensibly priced bedrooms by garden behind, good breakfast, open all day Sat, closed Tues lunchtime. *Recommended by Mr and Mrs W W Burke, Michael Dandy, Pam Service*

CHARLBURY SP3519   OX7 3PP
Bell
Church Street

Attractive two-room bar in small imaginatively refurbished 18th-c hotel, flagstones, stripped stonework and huge inglenook log fire, food from sandwiches up, Greene King and a guest ale, friendly welcoming service, restaurant, back family area including children's playroom; dogs welcome, suntrap terrace and pleasant garden down to stream, quiet refurbished bedrooms, open all day. *Recommended by Jon Carpenter, Mrs C A Murphy, Richard Greaves*

CHAZEY HEATH SU6979   RG4 7UG
Pack Horse
Just off A4074 Reading—Wallingford by B4526

Attractive 17th-c beamed pub (part of the Home Counties chain), good choice of enjoyable fairly priced food all day, real ales and lots of wines by the glass, friendly staff, polished tables on wood floors, built-in leatherette banquettes, big log fire in raised hearth; dogs welcome in main bar, disabled facilities, back garden. *Recommended by Sharon Dooley*

CHECKENDON SU6684   RG8 0TE
☆ Black Horse
Village signed off A4074 Reading—Wallingford

This charmingly old-fashioned country tavern (tucked into woodland away from main village) has been kept by the same family for 106 years; relaxing and unchanging series of rooms, back one with Hook Norton and West Berkshire tapped from the cask, one with bar counter has some tent pegs above fireplace (a reminder they used to be made here), homely side lounge with some splendidly unfashionable 1950s-look armchairs and another room beyond that, only filled rolls and pickled eggs; no credit cards; children allowed but must be well behaved, seats on verandah and in garden, popular with walkers and cyclists. *Recommended by the Didler*

CHURCH ENSTONE SP3725   OX7 4NN
☆ Crown
Mill Lane; from A44 take B4030 turn-off at Enstone

Pleasant uncluttered bar in beamed country pub, straightforward furniture, country pictures on stone walls, some horsebrasses, log fire in large fireplace, Fullers and Hook Norton beers, decent food, red-walled carpeted dining room, slate-floored conservatory with farmhouse furniture; children welcome, dogs in bar, white metal tables and chairs on front terrace overlooking lane, picnic-sets in sheltered back garden, closed Sun evening. *Recommended by Phil and Jane Hodson, Derek and Sylvia Stephenson, Barry Collett, Chris Glasson, Andy and Jill Kassube, JJW, CMW and others*

CHURCHILL SP2824   OX7 6NJ
☆ Chequers
Church Road; B4450 Chipping Norton—Stow-on-the-Wold (and village signed off A361 Chipping Norton—Burford)

Great welcome from licensees Assumpta and Peter Golding at this spic and span golden-stone village pub, front bar with modern oak furnishings on light flagstoned floor, some old timbers and country prints, exposed stone walls around big inglenook log fire, Hook Norton and up to three guests, decent wines, popular bar food, big back extension with soaring rafters and cosy upstairs dining area; children welcome, impressive church opposite, open all day. *Recommended by P and J Shapley, Martin and Pauline Jennings, Henry Midwinter, George Atkinson, Myra Joyce, Bernard Stradling and others*

CLANFIELD SP2802   OX18 2RG
☆ **Clanfield Tavern**
Bampton Road (A4095 S of Witney)

New licensees at this pleasantly extended pub and emphasis on traditional food; opened-up beamed interior keeping feel of separate areas, mostly carpeted with mix of pubby furniture including some old settles (built-in one by log fire), smallish bar with sofas in snug flagstoned area by woodburner, Banks's and a couple of guest ales, attractive dining conservatory; piped music; children welcome, dogs in bar, picnic-sets on small flower-bordered lawn looking across to village green, open all day weekends. *Recommended by anon*

CLIFTON SP4931   OX15 0PE
☆ **Duke of Cumberlands Head**
B4031 Deddington—Aynho

Warmly welcoming thatch and stone pub with big low-beamed lounge, good log fire in vast fireplace and simple furnishings, some emphasis on food from good reasonably priced bar snacks up (own pigs), friendly service, well kept Hook Norton and guests, good wine and whisky choice, cosy stripped-stone dining room, live music (classical/jazz) Sat night; children and dogs welcome, garden with barbecue, ten minutes' walk from canal, six bedrooms. *Recommended by Mrs Pat Parkin-Moore, Roy Hoing, Maurice Ricketts, David Jackman*

COLESHILL SU2393   SN6 7PR
☆ **Radnor Arms**
B4019 Faringdon—Highworth; village signposted off A417 in Faringdon and A361 in Highworth

Pub and village owned by NT, bar with cushioned settles, plush carver chairs and woodburner, back alcove with more tables, steps down to main dining area, once a blacksmith's forge with lofty beamed ceiling, log fire, dozens of tools and smith's gear on walls, Old Forge ales (brewed on site) and local Halfpenny, shortish choice of good well priced home-made food (not Sun evening), friendly efficient service; children and dogs welcome, garden with aunt sally and play area, open all day. *Recommended by Anne Morris, Graham Oddey, Jennifer and Patrick O'Dell, Simon Garfuncle*

CRAWLEY SP3412   OX29 9TW
☆ **Lamb**
Steep Hill; just NW of Witney

Refurbished 18th-c stone-built dining pub, simple beamed bar with polished boards and lovely fireplace, steps to candlelit dining room, good food from nice sandwiches and pubby dishes to more enterprising things, set menu deals Tues and Weds, good choice of wines by the glass, well kept Brakspears, helpful friendly service; piped music; children welcome, dogs in bar, views from tables on back terrace and lawn, pretty village, good walks – on Palladian Way, closed Sun evening. *Recommended by Ian Phillips, Alan Perry*

CRAYS POND SU6380   RG8 7SH
White Lion
Goring Road (B471 near junction with B4526, about 3 miles E of Goring)

Recently refurbished old green-shuttered country pub/restaurant, enjoyable interesting choice of food (not Sun evening) including good value set lunchtime menu, Greene King ales, friendly staff, traditional beamed interior with contemporary touches, log fires, dining conservatory; children welcome, big garden with play area, lovely countryside, open all day. *Recommended by Anne Pickering*

CROPREDY SP4646   OX17 1PB
Red Lion
Off A423 N of Banbury

Popular rambling 15th-c thatch-and-stone pub charmingly placed opposite pretty village's churchyard, good food and service, Hook Norton and a couple of guests, low beams, inglenook log fire, high-backed settles, brass, plates and pictures, unusual dining room murals, games room; piped music, limited parking; children allowed in dining part, picnic-sets on part-covered terrace, near Oxford Canal (Bridge 152). *Recommended by George Atkinson, Clive and Fran Dutson, Dr Kevan Tucker*

CUMNOR SP4503   OX2 9QH
☆ Bear & Ragged Staff
Signed from A420; Appleton Road

Extensive restaurant/pub dating from 16th c, clean contemporary décor in linked rooms with wood floors, leather-backed dining chairs and mix of tables, low lighting, good food from shared charcuterie and meze plates to pub standards and up, weekday lunch deals, good friendly service, flagstoned bar with log fire, well kept Green King ales, good wine choice, leather sofas and armchairs in airy garden room; children welcome, decked terrace, fenced play area, new bedrooms, open all day. *Recommended by Joan and Tony Walker, Bob and Angela Brooks, Richard Greaves, Jan and Roger Ferris*

CUXHAM SU6695   OX49 5NF
☆ Half Moon
4 miles from M40 junction 6; S on B4009, then right on B480 at Watlington

Lovely 17th-c restaurant/pub under new french landlord, freshly prepared french food using produce from own kitchen garden as well as french suppliers, two main eating areas with beams, cushioned settles, mirrors and prints, little fireplace in small tiled bar, Brakspears ales, house wines by the glass or pichet (460ml bottle); children and dogs welcome, seats in good-sized garden, sleepy village surrounded by fine countryside, open all day Sat, closed Sun evening, Mon. *Recommended by anon*

DEDDINGTON SP4631   OX15 0SH
☆ Deddington Arms
Off A4260 (B4031) Banbury—Oxford; Horse Fair

Beamed and timbered hotel with emphasis on sizeable contemporary back dining room doing very good food, comfortable bar with mullioned windows, flagstones and log fire, good food here, too, Adnams, Black Sheep and a guest, plenty of wines by the glass, attentive friendly service; unobtrusive piped music; attractive village with lots of antiques shops and good farmers' market fourth Sat of month, nice walks, comfortable chalet bedrooms around courtyard, good breakfast, open all day. *Recommended by Phyl and Jack Street, Michael Dandy, John Taylor*

DEDDINGTON SP4631   OX15 0SE
☆ Unicorn
Market Place

Welcoming recently refurbished 17th-c inn, beamed L-shaped bar, cosy snug with inglenook log fire, candlelit restaurant, good sensibly priced home-made food from snacks and pub favourites up (not Mon), well kept Hook Norton and Wells & Youngs, good choice of wines by the glass, proper coffee, daily papers and pub games; piped music; well behaved children welcome, cobbled courtyard leading to long walled back garden, good bedrooms and breakfast, open all day weekends (from 9am for good farmers' market – last Sat of month). *Recommended by MP, Roxanne Chamberlain*

DENCHWORTH SU3891   OX12 0DX
Fox
Off A338 or A417 N of Wantage; Hyde Road

Comfortable 17th-c thatched and beamed pub in pretty village, good choice of sensibly priced generous food including good Sun carvery (best to book), friendly efficient staff, well kept Greene King Old Speckled Hen, good house wines, two good log fires and plush seats in low-ceilinged connecting areas, old prints and paintings, airy dining extension; children welcome, tables under umbrellas in pleasant sheltered garden, peaceful village. *Recommended by D C T and E A Frewer*

DORCHESTER SU5794   OX10 7HH
George
Just off A4074 Maidenhead—Oxford; High Street

Handsome timbered hotel in lovely village, roaring log fire and charming furnishings in smart beamed bar, enjoyable food including OAP deals, ales such as Adnams, Brakspears and Wadworths, cheerful efficient service; piped music; children welcome, bedrooms, open all day. *Recommended by Jonnie Supper, John and Helen Rushton*

EAST HENDRED SU4688   OX12 8JN
Wheatsheaf
Signed off A417; Chapel Square

Attractive 16th-c black and white timbered village pub with big inglenook log fire in carpeted bar, other cosy rooms off, three well kept ales, good choice of wines, enjoyable food from pub standards up, restaurant; dogs allowed in bar, some tables out in front, more in pleasant garden behind, barbecues, open all day weekends. *Recommended by Russell Traynor*

FIFIELD SP2318   OX7 6HR
Merrymouth
A424 Burford—Stow

Simple but comfortable stone inn dating to 13th c, L-shaped bar, bay-window seats, flagstones, low beams, some walls stripped back to old masonry, warm stove, quite dark in some areas, good sensibly priced generous food including blackboard fish choice, Hook Norton and a couple of other ales, decent wine choice, cheery landlord and friendly staff: piped music; children and dogs welcome, tables on terrace and in back garden, nine stable-block bedrooms. *Recommended by Noel Grundy, P M Newsome, Stanley and Annie Matthews, Chris Glasson, Colin McKerrow*

FINSTOCK SP3616   OX7 3BY
☆ ## Plough
Just off B4022 N of Witney; High Street

Thatched low-beamed village pub nicely split up by partitions and alcoves, long rambling bar with leather sofas by massive stone inglenook, some unusual horsebrasses and historical documents to do with the pub, roomy dining room with candles and fresh flowers on stripped-pine tables, good food cooked by landlord, Adnams Broadside, Butts Organic Jester and a guest, traditional cider, several wines by the glass and 20 malt whiskies, bar billiards, board games; children at discretion of licensees, dogs allowed in bar (pub has two cats), seats in neatly kept garden, aunt sally, walks among local woodland and along River Evenlode, open all day Sat, closed Sun evening, Mon and maybe two weeks in Feb. *Recommended by Jon Carpenter, Mr and Mrs J C Cetti, George and Linda Ozols, D R Ellis, Ian and Helen Stafford*

FOREST HILL SP5807   OX33 1EH
White Horse
Wheatley Road (B4027)

Small friendly stone-built beamed village pub, two real ales, a dozen wines by the glass, good fairly priced thai food, other food including children's, central log fire in restaurant; handy for Oxfordshire Way; closed Mon. *Recommended by JJW, CMW*

FRILFORD SU4497   OX13 6QJ
Dog House
Faringdon Road

Comfortable hotel with beamed open-plan log-fire bar, restaurant and conservatory, enjoyable good value traditional food from sandwiches to specials, Greene King ales, friendly attentive young staff; children welcome, garden with heated terrace, 20 bedrooms. *Recommended by Ian Herdman*

FYFIELD SU4298   OX13 5LW

☆ **White Hart**

Main Road; off A420 8 miles SW of Oxford

Grand medieval hall with soaring eaves, huge stone-flanked window embrasures and minstrel's gallery, contrasting cosy low-beamed side bar with large inglenook, fresh flowers and evening candles throughout, civilised friendly atmosphere and full of history, good imaginative modern food (best to book) cooked by licensee using home-grown produce, Hook Norton, Loddon, Rebellion and Sharps Doom Bar (festivals during May and Aug bank holidays), around 16 wines by the glass (including champagne), several malt whiskies and home-made summer elderflower pressé; piped music; children welcome if well behaved, elegant furniture under smart umbrellas on spacious heated terrace, lovely gardens, good Thames-side walks, open all day weekends, closed Mon. *Recommended by Rochelle Seifas, David and Sue Atkinson, Graham and Toni Sanders, Malcolm Ward, Ewan Shearer and others*

GODSTOW SP4809   OX2 8PN

☆ **Trout**

Off A40/A44 roundabout via Wolvercote

Pretty 17th-c M&B dining pub in lovely riverside location (gets packed in fine weather), good bistro-style food all day (booking essential at busy times), four beamed linked rooms with contemporary furnishings, flagstones and bare boards, log fires in three huge hearths, Adnams and Timothy Taylors Landlord, several wines by the glass; piped music; children welcome till 7pm, plenty of terrace seats under big parasols (dogs allowed here), footbridge to island (may be closed), abbey ruins opposite, open all day. *Recommended by Robert Lorimer, A R Mascall, Ros Lawler, Tina and David Woods-Taylor, Andrea Rampley, Martin and Pauline Jennings and others*

GOZZARD'S FORD SU4698   OX13 6JH

☆ **Black Horse**

Off B4017 NW of Abingdon; N of A415 by Marcham—Cothill Road

Ancient traditional pub in tiny hamlet, sensibly short choice of good generous food (all day Sun) especially fish and seafood, well kept Greene King ales, decent wines, cheerful efficient service, carpeted beamed main bar partly divided by stout timbers and low steps, end woodburner, separate plainer public bar with darts and pool; nice garden, open all day. *Recommended by William Goodhart, John Pritchard*

GREAT TEW SP3929   OX7 4DB

☆ **Falkland Arms**

The Green; off B4022 about 5 miles E of Chipping Norton

Golden-stone thatched cottage in lovely village, unspoilt partly panelled bar with high-backed settles, diversity of stools and plain tables on flagstones or bare boards, one-, two- and three-handled mugs hanging from beam-and-boards ceiling, dim converted oil lamps, shutters for stone-mullioned latticed windows and open fire in fine inglenook, Wadworths and guests, Weston's cider, 30 malt whiskies, country wines, enjoyable bar food, snuff for sale, live folk Sun evening; children and dogs welcome, tables out at front and under parasols in back garden, small fair value bedrooms (no under-16s), open all day. *Recommended by Tich Critchlow, the Didler, George Atkinson, Andy and Jill Kassube, David Heath, Mr and Mrs P R Thomas and others*

HAILEY SP3414   OX29 9XP

Bird in Hand

Whiteoak Green; B4022 Witney—Charlbury

Attractive 17th-c extended stone inn, interesting food from shortish menu, helpful friendly service, well kept ales such as Ramsbury, beams and timbers, some stripped stone, comfortable armchairs on polished boards, large log fire, cosy corners in carpeted restaurant, lovely Cotswold views; parasol-shaded terrace tables, bedrooms, good breakfast, open all day. *Recommended by Nigel and Sue Foster, David Heath*

HAILEY SU6485   OX10 6AD
☆ King William IV
The Hailey near Ipsden, off A4074 or A4130 SE of Wallingford

Fine old pub in lovely countryside, beamed bar with good sturdy furniture on tiles in front of big log fire, three other cosy seating areas opening off (children allowed in two), enjoyable food including some interesting specials, Brakspears, friendly staff, miniature traffic lights on bar (red means bar closed, orange last orders, green open); dogs welcome, terrace and large garden enjoying wide-ranging peaceful views, may be red kites overhead, you can tether your horse in car park, Ridgeway National Trail nearby. *Recommended by Richard Endacott, Ray Carter, the Didler, Paul Humphreys*

HAMPTON POYLE SP5015   OX5 2QD
☆ Bell
Off A34 S, take Kidlington turn and village signed from roundabout; from A34 N, take Kidlington turn, then A4260 to roundabout, third turning signed for Superstore (Bicester Road); village signed from roundabout

Front bar with three snug rooms, lots of big black and white photoprints, sturdy simple furnishings, scatter cushions and window seats, a stove flanked by bookshelves one end, large fireplace stacked with logs the other, biggish inner room made lively by open kitchen with its wood-fired pizza oven, a couple of fireside leather armchairs, spreading dining room with plenty of tables on pale limestone flagstones, inventive food, good choice of wines by the glass, Fullers London Pride and Hook Norton Old Hooky, good service by uniformed staff, cheerful informal atmosphere; piped jazz; children welcome, dogs in bar, modern seats on sunny front terrace by quiet village lane, bedrooms, open all day. *Recommended by Rob Hubbard*

HANWELL SP4343   OX17 1HN
Moon & Sixpence
Main Street

Good food from pub favourites up in clean comfortable bar and dining area, friendly staff, well kept Hook Norton and decent wines by the glass; pretty garden, nice village setting. *Recommended by Graham and Nicky Westwood, Martin and Sue Radcliffe*

HARWELL SU4988   OX11 0LZ
☆ Kingswell
A417; Reading Road

Substantial hotel with dependably good imaginative bar food as well as restaurant meals, plenty of choice, helpful staff; comfortable bedrooms. *Recommended by Henry Midwinter*

HENLEY SU7682   RG9 1BH
Angel on the Bridge
Thames-side, by the bridge

Worth knowing for prime spot by Thames, with nice waterside deck (plastic glasses for this), small front bar with log fire, back bar and adjacent restaurant, Brakspears ales, good choice of wines by the glass, food from sandwiches and pubby things up, well organised staff; moorings for two boats, open all day at least in summer. *Recommended by David and Sue Atkinson*

HENLEY SU7582   RG9 2AA
Argyll
Market Place

Smartly comfortable and well run, with pleasant efficient service, enjoyable fairly priced pub food all day from sandwiches up, Greene King ales, decent wines by the glass, soft lighting, dark panelling; piped music; nice terrace garden behind, useful parking. *Recommended by Paul Humphreys*

HENLEY SU7882   RG9 2ED
Row Barge
West Street

Brakspears local under newish management, cosy low-beamed bar dropping down the hill
in steps, their ales kept well, tasty good value well presented pubby food, good helpful
service; sizable garden. *Recommended by Paul Humphreys*

HIGHMOOR SU7084   RG9 5DL
 ## Dog & Duck
B481

Appealing unspoilt 17th-c country pub, enjoyable food (not Sun evening) from nice
baguettes up, also good vegetarian options, Brakspears ales, decent choice of wines,
friendly efficient staff, log fires in small cosily furnished beamed bar and not much larger
flagstoned dining room with old pictures and prints, family room off; dogs welcome
(friendly pub labrador called Della), attractive long garden with some play equipment
and small sheep paddock, surrounding walks, open all day in summer, closed lunchtimes
in winter apart from Sun, may close Sun evening. *Recommended by Paul Humphreys, the Didler,
John Pritchard, David Lamb*

HOOK NORTON SP3534   OX15 5DF
☆ ## Gate Hangs High
N towards Sibford, at Banbury—Rollright crossroads

Snug tucked-away family-run pub, low-ceilinged bar with traditional furniture on bare
boards, attractive inglenook, good reasonably priced home-made food from bar snacks up,
well kept Hook Norton ales and a guest, decent wines, friendly helpful service, slightly
chintzy side dining extension (booking advised Sat evening and Sun); piped music; pretty
courtyard and country garden, four good value bedrooms, good breakfast, quite near
Rollright Stones. *Recommended by Colin McKerrow, George Atkinson*

HOOK NORTON SP3533   OX15 5NU
Pear Tree
Scotland End

Take-us-as-you-find-us village pub with engaging landlord and character locals, full Hook
Norton range kept well from nearby brewery, country wines, enjoyable bar food (not Sun
evening) from doorstep sandwiches to bargain Sun roast, knocked-together bar area with
country-kitchen furniture, good log fire, daily papers; occasional live music Tues, TV;
children and dogs welcome, attractive garden with play area, bedrooms, open all day.
Recommended by Steve Nye, Gene and Kitty Rankin, Jennifer and Patrick O'Dell, Barry Collett

KELMSCOTT SU2499   GL7 3HG
Plough
NW of Faringdon, off B4449 between A417 and A4095

Refurbished interior with ancient flagstones, stripped stone and log fire, wide choice of
food (more restauranty in evenings), beers such as local Halfpenny, Wye Valley and
Wychwood, farm cider; children, dogs and booted walkers welcome, tables out in covered
area and garden, lovely spot near upper Thames (good moorings a few minutes' walk
away), eight bedrooms, open all day weekends. *Recommended by Meg and Colin Hamilton,
Jennifer and Patrick O'Dell, R K Phillips*

KIDMORE END SU6979   RG4 9AU
New Inn
Chalkhouse Green Road; signed from B481 in Sonning Common

Newish licensees at this attractive black and white pub by church; beams and big fire,
enjoyable freshly made food including good value weekday set lunch, pleasant restaurant;
tables in large sheltered garden with pond, bedrooms. *Recommended by Bruce and Trish Field,
Paul Humphreys*

LAUNTON SP6022   OX26 5DQ
Bull
Just E of Bicester

Partly thatched modernised 17th-c village pub, welcoming and well managed, with
enjoyable food (not Sun evening) including OAP weekday lunch deals, three well kept
Greene King ales and a guest, Sun quiz; piped music; children allowed away from bar,
dogs on leads, wheelchair access from car park, disabled facilities, garden with terrace,
open all day. *Recommended by Bill Hawkins, Meg and Colin Hamilton*

LEWKNOR SU7197   OX49 5TH
☆ Olde Leathern Bottel
Under a mile from M40 junction 6; off B4009 towards Watlington

A popular place and useful for motorway, two heavy beamed bars, low ceilings,
understated décor and rustic furnishings, open fires, Brakspears, Marstons and
Wychwood, several wines by the glass, pubby bar food, family room separated by standing
timbers; dogs welcome, splendid garden with plenty of picnic-sets under parasols, play
area and boules, handy for walks on Chiltern escarpment. *Recommended by Roger and
Anne Newbury, Tina and David Woods-Taylor, Paul Humphreys, D and M T Ayres-Regan, Andy and
Jill Kassube and others*

LONG WITTENHAM SU5493   OX14 4QH
Plough
High Street

Friendly chatty local with low beams, inglenook fires and lots of brass, well kept ales
including Butcombe, good value wines by the glass, wide choice of generous well priced
food (all day weekends), good friendly service, dining room, games in public bar; dogs
welcome, Thames moorings at bottom of nice spacious garden with aunt sally, bedrooms.
Recommended by David Lamb

MAIDENSGROVE SU7288   RG9 6EX
Five Horseshoes
Off B480 and B481, W of village

16th-c dining pub set high in the Chilterns, rambling bar with low ceiling and log fire,
enjoyable food including salmon smoked by landlord and local game, friendly attentive
service, well kept Brakspears, good choice of wines by the glass, airy conservatory
restaurant; children and dogs welcome, plenty of garden tables and lovely views, wood-
fired pizzas on summer weekends (open all day then), good walks, closed Mon evening.
Recommended by Henry Midwinter, Philip Kingsbury, Tracey and Stephen Groves

MILTON SP4535   OX15 4HH
☆ Black Boy
Off Bloxham Road; the one near Adderbury

Neatly refurbished dining pub with good comfortable furnishings, but still plenty of oak
beams, exposed stonework, flagstones and a lovely big inglenook, good choice of enjoyable
home-made food, friendly licensees, good service, ales such as Hook Norton; piped music;
children and dogs welcome, narrow front terrace with heaters, tables across road in
spacious garden beyond car park, play area. *Recommended by Martin and Pauline Jennings*

MURCOTT SP5815   OX5 2RE
☆ Nut Tree
Off B4027 NE of Oxford, via Islip and Charlton-on-Otmoor

Refurbished beamed and thatched 15th-c dining pub, imaginative if not cheap food using
own produce including home-reared pigs, Hook Norton and a couple of guests, carefully
chosen wines, neat friendly staff; children welcome, dogs allowed in bar, pretty garden,
unusual gargoyles (modelled loosely on local characters) on front wall, ducks on village
pond, closed winter Sun evening, all day Mon. *Recommended by William Goodhart,
Laurence Smith, Paul Baxter*

NORTH MORETON SU5689   OX11 9AT
Bear at Home
Off A4130 Didcot—Wallingford; High Street

Dating from the 15th c with traditional beamed bar, cosy fireside areas and dining part
with stripped-pine furniture, enjoyable reasonably priced food from baguettes up, friendly
service, Timothy Taylors, a guest ale and a beer brewed for the pub (July beer festival),
Weston's cider, several wines by the glass; attractive garden overlooking cricket pitch,
pretty village, open all day Sat. *Recommended by Roy Hoing*

OXFORD SP5007   OX2 6TT
Anchor
Hayfield Road

Chef/landlord at this 1930s pub producing good quality interesting food using local
supplies, friendly efficient service, good value house wine, well kept Wadworths beers,
period furnishings, log fire, separate dining area; near Bridge 240 (Aristotle) on Oxford
Canal. *Recommended by David Gunn, Dr Kevan Tucker*

OXFORD SP5106   OX1 4DH
Chequers
Off High Street

Narrow 16th-c courtyard pub with several areas on three floors, interesting architectural
features, beams, panelling and stained glass, wide choice of rotating ales and of well
priced pubby food (sausage specialities), quick friendly service, games room with balcony;
walled garden. *Recommended by George Atkinson, Peter Lee*

OXFORD SP5106   OX1 3HB
Crown
In alley near MacDonalds, more or less opposite Boots

Refurbished Nicholson's pub with long narrowish rooms, popular food including speciality
pies, eight or so real ales, friendly attentive staff; courtyard seats. *Recommended by
George Atkinson*

OXFORD SP5106   OX1 3LU
☆ Eagle & Child
St Giles

Nicholson's pub with two charmingly old-fashioned panelled front rooms, well kept
Brakspears, Hook Norton and interesting guests, wide range of food all day from
sandwiches to Sun roasts, stripped-brick back dining extension and conservatory, Tolkien
and CS Lewis connections; games machine; children allowed in back till 8pm.
*Recommended by Tim and Ann Newell, G Jennings, Susan and Nigel Brookes, MP, the Didler, Clive and
Fran Dutson and others*

OXFORD SP5105   OX1 4LB
Head of the River
Folly Bridge; between St Aldates and Christchurch Meadow

Civilised well renovated pub by river, boats for hire and nearby walks; spacious split-level
downstairs bar with dividing brick arches, flagstones and bare boards, Fullers/Gales
beers, good choice of wines by the glass, popular pubby food from sandwiches up, good
service, daily papers; piped music; tables on stepped heated waterside terrace,
12 bedrooms. *Recommended by Michael Dandy*

OXFORD SP5106   OX1 3SP
☆ Kings Arms
Holywell Street

Dating from early 17th c, convivial, relaxed and popular with locals and students, quick
helpful service, well kept Wells & Youngs range and four guests, fine choice of wines by
the glass, eating area with counter servery doing good variety of reasonably priced food all

day, cosy comfortably worn-in partly panelled side and back rooms, interesting pictures and posters, daily papers; a few tables outside, open from 10.30am. *Recommended by Colin and Louise English, Andrea Rampley, the Didler, Tim and Ann Newell, Mr and Mrs M J Girdler, Revd R P Tickle and others*

OXFORD SP5106   OX1 3JS
Lamb & Flag
St Giles/Banbury Road

Old pub owned by nearby college, modern airy front room with light wood panelling and big windows over street, more atmosphere in back rooms with stripped stonework and low-boarded ceilings, a beer by Palmers for the pub (L&F Gold), Shepherd Neame Spitfire, Skinners Betty Stogs and guests, some lunchtime food including sandwiches and tasty home-made pies. *Recommended by Michael Dandy, the Didler, D W Stokes*

OXFORD SP5006   OX1 2EW
Oxford Retreat
Hythe Bridge Street

Civilised waterside pub with well kept Fullers London Pride, good choice of wines by the glass and cocktails, enjoyable well served food from pubby things up, restaurant with chunky tables and leather chairs overlooking river, attentive staff, log fire; garden with decking, open all day and till 3am Fri, Sat. *Recommended by Pippa Manley, Martin and Karen Wake*

OXFORD SP5106   OX1 3BB
☆ White Horse
Broad Street

Bustling and studenty, squeezed between bits of Blackwells bookshop, small narrow bar with snug one-table raised back alcove, low beams and timbers, ochre ceiling, beautiful view of the Clarendon building and Sheldonian, good choice of ales including Brakspears, St Austell, Timothy Taylors and White Horse, friendly staff, good value simple lunchtime food (the few tables reserved for this); open all day. *Recommended by Andrea Rampley, Terry and Nickie Williams, the Didler, Paul Humphreys, Nigel and Jean Eames and others*

PISHILL SU7190   RG9 6HH
☆ Crown
B480 Nettlebed—Watlington

Mainly 15th-c red-brick and flint pub, beamed bars with old local photographs and maps on part-panelled walls, nice old chairs around mix of wooden tables, lots of candles, three log fires, attractively presented food from sandwiches up, Brakspears and a couple of guests, cafetière coffee, friendly service, knocked-through back area with standing timbers, fine thatched 16th-c barn used for functions; dogs allowed in bar, picnic-sets under blue parasols in pretty garden, lots of nearby walks, bedrooms and self-contained cottage. *Recommended by Paul Humphreys, Penny and Peter Keevil, the Didler, Susan and John Douglas, Mrs Margaret Watson and others*

PLAY HATCH SU7477   RG4 9QU
Shoulder of Mutton
W of Henley Road (A4155) roundabout

Dining pub with low-ceilinged log-fire bar and large conservatory restaurant, good choice of enjoyable food including signature mutton dishes, well kept Greene King and guests such as Loddon; children welcome, picnic-sets in well tended walled garden with well, closed Sun evening. *Recommended by Paul Humphreys*

SATWELL SU7083   RG9 4QZ
☆ Lamb
2 miles S of Nettlebed; follow Shepherds Green signpost

16th-c country pub (originally two cottages) with low-beamed bar, nice pubby furniture on tiles, old photographs, agricultural and antique knick-knacks, inglenook log fire, Black

Sheep, Loddon and Timothy Taylors, several wines by the glass, separate cosy dining room and often interesting food (all day weekends); piped music; children welcome, dogs in bar, seats on lawn in large garden with chickens, boules and maybe summer barbecues, plenty of surrounding walks. *Recommended by Susan and John Douglas, Mr and Mrs P R Thomas, John Pritchard, Jeremy Whitehorn*

SHENINGTON SP3742   OX15 6NQ
☆ **Bell**
Off A422 NW of Banbury

Good wholesome home cooking in hospitable 17th-c two-room pub, nice sandwiches too, well kept Flowers and Hook Norton, good wine choice, fair prices, friendly informal service and long-serving licensees, relaxed atmosphere, heavy beams, some flagstones, stripped stone and pine panelling, coal fire, amiable dogs, cribbage, dominoes; children in eating areas, tables out in front, small attractive back garden, charming quiet village, good walks, simple comfortable bedrooms, generous breakfast, closed Sun evening, Mon. *Recommended by Graham and Nicky Westwood, George Atkinson, Sir Nigel Foulkes*

SHIPLAKE SU7476   RG4 9RB
Flowing Spring
A4155 towards Play Hatch and Reading

Newish licensees for this roadside pub (built on bank, all on first floor with slight slope front to back), open fires in small two-room bar, various bric-a-brac, good value home-made food (not Sun or Mon evenings) from sandwiches, wraps and pizzas up, special diets catered for, Fullers ales, Aspall's cider, modern dining room with floor-to-ceiling windows, tables out on covered balcony, various events including astronomy nights and occasional live music; children and dogs welcome, lawned garden bordered by streams, summer marquee and barbecues, open all day. *Recommended by Paul Humphreys*

SHIPTON-UNDER-WYCHWOOD SP2717   OX7 6DQ
☆ **Lamb**
High Street; off A361 to Burford

Mother and son team at this handsome stone inn, beamed bar with oak-panelled settle, farmhouse chairs and polished tables on wood-block flooring, stripped-stone walls, church candles, log fire, three changing beers and quite a few wines by the glass, well liked food, restaurant area; children welcome, dogs allowed in bar (there are two pub dogs), garden with contemporary furniture on terrace, bedrooms, open all day. *Recommended by Lawrence R Cotter, R K Phillips, Simon Collett-Jones*

SIBFORD GOWER SP3537   OX15 5RX
☆ **Wykham Arms**
Signed off B4035 Banbury—Shipston on Stour; Temple Mill Road

Cottagey 17th-c thatched and flagstoned dining pub, good food from light lunchtime menu up, friendly attentive staff, two changing well kept ales, plenty of wines by the glass, comfortable open-plan interior with low-beams and stripped-stone, glass-covered well, inglenook; children and dogs welcome, country views from big garden, lovely manor house opp, open all day Sun, closed Mon. *Recommended by John Levell, Edward Mirzoeff*

SOULDERN SP5231   OX27 7JW
Fox
Off B4100; Fox Lane

Pretty pub with good choice of enjoyable fairly priced food including the Fox Sandwich (roast beef between two yorkshire puddings), well kept Hook Norton and two guests (beer festivals), good choice of wines by the glass, comfortable open-plan beamed layout, big log fire, settles and chairs around oak tables, quiz nights; delightful village, garden and terrace tables, aunt sally, four bedrooms. *Recommended by David Lamb, Andy and Jill Kassube*

SOUTH NEWINGTON SP4033   OX15 4JE
Duck on the Pond
A361

Dining pub with tidy modern-rustic décor in small flagstoned bar and linked carpeted eating areas up a step, enjoyable food from wraps, melts and other light dishes to steak and family Sun lunch, changing ales such as Purity and Wye Valley, range of coffees, neat friendly young staff, woodburner; piped music; spacious grounds with tables on deck and lawn, aunt sally, pond with waterfowl, walk down to River Swere, open all day weekends. *Recommended by George Atkinson, Lucien Perring*

SPARSHOLT SU3487   OX12 9PL
Star
Watery Lane

Compact 16th-c country pub, comfortable beamed bar with eating area to one side, generous blackboard food, usually three real ales, quick friendly service; may be piped music; back garden, pretty village – snowdrops fill churchyard in spring. *Recommended by David Lamb, D C T and E A Frewer*

STANDLAKE SP3902   OX29 7RH
Black Horse
High Street

Three-room pub with low ceilings and old brick fireplaces, wide choice of enjoyable food including bargain lunchtime fixed-price menu and Sun carvery, well kept Hook Norton ales, decent wines; garden picnic-sets, open all day weekends. *Recommended by Eddie Edwards, DHV, Miss Teresa Evans*

STANTON ST JOHN SP5709   OX33 1EX
 ## Star
Pub signed off B4027; village signed off A40 E of Oxford

Pleasant old Wadworths pub tucked away at end of village; two small low-beamed rooms, one with ancient brick floor, other with close-set tables, up stairs to attractive extension (on same level as car park) with old-fashioned dining chairs around dark oak or elm tables, rugs on flagstones, shelves of good pewter, bookshelves either side of inglenook log fire, also family room and conservatory; piped music; children and dogs welcome, seats among flowerbeds in walled garden, some play equipment. *Recommended by John Robertson, Dennis and Doreen Haward, David Lamb, Dave Braisted*

STEEPLE ASTON SP4725   OX25 4RY
☆ ## Red Lion
Off A4260 12 miles N of Oxford

Welcoming village pub with plenty of cheerful customers, partly panelled neatly kept bar with beams, antique settle and other good furnishings, three real ales and decent wines, enjoyable popular bar food, helpful friendly service, back conservatory-style dining extension; well behaved children welcome lunchtime and until 7pm, dogs in bar, suntrap front garden with lovely flowers and shrubs, closed Sun evening. *Recommended by Brian Glozier, Ron and Sheila Corbett, Robert Watt, William Goodhart and others*

STOKE ROW SU6884   RG9 5QA
☆ ## Cherry Tree
Off B481 at Highmoor

Contemporary upscale pub/restaurant with particularly good and very popular food, Sun lunch till 5pm, attentive staff, well kept Brakspears ales, good choice of wines by the glass, minimalist décor and solid country furniture in four linked rooms with stripped wood, heavy low beams and some flagstones; TV in bar; seats in attractive garden, nearby walks, five good bedrooms in converted barn, open all day except Sun evening. *Recommended by Bob and Margaret Holder, Richard Endacott*

SUTTON COURTENAY SU5094   OX14 4NQ
Fish
Appleford Road

Civilised well run restaurant rather than pub, small front bar opening into attractive
three-part dining room, good freshly cooked food with some emphasis on fish, also bar
snacks and good value fixed-price menu, nice wines by the glass, Greene King Morland
Original, competent service from french staff, back conservatory; children welcome,
tables out in terrace arbour and on lawn, closed Sun evening, Mon. *Recommended by*
John and Helen Rushton

SWINFORD SP4308   OX29 4BT
Talbot
B4044 just S of Eynsham

Roomy and comfortable 17th-c beamed pub, wide changing choice of generous fresh food,
well kept Arkells ales direct from the cask, good choice of wines and soft drinks, friendly
landlord and staff, long attractive bar with some stripped stone, cheerful log-effect gas
fire, newspapers, some live jazz; may be piped music; children and dogs welcome, garden
with decked area overlooking Wharf Stream, pleasant walk along lovely stretch of the
Thames towpath, moorings quite nearby, eight good bedrooms. *Recommended by Meg and Colin*
Hamilton, Alistair and Joy Hamilton

SYDENHAM SP7201   OX39 4NB
Crown
Off B4445 Chinnor—Thame

Friendly low-beamed pub in picturesque village, good reasonably priced food cooked by
landlord, local ales, nice wines, open fires in long narrow bar; children welcome, small
garden, views of lovely church. *Recommended by Mr and Mrs E Hughes*

THAME SP7105   OX9 3HP
Cross Keys
Park Street/East Street

One-bar 19th-c local continuing well under present landlord, six ales including own good
Thame beers such as Mrs Tipples Ghost and Mr Splodges Mild, nice atmosphere;
courtyard garden. *Recommended by Tim and Ann Newell, Doug Kennedy*

THAME SP7006   OX9 2AD
Six Bells
High Street

Recently refurbished 16th-c black-beamed Fullers pub, friendly relaxed atmosphere with
cycling theme, interestingly varied menu (not Sun evening), good coffee, open fire;
children and dogs welcome, large terrace, open all day. *Recommended by Tim and Ann Newell*

THRUPP SP4815   OX5 1JY
☆ Boat
Brown sign to pub off A4260 just N of Kidlington

Attractive 16th-c stone building, low ceilings, old coal stove, bare boards or ancient
flooring tiles, good home-made food from panini and snacks to more upscale things, own
bread and ice-creams too, friendly landlord and efficient service, Greene King ales,
decent wine, restaurant; gets busy in summer; children and dogs welcome, fenced garden
behind with plenty of tables, nearby Oxford Canal moorings. *Recommended by Ian B, Meg and*
Colin Hamilton, Phil Lowther

UFFINGTON SU3089   SN7 7RP
Fox & Hounds
High Street

Traditional beamed village pub under newish ownership, enjoyable reasonably priced
pubby food (not Sun evening), changing real ales; children and dogs welcome, garden
picnic-sets, near Tom Brown's Museum and handy for White Horse Hill, open all day.
Recommended by R K Phillips

WALLINGFORD SU6089   OX10 0BS
George
High Street

Handsome extended 16th-c coaching inn, decent food in bistro, restaurant or beamed bar
with splendid log fireplace, good range of drinks, friendly service; tables in spacious
central courtyard, 39 bedrooms. *Recommended by David and Sue Atkinson*

WANTAGE SU3988   OX12 9AB
Lamb
Mill Street, past square and Bell; down hill then bend to left

Popular comfortable pub with low beams, log fire and cosy corners, well kept Fullers
London Pride and Greene King, wide choice of good generous food; children welcome,
disabled facilities, garden tables. *Recommended by anon*

WEST HENDRED SU4489   OX12 8RH
Hare
A417 Reading Road, outside village

Big welcoming open-plan village pub popular for its generous mainly traditional food (not
Sun evening), Greene King and a guest, efficient friendly staff, low-ceilinged main bar
with bare boards and terracotta tiles, timber dividers, comfortable parquet-floor dining
area; piped music; children welcome, colonnaded verandah, picnic-sets in side garden
with covered deck, open all day. *Recommended by D C T and E A Frewer*

WESTON-ON-THE-GREEN SP5318   OX25 3RA
Ben Jonson
B430 near M40 junction 9

Ancient stone-and-thatch country pub, beamed bar with oak furniture, woodburner, well
kept changing local ales, enjoyable food, newish dining room; children and dogs welcome.
Recommended by Laura Jones, Jane Sauyd

WESTON-ON-THE-GREEN SP5318   OX25 3QH
Chequers
Handy for M40 junction 9, via A34; Northampton Road (B430)

Extended thatched pub, homely and welcoming, with three areas off large semicircular
raftered bar, popular interesting food including game and some lovely puddings, well kept
Fullers and a guest, good wines by the glass; tables under parasols in attractive garden.
Recommended by Val and Alan Green, Martin and Alison Stainsby

WHITCHURCH SU6377   RG8 7EL
Greyhound
High Street, just over toll bridge from Pangbourne

Pretty former ferryman's cottage taken over recently by friendly enthusiastic licensees,
cosy low-beamed bar with fire, real ales including Hook Norton; small sheltered back
garden, attractive village on Thames Path, open all day weekends. *Recommended by N R White*

Half pints: by law, a pub should not charge more for half a pint than half the price of
a full pint, unless it shows that half-pint price on its price list.

WHITCHURCH HILL SU6378   RG8 7PG
Sun
Hill Bottom; signed from B471

Friendly unassuming brick-built pub in sleepy village, L-shaped bar with carpet and bare boards, white textured walls, dark woodwork, plush chairs and wall benches, enjoyable reasonably priced food including vegetarian choices, Brakspears, Hook Norton and Marstons ales; children welcome, couple of picnic-sets out at front, small side terrace, back lawn with play area. *Recommended by Phil Bryant*

WITNEY SP3509   OX28 4AZ
Fleece
Church Green

Smart civilised town pub on green, popular for its wide choice of good food including deli boards, friendly attentive service, Greene King ales, leather armchairs on wood floors, daily papers, restaurant; piped music; children welcome, tables out at front, ten bedrooms, open all day. *Recommended by Nigel and Sue Foster, R K Phillips*

WITNEY SP3510   OX28 6BS
☆ Three Horseshoes
Corn Street, junction with Holloway Road

Welcoming and accommodating staff in attractive 16th-c modernised stone-built pub, wide choice of good home-made food from pubby lunchtime things to more imaginative restauranty dishes, well kept Greene King ales and a guest, decent house wines, heavy beams, flagstones, well polished comfortable old furniture, log fires, separate dining room; back terrace. *Recommended by Nigel and Sue Foster, Sally Simon, Peter Lee*

WOLVERCOTE SP4909   OX2 8AH
Plough
First Turn/Wolvercote Green

Comfortably well worn-in pubby linked areas, friendly helpful service, bustling atmosphere, armchairs and Victorian-style carpeted bays in main lounge, well kept Greene King ales, farm cider, decent wines, enjoyable good value usual food in flagstoned former stables dining room and library (children allowed here), traditional snug, woodburner; picnic-sets on front terrace looking over rough meadow to canal and woods. *Recommended by Tony and Jill Radnor, Paul Humphreys*

WOOLSTONE SU2987   SN7 7QL
White Horse
Off B4507

Appealing old partly thatched pub with Victorian gables and latticed windows, plush furnishings, spacious beamed and part-panelled bar, two big open fires, Arkells ales, enjoyable good value food, restaurant; well behaved children allowed, plenty of seats in front and back gardens, secluded interesting village handy for White Horse and Ridgeway, bedrooms, open all day. *Recommended by Martin and Karen Wake, David Knowles, Jim and Frances Gowers, Jennifer and Patrick O'Dell*

ALSO WORTH A VISIT IN SURREY

Besides the region's top pubs, we recommend the following. Do tell us
what you think of them: **feedback@goodguides.com**

ABINGER COMMON TQ1146   RH5 6HZ
Abinger Hatch
Off A25 W of Dorking, towards Abinger Hammer

Modernised dining pub in beautiful woodland spot, popular food (not Sun evening) from
light dishes up, Fullers London Pride, Ringwood and Surrey Hills, heavy beams and
flagstones, log fires, pews forming booths around oak tables in carpeted side area, plenty
of space (very busy weekends when service can be slow); piped music, plain family
extension; dogs welcome, some disabled access, tables in nice garden, near pretty church
and pond, summer barbecues, open all day. *Recommended by CP, Ian Phillips*

ALBURY TQ0447   GU5 9AG
Drummond Arms
Off A248 SE of Guildford; The Street

Attractive recently refurbished country pub, Adnams, Courage, Fullers and Surrey Hills
ales, good choice of wines, food from sandwiches and light dishes up, good service,
opened-up bar with leather chesterfields, parquet-floored dining room, conservatory;
pretty streamside back garden with new furniture, duck island, summer barbecues and
hog roasts, pretty village with pleasant walks nearby, nine good bedrooms, open all day
weekends. *Recommended by Ian Phillips, John and Verna Aspinall*

ALFOLD TQ0435   GU6 8JE
Alfold Barn
Horsham Road

Beautifully preserved 16th-c building with bar and restaurant, good food including
bargain lunchtime deal, good service, a changing well kept ale, beams and rafters, mixed
furniture on flagstones or carpet, log fires; garden with play area, closed Sun evening,
Mon. *Recommended by Shirley Mackenzie, George James*

BANSTEAD TQ2559   SM7 2NZ
Woolpack
High Street

Well run and busy open-plan dining pub, well kept changing ales such as Sharps Doom
Bar, pleasant service; open all day. *Recommended by C and R Bromage*

BETCHWORTH TQ1950   RH3 7HB
Arkle Manor
Reigate Road

Smart M&B dining pub with enjoyable gently upscale food, attractive rambling layout with
easy chairs and so forth, real ales, good choice of wines by the glass, good service.
Recommended by C and R Bromage

BETCHWORTH TQ2149   RH3 7DW
Dolphin
Off A25 W of Reigate; The Street

16th-c village pub on Greensand Way, plain tables on ancient flagstones in neat front bar,
smaller bar, panelled restaurant/bar with blazing fire and chiming grandfather clock, nice
old local photographs, well kept Wells & Youngs ales, blackboard food, service can
struggle at times; children and dogs welcome, small front courtyard, weekend summer
barbecues in back garden, picturesque village (fine pre-Raphaelite pulpit in church),
open all day. *Recommended by Geoffrey Kemp, J R Osborne, LM, C and R Bromage*

BETCHWORTH TQ2150   RH3 7DS
Red Lion
Old Road, Buckland

Comfortable dining pub with good sensibly priced home-made food, friendly helpful staff, Adnams, Fullers London Pride and Sharps Doom Bar, rather old-fashioned carpeted bar with dark wood furniture, restaurant; children welcome, picnic-sets on lawn with cricket ground beyond, dining terrace, good bedrooms in separate modern block, open all day.
Recommended by Phil Bryant

BLETCHINGLEY TQ3250   RH1 4NU
Red Lion
Castle Street (A25), Redhill side

Old beamed village dining pub with fresh modern décor, well spaced tables, lots of racing prints, good reasonably priced mainly traditional food all day, friendly staff, well kept Greene King ales, good choice of wines by the glass, monthly quiz and some live music; no children after 6pm, tables under umbrellas on heated terrace, secret garden. *Recommended by John Atkins, Geoffrey Kemp, John Branston*

BUCKLAND TQ2250   RH3 7BG
☆ Jolly Farmers
Reigate Road (A25 W of Reigate)

Unusual place part pub/part restaurant/part deli, most customers come for the enjoyable all-day food using meticulously sourced local produce, but they do keep Harveys and Dark Star, local wines and home-made cordials, informal beamed and flagstoned bar with hops, smart leather sofas and armchairs, brick fireplace separating small dining room, three-room shop sells fresh vegetables, deli meats, cheeses, cakes and own range of produce, food market (Sat 9am-3pm); children welcome, tables on back terrace overlooking car park, open all day from 9.15am (breakfast served weekends). *Recommended by Derek and Maggie Washington, Derek Thomas, Colin and Louise English, Cathryn and Richard Hicks, LM, M G Hart and others*

BYFLEET TQ0661   KT14 7QT
Plough
High Road

Small pub with good range of changing ales, usually simple food from sandwiches to three or four bargain hot dishes lunchtime and Weds evening, friendly service, two log fires, rustic furnishings, farm tools, brass and copper, dominoes, more modern back area, sociable cat, no mobiles; terrace and small shady back garden. *Recommended by Ian Phillips*

CHARLWOOD TQ2441   RH6 0DS
Half Moon
The Street

Old pub next to churchyard, good-sized L-shaped bar with pubby furniture and a couple of sofas, front part open to original upstairs windows, good food from baguettes to substantial specials and enjoyable Sun lunch, friendly service, well kept ales such as Harveys and Wells & Youngs Bombardier, formal back dining room; piped music; tables out at front and in attractive courtyard area, nice village handy for Gatwick Airport.
Recommended by John Michelson, Phil Bryant, Barry Moses

CHILWORTH TQ0347   GU4 8NP
Percy Arms
Dorking Road

Refurbished partly 18th-c pub with south african influences in décor and food, good choice of wines by the glass, Greene King IPA and Abbot, front bar and lounge with steps down to dining area, efficient service despite being busy; children welcome, garden tables with pretty views over Vale of Chilworth to St Martha's Hill, good walks. *Recommended by Phil Bryant*

CHIPSTEAD TQ2757   CR5 3NP
Ramblers Rest
Outwood Lane (B2032)

M&B country dining pub with contemporary furnishings and cocktail-bar décor in partly 14th-c rambling building, panelling, flagstones, low beams and log fires, enjoyable up-to-date and more traditional food including popular Sun lunch, real ales, good value wines by the glass, young friendly staff, daily papers; children welcome, big pleasant garden with terrace, attractive views, good walks, open all day. *Recommended by Maureen and Keith Gimson, John Branston, C and R Bromage, Grmbj*

CHIPSTEAD TQ2757   CR5 3QW
White Hart
Hazelwood Lane

Refurbished L-shaped bar, tasty if not cheap food, half a dozen real ales, helpful staff; walled garden. *Recommended by C and R Bromage*

CLAYGATE TQ1663   KT10 0HW
Griffin
Common Road

Properly old-fashioned Victorian village local with well kept ales including Fullers London Pride, some interesting dishes as well as usual pub food freshly cooked and reasonably priced. *Recommended by Gordon Stevenson*

CLAYGATE TQ1563   KT10 0JL
Hare & Hounds
The Green

Renovated flower-decked Victorian/Edwardian village pub with small restaurant, good sensibly priced french food, fine wine choice, competent service; outside seating at front and in small back garden. *Recommended by Tom and Ruth Rees, Nick Stafford*

COBHAM TQ1058   KT11 3NX
☆ Cricketers
Downside Common; 3.75 miles from M25 junction 10; A3 towards Cobham, first right on to A245, right at Downside signpost into Downside Bridge Road, follow road into its right fork – away from Cobham Park – at second turn after bridge, then eventually turn into the pub's own lane, immediately before Common crossroads

Worth visiting for idyllic terrace views across village green; open-plan room areas much in need of redecoration, though lots of character with crooked standing timbers, low oak beams (some with crash-pads), wide oak ceiling boards and ancient plastering laths, log fire, Fullers, Greene King and a guest, bar food; piped music; children and dogs welcome, neatly kept garden, pretty hanging baskets, open all day. *Recommended by Conor McGaughey, Michael Cross, C and R Bromage, Ian Wilson, Ron and Sheila Corbett, Ian Phillips and others*

COBHAM TQ1059   KT11 3DX
Old Bear
Riverhill

Part of Wildwood restaurant chain and no longer pubby; enjoyable bistro-style food in various smartly refurbished contemporary dining rooms, beige plush button-back sofas, pale oak cushioned dining chairs and nice old farmhouse seats on light flooring, shelves of italian olive oil, pasta and flour, silver candelabra, large modern lamps (a huge movie one too), comfortable sitting room; seats out on raised terrace. *Recommended by Geoffrey Kemp*

If you have to cancel a reservation for a bedroom or restaurant, please telephone or write to warn them. You may lose your deposit if you've paid one.

COBHAM TQ1159   KT11 3EZ

Running Mare
Tilt Road

Attractive old pub overlooking the green, popular for its good food (very busy Sun lunchtime), well kept Fullers, Hogs Back and Wells & Youngs ales, good friendly service, two timbered bars and restaurant; children very welcome, a few tables out at front and on back rose-covered terrace. *Recommended by Colin McKerrow*

COLDHARBOUR TQ1544   RH5 6HD

Plough
Village signposted in the network of small roads around Leith Hill

Cosy two-bar pub with own-brewed Leith Hill ales and guests, Biddenden cider, several wines by the glass, pleasant service, open fires, light beams and timbering, snug games room (darts, board games and cards), food in bar and evening restaurant (Tues-Sat) specialising in steaks (not cheap); piped music, TV; children welcome if eating, dogs in bar, front terrace and quiet back garden overlooking fields, bedrooms (ones over bar noisy), open all day. *Recommended by Sara Fulton, Roger Baker, N R White*

 COMPTON SU9646   GU3 1JA

Withies
Withies Lane; pub signed from B3000

Carefully altered 16th-c pub, charmingly civilised and gently old-fashioned, with low-beamed bar, some 17th-c carved panels between windows, splendid art nouveau settle amongst old sewing-machine tables, log fire in massive inglenook, Adnams, Greene King and a guest, popular (not cheap) bar food served by efficient, helpful, bow-tied staff; children welcome, seats on terrace, under apple trees and creeper-hung arbour, flower-edged neat front lawn, on edge of Loseley Park and close to Watts Gallery, closed Sun evening. *Recommended by B and M Kendall, Ellie Weld, David London, LM, Helen and Brian Edgeley, Gerald and Gabrielle Culliford, Ian Herdman*

DORMANSLAND TQ4042   RH7 6PS

Plough
Plough Road, off B2028 NE

Hard-working licensees and friendly staff in traditional old pub in quiet village, well kept Fullers, Harveys and Sharps, Weston's cider, decent wines, good choice of enjoyable bar food including specials board, thai restaurant, log fires and original features; children welcome, disabled facilities, good-sized garden, barbecues. *Recommended by Richard Redgrove, David Clarke*

☆ EAST CLANDON TQ0551   GU4 7RY

Queens Head
Just off A246 Guildford—Leatherhead; The Street

Rambling dining pub in same small group as Duke of Cambridge at Tilford and Stag in Eashing, enjoyable food from light dishes up including set deals (Mon-Thurs), good friendly service, well kept ales such as Shepherd Neame Spitfire and Surrey Hills Shere Drop from fine old elm bar counter, comfortable linked rooms, big inglenook log-effect fire; children welcome, picnic-sets on pretty front terrace and in quiet side garden, handy for two NT properties, open all day Sat and till 9pm Sun. *Recommended by Geoffrey Kemp, Ian Phillips, Richard Tilbrook*

☆ EFFINGHAM TQ1153   KT24 5SW

Plough
Orestan Lane

Popular Youngs pub with consistently well kept ales from traditional bar, good choice of enjoyable if a little pricey food including Sun roasts, plenty of wines by the glass, nice staff, two coal-effect gas fires, beamery, panelling, old plates and brassware in long lounge, carpeted floors; plenty of tables on forecourt and in attractive garden, disabled parking, handy for Polesden Lacey (NT). *Recommended by Shirley Mackenzie*

ELLENS GREEN TQ0936   RH12 3AS
Wheatsheaf
B2128 N of Rudgwick

Family-run dining pub with good home-made food from lunchtime sandwiches up, good service, Badger ales and decent wines by the glass, tiled-floor bar with large fireplace, dining areas either side; dogs welcome, some seats in front, more on back terrace, open all day. *Recommended by Shirley Mackenzie*

ENGLEFIELD GREEN SU9771   TW20 0UF
Sun
Wick Lane, Bishopsgate

Well used, beamed local, Courage Best, Greene King Abbot and Wells & Youngs Bombardier and Bitter kept well, good blackboard wine choice, generous inexpensive pubby food from sandwiches up, friendly service, small wooden tables with banquettes and low stools, lots of pub bric-a-brac including interesting beer bottle collection, colourful photographs, open fire, conservatory; soft piped music; children welcome, biscuits and water for dogs, a few tables out at front, quiet garden with aviary, handy for Savill Garden and Windsor Park. *Recommended by LM, Ian Phillips*

EPSOM TQ2158   KT18 5LE
Derby Arms
Downs Road, Epsom Downs

Comfortably reworked M&B dining pub, their usual popular food, good range of wines by the glass, two real ales, open contemporary feel in bar and restaurant with horseracing theme, two-way log fire; picnic-sets outside, good views – opposite racecourse grandstand, open all day. *Recommended by John Branston, Miss Amy Jones*

EPSOM TQ2158   KT18 5LJ
Rubbing House
Langley Vale Road (on Epsom racecourse)

Popular restauranty dining pub with attractive modern décor, good value food promptly served even when busy, tables perhaps a little close together, Fullers London Pride and Greene King IPA, serious wine list, fantastic racecourse views, upper balcony; piped music; tables outside. *Recommended by Maureen and Keith Gimson, DWAJ, Ian Wilson*

ESHER TQ1364   KT10 9RQ
Bear
High Street

Thriving Youngs pub with their full range kept well, good choice of wines by the glass, prompt friendly service, popular reasonably priced food in bar and dining end, two landmark life-size bears behind roof parapet; big-screen sports TV; outside seating with awnings, comfortable bedrooms, open all day. *Recommended by Tom and Ruth Rees, Michael Dandy, Ian Phillips*

FARNHAM SU8547   GU9 9JB
Shepherd & Flock
Moor Park Lane, on A31/A324/A325 roundabout

Flower-decked pub on Europe's largest inhabited roundabout, welcoming landlord, eight interesting changing well kept ales, enjoyable food from baguettes up, simple up-to-date décor; they may try to keep your credit card while you eat; picnic-sets out in front and in pleasant enclosed back garden with barbecue, open all day weekends. *Recommended by Rosemary and Mike Fielder*

FARNHAM SU8545   GU10 3QT
Spotted Cow
Bourne Grove, Lower Bourne (towards Tilford)

Pleasant pastel-décor dining pub on edge of town in nice wooded setting, good choice of enjoyable food from pub standards to specials, friendly helpful staff, changing ales, several wines by the glass; children and dogs welcome, big garden, open all day weekends. *Recommended by Martin and Karen Wake*

FICKLESHOLE TQ3960
CR6 9PH
White Bear
Featherbed Lane/Fairchildes Lane; off A2022 Purley Road just S of A212 roundabout

16th-c country dining pub popular for its good value generous food (all day Fri and Sat, best to book weekends), lots of small rooms, beams, flagstones and open fires, friendly prompt service, four well kept changing ales; children welcome, picnic-sets on front terrace with stone bear, sizeable back garden, open all day. *Recommended by J M and R J Hope, John Branston, Lois Kench, Grahame Brooks*

☆ FOREST GREEN TQ1241
RH5 5RZ
Parrot
B2127 just W of junction with B2126, SW of Dorking

Genuinely aged village pub with cheerful atmosphere, heavy beams, timbers, flagstones and nooks and crannies hidden away behind inglenook, generous helpings of well liked food (not Sun evening) using produce from own farm, five well kept changing ales including Ringwood, 16 wines by the glass, local juice, efficient service; shop selling own meat, cheeses, cured hams, pies and so forth; dogs allowed in bar, attractive gardens with lovely country views, good walks nearby, open all day (till midnight Sat). *Recommended by Tom and Ruth Rees, Colin and Louise English, D M Jack, C and R Bromage, LM, John Branston and others*

FRIDAY STREET TQ1245
RH5 6JR
Stephan Langton
Off B2126

Prettily placed 1930s pub in tucked-away hamlet, new owners since 2009, enjoyable well presented food (not cheap – service charge added), ales including Fullers and Surrey Hills, log fire in bar, woodburner in large modern dining area; children and dogs have been welcome, smart seating at front, wooded setting with pond, good nearby walks. *Recommended by Ian Phillips, N R White, Jill Hurley*

GODSTONE TQ3551
RH9 8DX
Bell
Under a mile from M25 junction 6, via B2236

Good up-to-date and more traditional food in refurbished open-plan M&B family dining pub, good service, comfortably modern furnishings and lighting in handsome old building, separate bar with well kept Timothy Taylors Landlord, three open fires; back terrace and garden. *Recommended by David and Diane Young, Grahame Brooks, Mr and Mrs A Curry, Keith Sangster*

GOMSHALL TQ0847
GU5 9LA
Compasses
A25

Plain bar (open all day) and much bigger, neat and comfortable dining area, popular good value home-made food, real ales such as Surrey Hills Shere Drop, decent wines by the glass, friendly service; may be piped music; children welcome, pretty garden sloping down to roadside mill stream, open all day. *Recommended by DWAJ, Alan and Shirley Sawden*

GUILDFORD SU9949
GU1 3SA
Albany
Sydenham Road

Refurbished pub tucked away behind top of high street, Caledonian Deuchars IPA, Wadworths 6X and Wychwood Hobgoblin from original ornate counter, 20 wines by the glass, good varied choice of promptly served food including well priced lunchtime menu, leather tub chairs and sofas, bare boards, some striking wallpaper, raised dining area; tables on small front terrace and in secluded garden, four bedrooms. *Recommended by Phil Bryant*

GUILDFORD SU9949   GU2 4BL
Keystone
Portsmouth Road

Good choice of food (not Fri-Sun evenings) including deals, Black Sheep, Wadworths 6X and two guests, friendly helpful young staff, bistro atmosphere with simple décor and furnishings including a couple of settles and leather sofas; tables on heated back terrace (dogs allowed here only), open all day, closed Sun evening. *Recommended by John and Joan Nash, Tracey and Stephen Groves, Tony Hobden, Robin Bowen*

HAMBLEDON SU9639   GU8 4DR
Merry Harriers
Off A283; just N of village

Popular beamed country local with huge inglenook log fire and pine tables on bare boards, ales such as Hop Back, Palmers, Surrey Hills and Triple fff, decent wines, enjoyable generous pub food from sandwiches up, friendly staff, beer festivals and live music; children welcome, big garden with boules, llamas and wandering chickens, campsite, attractive walking countryside near Greensand Way. *Recommended by Phil Bryant*

HORLEY TQ2844   RH6 9LJ
Farmhouse
Langshott

17th-c former farmhouse, a pub since 1985, with linked beamed rooms, well kept ales such as Greene King Old Speckled Hen, pubby food all day including late-night pizzas; big child-friendly back garden, front smokers' shelter. *Recommended by John Branston*

HORSELL SU9959   GU21 4JL
Plough
Off South Road; Cheapside

Small friendly local overlooking wooded heath, relaxed atmosphere, well kept changing ales such as Hogs Back TEA and St Austell Tribute, good choice of wines by the glass and of malt whiskies, good value fresh food (all day Sat, not Sun evening) including fine range of home-made pies and vegetarian options, quiet dining area one side of L, games machines and TV the other; children and dogs welcome, tables in pretty garden with play area, open all day. *Recommended by Ian Phillips, David M Smith*

HORSELL COMMON TQ0160   GU21 5NL
☆ Sands at Bleak House
Chertsey Road, The Anthonys; A320 Woking—Ottershaw

Smart contemporary restauranty pub, grey split sandstone for floor and face of bar counter, brown leather sofas and cushioned stools, two dining rooms with dark wood furniture, good if not cheap food, Hogs Back TEA, Surrey Hills Shere Drop and a guest, fresh juices, friendly attentive uniformed staff, woodburners, daily newspapers; piped jazz, TV, lively acoustics; smokers' marquee in courtyard with picnic-sets, good shortish walks to sandpits which inspired H G Wells's *War of the Worlds*, seven bedrooms, open all day, till 8pm Sun. *Recommended by Ian Phillips*

IRONS BOTTOM TQ2546   RH2 8PT
Three Horseshoes
Sidlow Bridge, off A217

Welcoming renovated local, enjoyable good value home-made food, seven well kept ales such as Fullers, Harveys and Surrey Hills, darts; tables outside, summer barbecues. *Recommended by C and R Bromage*

'Children welcome' means the pub says it lets children inside without any special restriction; some may impose an evening time limit earlier than 9pm – please tell us if you find this.

LEATHERHEAD TQ1656
KT22 8AW
Edmund Tylney
High Street

Cosy Wetherspoons with standard good value food and wide choice of real ales, friendly service, big fire in upstairs library-style dining room; open all day. *Recommended by R C Vincent*

LIMPSFIELD TQ4053
RH8 0DR
Bull
High Street

Friendly village local dating from the 16th c, shortish choice of tasty reasonably priced food, good value wines, Adnams and Marstons Pedigree, helpful service, darts; sports TVs, juke box; children welcome, terrace tables. *Recommended by Simon Good, Grahame Brooks, Judy Brua, Christine and Neil Townend*

LINGFIELD TQ3844
RH7 6BZ
☆ Hare & Hounds
Turn off B2029 N at the Crowhurst/Edenbridge signpost

Smallish open-plan bar, bare boards and flagstones, mixed seating including button-back leather chesterfield, dining area, good wide-ranging food from french landlord, friendly efficient service, well kept ales such as Fullers London Pride and Harveys; children and dogs welcome, tables in pleasant split-level garden with decking, good walking country near Haxted Mill – leave boots in porch, open all day, closed Sun evening. *Recommended by Tony and Shirley Albert, Simon and Helen Barnes, Steven and Yvonne Parker, Derek Thomas, Melanie Alcock, Cathryn and Richard Hicks and others*

MERSHAM TQ3051
RH1 4EU
Inn on the Pond
Nutfield Marsh Road, off A25 W of Godstone

Popular dining pub doing enjoyable interesting food (all day Sun) including children's meals, well kept ales from Hogs Back, Kings and Sharps, Weston's cider, good choice of wines by the glass including champagne, comfortable casually contemporary dining room, back conservatory; sheltered terrace behind, views over pond and nearby cricket ground to North Downs. *Recommended by Fleur Perkie, John Branston, Peter Eyles, R K Phillips*

MICKLEHAM TQ1753
RH5 6EL
King William IV
Just off A24 Leatherhead—Dorking; Byttom Hill

Steps up to small nicely placed country pub, well kept Hogs Back TEA, Surrey Hills Shere Drop and Triple fff Alton's Pride, wide choice of food including blackboard specials, friendly service, pleasant outlook from snug plank-panelled front bar; piped music, outside gents'; children welcome, plenty of tables (some in heated open-sided timber shelters) in lovely terraced garden with great valley views, closed evenings Sun and Mon. *Recommended by LM, Phil Bryant*

MICKLEHAM TQ1753
RH5 6DU
☆ Running Horses
Old London Road (B2209)

Upmarket all-rounder with genuinely wide mix of customers (and dogs) and easy-going atmosphere, neatly kept open-plan bar with hunting pictures, racing cartoons and Hogarth prints, lots of race tickets hanging from beams, straightforward pubby furniture, inglenook with summer fresh flowers or winter fire, Fullers, Wells & Youngs and guests, wines by the glass from a serious list, good (not cheap) food from pubby meals to more elaborate choices, big formal restaurant with crisp white cloths and candles, competent service; children over 10 welcome, disabled facilities, busy front terrace with lovely tubs and hanging baskets, peaceful view of old church with stubby steeple, bedrooms, open all day, get there early for a seat or parking space. *Recommended by Conor McGaughey, Sheila Topham, Brian and Anna Marsden, Tony and Jill Radnor and others*

NEWDIGATE TQ2043   RH5 5DZ
☆ Surrey Oaks
Off A24 S of Dorking, via Beare Green; Parkgate Road

Cheery village pub with friendly landlord, well kept Harveys, Surrey Hills and three guests
from smaller breweries (beer festivals May and Aug), bottled continental beers and farm
cider/perry, well liked reasonably priced bar food (not Sun or Mon evenings), pubby
interior divided into four areas, older part has locals by the open fire in a snug beamed
room, standing area with unusually large flagstones and woodburner in inglenook, rustic
tables in light and airy main lounge, separate games room with pool, skittle alley; piped
classical music, TV and machines; children and dogs welcome, pleasingly complicated
garden has terrace, rockery with pools and waterfall, play area and two boules pitches,
open all day Sun. *Recommended by C and R Bromage, Roger and Donna Huggins, Pam and John Smith,
Peter Dandy, the Didler and others*

OCKLEY TQ1440   RH5 5TD
Inn on the Green
Billingshurst Road (A29)

Welcoming former 17th-c coaching inn on the green of a charming village, good fresh
traditional food, well kept Greene King and a guest like Kings Horsham, friendly attentive
service, slightly dated décor with usual pubby furniture, steps up to quiet eating area and
dining conservatory; tables in secluded garden, six comfortable bedrooms, good breakfast.
Recommended by Phil Bryant

OCKLEY TQ1439   RH5 5TH
☆ Old School House
Stane Street

Primarily a fish restaurant, but has thriving pubby eating area around small bar counter
with well kept Fullers ales, good wines by the glass including champagne, wonderful log
fire, buoyant atmosphere, prompt attentive young staff, good bar food from sandwiches
up; picnic-sets under cocktail parasols on sunny terrace with flowers around car park.
Recommended by Karen Eliot

OCKLEY TQ1337   RH5 5PU
☆ Punchbowl
Oakwood Hill, signed off A29 S

Attractive 16th-c tile-hung country pub with Horsham slab roof, welcoming relaxed
atmosphere, wide food choice (all day weekends) from sandwiches up, Badger ales,
central bar with huge inglenook, polished flagstones and low beams, restaurant area to
left and another bar to right with a couple of sofas, daily papers; children welcome away
from bar, picnic-sets in pretty garden, smokers' awning, quiet spot with good walks
including Sussex Border Path. *Recommended by Phil Bryant*

OTTERSHAW TQ0263   KT16 0LW
☆ Castle
Brox Road, off A320 not far from M25 junction 11

Friendly two-bar early Victorian local with big crackling log fires, country paraphernalia
on black ceiling joists and walls, half a dozen well kept ales such as Harveys, Sharps,
Surrey Hills and Timothy Taylors, Addlestone's cider, enjoyable bar food (not Sun
evening); TV, piped music; children welcome in conservatory till 7pm, dogs in bar, tables
on terrace and grass, open all day weekends. *Recommended by Ian Phillips*

OUTWOOD TQ3246   RH1 5PN
☆ Bell
Outwood Common, just E of village; off A23 S of Redhill

Attractive extended 17th-c country pub/restaurant, smartly rustic beamed bar with oak
and elm tables and chairs (some in Jacobean style), low beams and vast stone inglenook,
Fullers ales, decent wines by the glass, large range of liqueurs, enjoyable food including

plenty of fish (all day Sun); piped music, Tues quiz; children and dogs welcome, neat garden with play area, seats on sheltered lawn, nice country views, handy for windmill, open all day. *Recommended by Phil Bryant, John Atkins, M G Hart*

OUTWOOD TQ3146   RH1 5QU
Dog & Duck
Princluding of Wales Road; turn off A23 at station sign in Salfords, S of Redhill – OS Sheet 187 map reference 312460

Unhurried beamed country pub with good home-made food in bar or restaurant, welcoming service, well kept Badger ales, decent wines, warm winter fires, some live music; children welcome, garden with duck pond and play area. *Recommended by Sally Cullen, Richard Tilbrook*

OXTED TQ4048   RH8 0RR
Royal Oak
Caterfield Lane, Staffhurst Wood, S of town

Popular well managed pub, cheerful and comfortable, with good range of beers including Adnams, Harveys and Larkins, Biddenden cider, good value house wines, enjoyable locally sourced food including some imaginative dishes, back dining room; dogs welcome, nice garden with lovely views across fields, open all day weekends. *Recommended by John Branston, William Ruxton, N R White*

PYRFORD LOCK TQ0559   GU23 6QW
☆ # Anchor
3 miles from M25 junction 10 – S on A3, then take Wisley slip road and go on past RHS garden

Light and airy Badger family dining pub (can get very busy), food all day (small helpings available), lunchtime sandwiches too, good value wines, cheerful service, simple tables on bare boards, quieter more comfortable panelled back area, narrow-boat memorabilia, pleasant conservatory, daily papers; dogs allowed in part, splendid terrace in lovely spot by bridge and locks on River Wey Navigation (handy for RHS Wisley), fenced-off play area, open all day. *Recommended by John Saville, Peter Rozée, D Crook*

REIGATE HEATH TQ2349   RH2 8RL
Skimmington Castle
Off A25 Reigate—Dorking via Flanchford Road and Bonny's Road

Nicely located small country pub, emphasis on enjoyable home-made food, ales such as Adnams and St Austell, panelled beamed rooms, big working fireplace; children and dogs welcome. *Recommended by John Michelson, Gaynor Lawson, Phil Bryant, C and R Bromage*

RIPLEY TQ0456   GU23 6DL
Seven Stars
Newark Lane (B367)

Neat family-run traditional 1930s pub popular lunchtimes for enjoyable food from sandwiches to plenty of seafood, Brakspears, Fullers London Pride, Hook Norton Old Hooky and Shepherd Neame Spitfire, good wines and coffee, gleaming brasses, open fire; quiet piped music; picnic-sets in large tidy garden, river and canalside walks. *Recommended by Ian Phillips, Barrie and Mary Crees*

SEND TQ0156   GU23 7EN
New Inn
Send Road, Cartbridge

Well placed old pub by River Wey Navigation, long bar decorated to suit, Adnams, Greene King Abbot and one or two unusual guests, friendly landlord, good value food from sandwiches up, log-effect gas fires; large waterside garden with moorings and smokers' shelter. *Recommended by Ian Phillips*

SEND MARSH TQ0455   GU23 6JQ
☆ **Saddlers Arms**
Send Marsh Road

Genial and attentive licensees in unpretentious low-beamed local, homely and warm, with
Fullers London Pride, Hogs Back TEA, Shepherd Neame Spitfire and Wychwood
Hobgoblin, good value generous home-made food (all day Sun) from sandwiches to pizzas
and pubby favourites, roaring log fire, sparkling brassware, toby jugs, etc; dogs welcome,
picnic-sets out front and back. *Recommended by Ian Phillips, Shirley Mackenzie, DWAJ*

SHALFORD SU9946   GU4 8DW
Parrot
Broadford Road

Big warmly welcoming pub with wide range of enjoyable fairly priced food from good
snacks up, Fullers London Pride, Hogs Back TEA and Surrey Hills Shere Drop, friendly
attentive staff, rows of neat pine dining tables, some easy chairs around low tables,
pleasant conservatory; children welcome till 8pm, attractive garden, five bedrooms, handy
for Loseley Park. *Recommended by C and R Bromage*

SHALFORD TQ0047   GU4 8BU
☆ **Seahorse**
A281 S of Guildford; The Street

Gently upmarket M&B dining pub with wide choice of food from simple to more
sophisticated things, popular fixed-priced menu (weekday lunchtimes, early evenings),
friendly well trained young staff, Hogs Back TEA, good choice of wines and other drinks,
good contemporary furniture and artwork, smart dining room, comfortable part near
entrance with sofas and huge window; picnic-sets in big lawned garden, covered terrace,
open all day. *Recommended by MDN, Malcolm and Carole Lomax*

SHERE TQ0747   GU5 9HS
William Bray
Shere Lane

Major refurbishment and emphasis on good well presented locally sourced food, ales such
as Hogs Back, Sharps and Surrey Hills, good choice of wines, attentive service, roomy
contemporary bar with stone floor and woodburner, more formal airy restaurant with
comfortable leather chairs and large F1 racing photographs (owner was driver for Tyrell
and Lotus); very busy weekends; dogs welcome, tables on front split-level terrace, pretty
landscaped garden. *Recommended by Martin Stafford, J D Derry, N R White, Ian Phillips,
Tracey and Stephen Groves, Terry Buckland*

SOUTH GODSTONE TQ3549   RH9 8LY
Fox & Hounds
Tilburstow Hill Road/Harts Lane, off A22

Pleasant old tile-hung country pub with woodburner in low-beamed bar, welcoming staff,
enjoyable good value food from pubby staples up, well kept Greene King ales from tiny bar
counter, restaurant with inglenook; open all day. *Recommended by Conor McGaughey,
C and R Bromage*

SUTTON GREEN TQ0054   GU4 7QD
☆ **Olive Tree**
Sutton Green Road

Big rambling dining pub in quiet countryside, good honest fresh food (not Sun, Mon
evenings), cheaper bar menu including sandwiches, fireside leather sofas, relaxing back
dining room, bare boards and clean-cut pastel décor, well kept Fullers London Pride,
Ringwood and Timothy Taylors Landlord, good choice of wines by the glass, pleasant
helpful staff; terrace tables. *Recommended by LM, Paddy and Annabelle Cribb, Katherine Tonks,
Ian Phillips*

THAMES DITTON TQ1567   KT7 0QY
Albany
Queens Road, signed off Summer Road

M&B bar-with-restaurant in lovely Thames-side position, light airy modern feel, with good variety of food from sharing plates and pizzas to more upscale dishes, weekday fixed-price menu lunchtime and early evening, good choice of wines by the glass, cocktails, a couple of beers such as Sharps Doom Bar and Timothy Taylors Landlord, log fire, river pictures, daily papers; nice balconies and river-view terrace, moorings, open all day. *Recommended by Tom and Ruth Rees, Katherine Tonks, Jennie George*

THAMES DITTON TQ1666   KT7 0XY
Ferry
Portsmouth Road

Welcoming and relaxed bistro-style dining pub with good reasonably priced food from chef/landlord, well kept ales; some tables out at front. *Recommended by Tom and Ruth Rees, Lauren Bennett, Tim Grey*

TILFORD SU8743   GU10 2BU
Barley Mow
The Green, off B3001 SE of Farnham; also signed off A287

Opposite pretty cricket green, with woodburner in snug little low-ceilinged traditional bar, nice scrubbed tables in two small rooms set for food on left, interesting cricketing prints and old photographs, well kept ales such as Courage Best, Greene King Abbot, Hook Norton and Sharps Doom Bar, imaginative wine list, pubby food, weekend afternoon teas; darts and table skittles, no children except in back coach house; narrow front terrace, picnic-sets in back garden fenced off from Wey tributary, open all day Sun and, in summer, Sat. *Recommended by Phil Bryant, Rosemary and Mike Fielder*

TILFORD SU8742   GU10 2DD
Duke of Cambridge
Tilford Road

Civilised smartly done pub in same small local group as Stag at Eashing and Queens Head at East Clandon, enjoyable food with emphasis on local ingredients from standard fare to more imaginative things, children's menu, good choice of wines, Hogs Back TEA and Surrey Hills Shere Drop, efficient helpful service; terrace and garden with picnic-sets, good play area, open all day weekends. *Recommended by Canon George Farran, Martin and Karen Wake*

VIRGINIA WATER TQ9768   GU25 4QF
Wheatsheaf
London Road; A30

Several linked areas in large 18th-c inn (Chef & Brewer), reasonably priced food, real ales; children welcome, garden tables (traffic noise), by wooded entry to lake area, bedrooms, open all day. *Recommended by Rosemary and Mike Fielder*

WALTON-ON-THAMES TQ1065   KT12 1JP
Ashley Park
Station Approach/Ashley Park Road

Comfortable well run Ember Inn with good reasonably priced food, interesting choice of well kept ales, competent friendly service, good atmosphere; open all day, bedrooms in adjoining Innkeepers Lodge. *Recommended by Ron and Sheila Corbett, Ian Phillips*

WEST CLANDON TQ0451   GU4 7ST
☆ ## Bulls Head
A247 SE of Woking

Comfortable, spotless and unchanging, based on 1540s timbered hall house, popular especially with older people lunchtime for good value hearty food from sandwiches up including home-made proper pies (no food Sun evening), friendly helpful staff, Surrey

Hills Shere Drop, good coffee, small lantern-lit beamed front bar with open fire and some stripped brick, old local prints and bric-a-brac, simple raised back inglenook dining area, games room with darts and pool; no credit cards; children and dogs on leads welcome, disabled access, good play area in neat garden, handy for Clandon Park, good walks. *Recommended by David Lowe, DWAJ, Phil Bryant*

☆ **WEST HORSLEY** TQ0853   KT24 6HR
Barley Mow
Off A246 Leatherhead—Guildford at Bell & Colvill garage roundabout; The Street

Welcoming tree-shaded traditional pub, low beams, mix of flagstones, bare boards and carpet, leather sofas, two log fires, well kept ales such as Fullers London Pride, Greene King IPA and Shepherd Neame Spitfire, decent wines, good value food (not Sun evening) including nice lunchtime sandwiches, daily papers, vintage and classic car pictures (may be an AC Cobra or Jaguar XK outside), comfortable softly lit barn-like dining room; unobtrusive piped music, TV; dogs and children welcome, picnic-sets in good-sized garden, open all day. *Recommended by Ian Phillips, David Lowe, Brian Dawes, David M Smith and others*

WEST HORSLEY TQ0752   KT24 6BG
King William IV
The Street

Comfortable and welcoming early 19th-c pub with very low-beamed open-plan rambling bar, enjoyable food from baguettes up here and in conservatory restaurant, decent choice of wines by the glass, well kept Courage and a guest, good coffee, log fire, board games; piped music; children and dogs welcome, good disabled access, small sunny garden with decking and lovely hanging baskets. *Recommended by Ian Phillips, John Branston*

WEYBRIDGE TQ0864   KT13 9BN
Jolly Farmer
Princes Road

Attractive little low-beamed local opposite picturesque cricket ground, friendly efficient service, good value pubby food from sandwiches up, well kept ales such as Gales, Ringwood, St Austell and Sharps, good choice of wines by the glass, toby jugs and interesting old photographs; may be loud live music weekends; front terrace and nice back garden. *Recommended by Ian Phillips, Hunter and Christine Wright*

WEYBRIDGE TQ0965   KT13 9RW
Oatlands Chaser
Oatlands Chase

Big attractively modernised building in quiet residential road, rambling bar with stylish modern décor, pastels and unusual wallpaper, glazed panels, flagstones and painted boards, feature central fireplace, carefully mismatched furnishings mainly laid out for the wide range of enjoyable all-day food including bargain set menu, Sun roasts and proper children's meals, good service, three well kept changing ales, good wine choice, newspapers; disabled access, lots of tables out at front (some under trees), 19 immaculate bedrooms, open all day. *Recommended by Katherine Tonks, Minda and Stanley Alexander, Ian Phillips*

☆ **WEYBRIDGE** TQ0765   KT13 8LP
Old Crown
Thames Street

Comfortably old-fashioned three-bar pub dating from the 16th c, good value traditional food (not Sun-Tues evenings) from sandwiches to fresh fish, well kept Courage, Greene King and Wells & Youngs, good choice of wines by the glass, friendly efficient service, family lounge and conservatory, coal-effect gas fire; may be sports TV in back bar with Lions RFC photographs, silent fruit machine; children welcome, secluded terrace, smokers' shelter, steps down to suntrap garden overlooking Wey/Thames confluence, mooring for small boats. *Recommended by DWAJ, Jeremy King, Ian Phillips, LM and others*

WEYBRIDGE TQ0865
KT13 9NX

☆ **Prince of Wales**

Cross Road/Anderson Road off Oatlands Drive

Civilised and attractively restored flower-decked pub, good value generous pubby food from baguettes up, Sun roasts, beers from Adnams, Fullers, Wells & Youngs and one brewed for the pub, ten wines by the glass, relaxed lunchtime atmosphere, friendly service, daily papers, log-effect fire, tribal mask collection, stripped-pine dining room down a couple of steps; big-screen TVs for major sports events; well behaved children welcome, small pretty garden at side and back. *Recommended by Jeremy King, Ian Phillips*

WINDLESHAM SU9264
GU20 6PD

Bee

School Road

Stylishly refurbished with emphasis on eating, enjoyable if pricey upscale food but good value weekday set lunches, morning coffee and pastries, Sun roasts, good choice of wines by the glass, four well kept real ales; picnic-sets on small front terrace and in nice back garden with play area. *Recommended by Rosemary and Mike Fielder*

WINDLESHAM SU9363
GU20 6BN

☆ **Half Moon**

Church Road

Enjoyable if not cheap pub, much extended and mainly laid for pubby food from sandwiches up, well kept ales such as Fullers London Pride, Hogs Back TEA, Ringwood Fortyniner, Timothy Taylors Landlord and Theakstons Old Peculier, Weston's farm cider, decent wines, plenty of children's drinks, cheerful enthusiastic young staff, log fires, World War II pictures and modern furnishings, attractive barn restaurant out along covered flagstoned walkway; piped music, silenced games machine; big tidy garden with two terraces and play area. *Recommended by Guy Consterdine, Ian Phillips, Dr Martin Owton, Bertil Nygren*

WITLEY SU9439
GU8 5PH

White Hart

Petworth Road

Picture-book beamed Tudor local now owned by Wells & Youngs, their ales kept well, friendly helpful staff, enjoyable home-made food, log fire in cosy panelled inglenook snug where George Eliot drank, bar and restaurant; tables on cobbled terrace and in garden, open all day Fri and Sat (Sun 12-6pm). *Recommended by Richard Williams*

WORPLESDON SU9854
GU3 3RN

☆ **Jolly Farmer**

Burdenshott Road, off A320 Guildford—Woking, not in village

Old pub in pleasant country setting, dark-beamed carpeted bar with small log fire, Fullers and Gales beers, stripped-brick dining extension with rugs on bare boards, generous traditional food (not cheap and they may ask to swipe your credit if running a tab); piped music; children and dogs welcome, garden tables under parasols, open all day.
Recommended by Mrs Ann Gray, Gerry and Rosemary Dobson, Ian Phillips

---

If a pub tries to make you leave a credit card behind the bar, be on your guard. The credit card firms and banks that issue them condemn this practice. After all, the publican who asks you to do this is in effect saying: 'I don't trust you'. Have you any more reason to trust his staff? If your card is used fraudulently while you have let it be kept out of your sight, the card company could say you've been negligent yourself – and refuse to make good your losses. So say that they can 'swipe' your card instead, but must hand it back to you. Please let us know if a pub does try to keep your card.

ALSO WORTH A VISIT IN SUSSEX

Besides the region's top pubs, we recommend the following. Do tell us
what you think of them: **feedback@goodguides.com**

ALFRISTON TQ5203   BN26 5UE
☆ Olde Smugglers
Waterloo Square

Charming 14th-c inn, low beams and panelling, brick floor, sofas by huge inglenook,
masses of bric-a-brac and smuggling mementoes, various nooks and crannies, welcoming
licensees, wide range of good value bar food from sandwiches to imaginative specials, well
kept Dark Star, Harveys and a guest like Sharps Doom Bar, real cider, good choice of wines
by the glass; piped music, can get crowded – lovely village draws many visitors; children
in eating area and conservatory, dogs welcome, tables on well planted back suntrap
terrace and lawn, three bedrooms, open all day. *Recommended by Bruce Bird, MP,
John Beeken, Phil and Jane Villiers, N R White*

AMBERLEY SO0313   BN18 9NL
☆ Black Horse
Off B2139

Pretty pub with character main bar (dogs allowed), plenty of pictures, high-backed settles
on flagstones, beams over serving counter festooned with sheep bells and shepherds'
tools, lounge with many antiques and artefacts, log fires in both bars and restaurant,
straightforward bar food (all day Sun) from sandwiches up, well kept Greene King and
Harveys, friendly service; piped music, children must be well behaved, nice sheltered
raised garden, open all day. *Recommended by Bea Games, Michael and Deborah Ethier*

AMBERLEY TQ0211   BN18 9LR
Bridge
B2139

Popular open-plan dining pub, comfortable and relaxed even when busy, with welcoming
staff, pleasant bar and separate two-room dining area, decent range of reasonably priced
food from good sandwiches up, well kept ales including Harveys; children and dogs
welcome, seats out in front, more tables in side garden, handy for station, open all day.
Recommended by N R White

AMBERLEY TQ0313   BN18 9NR
☆ Sportsmans
Crossgates; Rackham Road, off B2139

Warmly welcoming licensees and friendly efficient young staff, good fairly priced food
including popular Sun roasts, well kept Dark Star, Harveys and other local ales (Aug
festival), three bars including a brick-floored one with darts, great views over Amberley
Wild Brooks from pretty back conservatory restaurant and tables outside; dogs welcome,
good walks, neat up-to-date bedrooms. *Recommended by LM, Miss Hazel Orchard, N R White,
Bruce Bird, PL*

ANGMERING TQ0704   BN16 4AW
☆ Spotted Cow
High Street

Generally well liked food from sandwiches up and good friendly service, ales such as
Fullers, Greene King, Harveys, Sharps and Timothy Taylors kept well, decent wines by the
glass, smallish bar on left, long dining extension with large conservatory on right, two
fires, sporting caricatures, smuggling history; children welcome, disabled access, big
garden with boules and play area, lovely walk to Highdown hill fort, open all day Sun

(afternoon jazz, sometimes, then). *Recommended by CP, Pam Adsley, Terry Buckland, Tony and Wendy Hobden, PL*

ARDINGLY TQ3430   RH17 6TJ
☆ Gardeners Arms
B2028 2 miles N

Reliable reasonably priced pub food in olde-worlde linked rooms, Badger beers, pleasant efficient service, standing timbers and inglenooks, scrubbed pine on flagstones and broad boards, old local photographs, mural in back part, nice relaxed atmosphere; children and dogs welcome, disabled facilities, attractive wooden furniture on pretty terrace, lots of picnic-sets in side garden, opposite South of England show ground and handy for Borde Hill and Wakehurst Place, open all day. *Recommended by Colin and Louise English, Chris Bell, C and R Bromage*

ARLINGTON TQ5507   BN26 6SJ
☆ Old Oak
Caneheath; off A22 or A27 NW of Polegate

17th-c former almshouse with open-plan L-shaped bar, beams, log fires and comfortable seating, Harveys and a guest tapped from the cask, traditional bar food (all day weekends), toad in the hole played here; piped music; children and dogs welcome, seats in quiet garden, walks in nearby Abbot's Wood nature reserve, open all day. *Recommended by anon*

ARLINGTON TQ5407   BN26 6RX
Yew Tree
Off A22 near Hailsham, or A27 W of Polegate

Neatly modernised Victorian village pub popular for its wide range of good value generous home-made food (booking advised), well kept Harveys Best and decent wines, prompt friendly service even when busy, log fires, hop-covered beams and old local photographs, darts in thriving bare-boards bar, plush lounge, comfortable conservatory; children welcome, nice big garden with play area, paddock with farm animals, good walks. *Recommended by John Beeken, Pam Adsley, Della Heath*

ARUNDEL TQ0208   BN18 9PB
☆ Black Rabbit
Mill Road, Offham; keep on and don't give up!

Comfortably refurbished riverside pub well organised for families and can get very busy, lovely spot near wildfowl reserve with timeless views of water meadows and castle; long bar with eating areas at either end, enjoyable fairly priced food all day from baguettes up, mixed recent reports on service, well kept Badger ales, several decent wines by the glass, log fires, newspapers; piped music; dogs welcome, covered tables and pretty hanging baskets out at front, terrace across road overlooking river, play area, boat trips and good walks, open all day. *Recommended by John Beeken, Colin McKerrow, N R White, David H T Dimock, Ann and Colin Hunt, Michael Butler and others*

ARUNDEL TQ0107   BN18 9AG
☆ Swan
High Street

Smart but comfortably relaxed open-plan L-shaped bar with attractive woodwork and matching fittings, friendly efficient young staff, well kept Fullers ales, good tea and coffee, good value enjoyable food from baguettes up, sporting bric-a-brac and old photographs, beaten brass former inn sign on wall, fire, restaurant, live jazz (third Sun of month from 5pm); 15 bedrooms, no car park, open all day. *Recommended by Tony and Wendy Hobden, Jestyn Phillips, Ann and Colin Hunt, Phil and Jane Villiers*

There are report forms at the back of the book.

ARUNDEL TQ0107   BN18 9JG
White Hart
Queen Street

Old tile-hung inn with several roomy linked areas, wood floors and stripped-pine tables, some contemporary touches, well kept Harveys ales, pubby food from short chalked menu, chatty landlord; covered terrace tables at back, bedrooms. *Recommended by Joan and Michel Hooper-Immins*

ASHURST TQ1816   BN44 3AP
☆ Fountain
B2135 S of Partridge Green

Attractive well run 16th-c country local with fine old flagstones, rustic tap room on right with some antique polished trestle tables and housekeeper's chairs by inglenook log fire, second inglenook in opened-up heavy-beamed snug, good well priced food including pub staples, Fullers, Harveys and two guests, folk music (second Weds of month), regular vintage car club meetings; no under-10s; dogs welcome, pretty garden with duck pond (pay ahead if you eat out here), open all day. *Recommended by John Redfern*

BALCOMBE TQ3033   RH17 6QD
Cowdray Arms
London Road (B2036/B2110 N of village)

Bright and airy main-road pub with good blackboard food using local suppliers, well kept Greene King and a guest, good value wines by the glass, comfortable settees in L-shaped bar, darts, conservatory restaurant; children and dogs welcome, large garden. *Recommended by David Zackheim*

BALLS CROSS SU9826   GU28 9JP
☆ Stag
Village signed off A283 at N edge of Petworth

Unchanging and cheery 17th-c country pub with friendly staff, fishing rods and country knick-knacks, tiny flagstoned bar with log fire in huge inglenook, a few seats and bar stools, Badger beers, summer cider and several wines by the glass, second tiny room and appealing old-fashioned restaurant with horsey pictures, pubby food (not Sun evening), bar skittles, darts and board games in separate carpeted room; veteran outside lavatories; well behaved children allowed away from main bar, dogs welcome, seats in front under parasols, more in good-sized back garden divided by shrubbery, bedrooms. *Recommended by John Robertson, Gerry and Rosemary Dobson, the Didler, N R White*

BARNS GREEN TQ1227   RH13 0PS
Queens Head
Chapel Road

Traditional welcoming village pub, decent choice of home-made pub food from baguettes up and some good local real ales, reasonable prices; children welcome, tables out at front, garden behind with play area. *Recommended by Peter Martin*

BEPTON SU8620   GU29 0LR
Country Inn
Severals Road

Old-fashioned friendly country local, well kept Banks's, Fullers and Wells & Youngs, good value food, heavy beams, stripped brickwork and log fire, darts-playing regulars; children welcome, tables out at front and in big garden with shady trees and play area, quiet spot. *Recommended by John Beeken, Tony and Wendy Hobden*

If you have to cancel a reservation for a bedroom or restaurant, please telephone or write to warn them. You may lose your deposit if you've paid one.

BERWICK TQ5105   BN26 6SP
☆ **Cricketers Arms**
Lower Road, S of A27

Charming local with three small unpretentious bars, huge supporting beam in each low
ceiling, simple country furnishings on quarry tiles, cricketing pastels and bats, two log
fires, well kept Harveys tapped from the cask, country wines, good coffee, tasty bar food
(all day weekends and summer weekdays), old Sussex coin game – toad in the hole;
children in family room only, dogs welcome, delightful cottagey front garden with picnic-
sets amongst small brick paths, more seats behind, Bloomsbury Group wall paintings in
nearby church, good South Downs walks, open all day in summer. *Recommended by*
Nick Lawless, Tony and Shirley Albert, Andrea Rampley, Conor McGaughey, the Didler, Michael and
Margaret Cross and others

BEXHILL TQ7208   TN39 4JE
Denbigh
Little Common Road (A259 towards Polegate)

Friendly local with enjoyable reasonably priced fresh food, well kept Harveys Best, decent
wine, cheery efficient service; enclosed side garden. *Recommended by MP, Christopher Turner,*
Sue Addison

BLACKBOYS TQ5220   TN22 5LG
☆ **Blackboys Inn**
B2192, S edge of village

Attractive old weatherboarded pub with bustling beamed locals' bar, lots of bric-a-brac
here and in main parquet-floored bar on right with beams, timbers and old photos on red
walls, log fire, similarly furnished restaurant; Harveys and guests, several wines by the
glass, good choice of food (all day weekends) using some own-grown produce, board
games; piped music; children and dogs welcome, contemporary furniture on terrace, more
seats under cover by sizeable pond, pretty gazebo on side lawn, Vanguard Way passes pub
and Wealdway is close by, Woodland Trust opposite, bedrooms, open all day (till 1am Fri,
Sat). *Recommended by Dr Martin Owton, John Atkins, the Didler*

BODLE STREET GREEN TQ6514   BN27 4RE
White Horse
Off A271 at Windmill Hill

Roomy country pub with friendly landlord, enjoyable homely food at varnished tables, well
kept Harveys, open fires; some tables outside. *Recommended by R and S Bentley, Merul Patel*

BOLNEY TQ2623   RH17 5RL
Bolney Stage
London Road, off old A23 just N of A272

Sizeable well refurbished 16th-c timbered dining pub, enjoyable varied food all day
including sandwiches, ales such as Dark Star, Fullers and Harveys, good choice of wines
by the glass, low beams and polished flagstones, nice mix of old furniture, woodburner
and big two-way log fire; children welcome, dogs in main bar, disabled facilities, tables on
terrace and lawn, play area, handy for Sheffield Park and Bluebell Railway. *Recommended by*
John Redfern

BOLNEY TQ2622   RH17 5QW
Eight Bells
The Street

Welcoming village pub with wide food choice from ciabattas and light dishes to enjoyable
specials, bargain OAP lunch Tues, Weds, well kept Harveys, Hop Back Summer Lightning
and an ale brewed for the pub, local wines from Bookers vineyard, brick-floor bar with
eight handbells suspended from ceiling, good log fire, timbered dining extension,
exemplary lavatories; tables under big umbrellas on outside decking with neatly lit steps,
bedrooms. *Recommended by Tony and Wendy Hobden, John Beeken*

BOSHAM SU8003   PO18 8LS
☆ Anchor Bleu
High Street

Waterside inn overlooking Chichester Harbour, two simple bars with some beams in low ochre ceilings, worn flagstones and exposed timbered brickwork, lots of nautical bric-a-brac, robust, simple furniture, up to six real ales and popular bar food; children and dogs welcome, seats on back terrace looking out over ducks and boats on sheltered inlet, massive wheel-operated bulkhead door wards off high tides, church up lane figures in Bayeux Tapestry, village and shore are worth exploring, open all day in summer.
Recommended by Terry and Nickie Williams, Val and Alan Green, Ann and Colin Hunt, Pam Adsley, Maureen and Keith Gimson and others

BREDE TQ8218   TN31 6EJ
Red Lion
A28 opposite church

Relaxed beamed village pub with plain tables and chairs on bare boards, candles, inglenook log fire, tasty reasonably priced food including local fish, changing ales such as Edge, Old Dairy and Wells & Youngs, friendly helpful staff, pub sheepdog called Billy; a few picnic-sets out at front, garden behind, narrow entrance to car park, open all day weekends. *Recommended by Mick B, Carol Wells, Peter Meister*

BRIGHTON TQ3104   BN1 4AD
☆ Basketmakers Arms
Gloucester Road – the E end, near Cheltenham Place; off Marlborough Place (A23) via Gloucester Street

Cheerful bustling backstreet local with eight changing ales, decent wines by the glass, over 100 malt whiskies and quite a choice of spirits, enjoyable very good value bar food all day (till 6pm weekends), two small low-ceilinged rooms, lots of interesting old tins, cigarette cards on one beam, whisky labels on another, and beermats, old advertisements, photographs and posters; piped music; children welcome till 8pm, dogs on leads, a few pavement tables, open all day (till midnight Fri, Sat). *Recommended by Conor McGaughey, Jeremy King, S T W Norton, the Didler, Colin Gooch, Peter Meister and others*

BRIGHTON TQ3104   BN1 1UF
Colonnade
New Road, off North Street; by Theatre Royal

Small richly restored Edwardian bar, with red plush banquettes, velvet swags, shining brass and mahogany, gleaming mirrors, interesting pre-war playbills and signed theatrical photographs, well kept Fullers London Pride and Harveys Best, lots of lagers, bar snacks, daily papers; tiny front terrace overlooking Pavilion gardens. *Recommended by Val and Alan Green, Jeremy King*

BRIGHTON TQ3104   BN1 1ND
☆ Cricketers
Black Lion Street

Cheerful and genuine town pub, friendly bustle at busy times, good relaxed atmosphere when quieter, cosy and darkly Victorian with lots of interesting bric-a-brac – even a stuffed bear; attentive service, well kept Fullers, Greene King, Harveys and Sharps tapped from the cask, good coffee, well priced pubby food (till 7.30pm weekends) from sandwiches up in covered former stables courtyard and upstairs bar, restaurant (where children allowed); piped and some live music; tall tables out in front, open all day. *Recommended by Dr and Mrs A K Clarke, Michael Butler, Ann and Colin Hunt, Nigel and Jean Eames*

BRIGHTON TQ3104   BN1 1HJ
Druids Head
Brighton Place

Brick and flint pub dating from the 16th c with smuggling history, well kept Harveys and guests, wide choice of enjoyable good value food; children welcome till 6pm, seats out in front under hanging baskets, open all day. *Recommended by Colin Gooch*

BRIGHTON TQ3004
BN1 3PB
☆ ## Evening Star
Surrey Street

Popular chatty drinkers' pub with up to four good Dark Star ales (originally brewed here), lots of changing guest beers including continentals (in bottles too), farm ciders and perries, country wines, lunchtime baguettes, friendly staff coping well when busy, simple pale wood furniture on bare boards, nice mix of customers; unobtrusive piped music, some live; pavement tables, open all day. *Recommended by the Didler, N R White, Peter Meister, Paul Davis*

BRIGHTON TQ3105
BN2 9UA
☆ ## Greys
Southover Street, off A270 Lewes Road opposite The Level (public park)

Certainly not a standard pub but does have basic simple furnishings on bare boards and flagstones, some wood panelling and a flame-effect stove, bar on right liked by regulars, dining side on left with flowers and candles on tables, Harveys and Timothy Taylors Landlord, several belgian bottled beers, carefully chosen wines, good food (not Sun evening, Mon or Fri) using local ingredients, live music Mon evening (tickets only), posters and flyers from previous performers on stair wall; no children; dogs in bar, seats under parasols on heated terrace, almost no parking on this steep lane or in nearby streets, open from 4pm, all day weekends. *Recommended by anon*

BRIGHTON TQ3103
BN2 1JN
Hand in Hand
Upper St James's Street, Kemptown

Brighton's smallest pub (can get crowded) brewing its own unusual Kemptown ales, also five weekly changing guests, plenty of bottled beers and Weston's cider, hot pies and sausage rolls, cockles and mussels Fri, cheerful service, dim-lit bar with tie collection and newspaper pages all over walls, photographs including Victorian nudes on ceiling, colourful mix of customers; veteran fruit machine, interesting piped music, live jazz Sun; open all day. *Recommended by Eddie Edwards*

BRIGHTON TQ3004
BN1 1AD
Pub du Vin
Ship Street

Next to Hotel du Vin, long and narrow with comfortable wall seating one end, soft lighting, local photographs, stripped boards, five well kept ales including Dark Star and Harveys from ornate pewter bar counter, good choice of wines by the glass, friendly helpful staff, enjoyable pubby food, modern grey leather-seated bar chairs and light oak tables, flame-effect fire, small cosy coir-carpeted room opposite with squashy black armchairs and sofas; marvellous original marble urinals worth a look; 11 comfortable bedrooms. *Recommended by Dr and Mrs A K Clarke, M E and F J Thomasson, Jeremy King*

BRIGHTON TQ3004
BN1 1AH
Victory
Duke Street

Bustling Lanes' corner local with lovely green-tiled façade and etched windows, long benches and medley of chairs and tables on bare boards, open fire in cosy snug, upstairs area, local ales such as Dark Star, real cider, generous food including some unusual things like zebra, live music, free wi-fi; children till 8pm, some pavement and courtyard tables, open all day (till 2am Fri, Sat). *Recommended by Val and Alan Green*

Tipping is not normal for bar meals, and not usually expected.

BURPHAM TQ0308   BN18 9RR
☆ George & Dragon
Off A27 near Warningcamp

Main emphasis in this busy 17th-c dining pub is on interesting modern food and the front part is restaurant, small area for drinkers, Arundel and Sharps ales, efficient service; children welcome, dogs in bar, some picnic-sets out in front, hilltop village and short walk from pub gives splendid views down to Arundel Castle and river. *Recommended by Karen Eliot, CP, Guy Vowles, Di and Mike Gillam, Tony Middis, Ben Samways and others*

BYWORTH SU9821   GU28 0HL
☆ Black Horse
Off A283

Popular and chatty country pub with smart simply furnished bar, pews and scrubbed tables on bare boards, pictures and old photographs, daily papers and open fires, ales such as Dark Star, Flowerpots, Langham and Wells & Youngs, well liked food (not winter Sun evening) from light lunchtime dishes up, children's menu, nooks and crannies in back restaurant, spiral staircase to a heavily beamed function room, games room with pool; dogs allowed in bar, attractive garden with tables on steep grassy terraces, lovely Downs' views, open all day. *Recommended by Bruce Bird, the Didler, Tony and Wendy Hobden, Ann and Colin Hunt*

CHAILEY TQ3919   BN8 4DA
☆ Five Bells
A275, 9 miles N of Lewes

Attractive rambling roadside pub, spacious and interesting, with enjoyable food putting unusual touches to good local and organic ingredients, well kept Harveys and Timothy Taylors Landlord, decent wine choice, young helpful staff, lots of different rooms and alcoves leading from low-beamed central bar with fine old brick floor, brick walls, inglenook, leather sofas and settles, live jazz Fri; piped music; pretty garden front and side with picnic-sets, closed Mon. *Recommended by John Beeken*

CHAILEY TQ3919   BN8 4BD
Horns Lodge
A275

Traditional former coaching inn, heavily timbered inside, with settles, horsebrasses and rural prints, log fires at each end of longish front bar, well kept Harveys and guests such as Dark Star and Dorking, good range of fairly priced bar food (not Tues) from sandwiches up, obliging staff, brick-floored restaurant, games room with darts and bar billiards, cribbage, dominoes and board games, too; piped music; children and dogs welcome, tables in garden with sandpit, bedrooms, open all day weekends. *Recommended by John Beeken, Tony and Wendy Hobden*

CHICHESTER SU8604   PO19 1LP
Old Cross
North Street

Refurbished open-plan pub in partly 16th-c building, bargain pubby food including pre-theatre weekday evening deals, friendly helpful staff, Ringwood Best and Wells & Youngs Bombardier from island bar, log fires. *Recommended by Alec Summers, Ann and Colin Hunt*

CHIDDINGLY TQ5414   BN8 6HE
☆ Six Bells
Village signed off A22 Uckfield—Hailsham

Cheerful unpretentious village local with long-serving licensees and plenty of loyal regulars, bars with shabby charm, simple seats, bric-a-brac, posters and pictures, log fires, more space in sensitive extension, well kept Courage, Harveys and a guest beer, well liked low-priced bar food (all day Fri-Sun), weekend live music; seats at back beyond goldfish pond, boules, monthly vintage car meetings, church opposite with interesting Jefferay monument, pleasant area for walks, open all day weekends. *Recommended by John Beeken, Mike Horgan, Di Wright, B and M Kendall, Nick Lawless, Tom Wexler*

CHILGROVE SU8116   PO18 9JZ

☆ **Royal Oak**

Off B2141 Petersfield—Chichester, signed Hooksway

Chatty long-serving licensee at this unchanging old country pub, popular with walkers and locals; two simple cosy bars, plain kitchen tables and chairs, log fires, Exmoor, Gales, Sharps and a guest beer, simple affordable food, cottagey dining room with woodburner, straightforward family room, shut the box; piped music, but live music second and last Fri of month; dogs welcome in bar, plenty of picnic-sets in big pretty garden, near South Downs Way, closed Sun evening, Mon and possibly from mid-Oct to mid-Nov. *Recommended by Ann and Colin Hunt, J A Snell*

CLIMPING SU9902   BN17 5RU

Oystercatcher

A259/B2233

Roomy part-thatched popular Vintage Inn dining pub, olde-worlde décor, friendly well trained young staff, wide choice of reasonably priced traditional food all day from sandwiches and starters doubling as light dishes up, good value set menu too, well kept Harveys Best, Shepherd Neame Spitfire and Timothy Taylors Landlord, good wines by the glass, nicely served coffee, log fires; disabled lavatories, picnic-sets in pleasant front garden (some traffic noise). *Recommended by David H T Dimock, N J Roberts, Graham Lewis*

COLEMANS HATCH TQ4533   TN7 4EJ

☆ **Hatch**

Signed off B2026, or off B2110 opposite church

Quaint and attractive little weatherboarded Ashdown Forest pub dating from 1430, big log fire in quickly filling beamed bar, small back dining room with another fire, very wide choice of good generous home-made food, well kept Harveys, Larkins and one or two guest beers, friendly quick young staff, good mix of customers including families and dogs; not much parking so get there early; picnic-sets on front terrace and in beautifully kept big garden, open all day Sat, Sun. *Recommended by Vernon Rowe, the Didler, Laurence Smith, Christian Mole, Bruce Bird*

COMPTON SU7714   PO18 9HA

Coach & Horses

B2146 S of Petersfield

Welcoming 17th-c two-bar local in pleasant village not far from Uppark (NT), pine shutters and panelling, woodburner, three or four interesting changing ales, enjoyable food from landlord/chef including two-for-one steak night Weds, bar billiards; children and dogs welcome, tables out by village square, good surrounding walks. *Recommended by Geoff and Linda Payne*

COOLHAM TQ1423   RH13 8GE

☆ **George & Dragon**

Dragons Green, Dragons Lane; pub signed off A272

Tile-hung cottage with cosy chatty bar, massive unusually low black beams (see if you can decide whether the date cut into one is 1677 or 1577), timbered walls, simple chairs and rustic stools, roaring log fire in big inglenook, Badger beers and decent pub food served by friendly staff, smaller back bar, separate restaurant; piped music – live music last Sun of month; children and dogs welcome, picnic-sets in pretty orchard garden, open all day weekends (till 8pm Sun). *Recommended by Philip and Cheryl Hill, Mrs J Ekins-Daukes, Ian Phillips*

COWBEECH TQ6114   BN27 4JQ
☆ **Merrie Harriers**
Off A271

White clapboarded village local, beamed public bar with inglenook log fire, high-backed
settle and mixed tables and chairs, old local photographs, carpeted dining lounge, well
kept Harveys Best and a guest, good food from nice bar snacks up, friendly service, brick-
walled back restaurant; a few picnic-sets out in front, rustic seats in terraced garden with
country views. *Recommended by Laurence Smith, Peter Meister, Tobias Sheppard, Gary Neate*

CROWBOROUGH TQ5130   TN6 1BB
Blue Anchor
Beacon Road (A26)

Improved and continuing well under brother licensees, well kept Shepherd Neame ales,
enjoyable fairly priced home-made food using local suppliers, friendly service; children
welcome, dogs in bar, big garden with terrace and play area, open all day. *Recommended by
Peter Meister, SRK*

CROWBOROUGH TQ5329   TN6 2NF
Wheatsheaf
Off Mount Pleasant

Friendly three-room 18th-c Harveys pub with their full range, reasonably priced home-
made food (not Fri-Sun evenings or Mon), open fires, beer and music festivals, other
events like leek and dog shows; side garden with seats under large tree, bedrooms in
adjacent cottage, open all day. *Recommended by Scott Walters*

CUCKFIELD TQ3025   RH17 5BS
Rose & Crown
London Road

17th-c beamed and panelled pub under new ownership, comfortably refurbished with
emphasis on spanish tapas, decent wines, well kept Harveys; children welcome, tables out
in front and in garden behind, open all day, closed Sun evening. *Recommended by
Terry Buckland, Mitch Clarke*

CUCKFIELD TQ3024   RH17 5JX
Talbot
High Street

Thriving under new management, light airy feel, imaginative food in bar and upstairs
restaurant, real ales, good service. *Recommended by Terry Buckland*

DALLINGTON TQ6619   TN21 9LB
☆ **Swan**
Woods Corner, B2096 E

Popular local with cheerful chatty atmosphere, well kept Harveys, decent wines by the
glass, enjoyable pubby food including deals, takeaway fish and chips (Tues), efficient
service, bare-boards bar divided by standing timbers, woodburner, mixed furniture
including cushioned settle and high-backed pew, candles in bottles and fresh flowers,
simple back restaurant with far-reaching views to the coast; piped music; steps down to
lavatories and smallish back garden. *Recommended by N R White, Mike and Eleanor Anderson*

DELL QUAY SU8302   PO20 7EE
Crown & Anchor
Off A286 S of Chichester – look out for small sign

Modernised 19th/20th-c beamed pub in splendid spot overlooking Chichester Harbour –
best at high tide and quiet times, can be packed on sunny days; comfortable bow-
windowed lounge bar, panelled public bar (dogs welcome), two log fires, lots of wines by
the glass, well kept Wells & Youngs ales and a guest such as Butcombe, enjoyable food all
day, friendly service; large terrace, nice walks. *Recommended by Ann and Colin Hunt, Jim and
Frances Gowers, Miss A E Dare, N J Roberts, J A Snell, Martin and Karen Wake*

DENTON TQ4502   BN9 0QB
☆ **Flying Fish**
Denton Road

Attractive 17th-c flint village pub by South Downs Way, floor tiles throughout, simple main
bar, tiny end room with facing sofas, nice middle room with little log fire by built-in wall
seats, long cushioned pews and mixed dining chairs, modern paintings, high-ceilinged
end dining room, Shepherd Neame ales, decent wines by the glass, fish and game and
more pubby food cooked well by french chef/landlord, reasonable prices, friendly service;
picnic-sets in front and on long back decking looking up to sloping garden, good
bedrooms. *Recommended by John Beeken, the Didler, Michael Rugman*

DEVILS DYKE TQ2511   BN1 8YJ
Devils Dyke
Devils Dyke Road

Vintage Inn set alone on Downs above Brighton and worth visiting for the spectacular
views night and day, their usual food, ales such as Harveys Best, Shepherd Neame Spitfire
and Timothy Taylors Landlord; children welcome, tables outside, NT pay car park, open all
day. *Recommended by Colin Gooch*

DITCHLING TQ3215   BN6 8TA
☆ **Bull**
High Street (B2112)

Handsome rambling old building, beams, old wooden furniture on bare boards, fire, well
kept Harveys, Timothy Taylors Landlord and two guests, home-made food from
sandwiches up including good Sun roasts, nicely furnished dining rooms with mellow
décor and candles, snug area with chesterfields; piped music – live folk music last Sun of
month; children welcome, dogs in bar, disabled access, attractive big garden and suntrap
terrace, barbecue, four nice bedrooms, good breakfast, open all day. *Recommended by
Nick Lawless*

EAST DEAN SU9012   PO18 0JG
☆ **Star & Garter**
Village signed with Charlton off A286 in Singleton; also signed off A285

Emphasis very much on good fresh seafood (other choices too) in this well run airy dining
pub, attractively furnished bar and restaurant with stripped panelling, exposed brickwork
and oak floors, furnishings from sturdy stripped tables and country kitchen chairs
through chunky modern to some antique carved settles, Arundel and guests tapped from
the cask, several wines by the glass, friendly young staff, daily papers; piped music;
children welcome, dogs in bar, teak furniture on heated terrace, smokers' shelter, steps
down to walled lawn with picnic-sets, peaceful village green position and near South
Downs Way, bedrooms, open all day weekends (food all day then too).
*Recommended by Nick Lawless, CP, Maureen and Keith Gimson, Henry Midwinter, Graeme Manson,
Christopher Turner and others*

EAST GRINSTEAD TQ3936   RH19 4AT
☆ **Old Mill**
Dunnings Road, S towards Saint Hill

Interesting 16th-c mill cottage over stream reworked as spacious informal Whiting &
Hammond dining pub; lots of panelling, old photographs and pictures, carpeted main
dining area with mix of old tables (each with church candle), steps down to ancient very
low-ceilinged part with fine timbers and inglenook woodburner, sizeable bar with long
curved counter and bright plush stools, library dining area off, enjoyable hearty fresh food
(all day), good choice of wines by the glass, Harveys ales including seasonal ones, friendly
efficient service; piped music; children welcome, picnic-sets in front garden, covered
decking next to working waterwheel, handy for Standen (NT). *Recommended by
N J Roberts, Andrew Hughes, Laurence Evans*

EAST HOATHLY TQ5216   BN8 6DR

☆ **Kings Head**

High Street/Mill Lane

Well kept 1648 ales (brewed here) and Harveys Best in long comfortably worn-in open-plan bar, some dark panelling and stripped brick, upholidaystered settles, old local photographs, log fire, wide choice of enjoyable sensibly priced hearty food, friendly helpful service, daily papers, restaurant; TV; garden up steps behind. *Recommended by John Beeken*

EAST LAVANT SU8608   PO18 0AX

☆ **Royal Oak**

Pook Lane, off A286

Restauranty dining pub in pretty Georgian house, really good imaginative food, home-baked breads, good wine list, low beams and crooked timbers, stripped brickwork, scrubbed tables and church candles, log fires, small drinking area with wall seats and sofas, ales such as Sharps and Skinners tapped from the cask; no dogs; tables on flagstoned front terrace with far-reaching views, comfortable bedrooms and self-catering cottages, open all day. *Recommended by Miss A E Dare, R and M Thomas, John Chambers*

EAST PRESTON TQ0701   BN16 1PD

Sea View

Sea Road

Hidden-away comfortable seaside pub, enjoyable good value home-made food (not Sun, Mon evenings), children's menu and OAP lunches (Mon, Tues), well kept ales including Arundel Castle, neat friendly staff; nice garden, limited parking, bedrooms. *Recommended by Tony and Wendy Hobden*

EASTBOURNE TV6199   BN22 7NE

Marine

Seaside Road (A259)

Spacious comfortable pub near seafront run by welcoming long-serving licensees, panelled bar, lounge with sofas and tub chairs, log fire, well kept ales such as Fullers London Pride and Wychwood Hobgoblin, good choice of wines and brandies, enjoyable pubby food from sandwiches up, back conservatory; children welcome. *Recommended by John Atkins, John Walker, Jon Baker, Matt Colson*

EASTERGATE SU9405   PO20 3UT

Wilkes Head

Just off A29 Fontwell—Bognor; Church Lane

Small friendly two-bar local with dining extension, flagstones and inglenook log fire, enjoyable reasonably priced food from sandwiches up, real ales such as Castle Rock Harvest Pale and Hop Back Summer Lightning, pleasant service, darts; tables in big garden with covered smokers' area, open all day weekends. *Recommended by Tony and Wendy Hobden*

ELSTED SU8320   GU29 0JT

Elsted Inn

Elsted Marsh

New welcoming licensees at this attractive country pub, enjoyable food from shortish menu, real ales such as Ballards, Otter and Sharps, two log fires, nice country furniture, old Goodwood racing photos (both horses and cars), dining area at back; plenty of seating in lovely enclosed Downs-view garden with big terrace, bedrooms, has been open all day weekends. *Recommended by Geoff and Linda Payne*

ELSTED SU8119   GU29 0JY

☆ **Three Horseshoes**

Village signed from B2141 Chichester—Petersfield; from A272 about 2 miles W of Midhurst, turn left heading W

A congenial bustle at this pretty white-painted old pub, beamed rooms, log fires and candlelight, ancient flooring, antique furnishings, fresh flowers and attractive prints and photographs, four changing ales tapped from the cask, summer cider, often interesting bar food including lovely puddings; well behaved children allowed, dogs in bar, delightful flowering garden with plenty of seats and fine views of South Downs, good surrounding walks. *Recommended by Tony and Jill Radnor, Karen Eliot, Henry Midwinter, D and J Ashdown, John Beeken and others*

ERIDGE STATION TQ5434   TN3 9LE

☆ **Huntsman**

Signed off A26 S of Eridge Green

Country local with two opened-up rooms, pubby furniture on bare boards, hunting pictures, ales from Badger and Gribble, over two dozen wines by the glass, popular bar food (not Sun evening, Mon) using some own-grown produce, friendly staff; children and dogs welcome, picnic-sets and heaters on decking, outside bar, more seats on lawn among weeping willows, parking can be difficult weekdays (lots of commuters cars), open all day weekends, closed Mon lunchtime. *Recommended by Heather and Dick Martin, Mrs J Ekins-Daukes, B J Harding, Peter Meister, N R White, Alan Franck and others*

FAIRWARP TQ4626   TN22 3BP

Foresters Arms

B2026

Chatty Ashdown Forest local handy for Vanguard Way and Weald Way, comfortable lounge bar, wide choice of enjoyable well priced food, friendly staff, Badger ales, farm cider, woodburner; piped music; children and dogs welcome, tables out on terrace and in garden, play area on small village green opposite. *Recommended by Mrs Diana Courtney*

FERNHURST SU9028   GU27 3HY

Red Lion

The Green, off A286 via Church Lane

Friendly wisteria-covered 16th-c pub tucked quietly away by green and cricket pitch near church, heavy beams and timbers, attractive furnishings, food from interesting sandwiches and snacks up, well kept Fullers ales and a guest, good wines, cheerful helpful service, restaurant; children welcome, pretty gardens front and back, open all day Sun. *Recommended by Chris Harrington, Ann and Colin Hunt*

FERRING TQ0903   BN12 6QY

Henty Arms

Ferring Lane

Six well kept changing ales (often an unusual one like Sadlers Wee Shimmy), generous attractively priced food (can get busy so best to book), breakfast from 9am Tues-Fri, neat friendly staff, opened-up lounge/dining area, log fire, separate bar with games and TV; garden tables. *Recommended by Tony and Wendy Hobden*

FINDON TQ1208   BN14 0TA

Gun

High Street

Low-beamed pub with friendly atmosphere, good fairly priced food (not Sun evening, Mon), well kept beers; children welcome, sheltered garden, pretty village below Cissbury Ring. *Recommended by Gerald and Gabrielle Culliford*

FINDON TQ1208   BN14 0TE
Village House
High Street; off A24 N of Worthing

Attractive converted 16th-c coach house, panelling, pictures and big open fire in large L-shaped bar, restaurant beyond, enjoyable fresh pubby food (not Sun evening) including blackboard specials and bargains for two, Arundel Gold, Gales HSB, Fullers London Pride and Harveys Best, fortnightly jazz, monthly quiz; small attractive walled garden, six comfortable bedrooms, handy for Cissbury Ring and downland walks. *Recommended by Trish McManus, Tony and Wendy Hobden*

FIRLE TQ4607   BN8 6NS
☆ ## Ram
Village signed off A27 Lewes—Polegate

Refurbished 16th-c village pub geared for dining but welcoming drinkers, popular if not particuarly cheap restaurany food including good Sun roasts, well kept Harveys with guests such as Dark Star and Sharps, real cider, friendly staff, three main areas with log fires, rustic furniture on wood floors, soft lighting; children and dogs welcome, picnic-sets out in front, big walled garden behind with fruit trees, play area, good walks, four stylish bedrooms, open all day. *Recommended by J A Snell, Alan Franck, N R White*

FISHBOURNE SU8304   PO19 3JP
☆ ## Bulls Head
Fishbourne Road (A259 Chichester—Emsworth)

Thoroughly traditional, with friendly staff, well kept Fullers/Gales ales, popular good value food (not Sun evening) changing daily, copper pans on black beams, some stripped brick and panelling, good log fire, daily papers, exemplary lavatories; unobtrusive piped music; children welcome, tables on heated covered deck, four bedrooms in former skittles alley. *Recommended by Terry and Nickie Williams, John Beeken, David H T Dimock, Miss A E Dare*

FLETCHING TQ4223   TN22 3ST
Rose & Crown
High Street

Well run 16th-c beamed village pub, inglenook log fire and comfortable wall banquettes in carpeted bar, wide range of enjoyable fairly priced home-made food from baguettes to generous Sun roasts, small restaurant, good attentive service, Harveys and guests; dogs welcome, tables in pretty garden, three bedrooms, open all day. *Recommended by C and R Bromage, Jason Bunce*

FULKING TQ2411   BN5 9LU
Shepherd & Dog
Off A281 N of Brighton, via Poynings

Old bay-windowed pub in beautiful spot below Downs, beams, panelling and inglenook, ales such as Dark Star, food from baguettes up; terrace and pretty streamside garden with well used picnic-sets, straightforward climb to Devils Dyke. *Recommended by Tim Loryman, John Redfern, Martin and Karen Wake*

FUNTINGTON SU7908   PO18 9LL
Fox & Hounds
Common Road (B2146)

Welcoming beamed family pub with cottagey rooms and huge log fire, wide choice of enjoyable food including popular Sun carvery (best to book weekends), good service, well kept Badger ales, reasonably priced wines and nice coffee, comfortable dining extension; garden behind, pair of inn signs – one a pack of hounds, the other a family of foxes. *Recommended by Terry and Nickie Williams, Ann and Colin Hunt*

GLYNDE TQ4508 BN8 6SS

☆ **Trevor Arms**

Over railway bridge S of village

Brick and flint village pub, impressive dining room with mix of high-backed settles, pews and cushioned dining chairs around mixed tables, carpeted middle room with Glyndebourne pictures leading to snug bar with small fireplace and fine downland views, reasonably priced food including OAP weekday lunch deals, well kept Harveys ales, friendly service, locals' bar with parquet flooring, panelled dado, old photographs of the pub, darts and toad in the hole; big garden with rows of picnic-sets and Downs backdrop, popular with walkers, railway station next door, open all day. *Recommended by John Beeken*

HAMMERPOT TQ0605 BN16 4EU

☆ **Woodmans Arms**

On N (eastbound) side of A27

Well kept pretty thatched pub rebuilt after 2004 fire, beams and timbers, good choice of enjoyable food from sandwiches up (smaller helpings available), Fullers/Gales and a guest beer, neat polite staff, woodburner in inglenook; no dogs inside; children welcome if eating, garden tables, open all day, closed Sun evening. *Recommended by Jo Connelly, Ann and Colin Hunt, Tony and Wendy Hobden*

HEATHFIELD TQ5920 TN21 9AH

☆ **Star**

Church Street, Old Heathfield, off A265/B2096 E

Good mix of locals and visitors in this characterful country pub by village church, two main bar rooms (one more set up for eating) with heavy beams, built-in settles and window seats, panelling, inglenook log fire in one, woodburner in other, well kept Harveys, Shepherd Neame and a guest, decent wines by the glass, good choice of enjoyable blackboard food, upstairs dining room; piped music, pleasant helpful staff; children welcome in eating areas, dogs in bar, prettily planted garden with rustic seats under parasols and lovely view over rolling countryside (Turner thought it fine enough to paint), open all day. *Recommended by Laurence Smith, Mike Gorton*

HENFIELD TQ2116 BN5 9HP

White Hart

High Street (A281)

Friendly 17th-c village pub (former coaching inn), Badger beers and enjoyable locally sourced food including good value weekday set menu, decent wines, comfortable L-shaped lounge, log fire in stone fireplace, dark beams and panelling, pine furniture on parquet floor, chess and draughts, large civilised dining area; children welcome, picnic-sets in small pleasant courtyard garden, open all day weekends (food all day then, too). *Recommended by Dr and Mrs M Davies, Martin Sayers*

HENLEY SU8925 GU27 3HQ

☆ **Duke of Cumberland Arms**

Off A286 S of Fernhurst

Wisteria-covered 15th-c stone-built pub with log fires in two small rooms, low ceilings, scrubbed oak furniture on brick or flagstoned floors, rustic decorations, well kept Harveys and a couple of guests tapped from the cask, popular often interesting bar food (not Sun evening), separate restaurant, friendly attentive staff; well behaved children and dogs welcome, seats on terrace, lovely hill views, charming sloping garden and trout ponds, open all day. *Recommended by Bruce Bird, Richard Follett, Henry Midwinter, the Didler, Chris Harrison, Miss A E Dare and others*

All *Guide* inspections are anonymous. Anyone claiming to be a *Good Pub Guide* inspector is a fraud. Please let us know.

HOUGHTON TQ0111   BN18 9LW
George & Dragon
B2139 W of Storrington

Elizabethan beams and timbers, attractive old-world bar rambling up and down steps,
Arun Valley views from back extension, reasonably priced generous food (all day
weekends), friendly service, Marstons-related ales and decent wines, note the elephant
photograph above the fireplace; piped music; children welcome, charming well organised
sloping garden, good walks. *Recommended by Michael and Deborah Ethier*

HURSTPIERPOINT TQ2816   BN6 9RQ
 ## New Inn
High Street

Popular 16th-c beamed pub under same management as Bull in Ditchling, well kept ales
including Harveys, good wines by the glass, enjoyable food with plenty for vegetarians,
good friendly young staff, contrasting linked areas including oak-panelled dim-lit back
part with bric-a-brac and open fire, and a smart apple-green dining room; sports TV;
children and dogs welcome, garden tables, open all day. *Recommended by Terry Buckland,*
Tim Loryman

ICKLESHAM TQ8716   TN36 4BL
☆ ## Queens Head
Off A259 Rye—Hastings

Friendly well run country pub, extremely popular locally (and at weekends with cyclists
and walkers), open-plan areas around big serving counter with high beamed walls,
vaulted roof, shelves of bottles, plenty of farming implements and animal traps, pubby
furniture on brown pattered carpet, other areas with inglenooks and a back room with old
bicycle memorabilia, Greene King, Harveys and a couple of guests, local cider, several
wines by the glass, straightforward reasonably priced bar food (all day weekends); piped
jazz or blues, live 4-6pm Sun; well behaved children allowed away from bar till 8.30pm,
dogs welcome in bar, picnic-sets, boules and play area in peaceful garden with fine Brede
Valley views, you can walk to Winchelsea, open all day. *Recommended by V Brogden,*
Robert Kibble, Peter Meister, Tom and Jill Jones, N R White, Colin and Louise English and others

ICKLESHAM TQ8716   TN36 4BD
☆ ## Robin Hood
Main Road

Friendly no-frills beamed pub with enthusiastic landlord and cheerful attentive staff,
great local atmosphere, good value unpretentious home-made food including
blackboard specials, six well kept changing ales (many from small breweries), hops
overhead, lots of copper bric-a-brac, log fire, games area with pool, back dining
extension; big garden with Brede Valley views. *Recommended by Tom and Jill Jones, Bruce Bird,*
Conrad Freezer, Peter Meister

ISFIELD TQ4417   TN22 5XB
Laughing Fish
Station Road

Opened-up Victorian local, jovial landlord and friendly staff, good value home-made pubby
food (not Sun evening), Greene King and guests, extensive wine list, open fire, traditional
games, events including entertaining beer race Easter bank holiday Mon; children and
dogs welcome, disabled access, small pleasantly shaded walled garden with enclosed play
area, right by Lavender Line, open all day. *Recommended by John Beeken*

JEVINGTON TQ5601   BN26 5QB
Eight Bells
Jevington Road, N of East Dean

Village pub with simple furnishings, heavy beams, panelling, parquet floor and inglenook
flame-effect fire, good choice of popular home-made food (all day Sun – best to book

weekends) from sandwiches up, nice puddings, Adnams Broadside, Flowers Original and Harveys Best; piped music; dogs welcome, front terrace, secluded Downs-view garden with some sturdy tables under cover, adjacent cricket field, good walking country, open all day. *Recommended by Pam Adsley*

KINGSFOLD TQ1635 RH12 3SA
Wise Old Owl
Dorking Road (A24 Dorking—Horsham, near A29 junction)

Nicely rambling olde-worlde reworking of 1930s pub, standing timbers dividing seating areas, Dark Star and Hepworth from long planked counter, good choice of wines by the glass, enjoyable well priced food from sandwiches up including popular Sun lunch, cream teas, good friendly service, contemporary restaurant with high-backed wicker chairs and mixed tables on coir or wood flooring, some modern art, church candles and fresh flowers, log fires, deli/farm shop; piped music, sports TV, games machines in bar alcove, upstairs lavatories; children welcome, picnic-tables on fenced-off gravel areas, open all day from 9.30am. *Recommended by Ian Phillips*

KINGSTON TQ3908 BN7 3NT
 ### Juggs
Village signed off A27 by roundabout W of Lewes

Popular rose-covered village pub, heavy 15th-c beams and very low front door, lots of neatly stripped masonry, sturdy wooden furniture on bare boards and stone slabs, smaller eating areas including a family room, wide choice of enjoyable food including plenty of fish and good vegetarian options, well kept Shepherd Neame and a beer brewed for the pub, good coffee and wine list, friendly helpful staff, log fires; piped music; children and dogs welcome, disabled facilities, nice covered area outside with heaters, lots of hanging baskets, play area, good walks, open all day. *Recommended by John Beeken, Ann and Colin Hunt, Evelyn and Derek Walter, Mr and Mrs John Taylor, PL and others*

LEWES TQ4210 BN7 2RD
Dorset
Malling Street

Light, airy and comfortable with large mellow area around central bar, smaller snug, lots of bare wood, welcoming competent staff, good varied choice of fairly priced food, well kept Harveys, smart restaurant; large back terrace, six bedrooms. *Recommended by Ann and Colin Hunt*

LEWES TQ4210 BN7 2AN
Gardeners Arms
Cliffe High Street

Warmly welcoming, unpretentious small local opposite brewery, light and airy, with plain scrubbed tables on bare boards around three narrow sides of bar, well kept Harveys and interesting changing guests, farm ciders, some lunchtime food including good pies, Sun bar nibbles, newspapers and magazines, toad in the hole played here; open all day. *Recommended by Mike and Eleanor Anderson, the Didler, N Wiseman, Ann and Colin Hunt*

LEWES TQ4210 BN7 2AN
John Harvey
Bear Yard, just off Cliffe High Street

No-nonsense tap for nearby Harveys brewery, all their beers including seasonals kept perfectly, some tapped from the cask, good well priced food from huge lunchtime sandwiches, baked potatoes and ciabattas up, friendly efficient young staff, basic dark flagstoned bar with one great vat halved to make two towering 'snugs' for several people, lighter room on left; piped music and machines; a few tables outside, open all day, breakfast from 10am. *Recommended by Gene and Kitty Rankin, Ben Williams, Ann and Colin Hunt and others*

LEWES TQ4110   BN7 1YH
☆ **Lewes Arms**
Castle Ditch Lane/Mount Place – tucked behind castle ruins

Cheerful unpretentious little local with half a dozen real ales, 30 malt whiskies and good choice of wines by the glass, really good reasonably priced bar food (all day Sat, not Sun evening), tiny front bar on right with stools along nicely curved counter and bench window seats, two other simple rooms hung with photographs and information about the famous Lewes bonfire night, beer mats pinned over doorways, poetry and folk evenings; children (not in front bar) and dogs welcome, picnic-sets on attractive two-level back terrace, open all day (till midnight Fri, Sat). *Recommended by the Didler, Ann and Colin Hunt, John Beeken, Mike and Eleanor Anderson and others*

LEWES TQ4210   BN7 2BU
Snowdrop
South Street

Tucked below the cliffs and doing well under present owners, narrowboat theme with brightly painted bar front and colourful jugs, lanterns etc hanging from planked ceiling, well kept Dark Star, Harveys, Hogs Back and Rectory, hearty helpings of enjoyable good value local food including good vegetarian choice, friendly efficient service, live jazz Mon; they may ask to keep your credit card while running a tab; dogs very welcome (even a menu for them), small garden and terrace, open all day. *Recommended by John Beeken, Ann and Colin Hunt*

LITTLEHAMPTON TQ0202   BN17 5DD
☆ **Arun View**
Wharf Road; W towards Chichester

Airy attractive 18th-c pub in lovely harbour spot with busy waterway directly below windows, very popular lunchtimes with older people (younger crowd in evenings) for its enjoyable interesting food (all day Sun) from sandwiches to good fresh fish, well kept Arundel ASB, Fullers London Pride and Ringwood Best, 20 wines by the glass, cheerful helpful service, lots of drawings, caricatures and nautical collectables, flagstoned and panelled back bar with banquettes and dark wood tables, large waterside conservatory; piped and some live music, two TVs, pool; disabled facilities, flower-filled terrace, summer barbecues, interesting waterside walkway to coast, four redone bedrooms, open all day. *Recommended by Trevor and Sheila Sharman, Roger Laker*

LITTLEHAMPTON TQ0202   BN17 5EG
Crown
High Street

No-frills town-centre pub with six changing ales including own Anchor Springs, good value pubby food. *Recommended by Tony and Wendy Hobden*

LODSWORTH SU9223   GU28 9BZ
☆ **Hollist Arms**
Off A272 Midhurst—Petworth

200-year-old village pub under new management, small snug room on right with tables by open fire, public bar on left with stools against pale counter, comfortable window seat and a few tables, well kept Kings, Langhams and Timothy Taylors Landlord, enjoyable bar food, L-shaped dining room with sofas by inglenook, elegant dining chairs and wheelbacks on wood-strip floor, interesting prints and paintings; children and dogs welcome, up steps to pretty cottagey back garden, picnic-sets on terrace or you can sit under a huge horse chestnut on the green, good walks nearby, open all day. *Recommended by Neil Ivens, Tony and Wendy Hobden, Martin and Karen Wake*

LOWFIELD HEATH TQ2539   RH11 0QA
Flight
Charlwood Road

Pictures and models of aircraft, friendly helpful staff, well kept beers, enjoyable generously served food including home-made cakes and scones; caters well for children in conservatory, with view of planes taking off from Gatwick, plenty of tables outside, too. *Recommended by R C Vincent*

LOXWOOD TQ0331   RH14 0RD
Onslow Arms
B2133 NW of Billingshurst

Comfortable and welcoming with popular food from doorstep sandwiches up, Badger ales, good house wines, coffees and teas, daily papers and lovely log fires; dogs welcome, picnic-sets in good-sized garden sloping to river and nearby restored Wey & Arun Canal, good walks and boat trips. *Recommended by Terry and Nickie Williams, Ian Phillips*

LYMINSTER TQ0204   BN17 7PS
Six Bells
Lyminster Road (A284), Wick

Unassuming flint pub, enjoyable elegantly presented food from weekday soups and sandwiches and daily roast bargains to some interesting specials, helpful staff, well kept Fullers London Pride and Greene King Abbot, good house wine, low black beams and big inglenook, pubby furnishings, friendly welcoming service; terrace and garden seating. *Recommended by Tony and Wendy Hobden*

MARESFIELD TQ4623   TN22 2EH
Chequers
High Street

Imposing three-floor Georgian coaching inn stylishly reworked under the Marco Pierre White Wheeler's of St James brand, good food including cheaper set menus in various linen-clothed dining areas – one with high-raftered ceiling, another with collection of Jak's cartoons on white-panelled walls, well kept Harveys in bare-boards oyster bar with beams and open fire; two decked areas in walled garden, ten refurbished bedrooms. *Recommended by Michael Butler*

MAYFIELD TQ5826   TN20 6AB
Middle House
High Street

Handsome 16th-c timbered inn, L-shaped beamed bar with massive fireplace, several well kept ales including Harveys, local cider, decent wines, quiet lounge area with leather chesterfields around log fire in ornate carved fireplace, good choice of food, panelled restaurant; piped music; children welcome, terraced back garden with lovely views, five bedrooms, open all day. *Recommended by Steve Godfrey*

MAYFIELD TQ5927   TN20 6TE
☆ # Rose & Crown
Fletching Street

Pretty 16th-c weatherboarded cottage with two cosy front character bars, low ceiling boards (coins stuck in paintwork), bench seats built into partly panelled walls, stripped floorboards and inglenook log fire, small room behind servery and larger lower room (less character), Harveys and a guest, ten wines by the glass, bar food all day; children welcome and dogs (resident chocolate labrador called Bob), picnic-sets under parasols on front terrace, open all day (till midnight Sat). *Recommended by Ingrid and Peter Terry*

MID LAVANT SU8508   PO18 0BQ
Earl of March
A286

Refurbished and extended with emphasis on eating but seats for drinkers in the flagstoned log-fire bar serving ales such as Ballards, Harveys and Hop Back, good if pricey food, much sourced locally, in plush dining area and conservatory with seafood bar, polite efficient staff; nice view up to Goodwood from neatly kept garden with good furniture, local walks. *Recommended by Miss A E Dare, Tracey and Stephen Groves*

MIDHURST SU8821   GU29 9BX
Wheatsheaf
Wool Lane/A272

Cosy low-beamed and timbered pub dating from the 16th c, friendly local atmosphere, good range of enjoyable reasonably priced food, well kept local ales, restaurant. *Recommended by Geoff and Linda Payne*

MILTON STREET TQ5304   BN26 5RL
☆ Sussex Ox
Off A27 just under a mile E of Alfriston roundabout

Extended country pub (originally a 1900s slaughterhouse) with magnificent Downs views – particularly popular at weekends; bar area with a couple of high tables and chairs on bare boards, old local photographs, Dark Star and Harveys, good choice of wines by the glass, lower brick-floored room with farmhouse furniture and woodburner, similarly furnished hop-draped dining room (children allowed here), further two-room front dining area with high-backed rush-seated chairs, bistro-style bar food, friendly service; dogs welcome in bar, teak seating on raised back deck taking in the view, picnic-sets in garden below and more under parasols at front, closed Sun evening in winter and between Christmas and New Year. *Recommended by Helen Greatorex, Jeremy Christey, Laurence Smith*

NUTBOURNE TQ0718   RH20 2HE
Rising Sun
Off A283 E of Pulborough; The Street

Unspoilt creeper-clad village pub dating partly from the 16th c, beams, bare boards and scrubbed tables, friendly helpful licensees (same family ownership for 30 years), well kept Fullers London Pride and guests such as Hogs Back and Langham, good range of bar food and blackboard specials, big log fire, daily papers, enamel signs and 1920s fashion and dance posters, cosy snug, attractive back family room, some live music; dogs welcome, garden with small back terrace under apple tree, smokers' shelter, listed outside lavatory. *Recommended by John Beeken*

OFFHAM TQ3912   BN7 3QD
☆ Blacksmiths Arms
A275 N of Lewes

Civilised and comfortable open-plan dining pub with chef/owner doing wide choice of good food including bargain two-course specials and nice vegetarian choices, well kept Harveys Best and a seasonal beer, good friendly uniformed staff, huge end inglenook; french windows to terrace with picnic-sets, four bedrooms. *Recommended by Ann and Colin Hunt, Tom and Ruth Rees*

OFFHAM TQ4011   BN7 3QF
☆ Chalk Pit
Offham Road (A275 N of Lewes)

Former late 18th-c chalk pit office building on three levels, well kept Harveys and a guest ale, decent wines by the glass, good choice of popular home-made food including OAP bargains, attentive cheerful staff, neat restaurant extension, skittle alley, toad in the hole played Mon nights; children welcome, garden with terrace seating, smokers' shelter with pool table, three bedrooms, open all day Fri-Sun (usually food all day then, too). *Recommended by Ann and Colin Hunt, PL, John Beeken*

OVING SU9005   PO20 2BP

☆ Gribble Inn

Between A27 and A259 E of Chichester

16th-c thatched pub with own-brewed beers and guests, chatty bar with lots of heavy beams and timbering, old country-kitchen furnishings and pews, other linked rooms with cottagey feel, huge winter log fires, home-made food (not Sun evening) using own ale in some dishes, skittle alley with bar, live jazz (first Tues of month); children in family room, dogs allowed in bar, seats outside under covered area, more in pretty garden, open all day weekends. *Recommended by Ian and Barbara Rankin, Guy Vowles, Susan and John Douglas, the Didler, David H T Dimock and others*

PARTRIDGE GREEN TQ1819   RH13 8JT

☆ Green Man

Off A24 just under a mile S of A272 junction – take B2135 at West Grinstead signpost; pub at Jolesfield, N of Partridge Green

Relaxed gently upmarket dining pub with enterprising food, several champagnes by the glass and other good wines, Dark Star and Harveys Best, truly helpful service; unassuming front area by counter with bentwood bar chairs, stools and library chairs around one or two low tables, old curved high-back settle, main eating area widens into another area with pretty enamelled stove and a pitched ceiling on left, more self-contained room on right with stag's head, minimal decoration but plenty of atmosphere; cast-iron seats and picnic-sets under cocktail parasols in neat back garden. *Recommended by David Cosham, Terry Buckland, Ron and Sheila Corbett, Philip Stott*

PETT TQ8613   TN35 4HB

Two Sawyers

Pett Road; off A259

Family run with meandering low-beamed rooms including bare-boards bar with stripped tables, tiny snug, passage sloping down to restaurant allowing children, enjoyable good value freshly made food, friendly service, well kept Harveys with guests like Dark Star and Ringwood, local farm cider and perry, wide range of wines; piped music; dogs allowed in bar, suntrap front brick courtyard, back garden with shady trees and well spaced tables, three bedrooms, open all day. *Recommended by Peter Meister, Ellie Weld, David London, Kevin Booker, Julia Atkins*

PETWORTH SU9721   GU28 0AH

Star

Market Square

Airy open-plan pub in centre, Fullers ales, decent wine, enjoyable reasonably priced food, good coffee, leather armchairs and sofa by open fire, friendly atmosphere. *Recommended by Lindsey Hedges, Richard Griffiths, Ann and Colin Hunt*

PETWORTH SU9921   GU28 0HG

☆ Welldiggers Arms

Low Heath; A283 E

Unassuming L-shaped bar, low beams, log fire, pictures askew on shiny ochre walls, long rustic settles with tables to match, some stripped tables laid for eating, side room, no music or machines, enjoyable food (not always cheap), Wells & Youngs, decent wines, friendly landlord; children (in family area) and dogs welcome, plenty of tables on attractive lawns and terrace, nice views, closed Mon, also evenings Tues, Weds, Sun. *Recommended by Mrs Blethyn Elliott, Richard Tilbrook*

If you stay overnight in an inn or hotel, they are allowed to serve you an alcoholic drink at any hour of the day or night.

PLUMPTON TQ3613   BN7 3AF

Half Moon
Ditchling Road (B2116)

Enlarged beamed and timbered dining pub with interesting home-made food using local produce, children's menu, Sun roasts, local ales and wines (even an organic Sussex lager), good service, log fire with unusual flint chimneybreast; piped music – live music Thurs; dogs welcome, tables in wisteria-clad front courtyard and on new back terrace, big Downs-view garden with picnic area, summer family days (last Sun of July and Aug) with face painting and bouncy castle, good walks, open all day. *Recommended by Dominic and Claire Williams*

RINGMER TQ4415   BN8 5RP

Old Ship
Uckfield Road (A26 Lewes—Uckfield, outside village S of Isfield turn-off)

Sizeable low-beamed roadside pub with emphasis on dining, wide choice of enjoyable home-made food all day from sandwiches and baked potatoes to steaks and fresh fish, children's menu, friendly service, Harveys Best, Biddenden cider, nautical pictures and memorabilia; dogs welcome, good-sized attractive garden with play area, open all day. *Recommended by Nigel and Jean Eames, Ian Forbes*

ROBERTSBRIDGE TQ7323   TN32 5AW

☆ George
High Street

Attractive contemporary dining pub, armchairs and sofa by inglenook log fire on right, friendly helpful licensees, Adnams, Harveys, Hop Back and Rother Valley, good wines by the glass, enjoyable locally sourced food from tasty baguettes to some enterprising main dishes, bustling chatty atmosphere; piped music – live music lunchtime (last Sun of month); children welcome and dogs (they have one called Stanley), back courtyard, four bedrooms. *Recommended by Simon Tayler, David and Sally Cullen, Mrs A S Crisp, Nigel and Jean Eames*

ROGATE SU8023   GU31 5EA

☆ White Horse
East Street; A272 Midhurst—Petersfield

Rambling heavy-beamed local in front of village cricket field, civilised and friendly, with Harveys full range kept particularly well, relaxed atmosphere, flagstones, stripped stone, timbers and big log fire, attractive candlelit sunken dining area, good range of enjoyable reasonably priced food (not Sun evening), friendly helpful staff, traditional games (and quite a collection of trophy cups), no piped music or machines; quiz and folk nights; some tables on back terrace, open all day Sun. *Recommended by D and J Ashdown, Geoff and Linda Payne*

ROWHOOK TQ1234   RH12 3PY

☆ Chequers
Off A29 NW of Horsham

Attractive welcoming 16th-c pub, relaxing beamed and flagstoned front bar with portraits and inglenook fire, step up to low-beamed lounge, well kept Fullers London Pride, Harveys and guests such as Weltons, decent wines by the glass, good coffee, good food from ciabattas up, separate restaurant; piped music; children and dogs welcome, tables out on front terraces and in pretty garden behind with good play area, attractive surroundings. *Recommended by Steve and Hilary Nelson, Ian Phillips, Ian and Rose Lock*

RUDGWICK TQ0934   RH12 3EB

Kings Head
Off A281; Church Street (B2128)

Beamed 13th-c pub by fine old church in pretty village, well kept Fullers, Shepherd Neame and Harveys, good italian cooking including lots of seafood, reasonable prices; flower-decked seating area at front, more seats behind. *Recommended by John Beeken*

RUSHLAKE GREEN TQ6218   TN21 9QE
☆ **Horse & Groom**
Off B2096 Heathfield—Battle

Cheerful village-green local, little L-shaped low-beamed bar with brick fireplace and local
pictures, small room down a step with horsey décor, simple beamed restaurant, enjoyable
home-made food, Shepherd Neame ales, decent wines by the glass; children and dogs
welcome, attractive cottagey garden with pretty country views, nice walks. *Recommended by*
Chris Saunders

RUSPER TQ1836   RH12 4QA
☆ **Royal Oak**
Friday Street, towards Warnham – back road N of Horsham, E of A24 (OS Sheet 187
map reference 185369)

Old-fashioned and well worn-in tile-hung pub in very rural spot on Sussex Border Path,
small carpeted top bar with leather sofas and armchairs, log fire, steps down to long
beamed main bar with plush wall seats, pine tables and chairs and homely knick-knacks,
well kept Surrey Hills Ranmore and six changing guests, farm ciders and perries, short
choice of enjoyable home-made lunchtime food (evenings and Sun lunch by
prearrangement), local farm produce for sale, plain games/family room with darts; a few
picnic-sets on grass by road and in streamside garden beyond car park, roaming chickens,
open all day Sat, till 9pm Sun. *Recommended by Bruce Bird, Conor McGaughey, the Didler and others*

RYE TQ9220   TN31 7JT
George
High Street

Sizeable hotel with lively up-to-date feel in bar and adjoining dining area, beams, bare
boards and log fire, leather sofa and armchairs, a couple of quirky sculptures, Adnams,
Greene King Old Speckled Hen and Harveys Best, continental beers on tap too, enjoyable
interesting food, popular afternoon tea, pleasant courteous staff (some french); soft piped
jazz; good bedrooms, open all day. *Recommended by Colin and Louise English, John Atkins*

RYE TQ9220   TN31 7EY
☆ **Mermaid**
Mermaid Street

Lovely old timbered hotel on famous cobbled street with civilised antiques-filled bar,
Victorian gothick carved chairs, older but plainer oak seats, huge working inglenook with
massive bressumer beam, Fullers, Greene King and Harveys, good selection of wines and
malt whiskies, short bar menu, more elaborate restaurant choices; piped music; children
welcome, seats on small back terrace, bedrooms, open all day. *Recommended by*
Terry Buckland, the Didler, Colin and Louise English, N J Roberts, Richard Mason, Meg and Colin Hamilton
and others

RYE TQ9220   TN31 7LH
Queens Head
Landgate

Friendly old pub refurbished under newish licensees, good selection of changing ales and
ciders (regular festivals), short choice of enjoyable low-priced home-made food, live
music; small area out at back for smokers, bedrooms. *Recommended by Peter Meister, Mike and*
Eleanor Anderson

RYE TQ9220   TN31 7HH
☆ **Ypres Castle**
Gun Garden; steps up from A259, or down past Ypres Tower

Traditional pub perched above river, bustling bars with various old tables and chairs, local
artwork and log fire, informal almost scruffy feel which adds to character, straightforward
promptly served bar food (all day Sat, not Sun evening), well kept Fullers, Harveys and
Timothy Taylors Landlord; piped and some live music, no dogs inside; children welcome

lunchtime, seats in sheltered garden, boules, open all day, Sun till 8pm (6pm winter). *Recommended by Robert Kibble, Sue and Mike Todd, Sue Callard, Barry Collett, Richard Mason, Tony and Wendy Hobden and others*

SELSFIELD COMMON TQ3433   RH19 4RA
White Hart
B2028 N of Haywards Heath, near West Hoathly

14th-c century cottage restaurant and large attached Sussex barn (bar here), welcoming staff, well kept Harveys, Shepherd Neame and Wells & Youngs Bombardier, Weston's cider, several wines by the glass, traditional bar food, more upmarket dishes in restaurant with inglenook log fire; piped music in barn – live music Fri; garden picnic-sets, handy for Wakehurst Place, open all day, closed Sun evening. *Recommended by M Vingoe, C and R Bromage, Terry Buckland*

SHOREHAM-BY-SEA TQ2105   BN43 5TE
Red Lion
Upper Shoreham Road

Modest dimly lit low-beamed and timbered 16th-c pub with settles in snug alcoves, wide choice of good value pubby food including speciality pies, half a dozen well kept changing ales such as Adur, Arundel and Hepworths (Easter beer festival), farm cider, decent wines, friendly efficient staff, log fire in unusual fireplace, another open fire in dining room, further bar with covered terrace; pretty sheltered garden behind, old bridge and lovely Norman church opposite, good Downs views and walks. *Recommended by Tim Loryman, Tony and Wendy Hobden, Bruce Bird*

SIDLESHAM SZ8697   PO20 7NB
☆ ## Crab & Lobster
Mill Lane; off B2145 S of Chichester

Restaurant-with-rooms rather than pub but walkers and bird-watchers welcome in small flagstoned bar for a light meal, Harveys and Sharps, 17 wines by the glass including champagne, stylish upmarket restaurant with good imaginative (and pricey) food including local fish, friendly efficient staff; piped music; children welcome, tables on back terrace overlooking marshes, smart bedrooms, self-catering cottage, open all day (food all day weekends). *Recommended by Graeme Manson, Peter La Farge, Peggy and Alec Ward, Susan and John Douglas, Richard Tilbrook, N R White and others*

SLINDON SU9708   BN18 0NE
Spur
Slindon Common; A29 towards Bognor

Civilised, roomy and attractive 17th-c pub, good choice of upmarket but good value food changing daily, well kept Courage Directors, cheerful efficient staff, welcoming atmosphere, two big log fires, pine tables, large elegant restaurant, games room with darts and pool, friendly dogs; children welcome, pretty garden (traffic noise). *Recommended by David H T Dimock*

SMALL DOLE TQ2112   BN5 9XE
Fox
Henfield Road

Popular open-plan village local on busy road, good choice of reasonably priced bar food from sandwiches up, well kept Harveys Best and Wells & Youngs Bombardier, friendly staff coping well at busy times, raised dining areas; piped music; tables on small front terrace, handy for downland walks. *Recommended by John Beeken*

Most pubs with any outside space now have some kind of smokers' shelter. There are regulations about these – for instance, they have to be substantially open to the outside air. The best have heating and lighting and are really quite comfortable.

SOMPTING TQ1605   BN15 0AR
Gardeners Arms
West Street

Smartened up by friendly licensees, just off main coast road (the famous Saxon church is unfortunately on the far side of the dual carriageway), good choice of tasty food all day including some bargains (the railway-carriage restaurant is not currently in use), well kept Bass, Harveys, Sharps Doom Bar and a guest, log fire; piped music; dogs welcome, smokers' terrace. *Recommended by Bruce Bird, Tony and Wendy Hobden*

SOUTHWATER TQ1528   RH13 0LA
Bax Castle
Two Mile Ash, a mile or so NW

Popular early 19th-c flagstoned country pub pleasantly extended with former barn restaurant, big log fire in back room, Ringwood, Jennings and Wychwood ales, good value generous home-made food including good Sun lunch (best to book); some piped music; children and dogs welcome, picnic-sets on two pleasant lawns, play area, near Downs Link Way on former rail track. *Recommended by Tony and Wendy Hobden, Ian Phillips*

ST LEONARDS TQ8008   TN38 0EB
Horse & Groom
Mercatoria

Friendly traditional town local in old Maze Hill area, carved horseshoe bar serving front and back rooms, Adnams, Greene King, Harveys and guests, interesting pictures, no food but connecting restaurant next door; small garden. *Recommended by Steve Long*

STAPLEFIELD TQ2728   RH17 6EF
Jolly Tanners
Handcross Road, just off A23

Neatly kept split-level local by cricket green, welcoming landlord and pub dogs, two good log fires, padded settles, lots of china, brasses and old photographs, well kept Fullers London Pride, Harveys and guests (always a mild; three beer festivals), real ciders, pubby food, chatty atmosphere; piped music, jazz Sun evening, quiz Thurs; children welcome and dogs (may be a treat), attractive suntrap garden with plenty of space for kids, quite handy for Nymans (NT). *Recommended by Sheila Topham, Mike and Eleanor Anderson*

STEYNING TQ1711   BN44 3RE
Chequer
High Street

Rambling low-beamed Tudor coaching inn, five or so well kept ales such as Cottage, Dark Star, Gales, Harveys and Timothy Taylors, good choice of wines, enjoyable well priced usual food (not Sun evening) from sandwiches up including breakfast from 10am, log fire, antique snooker table, large painting featuring locals, some live music; smokers' shelter, bedrooms, open all day. *Recommended by Bruce Bird, Greta and Christopher Wells, Richard Wilkie, Tony and Wendy Hobden*

STEYNING TQ1711   BN44 3YE
White Horse
High Street

Smart contemporary bar in creeper-covered former coaching inn, enjoyable interesting food, good choice of wines by the glass, Greene King ales, good courteous uniformed service; children welcome, spacious terrace. *Recommended by John Redfern*

STOUGHTON SU8011   PO18 9JQ
Hare & Hounds
Signed off B2146 Petersfield—Emsworth

Airy pine-clad country dining pub with simple contemporary décor, good reasonably priced fresh food including doorstep sandwiches and Sun roasts (till 4pm), four well kept changing ales, real cider, good helpful service, big open fires, public bar with darts, quiz nights; children in eating areas, dogs welcome, tables on pretty front terrace and on grass behind, lovely setting near Saxon church, good local walks. *Recommended by Rodney and Mary Milne-Day, Martin and Karen Wake, Paul Smurthwaite, R and R Goodenough*

SUTTON SU9715   RH20 1PS
☆ White Horse
The Street

Opened-up country inn with minimalist contemporary décor, island servery separating bar from two-room barrel-vaulted dining area with modern hardwood chairs and tables on coir, church candles and several open fires, ales such as Harveys and Sharps, decent wines by the glass, bar food with bistro touches; children and dogs welcome, steps up to garden with plenty of picnic-sets, walks in lovely surrounding countryside right from the door (packed lunches on request), Bignor Roman villa close by, bedrooms, closed Sun and Mon evenings. *Recommended by A N Bance, Nick Lawless, J A Snell*

THAKEHAM TQ1017   RH20 3EP
White Lion
Off B2139 N of Storrington; The Street

Tile-hung 16th-c two-bar village local, good robust home-made food (not Sun-Weds evenings) from open kitchen, friendly informal service, real ales such as Arundel, Fullers, Harveys and St Austell, good choice of wines by the glass, heavy beams, panelling, bare boards and traditional furnishings including settles, pleasant dining room with inglenook woodburner, fresh flowers; dogs welcome, sunny terrace tables, more on small lawn, wendy house and rabbits, small pretty village, open all day. *Recommended by Mike and Eleanor Anderson*

TILLINGTON SU9621   GU28 9AF
☆ Horse Guards
Off A272 Midhurst—Petworth

Prettily set dining pub converted from three cottages, some traditional dishes as well as fancier pricier things, home-baked bread, Harveys and a guest, good choice of wines by the glass, friendly helpful service, log fire and country furniture in neat low-beamed front bar, lovely views from bow window, simple pine tables in dining room with fire, own and local produce for sale; children welcome, terrace tables and sheltered garden behind, attractive ancient church opposite, three bedrooms, good breakfast. *Recommended by Richard Tilbrook, Colin McKerrow, Barry Steele-Perkins, Martin Walker, Ann and Colin Hunt*

TROTTON SU8322   GU31 5ER
☆ Keepers Arms
A272 Midhurst—Petersfield

Pretty cottage above River Rother with beamed and timbered L-shaped bar, comfortable sofas and old winged-back leather armchairs around big log fire, simple rustic tables on oak flooring, other interesting old furniture, two dining rooms, one with woodburner, tasty bar food, Ballards, Dark Star and a guest ale; children welcome (no babies or toddlers in evening), dogs allowed in bar, seats on south-facing terrace, closed Sun evenings in Jan and Feb. *Recommended by Angus Wilson, John Branston*

TURNERS HILL TQ3435   RH10 4NU
☆ Red Lion
Lion Lane, just off B2028

Old-fashioned and unpretentious country local with snug, curtained, parquet-floored bar, plush wall benches, homely memorabilia and small open fire, steps up to carpeted area with inglenook log fire, cushioned pews and settles forming booths, Harveys ales, generous home cooking, friendly staff, daily papers; piped music (some live music in summer), games machine; children (away from bar) and dogs welcome, picnic-sets on side grass overlooking village, open all day, Sun till 10pm (8pm in winter). *Recommended by Terry Buckland, John Branston, Nick Lawless, N J Roberts, Colin and Louise English and others*

UPPER BEEDING TQ1910 BN44 3HZ
Kings Head
High Street

Old pub opened up but keeping some intimate seating areas, more formal dining area at
one end, well kept Fullers London Pride and Harveys Best, decent pubby food, good
service, warming log fire; children, dogs and walkers welcome, attractive back garden
with beautiful downland views, play area and access to River Adur. *Recommended by*
Tim Loryman, Tony and Wendy Hobden

UPPER BEEDING TQ1910 BN44 3TN
Rising Sun
Shoreham Road (A2037)

Friendly old pub (just off South Downs Way) smartened up by newish landlord, enjoyable
home-made food, well kept Fullers London Pride, Harveys and guests, good welcoming
service, cosy rooms, small dining conservatory; big garden with downland views.
Recommended by Bruce Bird

VINES CROSS TQ5917 TN21 9EN
Brewers Arms
Vines Cross Road off B2203, then left at T junction; 1 mile E of Horam

Victorian country pub redecorated under new management; sizeable public bar, stools by
counter, quite a mix of dining chairs, benches and settles around wooden tables on
stripped boards, three similarly furnished connecting rooms, one with open fire, another
with woodburner, Greene King and guests, several wines by the glass, good food from
pubby dishes up, helpful staff; children and dogs welcome, some picnic-sets in front and
to the side, open all day. *Recommended by anon*

WADHURST TQ6131 TN5 6JH
Best Beech
Mayfield Lane (B2100 a mile W)

Dining pub taken over by twin brothers and reopened in 2010 after fresh contemporary
refurbishment, good well priced food from traditional choices up, fixed-price menus
including Sun lunch, Shepherd Neame ales and several wines by the glass, friendly
service; children welcome, garden, six comfortably updated bedrooms, open all day Sat,
closed Sun evening. *Recommended by Steven Tait*

WALDERTON SU7910 PO18 9ED
Barley Mow
Stoughton Road, just off B2146 Chichester—Petersfield

Country pub with good value generous food from lunchtime sandwiches up including Sun
carvery, well kept ales such as Arundel, Harveys and Ringwood, good wine choice, friendly
service even on busy weekends, two log fires and rustic bric-a-brac in U-shaped bar with
roomy dining areas, live jazz suppers (third Tues of month), popular skittle alley; children
welcome, big pleasant streamside back garden, good walks, handy for Stansted House.
Recommended by J A Snell, R and R Goodenough

WALDRON TQ5419 TN21 0RA
Star
Blackboys—Horam side road

Big inglenook log fire in candlelit, beamed and panelled bar, padded window seat and
nice mix of furniture including small settle on bare boards and quarry tiles, old prints and
photographs, snug off to left, well kept Harveys and a guest such as 1648 or Bass, reliable
food from good lunchtime sandwiches up, friendly prompt service, separate back dining
room; picnic-sets in pleasant garden, a couple more at front overlooking pretty village.
Recommended by PL

WARNINGLID TQ2425   RH17 5TR

 Half Moon

B2115 off A23 S of Handcross or off B2110 Handcross—Lower Beeding

Good modern cooking (not Sun evening) in this informal simply furnished brick and stone dining pub, Harveys, a changing guest and decent wines by the glass, bustling bare-boards locals' bar with small fireplace, room off with 18th-c beams and flagstones, steps down to unpretentious main bar, panelling, bare brick and photos of the village, down again to smaller carpeted area with big paintings; no children inside; dogs allowed in bar, picnic-sets on lawn in sizeable garden with spectacular avenue of trees, open all day weekends.
Recommended by Brian Dawes, Pat and John Carter, Terry Buckland, Ian Wilson and others

WARTLING TQ6509   BN27 1RY

☆ **Lamb**

Village signed with Herstmonceux Castle off A271 Herstmonceux—Battle

Family-run country pub with three log fires, small entrance bar leading through to beamed and timbered snug with comfortable leather sofas, Harveys and Sharps, several wines by the glass, enjoyable food served by friendly staff, separate restaurant; children welcome away from bar, dogs away from restaurant, up steps to flower-filled back terrace, closed Sun evening, Mon. *Recommended by John Atkins, N J Roberts*

WEST ASHLING SU8007   PO18 8EA

Richmond Arms

Just off B2146; Mill Road

Newly refurbished village dining pub in quiet pretty setting near big mill pond with ducks and geese, good food from bar snacks up, Harveys ales; no dogs; children welcome, two smart bedrooms, closed Sun evening, Mon and Tues. *Recommended by Bill Oliver*

WEST WITTERING SZ8099   PO20 8QA

Lamb

Chichester Road; B2179/A286 towards Birdham

Welcoming 18th-c tile-hung country pub doing well under present landlord, good choice of enjoyable food from light meals to giant fish and chips, Badger ales, good service even during busy summer months, rugs on tiles, blazing fire; children and dogs welcome, tables out in front and in small sheltered back garden. *Recommended by David H T Dimock, Tony and Wendy Hobden*

WEST WITTERING SZ7798   PO20 8AD

Old House At Home

Cakeham Road

Roomy and cheerfully brightened up with three bar areas on two levels, wood floors and modern décor, well kept ales including Fullers London Pride, enjoyable if a little pricey food, friendly staff, log fires; children and dogs welcome, garden with play area, three bedrooms. *Recommended by John Whitney, Michael Butler*

WILMINGTON TQ5404   BN26 5SQ

☆ **Giants Rest**

Just off A27

Busy country pub with affable long-serving landlord, long wood-floored bar, adjacent open areas with simple furniture, log fire, well kept Harveys, Hop Back and Timothy Taylors, quite a choice of bar food (all day weekends), wooden puzzles and board games; piped music; children and dogs welcome, lots of seats in front garden, surrounded by South Downs walks and village famous for chalk-carved Long Man, bedrooms. *Recommended by Evelyn and Derek Walter, John Beeken, Mark Jiskoot*

WINCHELSEA TQ9017
TN36 4EN
New Inn
German Street; just off A259

Attractive pub with L-shaped front bar mainly laid for dining – new owners concentrating on good, fair value food, some slate flagstones and log fire, well kept Greene King ales, friendly helpful staff, separate back bar with darts and TV; piped music; children welcome, pleasant walled garden, delightful setting opposite church – Spike Milligan buried here, comfortable bedrooms, good breakfast. *Recommended by Michael Butler, Mr and Mrs Price*

WITHYHAM TQ4935
TN7 4BD
☆ # Dorset Arms
B2110

Unpretentious 16th-c pub handy for Forest Way walks, friendly service, well kept Harveys ales, decent wines including local ones, good choice of fairly priced food, sturdy tables and simple country seats on wide oak boards, good log fire in Tudor fireplace, darts, dominoes, shove-ha'penny, cribbage, carpeted restaurant; piped music; dogs welcome, white tables on brick terrace by small green, closed Mon. *Recommended by Peter Meister, the Didler*

WORTHING TQ1204
BN13 1QY
North Star
Littlehampton Road (A259)

Comfortable Ember Inn with competitively priced food from noon to 8pm, real ales such as Greene King, Harveys, Purity and Shepherd Neame, good choice of wines by the glass, friendly service. *Recommended by Tony and Wendy Hobden*

WORTHING TQ1502
BN11 2DB
Selden Arms
Lyndhurst Road, between Waitrose and hospital

Friendly chatty local with welcoming long-serving licensees, well kept Dark Star Hophead and several changing guests, belgian beers and farm cider, bargain lunchtime food (not Sun) including doorstep sandwiches, log fire, lots of old pub photographs, occasional live music; dogs welcome, open all day. *Recommended by Tony and Wendy Hobden*

WORTHING TQ1502
BN11 1DN
Swan
High Street

Villagey atmosphere with good mix of customers in big open-plan pub, welcoming long-serving licensee, reasonably priced pubby lunchtime food and specials, several well kept ales including Harveys and Hop Back, old-fashioned interior with beams and some stained glass, regular entertainment from folk nights to quizzes; handy for hospital. *Recommended by Bruce Bird*

PUBS NEAR MOTORWAY JUNCTIONS

The number at the start of each line is the number of the junction. Detailed directions are given in the entry for each pub.

M3

1: Sunbury, Flower Pot 1.6 miles
3: West End, Inn at West End 2.4 miles
5: North Warnborough, Mill House
   1 mile; Hook, Hogget 1.1 miles
7: North Waltham, Fox 3 miles
9: Easton, Chestnut Horse 3.6 miles

M4

9: Bray, Crown 1.75 miles; Bray, Hinds
   Head 1.75 miles
13: Winterbourne, Winterbourne Arms
    3.7 miles
14: East Garston, Queens Arms 3.5 miles

M20

11: Stowting, Tiger 3.7 miles

M25

13: Laleham, Three Horseshoes 5 miles
16: Denham, Swan 0.75 miles
18: Chenies, Red Lion 2 miles

M40

2: Hedgerley, White Horse 2.4 miles;
   Forty Green, Royal Standard of
   England 3.5 miles

PUBS SERVING FOOD ALL DAY

We list here all the top pubs that have told us they plan to serve food all day, even if it's only one day of the week. The individual entries for the pubs themselves show the actual details.

London

Central London:
   Bountiful Cow, Old Bank of England,
   Olde Mitre, Seven Stars
Outer London:
   Bishop Out of Residence, Old Orchard
South London:
   Telegraph

Berkshire

Sonning, Bull
White Waltham, Beehive

Buckinghamshire

Coleshill, Harte & Magpies
Forty Green, Royal Standard of England
Grove, Grove Lock
Wooburn Common, Chequers

Hampshire

Bransgore, Three Tuns
Southsea, Wine Vaults

Isle of Wight

Arreton, White Lion
Shorwell, Crown

Kent

Brookland, Woolpack
Langton Green, Hare
Penshurst, Bottle House
Sevenoaks, White Hart
Stalisfield Green, Plough
Stowting, Tiger

Oxfordshire

Kingham, Plough
Oxford, Bear, Turf Tavern
Stanton St John, Talk House

Surrey

Blindley Heath, Red Barn
Elstead, Mill at Elstead
Horsell, Red Lion
Milford, Refectory

Sussex

Alfriston, George
Charlton, Fox Goes Free
East Chiltington, Jolly Sportsman
Horsham, Black Jug
Ringmer, Cock

Maps

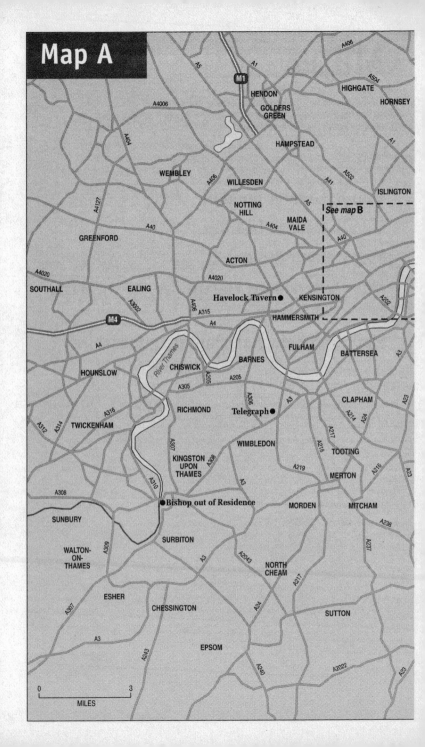

Map A

M1

HENDON

GOLDERS GREEN

A5

A1

A406

A504

HIGHGATE

HORNSEY

A4006

A404

HAMPSTEAD

A1

WEMBLEY

A406

WILLESDEN

A502

A41

NOTTING HILL

A5

ISLINGTON

MAIDA VALE

See map **B**

A4127

A40

A404

GREENFORD

A40

A4020

ACTON

SOUTHALL

EALING

A4020

Havelock Tavern ●

KENSINGTON

A202

A4020

A406

A3002

A315

HAMMERSMITH

M4

A4

FULHAM

BATTERSEA

A3

A4

River Thames

CHISWICK

BARNES

HOUNSLOW

A305

A205

A205

A306

A3

CLAPHAM

A23

A316

RICHMOND

Telegraph ●

A214

A24

TWICKENHAM

A312

A314

A307

WIMBLEDON

A217

A218

TOOTING

A216

A23

KINGSTON UPON THAMES

A308

A310

A3

A219

MERTON

●**Bishop out of Residence**

MORDEN

MITCHAM

A236

SUNBURY

SURBITON

A308

A309

A3

A24

A237

WALTON-ON-THAMES

NORTH CHEAM

A217

ESHER

CHESSINGTON

A24

SUTTON

A307

A3

A243

EPSOM

A240

A2022

A23

0   3

MILES

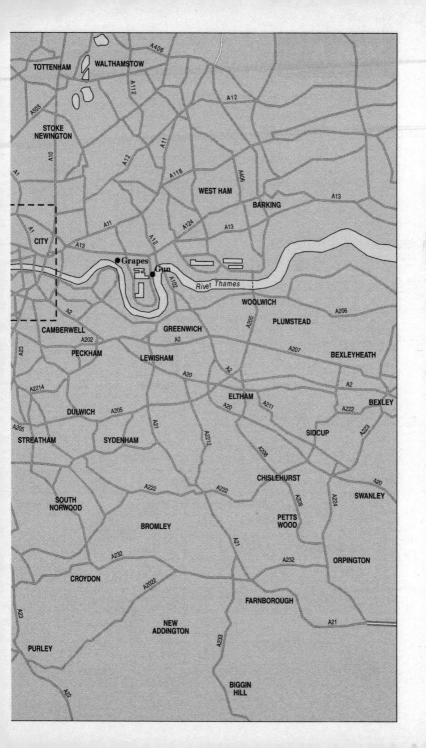

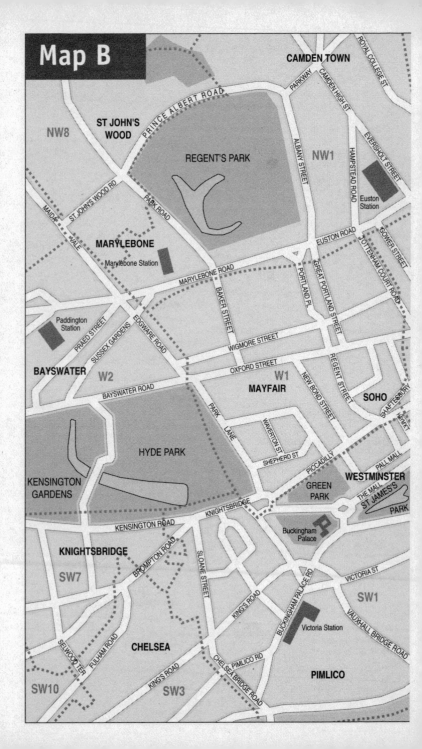

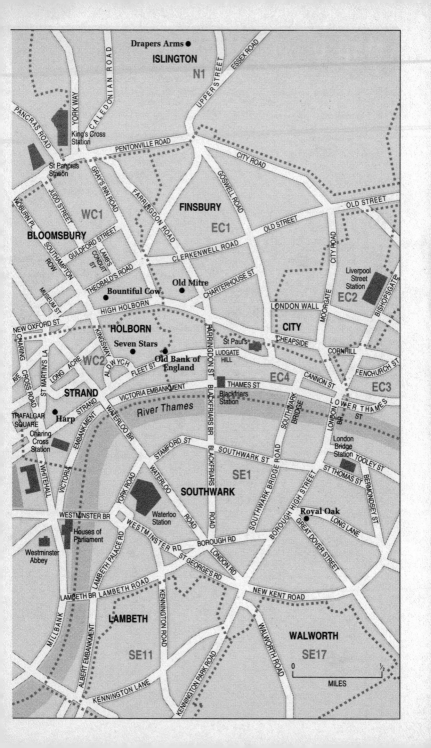

Map C

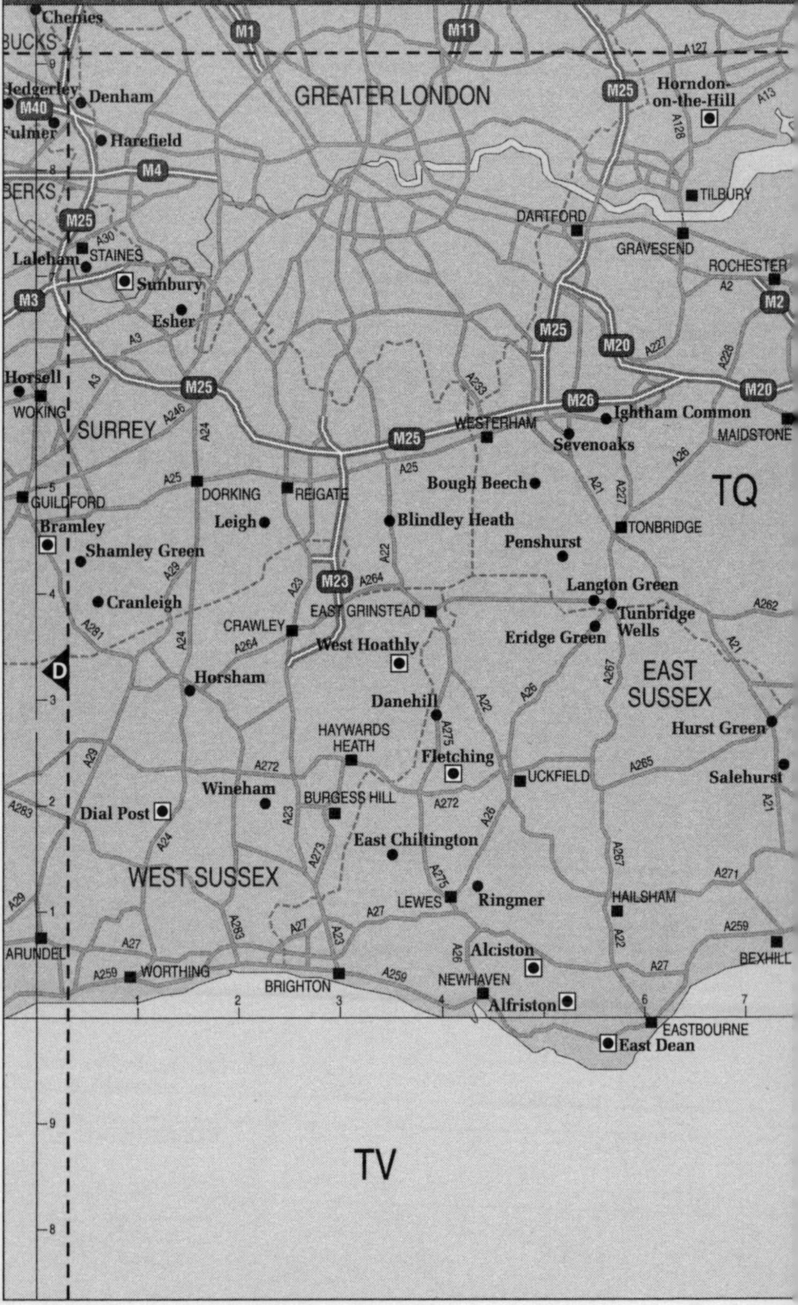

BUCKS
Chenies
Hedgerley
Denham
Fulmer
M40
Harefield
GREATER LONDON
M1
M11
M25
Horndon-on-the-Hill
A13
A127
M4
BERKS
M25
Laleham
STAINES
Sunbury
Esher
DARTFORD
TILBURY
GRAVESEND
ROCHESTER
A2
M2
A30
M3
A3
Horsell
WOKING
A3
A246
SURREY
M25
A24
WESTERHAM
M25
A25
M26
Ightham Common
MAIDSTONE
Sevenoaks
A26
A225
M20
A227
M20
A228
A25
GUILDFORD
Bramley
Shamley Green
Cranleigh
A281
DORKING
REIGATE
Leigh
A25
Bough Beech
Blindley Heath
Penshurst
TONBRIDGE
TQ
A22
M23
A264
EAST GRINSTEAD
Langton Green
Tunbridge Wells
A262
A25
A21
A281
A24
CRAWLEY
A26A
West Hoathly
Eridge Green
A267
EAST SUSSEX
A26
D
Horsham
Danehill
A275
Hurst Green
HAYWARDS HEATH
Fletching
A20
A26
Salehurst
A21
A23
A272
UCKFIELD
A265
Wineham
BURGESS HILL
A272
A26
A267
A271
Dial Post
A24
East Chiltington
A275
HAILSHAM
A22
WEST SUSSEX
A273
LEWES
Ringmer
A29
A283
A27
ARUNDEL
A27
A23
A27
Alciston
A259
BEXHILL
A259
WORTHING
A283
BRIGHTON
A259
NEWHAVEN
Alfriston
A27
EASTBOURNE
East Dean

TV

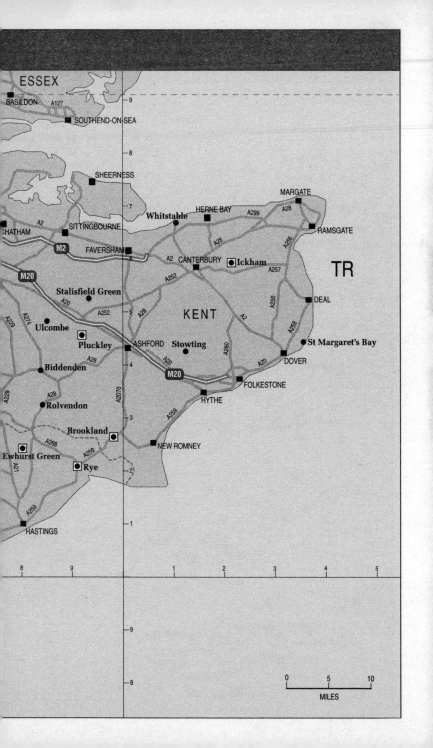

Map D

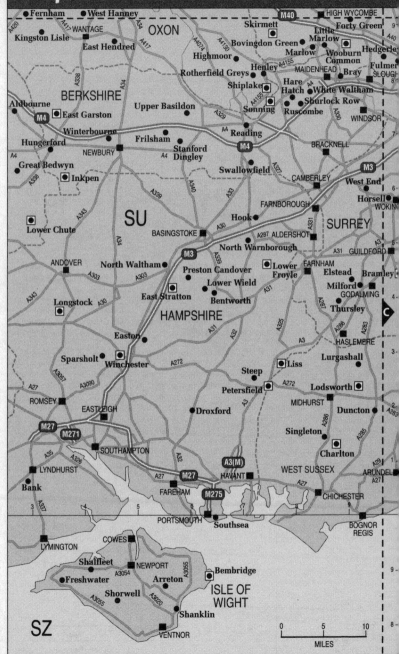

Fernham • West Hanney • HIGH WYCOMBE ■ M40

Kingston Lisle • WANTAGE OXON Skirmett • Forty Green •
East Hendred • Bovingdon Green • Little Marlow ■ Hedgerley •
Highmoor • Marlow Wooburn Common Fulmer •
Rotherfield Greys • Henley • MAIDENHEAD SLOUGH
Shiplake • Hare Hatch Bray WINDSOR
BERKSHIRE Sonning White Waltham
Aldbourne • M4 East Garston ■ Sherlock Row
Upper Basildon • Ruscombe •
Winterbourne • Reading BRACKNELL
Hungerford • Frilsham • M4
NEWBURY Stanford Dingley CAMBERLEY M3
Great Bedwyn • Swallowfield • West End •
Inkpen ■ Horsell •
Lower Chute ■ SU Hook WOKIN
BASINGSTOKE ■ FARNBOROUGH SURREY
North Warnborough • ALDERSHOT GUILDFORD ■
ANDOVER ■ M3 FARNHAM A31
North Waltham • Lower Froyle ■ Elstead • Bramley •
Preston Candover • Milford •
Lower Wield • GODALMING
Longstock ■ East Stratton ■ Bentworth • Thursley •
HAMPSHIRE HASLEMERE
Easton • Lurgashall •
Sparsholt • Liss ■ Lodsworth ■
Winchester ■ Steep •
ROMSEY ■ Petersfield • MIDHURST Duncton •
EASTLEIGH ■ Droxford • Singleton •
M27 Charlton ■
M271 SOUTHAMPTON ■
LYNDHURST ■ A3(M) WEST SUSSEX
Bank • HAVANT ■ ARUNDEL ■
FAREHAM ■ M275 CHICHESTER
PORTSMOUTH ■ BOGNOR REGIS
Southsea COWES ■
LYMINGTON ■ NEWPORT ■ Bembridge ■
Shalfleet • Arreton •
Freshwater • ISLE OF WIGHT
Shorwell •
Shanklin •
SZ VENTNOR ■

0   5   10
MILES

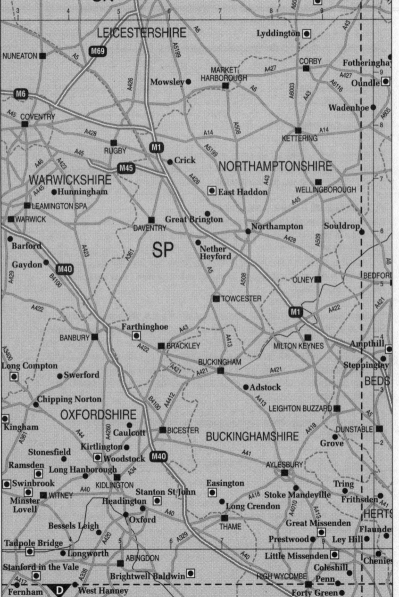

Map E

Report Forms

We need to know about pubs in this edition, pubs worthy of inclusion and ones that should not be included. Sometimes pubs are dropped simply because very few readers have written to us about them. You can use the cut-out forms on the following pages, email us at **feedback@goodguides.com** or write to us and we'll gladly send you more forms:

The Good Pub Guide
FREEPOST TN1569
WADHURST
East Sussex TN5 7BR

Though we try to answer all letters, please understand if there's a delay (particularly in summer, our busiest period). We'll assume we can print your name or initials as a recommender unless you tell us otherwise.

FULL ENTRY OR OTHER GOOD PUBS?

Please try to gauge whether a pub should be a top pub with a full entry or whether it should be in the Also Worth a Visit section (and tick the relevant box). Full entries need qualities that would make it worth other readers' while to travel some distance to them. If a pub is an entirely new recommendation, the Also Worth a Visit section may be the best place for it to start its career in the *Guide* – to encourage other readers to report on it.

The more detail you can put into your description of a pub, the better. Any information on how good the landlord or landlady is, what it looks like inside, what you like about the atmosphere and character, the quality and type of food, whether the real ale is well kept and which real ales are available, whether bedrooms are available, and how big/attractive the garden is. Other things that help (if possible) include prices for food and bedrooms, food service and opening hours, and if children or dogs are welcome.

If the food or accommodation are outstanding, tick the **FOOD AWARD** or the **STAY AWARD** box.

If you're in a position to gauge a pub's suitability or otherwise for **disabled people**, do please tell us about that.

If you can, give the full address or directions for any pub not yet in the *Guide* – best of all please give us its post code. If we can't find a pub's post code, we don't include it in the *Guide*.

I have been to the following pubs in *The Good Pub Guide 2012* in the last few months, found them as described, and confirm that they deserve continued inclusion:

Continued overleaf

PLEASE GIVE YOUR NAME AND ADDRESS ON THE BACK OF THIS FORM

Pubs visited continued...

By returning this form, you consent to the collection, recording and use of the information you submit, by The Random House Group Ltd. Any personal details which you provide from which we can identify you are held and processed in accordance with the Data Protection Act 1998 and will not be passed on to any third parties.

The Random House Group Ltd may wish to send you further information on their associated products. Please tick box if you do not wish to receive any such information.

Your own name and address *(block capitals please)*

Postcode

In returning this form I confirm my agreement that the information I provide may be used by The Random House Group Ltd, its assignees and/or licensees in any media or medium whatsoever.

Please return to
The Good Pub Guide,
FREEPOST TN1569,
WADHURST,
East Sussex
TN5 7BR

IF YOU PREFER, YOU CAN SEND US REPORTS
BY EMAIL:
feedback@goodguides.com

I have been to the following pubs in *The Good Pub Guide 2012* in the last few months, found them as described, and confirm that they deserve continued inclusion:

Continued overleaf

PLEASE GIVE YOUR NAME AND ADDRESS ON THE BACK OF THIS FORM

Pubs visited continued...

Your own name and address *(block capitals please)*

Postcode

Please return to
The Good Pub Guide,
FREEPOST TN1569,
WADHURST,
East Sussex
TN5 7BR

IF YOU PREFER, YOU CAN SEND US REPORTS
BY EMAIL:
feedback@goodguides.com

I have been to the following pubs in *The Good Pub Guide 2012* in the last few months, found them as described, and confirm that they deserve continued inclusion:

Continued overleaf

PLEASE GIVE YOUR NAME AND ADDRESS ON THE BACK OF THIS FORM

Pubs visited continued...

By returning this form, you consent to the collection, recording and use of the information you submit, by The Random House Group Ltd. Any personal details which you provide from which we can identify you are held and processed in accordance with the Data Protection Act 1998 and will not be passed on to any third parties.

The Random House Group Ltd may wish to send you further information on their associated products. Please tick box if you do not wish to receive any such information.

Your own name and address *(block capitals please)*

Postcode

In returning this form I confirm my agreement that the information I provide may be used by The Random House Group Ltd, its assignees and/or licensees in any media or medium whatsoever.

Please return to
The Good Pub Guide,
FREEPOST TN1569,
WADHURST,
East Sussex
TN5 7BR

IF YOU PREFER, YOU CAN SEND US REPORTS
BY EMAIL:
feedback@goodguides.com

I have been to the following pubs in *The Good Pub Guide 2012* in the last few months, found them as described, and confirm that they deserve continued inclusion:

Continued overleaf
PLEASE GIVE YOUR NAME AND ADDRESS ON THE BACK OF THIS FORM

Pubs visited continued...

Your own name and address *(block capitals please)*

Postcode

Please return to
The Good Pub Guide,
FREEPOST TN1569,
WADHURST,
East Sussex
TN5 7BR

IF YOU PREFER, YOU CAN SEND US REPORTS
BY EMAIL:
feedback@goodguides.com